DISCARDED

Chow Chop Suey

Arts and Traditions of the Table: Perspectives on Culinary History

Arts and Traditions of the Table: Perspectives on Culinary History

Albert Sonnenfeld, Series Editor

For a full list of titles in this series, see pages 331–32.

Chow Chop Suey

Food and the Chinese American Journey

Anne Mendelson

Columbia University Press
New York

Columbia University Press
Publishers Since 1893
New York   Chichester, West Sussex
cup.columbia.edu
Copyright © 2016 Anne Mendelson
All rights reserved

Library of Congress Cataloging-in-Publication Data

Names: Mendelson, Anne, author.
Title: Chow chop suey : food and the Chinese American journey / Anne Mendelson.
Description: New York : Columbia University Press, [2016] |
Series: Arts and traditions of the table : perspectives on culinary history |
Includes bibliographical references and index.
Identifiers: LCCN 2016020958 | ISBN 9780231158602 (cloth : alk. paper) |
ISBN 9780231541299 (e-book)
Subjects: LCSH: Cooking, Chinese—History. | Chinese Americans—Food—History. |
Food habits—Unites States. | Emigration and immigration—United States—History. |
Chinese American families—History.
Classification: LCC TX724.5.C5 M376 2016 | DDC 641.5951—dc23
LC record available at https://lccn.loc.gov/2016020958

∞

Columbia University Press books are printed on permanent and durable acid-free paper.
Printed in the United States of America

COVER DESIGN: Jason Heuer
COVER IMAGE: © Everett Historical/Shutterstock; Symbols: © lightmood/Shutterstock

In loving memory of my husband,

Martin Iger,

who taught me to love Chinese food.

炒雜碎

(Pronounced "chau tsap sui" in Cantonese, "chao za sui" in Mandarin)

Stir-fried (炒) *jumbled* (雜) *fragments* (碎), a phrase garbled by late-nineteenth-century English-speaking patrons of Chinese restaurants into "chop suey," with the crucial word "chau" or "chao" omitted.

Contents

Acknowledgments

The number of people who helped in my research is beyond counting. Let me begin with the four members of the Coe-Ziegelman family. Andrew Coe's seminal work *Chop Suey: A Cultural History of Chinese Food in the United States* inspired my own hope of some day writing about this subject, and he has offered encouragement at every step of the way. Jane Ziegelman had something penetrating to contribute whenever Chinese food was being discussed. I must thank their children, Buster and Edward, for being cheerful and intelligent participants in many talk-filled lunches in Flushing, Manhattan Chinatown, and elsewhere. Among the many friends who over the last few years shared in the eating, talking, and thinking, special thanks to Michael Gray and Patricia A. Andrews, Kian Lam Kho and Warren Livesley, Regina Schrambling and Bob Sacha, Danielle Gustafson and Bradley Klein, Cara De Silva, Madeleine Lim, and Ame Gilbert.

Many other writers and scholars generously shared ideas and information with me. I am especially indebted to Lucey Bowen, Ava Chin, Karen Christensen, Janet Chrzan, Fuchsia Dunlop, Nathalie Dupree, Jonathan Gold and Laurie Ochoa, Bruce Kraig, Rachel Laudan, Elizabeth L. Mo, Alejandro and Maricel Presilla, Jacqueline M. Newman, Molly O'Neill, Erica J. Peters, Valerie Saint Rossy, Ed Schoenfeld, Scott Seligman, Richard Tan, Grace Young, and Willa Zhen.

My left-hand man, neurologist Dr. Gary Alweiss, kept this writer's-cramp-afflicted southpaw more or less able to hold a pen throughout the writing process. Thanks, Gary!

I am grateful for moral support from my nephew Jorj Bauer and his wife, Susan Talbutt. Jorj's expertise also got me through several computer emergencies.

Thanks to Susan B. Carter for allowing me to cite important findings from her own forthcoming book on the Chinese in America, and to Zanne Stewart (at a very difficult moment in her life) and Suzi Arensberg Diacou for sharing firsthand recollections of some pivotal events during the 1970s and 1980s.

My work has been immeasurably helped by access to the collections of the Bobst Library at New York University, the New York Public Library, and the Firestone Library at Princeton University. I am also grateful to the Bergen County (New Jersey) Cooperative Library System and the North Bergen Public Library for the kind of help we would all like to have from local taxpayer-supported libraries.

A grant from the John Simon Guggenheim Memorial Foundation supported the first stages of my research. The Taiwan Tourism Bureau made it possible for me to visit Taiwan in 2010; sincere thanks to Marian Goldberg, Polly Yang, and the extraordinarily knowledgeable Helen Wong.

Paul Freedman and Eugene N. Anderson read versions of the text in manuscript. Their discerning comments (and Gene Anderson's profound knowledge of Chinese culinary history) have greatly enhanced the final result.

My agents, Jane Dystel and Miriam Goderich, have been towers of strength as this project straggled from first idea to completion. Heartfelt thanks to everyone at Dystel & Goderich.

Finally, I am grateful to my editor, Jennifer Crewe, for seeing some merit in my original proposal and patiently steering the project to a long-delayed conclusion. My best thanks to Kathryn Schell, Jonathan Fiedler, Kathryn Jorge, and all of the Columbia University Press team. And a special shout-out to attentive copy editor Patti Bower, who had my back from first to last page.

A Note on Romanization
and Terminology

I have given most Chinese words and names in today's pinyin system for romanizing the pronunciation of *putonghua* or the "common speech," a form of the Beijing dialect that the People's Republic officially declared the national spoken language in 1955. However, no adequate system exists for converting the many sublanguages and dialects of Cantonese into the Roman alphabet. Since scholarly consistency is nearly impossible, I have generally followed the path of least resistance by using the spellings that tended to be most popular among Cantonese Americans or familiar in the English-language American press (e.g., Sze Yup instead of Sei Yap). I also generally adopt the English spellings preferred by the owners of proper names (thus, Yuenren Chao instead of Yuanren Zhao) and refer to the northern dialect by the convenient term of "Mandarin" instead of trying to follow the twists and turns of various names proposed for it after the 1911 revolution.

Introduction

There is a Chinese phrase rendered as *xiang banfa* in today's official Mandarin romanization system, *seung bahnfat* in the Cantonese equivalent. It is invoked when people find themselves facing any kind of difficulty and means something like "find a solution" or "come up with a plan."

"*Xiang banfa!*" urges a mother listening to a child's complaints about playground aggressors. A MacGyver of any race or nation who improvises a desert-island fix for an outboard motor out of duct tape and old bicycle parts is a *xiang banfa* practitioner. So was the defier of former laws prohibiting Chinese laborers from entering the United States who more than a century ago hid secret instructions for establishing a fake identity inside a banana skin.[1] In 1970s Indianapolis, a young girl saw her immigrant parents confront the terrible absence of Chinese tofu, tell themselves "*Xiang banfa,*" and arrive at an excellent homemade version based on ground soybeans and calcium sulfate.[2] The instinct was well developed among the Chinese peoples before a few hundreds, then many thousands of men—but almost no women—started sailing across the Pacific to the land they called "Gold Mountain." Nearly all were Cantonese, meaning natives of Guangdong Province in the far south.

The phrase *xiang banfa* was just one of many things I'd never heard of when I set out to write a book on the history of Chinese food in America from the Gold Rush to the end of the Cold War. What I planned was a cook's eye view of a remarkable immigrant cuisine. For the purpose,

I expected to draw on my knowledge of English-language Chinese cookbooks and experience of the Chinese American restaurant scene— admittedly a narrow experience, since my Chinese-language skills extend only to reading some food-related characters and looking up terms in Chinese–English dictionaries.

This plan went astray almost at once. To my surprise, I became convinced that Chinese American food was *not* an immigrant cuisine on terms comparable to any other. How could it have been, when for about a century and a half virtually all Chinese-born people who had made it to America were specifically banned from becoming immigrants, in the sense of people who can exchange birthright citizenship in one country for adoptive citizenship in another? The shadow of threatened deportation hung over the community until World War II, when for the first time Chinese-born residents were explicitly allowed to apply for American citizenship.

The cooking that white and sometimes black Americans fell in love with after about 1895—still popular today among millions who happily ignore culinary snobberies—did not accompany the Chinese across the ocean. It did not enter American foodways in the natural course of an immigrant group's incorporation into this nation's life. The Chinese themselves concocted it for non-Chinese patrons, equipped with a phenomenal insight into the American palate that I discovered to be a crucial part of the story in its own right.

In effect, the late-nineteenth-century restaurant pioneers invented a new quasi-Chinese culinary idiom often summed up as the food of the chop suey era. They did this during a time of great and often deadly threats visited on them under the law barring Chinese workers from entering the United States, the 1882 Chinese Exclusion Act. It was an extraordinary instance of the *xiang banfa* instinct deployed at the moment of greatest need. The new cuisine itself stands as a historic turning point in race relations, improvised to please a white majority that could not have foreseen itself ever becoming a minority (an event now predicted to occur in less than two generations). White reviewers and gourmets pronouncing judgment on all-the-rage Chinese restaurants for the benefit of other whites failed—and often still fail—to notice the oddity of the underlying racial dynamic, or the fact that it isn't some unchanging historical given.

Any adequate history of Chinese American cooking must begin with the principles of Chinese cuisine as understood by the Cantonese-speaking men who first arrived here from Guangdong Province—a place, for nearly all Chinese, almost synonymous with excellent food. It must describe the more recent arrival of Mandarin-speaking newcomers and their impact on the late-twentieth-century Chinese culinary scene in America. It must explain why the entire system of Chinese cooking has historically been so difficult for non-Chinese to grasp, and how it came to be somewhat intelligibly "translated" for the American mind during the twentieth century. It also has to point out just what differentiates the made-up chop suey cuisine from Cantonese or any other version of Chinese cooking.

But this is not a story that can be adequately presented in measuring-spoon or restaurant-menu terms. Eventually I saw that I would have to devote a great deal of space to realities of the Exclusion era that have nothing to do with cooking, troubles that deeply stamped the lives of the men who kept Cantonese food culture alive among themselves through the worst of times.

It may seem unnecessary for a food historian to rehash events that have been abundantly chronicled by political and social historians. But I believe that readers of a book on Chinese American food will be well served by being asked to recognize these matters. There is great food for thought in—among other things—how the Cantonese in America came to be an almost all-male society hindered from forming family ties on American soil, what large roles opium and prostitutes played in the community, and how murderous persecution eventually drove many thousands into Chinatowns throughout this country. In addition, it is important to frame the Chinese American story within the context of geopolitical questions such as civil strife in China before and after the fall of the Qing Empire, or U.S. relations with the Nationalist regime on Taiwan during World War II and the Cold War. Rivalries between the Cantonese American community and later Mandarin-speaking arrivals also deserve to be taken into account.

In short: The story when finished had almost nothing to do with the one I had thought I was going to write.

The book is divided into two parts. The first, in which historical incidents play the more prominent role, broadly covers events from the mid-eighteenth to the early twentieth century, moving from Qing-era China to areas of Cantonese settlement on the American West Coast. The second focuses more extensively on culinary issues as reflected in Chinese American restaurants and English-language Chinese cook-books from the late 1890s up to roughly 1990. But culinary and political history are interwoven throughout both sections.

A brief road map may be in order. The opening chapter suggests some of the remarkable qualifications that equipped people from southern Guangdong for fortune seeking on Gold Mountain. The second examines the features of Chinese cuisine that made it so deeply incomprehensible to Westerners while the Cantonese, for their part, learned to reproduce Western cooking with uncanny skill. The next two chapters follow the growing Cantonese community in America from hopeful early years marked by impressive San Francisco restaurant success to an era of savage persecution. The incipient American labor movement whipped up a racist campaign that ended by drubbing Chinese manual labor out of the U.S. labor market, with the 1882 Chinese Exclusion Act as principal weapon.

Using any means they could find in the struggle to survive, the Cantonese became pioneers in West Coast fishing and produce gardening. Before being blacklisted from manual employment, they did the swamp clearing that made the beginnings of California agribusiness possible and completed the transcontinental railroads that linked industrial-scale farms with eastern and midwestern markets. In the true *xiang banfa* spirit, many found jobs cooking for white employers while others evaded legal strictures against laborers by reinventing themselves as self-employed persons conducting small businesses, with laundries being the usual choice for a few decades.

It was during this period that America's Chinatowns were formed, Chinese American culinary professionals started to invent the all-important "chop suey" cuisine as an irresistible draw for a white clientele, and restaurants gradually supplanted laundries as the preferred bulwark against deportation. The community's one great legal victory, the 1898 *United States v. Wong Kim Ark* decision in which the Supreme Court declared on Fourteenth Amendment grounds that a child born to Chinese parents on U.S. soil is automatically an American citizen, laid down the later foundation for converting an almost wholly male

Chinese-born population to something resembling a community of true immigrants.

Part 2 opens with a chapter describing both the important features of "chop suey" cuisine as a construct deliberately tailored to non-Chinese preferences and the further changes wrought by white enthusiasts who tried (with muddled understanding) to teach other fans how to cook "chop suey." As I explain, the phrase originated as a garbled English rendering of "chow chop suey," with "chow" indicating the stir-fry method. Though the term "chop suey" later went on to a freewheeling life of its own in non-Chinese minds, in early days it clearly stood for the general category of Chinese dishes cooked by stir-frying—a technique that at the time was wholly unintelligible to American cooks and could not have been explained in English. Had white patrons of late-nineteenth-century Chinese restaurants happened to latch onto "chow" rather than "chop suey" to identify the most popular class of dishes, everyone would have been spared much later confusion. Non–Chinese Americans would then have accurately used terms like "chow duck," "chow clams," and so forth instead of ignorantly inserting the phrase "chop suey" where it made no sense.

The next chapter describes how improved understanding between educated Americans and American-educated, Chinese-born Chinese led to the first truly insightful English-language Chinese cookbook: *How to Cook and Eat in Chinese* (1945).

The last three chapters survey the changing American restaurant and cookbook-publishing scene from the aftermath of World War II until the fall of the Iron Curtain. Chapter 7 focuses on prominent and influential restaurants; chapter 8, on prominent and influential books as well as cooking schools. Taiwanese–American relations are crucial to this part of the story. Thanks to the U.S. alliance with the Nationalist government-in-exile on Taiwan, a comparative handful of Mandarin-speaking, non-Cantonese restaurateurs and teachers acquired a commanding position as interpreters of Chinese cuisine to American diners and cooks during the Cold War. Cookbook publishing on Taiwan also helped set the stage for some important developments in English-language Chinese instruction here. Chapter 7 focuses on a Chinese restaurant vogue that reached its height during the 1960s and 1970s. Chapter 8 covers a corresponding vogue of Chinese cooking schools and increasingly ambitious cookbooks, partly foreshadowed by similar developments on Taiwan and in burgeoning stateside Taiwanese communities.

The concluding chapter shows Chinese cuisine fading somewhat from the American media limelight just as the Chinese culinary presence on U.S. soil was about to be lastingly transformed by the Hart-Celler immigration reforms of 1965 and many Far Eastern geopolitical convulsions. Between about 1970 and 1990, surprisingly self-reliant enclaves of Chinese immigrants from diverse geographical backgrounds began appearing in and beyond the old American Chinatowns—and producing restaurants that didn't need white patronage to survive and prosper. In a pattern hinting at deeper changes that are predicted to strengthen when whites become an American racial minority by about 2060, these establishments owed their existence to clienteles of new ethnic Chinese immigrants who shared the owners' regional origins, particular languages, and culinary frames of reference. Meanwhile, the old—and often very inequitable—racial-exchange models of the Chinese restaurant business that many white (and black) people grew up on were gradually disappearing, and have continued to do so. Strange though it may sound, there are many things that young or middle-aged Chinese Americans with unfettered access to any career from astrophysicist to news reporter would rather do for a living than go on cooking to please outsiders.

It remains to be said that the historiography of Chinese American food is also destined to grow in the near future—in fact, is growing swiftly at this moment. I know of half a dozen important research projects now in progress or about to be published. A tremendous new factor is coming into play: a generation of bilingual historians with serious scholarly training who, unlike me, can comb through original Chinese-language sources. Such quarries might include newspapers from California or Hong Kong, importers' business records, store inventories, or the letters and diaries of people who lived the Cantonese American experience during Exclusion. This previously untapped material constitutes a whole new Gold Mountain of potential evidence. I can confidently predict that in a very few years, readers interested in this story will have access to broader and deeper accounts than anything yet published.

Prologue

A Stroke of the Pen

Lyndon Johnson might have ordered the weather himself on the sunny Sunday afternoon of October 3, 1965. He *had* ordered the stage backdrop. After canny presidential carrot-and-stick persuasions had successfully pushed one of his most cherished bills through Congress on Thursday, the fiat had gone forth to transfer the signing ceremony from the White House to the Statue of Liberty National Monument. Several days of rapid scurrying in Washington and New York had gotten all the necessary props and security measures in place and dispatched boatloads of politicians, reporters, and onlookers across New York Harbor in time to greet the chief executive.

Among the officeholders watching the White House helicopter bear down on Liberty Island under brilliant autumn skies were four men who cared as deeply about the new legislation as Johnson himself. For senators Robert Kennedy and Edward Kennedy, the signing ceremony marked the triumph of a cause dear to their fallen brother, the late president John F. Kennedy. For Brooklyn representative Emanuel Celler, it spelled the end of a stubborn, often thankless campaign begun during his freshman term more than forty years earlier and finally brought to fruition with the co-sponsorship of an ally who personified the liberal conscience of the age, Michigan senator Philip Hart. H.R. 2580, the Hart-Celler Act, had eventually carried both houses of Congress by wide margins as the Immigration and Naturalization Act of 1965.[1]

The helicopter doors opened to disgorge Johnson, Vice President Hubert Humphrey, and their wives. A gaggle of functionaries followed, among them the new White House press secretary, thirty-one-year-old Bill Moyers. Cameras zeroed in from different angles at 3:08 P.M. as Lyndon Johnson, the statue towering over him, marched to the podium to deliver a speech mostly drafted by Moyers.

Surviving photographs show scarcely a non-Caucasian face in the audience.[2]

"The bill that we will sign today is not a revolutionary bill," the president announced. "It does not affect the lives of millions. It will not reshape the structure of our daily lives, or really add importantly to either our wealth or our power."

No American politician has ever been more deeply wrong about anything—nor more deeply right—than was Johnson as he went on to say that the new law was nevertheless "one of the most important acts of this Congress and of this administration," adding, "For it does repair a very deep and painful flaw in the fabric of American justice. It corrects a cruel and enduring wrong in the conduct of the American Nation."[3]

The wrong in question had been hammered into law in 1924, over the opposition of young Manny Celler, by the joint efforts of Washington State representative Albert Johnson and the equally racist senator David Reed of Pennsylvania. In response to a powerful nativist mood then sweeping the land, the Johnson-Reed Act (or National Origins Act) established the general ethnic makeup of America in 1890—that is, before the greatest influxes of "refuse" from such "teeming shores" as Italy and the Jewish Pale of Settlement—as a template to set future quotas of immigrant labor.[4] Certain people could argue for exemption: merchants, skilled artisans with demonstrable mastery of a trade, students, and professionals like doctors or lawyers. But the numbers of people in these categories who wanted to come to America were fairly limited. Johnson-Reed was meant to (and did) prevent masses of unskilled workers from anywhere in the world except northwestern Europe and the British Isles from competing with birthright Americans. One section broadened the existing provisions of the overtly Sinophobic 1882 Chinese Exclusion Act to apply to other Asians, thus imposing especially vigilant barriers to keep out manual labor from the Far East.[5] The new law never achieved 100 percent success in heading off newcomers deemed to be the scum of humanity, but it would drastically remold the course of immigration for forty-plus years.

Manny Celler's stance against locking out unskilled immigrants on the basis of where they had been born began to attract influential allies in the decade after World War II. In 1952 Congress roused itself to pass the McCarran-Walter Act, no thoroughgoing repudiation of Johnson-Reed's exclusionary intent but at least a tentative break with a white-supremacist rationale that had governed all immigration policy since the 1790 Naturalization Act.[6] In 1958 rising Democratic star John F. Kennedy (whose family knew something about anti-immigrant prejudice) wrote an essay titled "A Nation of Immigrants" on behalf of the Anti-Defamation League. Reform of the nation's immigration laws was one of the Kennedy causes that Lyndon Johnson had most sincerely embraced on entering the White House. As with the denial of voting rights to black citizens, he saw both an opportunity and a moral imperative to right an historic injustice.

The ceremony at Liberty Island passed entirely unnoticed by anyone writing about American food and cooking. At the time, few Americans had ever had occasion to consider Chinese food anything but an odd scrap of cultural wallpaper in the nation's attic. Forty years after the Johnson-Reed Act had slammed the door on immigration from most of the world, people had generally stopped expecting further chapters to unfold in the story of immigrant cooking. Not even culinary snobs had reason to suppose that the new law would ever affect anybody's ideas of what to have for dinner in Minneapolis, Tallahassee, Boise, Spokane, Houston, or New York.

In 1965 all large American cities, most mid-sized municipalities, and some fairly small towns had either a sprinkling of Chinese restaurants or at least one. Except in cities with Chinatowns big enough to supply hired labor, virtually all were small, family-owned businesses built on the unending drudgery of every member old enough to chop vegetables or wash dishes. (The only difference in larger restaurants was at least nominal wages for equally grueling, generally nonunionized toil.) What is worth pondering is that outside of Chinatown—and often even there—the target clientele was, and long had been, almost wholly non-Chinese. Few people stopped to wonder why.

The reasons lay eighty or a hundred years in the past. They were as good as invisible to most well-meaning Americans in 1965. The ease with which the Hart-Celler Act had been carried suggested that politicians expected it to produce little more than a peaceful sprinkling of new faces to tell the rest of us how big-hearted we were. The public at large had managed to mislay memories of the inflamed xenophobia originally responsible for the 1882 and 1924 bills, not to mention many other exclusionary measures written into law during the long reign of "America for Americans" rhetoric that really meant "America for Decent White Protestant Americans."

True, race relations were again erupting into violent confrontation—but in most of the country the very concept of race relations had shrunk to include only two home-grown cohorts, blacks and whites. Earlier controversies over immigrant labor had faded so thoroughly from the national awareness that many otherwise well-educated citizens had no idea of how the Chinese had been treated. The subject was a gigantic blank in public-school curricula and not much better covered in college American history courses.

It took several decades for most Caucasian Americans to notice that the racial makeup of the United States was being profoundly transformed, or to rearrange their mental images of certain groups that the Old World's teeming shores had sent us generations earlier. Who exactly were the Greeks, Italians, Poles, or Russian Jews who crossed the Atlantic to America's East Coast before 1924? We can now recognize that they were greatly misperceived for decades—yet never as misperceived as the Chinese who crossed the Pacific to the West Coast during the same period. Even today few white or black Americans know anything about the circumstances that originally dispatched more than two hundred thousand men and a handful of women to this country in the late nineteenth century from one small corner of China.

PART I

ONE

Origins

The Toisan–California Pipeline

THE WAYWARD PROVINCE OF GUANGDONG

August 29, 1842, came and went no more eventfully than other Mondays in the twenty-six United States and a negligible hamlet called Yerba Buena in the Alta California territory of Mexico. On the other side of the world, however, the balance of East/West realpolitik was being permanently realigned at the city of Nanjing on the Yangzi River, about eighty-five miles from the eastern coast of China. Attended by phalanxes of British military and naval officers along with a bored-looking spaniel, the representatives of Queen Victoria and China's Daoguang Emperor sat at a table in the state cabin of HMS *Cornwallis* to sign the Treaty of Nanjing.[1] This lopsided bargain ended the First Opium War by imposing a long string of British demands on China in return for nothing. It was a decisive defeat in the Qing dynasty's attempt to turn back, or at least partly contain, the tide of an emerging global economy dominated by stronger and more ruthless powers.

The Qing were the descendants of non-Han aliens, Manchu invaders from beyond China's northern borders who had seized the imperial throne less than two centuries earlier, in 1644. In many ways, the timing of the new dynasty's arrival could not have been worse. The business of putting their new empire in order collided from the start with disruptive

Western trading interests, now firmly pitched throughout the maritime Far East and scrambling with each other for advantage.

The lands the Qing intended to govern would have presented fearsome challenges in any case. Then as now, China's climatic, topographical, and human barriers to unification dwarfed those of any other nation on earth. By claim at least, the empire took in the sky-piercing Himalayas in the far west along with innumerable ranges of lesser mountains and hills scattered across twenty-plus provinces; huge deserts and dry steppes stretching far along the old Silk Road in the northwest; the two greatest watercourses of Asia, the Yellow and the Yangzi Rivers, each winding to the Pacific Ocean throughout several thousand miles of stupendously varied terrain; a large, humid tropical and subtropical zone in the far south; and more than nine thousand miles of coastline. It also embraced literally dozens of different ethnicities and languages. The latter included not only a host of speech groups belonging to non-Han minority peoples but at least ten major Han Chinese languages with untold constellations of local sublanguages and dialects. (All the Han tongues were mutually intelligible as written in Chinese characters, but in spoken form might be further apart than Romanian and Portuguese.)

For the Qing authorities in Beijing, one annoying stretch of coastline, the people who lived along it, and the two major languages they spoke spelled particular trouble. The imperial court was obliged to call in interpreters to translate the uncouth speech of functionaries from the far south-southeastern regions—the provinces of Guangdong and Fujian, which lay along what Beijing considered the empire's most dangerous maritime frontier.

Between them, these two provinces would account for the lion's share of emigration from China to the rest of the world until after World War II. But while the Qing were struggling to unseat the doomed Ming dynasty in the early seventeenth century, the very concept of emigration was almost impossible to reconcile with some aspects of a widely prevailing Chinese world view. Recent interlopers though they were, the Qing, once victorious, were determined to enforce most of that view.

By Ming and Qing lights, the mere act of travel to foreign parts, at least by sea, implicitly threatened a system of belief that placed China (the "Middle Kingdom") and its ruler (the "Son of Heaven") at the center of the universe, with other realms and peoples occupying different peripheral ranks from semicivilized to subhuman.[2] Even when seagoing Western aliens had proved to be a permanent fact of life, official attitudes toward the planet at large were a strange amalgam of xenophobia and ambivalent acceptance. Leaving the ancestral realm without official clearance was, in theory at least, punishable by beheading.[3] After all, it could serve little purpose except treason or merchant enterprise. The second ranked as the least honorable of all lawful human activities on the scale of Confucian values.

Nowhere in the Middle Kingdom did people more openly flout such doctrines than in Fujian and Guangdong. For centuries they had understood that their coastal waters offered unparalleled access to all of Southeast Asia. They further knew that China could not very well do without many articles of trade shipped from those regions—the "Nanyang," or "Southern Ocean," as the lands from Vietnam to beyond the Spice Islands were collectively called—or the revenue from commercial traffic.

The ethnic makeup of Fujian and Guangdong was complex and unruly even by Chinese standards. At different times over many centuries, successive Han Chinese groups had migrated to both provinces from the north, first colonizing farmland, later seeking refuge from northern invaders or a healthy distance from imperial oversight. The Guangdong residents—or "Cantonese," as the English would later call them—considered themselves more truly Chinese than their northern rulers. Indeed, the difficult spoken languages of both Guangdong and Fujian are believed to resemble the most ancient forms of Han Chinese more closely than counterparts elsewhere, and non-Han genetic admixtures appear to be less prevalent in the southeast than in most of China.[4]

In any case, both provinces were hotbeds of smuggling, piracy, merchantry, and other dubious pursuits. Fujian—pronounced "Hokkien" in the most widespread of the local dialects—was the more active in establishing trading networks throughout the Nanyang. Unofficial Hokkienese outposts had long existed in many corners of today's Vietnam, Thailand, Malaysia, Singapore, Indonesia, and the Philippines. People from Guangdong sometimes founded settlements in the Nanyang. But they also were the more adroit at exploiting the arrival of European traders in Chinese waters.

Guangdong, China's southernmost province, lies about half north and half south of the Tropic of Cancer. It was the southern, or fully tropical, half that eventually would drag China willy-nilly into the early modern global economy. The dominant feature here is the massive delta of the Pearl River, or Zhu Jiang, flowing through verdant hill country into the South China Sea. It furnishes a convenient water route from Southeast Asia as far inland as the port of Guangzhou (Canton city), the provincial capital.

South of Guangzhou, the Pearl River Delta is a perplexed, hilly welter of innumerable tidal channels interspersed with dikes, fish ponds, and pieces of reclaimed ground. In this region, land flat enough for farming was less easily come by than in central or northern parts of the province. There was some cultivation of rice and a newer staple crop, the hugely important sweet potatoes introduced from the Americas in the seventeenth century. Sugar cane was the major cash crop; local tree fruits from oranges to litchis were reputedly among the finest in the kingdom.[5] In rural districts nearly everyone had a small plot to supply kitchen needs. But the area was less self-sufficient in agriculture than the rest of Guangdong, and the locals had more of a nose for trade.

Only with difficulty could imperial officialdom stop delta residents from welcoming foreign vessels while barely preserving the dignified fiction that goods entering China from elsewhere were really tributary missions to the current Son of Heaven. The mazy backwaters between the sea and the port city were scant barrier to commercial interchange between determined outsiders and equally eager locals and offered endless aid and comfort to smugglers. For centuries, Guangzhou merchants had been selling porcelains, silks, and tea—with or without official sanction—to the Arab traders who plied the Southeast Asian coasts. They hoped to do likewise with the European voyagers who began seeking a piece of the action during the final Qing and Ming struggles for the throne.

It took the Qing six years to conquer the wayward province after coming to power. Afterward, Cantonese readiness to collude with the Portuguese and other foreigners made the situation difficult to monitor from Beijing, more than a thousand miles away. The imperial masters were almost as much at a loss to read the minds of these refractory subjects as U.S. and Canadian authorities later would be in the Far West.

The character of the southeastern Chinese and particularly the Pearl River Delta Cantonese, as it appeared not only to northerners but later to many British and American chroniclers, was indomitably hardy, persistent, stoical, practical, wily, and resourceful. No group more completely personified the *xiang banfa* instinct. From decades if not centuries pursuing trade opportunities in the Nanyang, they were used to organizing expeditions to foreign parts, where they knew how to hit the ground running. They could endure dreadful conditions with an apparent indifference that non-Chinese often interpreted as a penchant for squalor.

Representatives of the West would soon marvel at the south Guangdong natives' genius for improvisation and imitation in new surroundings while—like representatives of Beijing—often being frustrated by their skill at getting their own way by open or devious means. In the context of other people's mores, they could look like congenital liars and lawbreakers. Probably it is more accurate to say that their lives were ruled by a consciousness of community and self almost impossible to communicate to outsiders but ineradicably bred into them as birthright members of tight-knit individual villages and clans in the delta backwaters. This instinctive identification with place and lineage was all the stronger for the spectacular fragmentation of Han sublanguages and dialects in Guangdong. Often people living in one administrative district could barely understand the speech of people from the next.[6] The more educated might have some command of Cantonese as spoken in Guangzhou. This was officially the standard language of the province, but local speech was a token of jealously ingrained local loyalties expressed in frequent feuds.

It is not surprising, then, that even more than most Chinese, natives of the Pearl River Delta could travel and (for a time) settle anywhere in the world without ceasing to be citizens of some unshakably internalized ancestral domain.

THE CANTON SYSTEM

A sometimes neglected truth underlying the Chinese diaspora of modern times is that from the moment the first Portuguese voyagers appeared in Chinese coastal waters not long after 1500, Chinese and

Western economic influences throughout the Far East fed each other in a powerful synergy. While Portuguese, Dutch, and English entrepreneurs founded local beachheads and trafficked in an ever-expanding range of goods, Chinese entrepreneurs were doing likewise in all parts of the Nanyang.[7] Of course most of these exporter-importers were from the untrustworthy provinces of Fujian and Guangdong. Quietly ignoring official prohibitions on leaving the shores of the Middle Kingdom, Hokkienese and Cantonese established berths at useful locations in incipient Western colonies from the Malay peninsula to the Philippines, buying or selling or brokering anything from metal ores to rice. The imperial court frequently viewed these activities as a form of organized crime, and sometimes with reason.

The Ming and (after 1644) Qing emperors uneasily sought to control an expanding flow of goods and people along the long Chinese coastline. Some form of triage was obviously necessary. Since the port of Guangzhou and the shoreline around the Pearl River Delta offered the easiest access to the interior anywhere in the kingdom, Beijing poured more effort into supervising this maritime area than any other. Arriving foreigners were considered national security threats until proved otherwise. The hope was that funneling them into one manageable zone would make other coasts safer.[8]

As early as 1557 the Ming authorities had permitted Portugal to establish the tiny trading outpost of Macau (later to receive the Chinese name of Aomen) on the western shore of the river mouth for regular access to Guangzhou, some seventy miles inland as the crow flies. The real distance upriver was much greater. The difficulty of navigating the shallow, tortuous channels between Macau and the port city without local help offered a good rationale for correspondingly tortuous bureaucratic oversight.[9]

In 1757, realizing that more drastic measures were needed to stop outsiders from doing business in other cities, the Qing regime declared all ports except Guangzhou closed to foreign vessels. This move annoyed both the British East India Company—now the most important Western commercial presence in the Far East—and merchants from every tea-drinking (and to a lesser extent, porcelain- and silk-importing) European nation. But all were obliged to operate under what came to be known as the "Canton system," a procedural gauntlet that had begun to take shape at around 1700 and would reach full flowering between the 1757 decree and 1800.[10]

The system was so obstacle-ridden, and so maddeningly tailored to maintain Western trade deficits, that one of its eventual effects would be to awaken British minds to the charms of opium smuggling. It depended on incessant supervision by numberless functionaries.

The mere size of Western oceangoing ships barred open sailing (or surreptitious sneaking) upriver to the port city. Even going with the tide, the keels of the largest sailing vessels when fully loaded barely cleared the bottom of the deepest channels as far north as the anchorage at Huangpu ("Whampoa" to the English), about twelve miles short of Guangzhou. By law, non-Chinese vessels and personnel had to be attended at all times by successive troops of fee-collecting agents who oversaw every stage of their mission, starting with the hiring of local pilots licensed to take foreign ships upriver from Macau to Huangpu. There the cargoes were off-loaded to smaller "chop boats" leased from Cantonese merchants, for transport through a series of "chops" (toll stages) to the wharves at Guangzhou. All these procedures were under the ultimate control of the Hoppo, or Guangzhou-based imperial customs supervisor, who also superintended the performance of the same steps in reverse order for departing cargoes.[11]

Foreigners were too dangerous to be left unsupervised for a minute, even for the purpose of going to buy food in Guangzhou, Huangpu, or anywhere else. That job and many others were ultimately controlled by the "*cohong*," a consortium of Guangzhou merchants through whom Western merchant captains and supercargoes were obliged to channel all transactions. On behalf of individual European delegations, the different members of the *cohong* made official arrangements with local purveyors known as "compradors," a name borrowed from Portuguese. Among other duties, the compradors bought each day's food supplies for foreign ships' crews and merchant delegations throughout their stay. Sometimes they also arranged for the hiring of local cooks to prepare Western meals to the visitors' taste. After several decades the imperial court and the *cohongs* decided to house the Western merchant staffs in quarters of their own, and built a compound of "factories" (mansions-cum-warehouses) along the Guangzhou waterfront. Traders—originally obliged to return to Macau as soon as possible after finishing a mission—were eventually permitted to occupy these lodgings at certain seasons of the year.[12]

The barriers to East–West communication were many. Viewing unfettered talk between imperial subjects and nonsubjects as an invitation to trouble, Beijing harshly discouraged bilingual proficiency on both sides. Locals were officially forbidden to teach Chinese (including both Cantonese and Mandarin) to any European, and any acquisition of foreign languages by the Guangzhou citizenry at large seems to have been thought treasonous. For the purpose of business transactions with the English, numbers-crunching and other exchanges of necessary information were supposed to be carried out only by official interpreters through the sanctioned medium of pidgin English (modeled on the pidgin Portuguese that had been the first transcultural lingua franca of the delta). Nonetheless, some Westerners managed to pick up a little Cantonese, and some employees of the *cohong* got well beyond pidgin.[13]

The scene became more complicated after the Revolutionary War half a world away. American merchants had been hungrily coveting worldwide markets well before the signing of official peace treaties. The *Empress of China*, the first merchant ship bound for Chinese waters under the Stars and Stripes, sailed out of New York Harbor in February 1784, less than three months after the last British troops had evacuated the city. In a few years an official American "factory" had joined those of various European nations along the Guangzhou waterfront, and the merchants of the *cohong* were adjusting their ideas of foreigners to take in the interesting fact that the newcomers, though they ate like Englishmen, belonged to some other anomalous branch of humanity.

But the Canton factory system was already fraying, and with its decline Guangzhou would be relegated to a lesser role in a more intensive, more freely conducted international commerce. The first English-built steamships arrived in the region in the early 1830s. They drastically changed the terms on which foreign traffic could come and go throughout the Pearl River Delta. Not only could they sail in a dead calm, but they didn't need deep keels to avoid pitching over in strong crosswinds. Large but shallow-bottomed cargo vessels could now bypass Huangpu along with native pilots and the entire "chop" gauntlet and travel directly upriver from any spot near the Pearl River mouth to Guangzhou.[14] The

British were thus able not just to navigate local waters with self-reliance but to graduate from opium smuggling to brazenly forcing the noxious trade on China in a series of armed naval initiatives that became the First Opium War of 1839–1842.

THE THRESHOLD OF THE GOLD RUSH

The First Opium War and the Treaty of Nanjing coincided with a cascade of domestic evils ravaging Guangdong along with the rest of China. An epoch of nationwide prosperity, peaking around and after the mid-eighteenth century, had contributed to a swift, drastic population growth that proved unsustainable. (By some scholarly estimates, China's total population may have doubled from about 200 million to more than 400 million between 1750 and 1850.[15]) At the same time, opium trafficking, though still illicit, had assumed large enough dimensions to not only offset but outweigh the immense revenues derived from the export of Chinese tea and textiles. The hated treaty did not legitimize the trade—a blow made possible only by further wars leading to the 1860 Convention of Beijing—but it left the Qing regime helpless to stem an ever-increasing influx of British-conveyed Indian opium that would bring the economy to the brink of ruin.

Meanwhile, successive floods along several great rivers after the start of the century had begun triggering catastrophic soil loss. Devastating droughts alternated with floods. In the south, years of reduced or failed rice harvests ensued along with intermittent starvation. At the time of the Nanjing accord, remaining arable land in Guangdong was being more and more bitterly fought over by clans belonging to the Cantonese majority and a Han minority whom they despised as greedy northern carpetbaggers: the Hakka people, who had arrived in the southeastern provinces a few generations earlier, bringing their own language and habits.

During the 1850s the Punti (Cantonese) and Hakka conflict would reach the level of warfare, particularly in the Pearl River Delta.[16] But it was dwarfed by more wide-reaching civil wars that broke out at the same time and nearly toppled the Qing dynasty. The bloodiest of these was led by a deranged Hakka who believed himself to be Jesus Christ's younger brother and who preached a messianic gospel inspired by smatterings of Christian missionary teachings. Sweeping across many provinces between 1851 and 1864, the so-called Taiping ("Great Peace") Rebellion is thought to have claimed some 20 million lives.[17] Staggering though this figure sounds, it probably represents less than half the overall toll of midcentury turf wars and armed rebellions. The carnage barely made a dent in China's ruinous labor surplus.

The First Opium War formed a grim prelude to these events. It began in 1839 with a Beijing-appointed commissioner destroying twenty thousand chests of opium confiscated from British factories at Guangzhou. It ended three years later at Nanjing with the first of many "unequal treaties" that foreign powers would exact from the hapless Qing rulers before the end of the century. Among other provisions, Great Britain was to receive unfettered commercial access to five port cities in which British and other foreign nationals would occupy their own quarters under their own laws, unanswerable to any Chinese authority. Guangzhou was the most important of these extraterritorial concessions. The remaining four were Shanghai, its slightly southerly neighbor Ningbo, and two cities locally called Amoy and Hokchiu (Xiamen and Fuzhou in pinyin, today's official transliteration of the Mandarin language) situated on the Straits of Taiwan in Fujian Province. In addition, China was required to cede control of an obscure island named "Fragrant Harbor," or Hong Kong in Cantonese (Xiang Gang in pinyin).[18] The new British possession lay along the eastern side of the widening Pearl River mouth where it debouches into the South China Sea, some forty miles from Macau on the opposite side.

The harbor was the finest anywhere on the Chinese coastline south of Shanghai. The location had every advantage over Guangzhou, which soon was relegated to a secondary staging role as the four other mainland ports assumed their own importance. International traders and navigators rejoiced at being spared the tricky journey up and down the Pearl River. Still, the river's supremacy as a conduit of goods moving between the interior and the seven seas continued unthreatened for some decades. What no one had foreseen was that the river and Hong Kong together would also become the great nineteenth-century conduit for *people* moving between China and the outside world.

For several years after its founding, Hong Kong remained an unpromising small settlement. What triggered its rise to a uniquely multicultural and cosmopolitan entrepôt was the discovery of gold a few days' journey from the even more obscure village of Yerba Buena, situated next to an equally excellent harbor on the other side of the Pacific. For a few frenetic decades, the little British colony and the California hamlet—now rechristened "San Francisco"—grew like siblings linked through a kind of transoceanic symbiosis.[19]

The race to California (by now a territory of the United States) from all parts of the Old and New Worlds got under way in earnest in 1849. An Australian gold rush followed in 1851, a brief stampede to the Canadian diggings at Fraser Canyon in 1858. Short-lived though they were, all three presaged a new era of Western-driven progress whose world-spanning wheels would be turned by brute manpower, recruited from wherever it could be found and massively deployed on every continent in such different arenas as mining, plantation-scale food production, and tremendous engineering projects. Today's global Chinese diaspora is rooted in that epoch.

Never in history had there been a mass exodus of surplus manual labor from the Middle Kingdom to other nations. But there never had been anything like the mid-nineteenth-century fusion of circumstances in war-torn southern China. Among the dazzling range of goods circulating through Hong Kong during and after the Gold Rush, the most important export came to be human beings.

From the start, southern Cantonese in Hong Kong hugely outnumbered British-born colonists, usually by more than fifteen to one.[20] Ignoring cries of *hanjian* ("Traitor!") from more tradition-minded Chinese, Pearl River Delta natives had soon begun heading to the new port in defiance of the ineffectual imperial ban on emigration. Few if any meant to make it their home for good; the idea of seeking permanent citizenship anywhere beyond one's native village or district was all but unintelligible in southern Chinese culture. On the other hand, no one hesitated to temporarily exploit advantageous opportunities elsewhere, and Hong Kong was an ideal roost in which to look for or create them.[21]

Hong Kong was nothing like Guangdong under the Canton system. It offered relief from stifling layers of neo-Confucian bureaucracy, with unsupervised direct communication in several languages between private parties to contracts. Like San Francisco, it welcomed go-getters, a role to which Pearl River inhabitants seemed to have been born.

HONG KONG, THE TOISANESE, AND OVERSEAS SOJOURNING

The new order of things resulting from the encounter of an underfed, overpopulated China with Western colonial powers in late-Qing times introduced complexities to which Chinese and English terms are equally inadequate. It should first be understood that the custom of transplanting merchant communities to overseas dominions, either temporarily or semipermanently, was widespread throughout the Old World centuries before the Gold Rush. Armenians and Jews were the greatest (though not only) founders of trading diasporas as far east as India; Cantonese and Hokkienese almost as far west. The practice does not correspond to notions of emigration or immigration rooted in any modern view of the nation-state. The Mandarin Chinese name for such voyages, as well as voyagers, is *qiao* (Cantonese, *kiuh*), rendered in English as "sojourn" and "sojourners." This translation has had its critics. But the words "emigration" or "immigration" and "emigrants/immigrants," as usually understood in the United States, are much more distorting.

In any case, everything connected with sojourning outgrew manageable categories during the Qing era. The historian Wang Gungwu has proposed the convenient Mandarin term *"hua shang"* for the general class of Chinese entrepreneurs, middlemen, and brokers who came to prominence with the arrival of European adventurers in the sixteenth century and spread throughout the Nanyang, stimulating the circulation of money and goods.[22] Immigration officials in California later sought to classify them as "merchants," with some awkwardness. I have preferred Wang's phrase because these agents' and traffickers' activities far exceed any conventional Western notion of merchantry. The *hua shang* are better described as the whole tribe of operators who converted plans—large or small, honorable or shady—into profitable action. They included many sorts of wheeler-dealers who would have a longstanding role in diffusing foods between China and other Asian regions.

The turmoil of late-Qing China helped to create another overseas contingent with no real counterpart in prior Chinese history. Wang refers to them as the *hua gong*, roughly corresponding to "Chinese manual labor" or "Chinese workers."[23] In mere numbers, they soon surpassed the *hua shang*. But the two groups' fortunes would be complexly intertwined.

When Hong Kong became the undisputed magnet city for East–West commerce, an ambitious group of new arrivals from Guangzhou and the delta quickly made themselves indispensable to both their compatriots and the island's new rulers, as *hua shang* engaged in a slew of business enterprises. With a resourcefulness and adaptability that astonished their supposed masters, they seized on any role that might have a future. In no time they had turned themselves into wholesale jobbers or retail shopkeepers, building contractors, artisans, makers of sampans and junks, carpenters and outfitters for Western seagoing vessels, restaurateurs, brothel keepers, landlords, bankers, currency dealers, and facilitators of traffic in many wares including two major foundations of Hong Kong's future prosperity: opium and human beings.[24] Meanwhile, nearly anyone with a head for business also cultivated the knack of networking with all sorts of Westerners. Pearl River natives might be found managing wealthy English households as steward-factotums or handling entire departments of large European firms.

Other aggressive operators from all Western nations were now converging on Hong Kong, hoping to cash in on some facet of its many-dimensional boom. The Guangzhou and delta Cantonese were not alone. But they understood local resources and the *xiang banfa* mentality better than anyone else. They had huge advantages in already speaking and writing the language. Veterans of the earlier Canton trade in Guangzhou could steer them to supply webs for especially desirable porcelain goods, teas, or other trade articles as well as basic shipboard necessities. Still better, the *hua shang* could read the local labor market with unparalleled accuracy and recruit *hua gong* from particular districts in order to keep townsmen or clansmen clustered together on the other side of the sea—an all but obligatory aid to both morale and ease of communication.[25]

The dozen or so southern counties of the delta encompassed different sublanguages or dialects as well as strong contrasts between haves and have-nots. The better-off mostly lived in Guangzhou and three somewhat urbanized counties or districts (Mandarin, *xian*; Cantonese, *sin*) to the south, on the west side of the river. Their names were, in modern pinyin, Nanhai, Panyu, and Shunde. Beyond Shunde, another county called Zhongshan stretched southward toward the port at Macau. Xinhui county was situated on Zhongshan's western border; west of that lay a group of three other counties. Their names were Kaiping, Enping, and—the southernmost and poorest of the lot—Xinning on the South China Sea coast. These eight counties would account for almost all Chinese immigration to the United States before, and long after, the 1882 Chinese Exclusion Act.[26]

The importance of Xinning, which was officially renamed Taishan in 1914, is unique enough to warrant some inconsistency in rendering Chinese names. The community's own pronunciations were "Sunning" and "Toishan," or more commonly "Toisan" or "Hoisan"; "Toisan" and "Sunning" are the versions probably most familiar today to people with ancestral links to the county. Of course nobody there spoke Mandarin, and even the Cantonese of Guangzhou was strange to the local ear. As the memoirist William Poy Lee has observed in our own time, the seven-toned "Big City Cantonese" was positively "melodic, like a stanza of music," while Toisanese sentences were unleashed at piercing volume "like a mortar barrage, with consonants, vowels, all the tones meshed into a tight, barbed clump of earthy linguistics."[27] (Many Mandarin-speakers felt the same about *all* versions of Cantonese.)

Workers leaving Toisan and the other counties transplanted jealous parochial loyalties to California and other parts of the United States. Most people firmly identified with either the prosperous Three Counties ("Sam Yup" in Cantonese or "San Yi" in Mandarin) of Nanhai, Panyu, and Shunde or the less fortunate Four Counties ("Sze Yup" or "Si Yi") of Xinhui, Kaiping, Enping, and Sunning, the future Toisan. (Zhongshan also had some representation in California but sent more workers to Hawaii.) They clung proudly to their own county or even village speechways—indeed, their deepest allegiance was to people of the same surname, indicating descent from a common lineage.

The Hong Kong labor recruiters dispatched more people to California from Toisan than anywhere else in China.[28] Unfortunately, exact statistics are impossible to reconstruct, and I have found wildly different numbers published with little documentation. But it is beyond dispute that nearly all the Chinese who came to California in the nineteenth century were from the Pearl River Delta, Four Counties natives greatly outnumbered Three Counties natives, and by far the largest Four Counties contingent was Toisanese.

The human traffic out of late-Qing-era China was not limited to Hong Kong and reached many parts of the world besides California. For sheer brutality, much of this lucrative shipping business came second only to the African slave trade that it replaced. Pearl River Delta Cantonese making the Hong Kong to San Francisco voyage were luckier than many others. Most went of their own will, as a conscious risk in pursuit of gain. For a few years the chief object was gold; from 1849 on, America was the "Gold Mountain" (Cantonese, *gum saan*; Mandarin, *jin shan*) in Chinese dreams. A more lasting goal was to earn money for the support of families back in Guangdong, and ideally for final return to one's native village, alive or dead. (When possible, delta-born sojourners made advance arrangements to have their bones shipped home for burial; again, Hong Kong was the usual conduit.) Enough Toisanese families ended up receiving steady remittances from Gold Mountain for several generations to outweigh all other contributions to the district's economy and leave it completely dependent on sojourning sons, husbands, and fathers.[29]

The story was very different for millions of other *hua gong*. The worldwide demand for manual labor had ramped up just as slavery was being abolished throughout the Americas and elsewhere. Filling the manpower shortage became an urgent concern for all the colonial powers as well as entrepreneurs in newly independent states. A notorious system of press-ganging sprang up in all the Chinese ports opened to international trade in 1842, and eventually in the many other ports where Westerners grabbed similar concessions in the next decades.

Bands of "crimps"—thugs hired to recruit people for either Western or Chinese labor brokers—kidnapped or decoyed able-bodied men to confined harborside coops known to Westerners as "barracoons" and to Chinese as "pigsties" (*zhu zi juan*). There they were gulled or beaten into signing indentures for a certain term of servitude and crammed like animals onto ships bound for foreign plantations, mines, or railway projects. If they were lucky or unlucky enough to survive the voyage, their indentures were made over to new masters and they served out their terms under conditions as brutal as those formerly visited on black slaves.

The most notorious points of origin were Macau, Xiamen (Amoy) in Fujian Province, and Shanghai (which gave its name to the usual recruiting technique). The most terrible destinations were Peru, Cuba, and the West Indies. The semi-enslaved victims of the trade came to be known as "coolies," a word that made its way from several Indian languages into several Chinese languages as well as English. Originally the English term carried only the neutral meaning (carried over from Indian usage) of "hired worker." But as the barbarous indenture system spread, it took on inflamed emotional overtones. Angry debates about the word's exact application spread to Western political theaters.[30]

Hong Kong had some share in this evil traffic. But it would also be the scene of the first British efforts to clean up the coolie trade. Besides, a large proportion of *hua gong* leaving Hong Kong were voluntarily embarked for the United States, Australia, and Canada. Conditions aboard many ships bound for those destinations might be hard to endure, but they were less monstrous than on the notorious "floating hells" that carried thousands to early deaths in South American guano mines or Cuban sugar plantations. Instead of being forced or duped into signing indentures, passengers without ready money usually traveled under "credit ticket" arrangements by which their fare was advanced to the shipping company by a labor broker or other third party, to be repaid with interest out of their eventual earnings.[31] Nearly all Toisanese newcomers to Gold Mountain had shipped as credit ticket passengers.

It would be a mistake to think of the Toisanese and their Four Counties neighbors as hapless yokels with no understanding of the modern world. Perhaps because the Four Counties had the poorest soil and most marginal farm incomes in the delta, local people already had a history of frequently turning their hand to other trades in Three Counties manufacturing centers on the outskirts of Guangzhou (for instance, iron works in the town of Foshan, a major source of woks). Between growing seasons, many Toisanese routinely traveled to the Three Counties for temporary jobs at foundries or textile mills.[32] After 1849 they would set out for Hong Kong and America not as unworldly naïfs but as possessors of survival skills on several different levels.

Certainly they did not arrive in San Francisco like friendless shipwreck victims. From the start, many Pearl River Delta and Hong Kong *hua shang* were involved in the California traffic not just as planners and facilitators but as passengers who would climb off the schooner or steamer ready to start re-creating practical home comforts within weeks or days.[33] Thanks to them, many other Chinese fresh off the boat found themselves better equipped to survive in the rude beginnings of San Francisco than many or most Yankees arriving from the East Coast or Midwest.

The factotums seem to have had an extraordinary sense of organization. Their grasp of what people would need on the other side extended from clothes and shoes to soy sauce and prefabricated houses. In both Hong Kong and San Francisco, these wheeler-dealers were equally quick to discern the developing contours of the local "service" economy and managed to have crucial personnel at hand in time to start playing a part in it. Among these were cooks. Who they were and how they were recruited are not questions that ever troubled any contemporary record keeper on either side of the Pacific. But there can be no doubt that experienced professional cooks were part of the San Francisco Chinese community from the start of its existence, and they were already familiar with Western appetites.

The Culinary "Language" Barrier

The mental distance between the English language and any member of the Han Chinese language groups is almost inconceivable. This barrier in itself accounts for much of the mutual bafflement and aversion that marked the relations of Chinese and Americans in this country for generations after the first gold seekers from Toisan climbed aboard ships bound for Gold Mountain. We cannot compare the process of bridge building across the linguistic divide to anything in prior Western history. It was many times more difficult to be bilingual in Toisanese (or any other version of Cantonese) and English than, say, German and English, Spanish and English, or Polish and English. For both parties, the difficulty of reading and writing was exceeded only by the difficulty of speaking.

Westerners who realized that written Chinese, with its thousands of ideogrammatic characters, could not be mastered through simple study like any European language seldom tried to rationally understand what was different about it. More often they were content with condescending shrugs at its hopeless mysteries. Educated people and ignoramuses both giggled over the spoken Cantonese sublanguages—especially Toisanese—as monkey jabber.

The Wade-Giles system of romanizing words as pronounced in Mandarin was not regularized until after 1890, and even then had trouble reaching more than a handful of scholars and librarians. Today's pinyin system for approximating the pronunciation of spoken Mandarin and indicating its four "sung" tones was a long way in the future. The more complex Cantonese, with still more tones and other unique features, was hopeless; even today all systems for converting any of the numerous spoken versions into Western vowels and consonants are breathtaking in their confusion and inadequacy. Cantonese dialects and regional subdialects with their many sung tones were confounding enough to Westerners. Alphabetical writing and "toneless" speech were equally mystifying ideas to men from the Pearl River Delta.

I submit that these blocks to purely verbal communication were matched (and exacerbated) by equally serious mutual misapprehensions about the business of cooking and eating.

Anyone trying to understand the history of history of Chinese food in this country should start by recognizing that any cuisine forms a system of skills and practices that can be figuratively described as a "syntax" and "vocabulary," analogous to spoken or written language. Many students of anthropology and semiotics have discussed cooking systems— not cooking terminology as such but the act of deploying implements and techniques in prelearned patterns in order to accomplish particular ends—as "languages." I have nothing to add to that highly theory-laden conversation. But it cannot be too strongly stated that the gaps between Cantonese and American culinary "idioms" were just as frustrating as those between actual linguistic idioms—a fact glimpsed in the twentieth century by a few cookbook authors who wrote of cooking "in Chinese."[1]

For Chinese and Westerners to make sense out of each other's gastronomic mindsets is far from easy even now, in an age of painstakingly detailed cookbooks and rapidly exchanged information. Two and a half centuries ago, it must have been like attempted messages between extraterrestrials from different galaxies.

Against all odds, one party had succeeded in the effort by the mid-eighteenth century. At that point, Chinese cooks in the vicinity of Guangzhou had mastered enough English culinary skills to present more than acceptable meals to representatives of the British East India Company who were trading at Guangzhou under the restrictive Canton system.

Neither the English nor any other Westerners tried to reciprocate until long after the colonial era. During the second half of the nineteenth century at least some English and Americans, ignoring the reflexive shudders and jeers of many others, learned to enjoy Chinese food. But they did not go so far as to try re-creating it in their own kitchens through either deliberate analysis of the crucial principles or hands-on practice in pursuit of the right reflexes.

It is surely impossible to trace the stages through which Pearl River Delta cooks felt their way into applied skills in English cookery. But Westerners were generally agreed that the southeastern Chinese flair for mimicry and improvisation at any useful task whatever bordered on wizardry. Visiting Englishmen had not had the concept of *xiang banfa* explained to them, but they knew it when they saw it in action.

Later, as Western steam-powered machinery reached Far Eastern colonies in the late nineteenth century, entrepreneurially minded Chinese "sojourners" might learn to copy it well enough to dominate some regional industry within a few decades. (This would happen with the rice-milling business in Thailand.[2]) At a humbler socioeconomic level but in just the same spirit, southern Guangdong locals—always men, since there was almost no communication permitted between foreigners and Chinese women—had picked up British and other European culinary skills after only a few generations of contact with Westerners. This nimble address presaged a mastery suggested in the following three instances:

• In an account of Far Eastern voyages in the years 1747 and 1748, the colonial administrator Charles Frederick Noble noted the highly satisfactory cooking arrangements for his visiting party at the British "factories" in Guangzhou:

> Our porter business was all performed by Chinese *cowlies*, whom we hired for a small matter, and most of whom spoke a little English; which we found very convenient. We had likewise several Chinese cooks to assist our own, who, as they had been long employed by the English ships, and could speak the English language pretty well, dressed our victuals after the English manner, as well and as expeditiously as our own cooks.[3]

• More than a century later, the *London Times* correspondent George Wingrove Cooke was able to make a far more glowing report about what Chinese cooks were capable of when not led astray by awful English teaching:

> Every Chinaman has a natural aptitude for cookery. I know one little, lean, thread-paper anatomy at Hongkong, whose only teaching has been half a dozen lessons administered to him from a French cookery-book, and who will send you up a consommé aux oeufs pochés, a filet de boeuf aux champignons, a salmi of teal, a salad, waferlike fried potatoes, and a sweet omelette in a style certainly not inferior to Vefour; for the salmi I'd back him against the world, and for the salad against any Englishman who ever inverted that best of Italian proverbs, "Molto d'olio, poco d'aceto."[4]

• At the Hotel Gladstone in Portland, Oregon, during the late 1890s, an ambitious and very food-savvy proprietress named Elizabeth Brennan decided to upgrade the kitchen by replacing the French staff with a trio of Chinese cooks. One of them, Jue Let, would eventually become her own family cook after her marriage to John Beard. More than half a century later, her son James (born in 1903) vividly recalled the excellence of Let's yeast rolls, chicken pie, pot-au-feu, and Welsh rabbit, and the assurance with which he taught the English-born Elizabeth to make English-style pound cake, seed cake, and "ladyfingers as light as ghosts' footsteps." Sometimes Let would treat the Beards to his own Chinese cooking, but "Mother never mastered the dishes."[5] Nor did James Beard throughout his career ever venture to present serious recipes for Chinese fare.

This one-way street is worth thinking about. It would be the rule in all Chinese–Western culinary encounters until well into the twentieth century. I doubt that the inequality of the exchange can be entirely chalked up to American (or English) ignorance and xenophobia, glaring though they were until the aftermath of World War II. There was something about Chinese cuisine that even so practiced, clever, and willing a cook as Elizabeth Beard couldn't or wouldn't get the hang of, despite all Jue Let's expertise—while not just a few but many Chinese became supremely skilled at reproducing the nuances of English, American, and French cookery.

To understand the reasons behind this long and oddly asymmetrical impasse of understanding, we should discard the smirky, patronizing attitudes toward WASP predecessors that Caucasian followers of today's food fashions often strut as badges of their own sophistication. Better to start by putting ourselves in the position of people who were no brighter or stupider than we are but understandably enough had never tasted any kind of Chinese cooking. Even today a few non-Chinese Americans can remember blank bewilderment or instinctive dislike on first encounters with the food of some long-ago "Dragon Pavilion" or "Golden Sampan." I am one.

I have long forgotten most details of the meal in Philadelphia's tiny Chinatown that I was taken to as a child, probably during the early 1950s. But the sense of an alien quality, something disturbingly *different* about the food, is as sharp as ever in my memory. I have never involuntarily flinched in the same way from Indian, Japanese, or any other "foreign" cuisine. It took me a quarter of a century to get over that first instinctive unease, in a sudden "Eureka!" moment at a 1970s New York dim sum parlor.

Today I can make a good retrospective guess at the main reasons for my original distaste. They are instructive because in a negative way they exactly mirror some true and important qualities of Chinese cuisine, or the quasi-Cantonese version of it that would have been on display at my Philadelphia encounter. They also are likely to have been just the things that many Gold Rush Californians promptly and instinctively rejected on first exposure to what they liked to call "Celestial" cooking.

I would have made a mess of putting my initial objections into words. So would (and did) those disapproving Gold Rushers. For rookies like them and me, the whole experience was one huge, contorted mystery that defied disentangling in lucid terms. Popular assumptions about food are always cruder and less thought-out than the lessons laid down by cookbook writers. Their very instinctiveness is just what makes them difficult to articulate to anyone else.

Now, people previously acquainted with one cuisine who suddenly encounter another will of course miss certain accustomed features and wonder at other things that are unfamiliar. But with Chinese cuisine, what is unfamiliar is not only a great mass of details but the underlying "language" mentioned before—a system with a far more complex "grammar" than any Western counterpart. In fact, this culinary idiom is as stunningly *remote* from other systems of cookery as the Chinese written language is from all other writing systems, and as heterogeneous as the constellation of different Han Chinese spoken languages. (Written Chinese is a sui generis mixture of ideographs and phonetic elements; instead of one spoken Han language, China possesses a plethora of separate Han languages, sublanguages, and dialects probably outnumbering all the languages of Europe.) Uninitiated Western cooks trying to get to first base in Chinese culinary "syntax" and "vocabulary" have a far more bewildering task than Chinese cooks trying to master some English, French, American, or other Western dishes. Uninitiated Western eaters face the same impasses from another angle.

The main culinary touchstones that Gold Rush eaters would have missed in southern Cantonese-style cooking in California, and that I would miss in a later, watered-down version of the same cuisine in Philadelphia, were

- Identifiable principal ingredients retaining original sizes and shapes;
- Recognizable textures or consistencies in the components of dishes;
- Recognizable original flavors or seasonings; and
- Cooking techniques designed with any of the above criteria in mind.

To my best ex post facto conjecture, the features marking the foreign "language" of the cooking were

- An inexplicable, off-putting smell, most likely produced by some unfamiliar and unwelcome fat;
- Nameless bits of this or that, cut up smaller or thinner than food "should" have been;
- Brazen juxtapositions of ingredients—animal and vegetable—in what appeared to be ill-assorted jumbles; and
- A peculiarly dense, complicated intertwining of several unfamiliar flavors at once, especially ones produced by strange kinds of fermentation.

Of course, millions of non-Chinese diners have come, with repeated exposure, to love all the qualities that some of us once hated. We have learned to respond to bits of a new "language," with or without actively grasping what makes it tick, and we tend to smile at the ignorance of people who haven't acquired our sophistication. But it makes sense to use such reactions as windows into major differences between two kinds of kitchen idiom instead of dismissing them as senseless.

DISCREPANT APPROACHES AND ATTITUDES

On the Western side, the main cooking methods recognized by ordinary English and American home cooks and eaters at around 1850 were boiling, baking, roasting, frying, and broiling. To these, as set forth in 1817 by the English authority Dr. William Kitchiner in an influential manual titled *The Cook's Oracle*, some people would have added stewing as a variant of boiling. Baking was a relative newcomer to family cooking, dependent on the presence of home ovens, and at this time certainly was not synonymous with roasting. The latter was mostly done on spits in front of an open fire, whose management was well understood by some cooks and botched by others. Frying, in popular understanding as well as in Kitchiner's usage, meant "boiling in fat."[6]

Food meant to undergo any of these processes was usually left whole or (depending on size) divided into rather large pieces. Poultry might be cooked whole or cut into joints. Meats were usually prepared as joints or sliced into steaks or cutlets; only for especially elegant presentations were vegetables cut into anything finer than a few chunks. (Indeed, kitchen knives with straight edges suitable for efficient chopping and dicing were rare in American home kitchens until late in the nineteenth century.) All but very large fish were usually cooked whole.

Cooks with sufficient means and interest might have a large selection of aromatics and other seasonings at their disposal. But there was no universal idea that any were really mandatory except salt, pepper, and a few "sweet" spices for cakes and pastries. If my own family's habits as late as the mid-twentieth century are any guide, many middle-class cooks ignored nearly all herbs as needless folderol.

In most kitchens, the core elements of the diet were understood to be two. Bread or sometimes potatoes most essentially represented the starch-based side of things, which was well enough liked but didn't command the prestige of the protein-based side—meaning poultry or meat, especially beef, preferably cooked by any method but boiling. (The much cheaper pork had less cachet than most other meats.) People also ate either a handful (for the poor) or a sizable range (for the better-off) of fruits and vegetables. But there was little mistaking the fact that roast or broiled meat was king on the scale of popular American dietary priorities. (Anti-Chinese rabble-rousers would later intimate that it was the birthright of American manhood.)

The Chinese approach was incompatible with the practices or attitudes described above. It started with the unspoken, instinctive premise that in everyday meals prepared by the major everyday methods, any one ingredient should be cooked for *the shortest possible time needed for it to reach a certain optimum flavor and texture over briefly applied high heat*. Given that nearly all cooking involves more than one ingredient, working by this principle requires superefficient prior organization incomprehensible to untutored outsiders.

Chinese cognoscenti and theorists recognized many subtly differentiated cooking methods (not all conforming to the shortest-possible-time rule) under a host of individual names. But for the plain, everyday cooking of the southern Guangdong natives who came to California, the three crucial ones were

- Stir-frying (Mandarin, *chao*; Cantonese, *chau*, often anglicized by Americans as "chow"): Stirring and tossing particular combinations of ingredients in an appropriately sized, bowl-shaped shallow pan (Mandarin, *huo*; Cantonese, *wok*) with a little very hot fat over very high heat, at blitzkrieg speed. It is the single most important Chinese cooking method, considered by many to have reached its highest form in southern Guangdong.
- Steaming (Mandarin, *zheng*; Cantonese, *jing*): Here the food to be prepared is set on perforated trays or slatted bamboo platforms (sometimes bowls or plates perched on racks) over boiling water in a covered vessel, to cook in the rising steam. Steaming occasionally involves fairly time-consuming items (e.g., a whole chicken or duck) but is most often applied to quicker-cooking foods like dumplings and whole fish. This method is admired for preserving an intrinsic purity and immediacy (Mandarin, *xian*; Cantonese, *sin*) of fresh natural flavors; it is particularly important in southern Guangdong.

- A form of controlled boiling or combination of boiling and steaming used, with a final resting-and-absorption period, for rice.

Of these, stir-frying and Chinese-style steaming were perfectly unknown in Western kitchens, and the care taken with rice-cooking baffled any non-Chinese who hadn't grown up in rice country. The most "untranslatable" aspects of all three methods were the minutiae of advance organization and the signs marking the critical moment of doneness—and, beyond these, the very idea of what a meal is.

A CIVILIZED MEAL

As George Wingrove Cooke astutely remarked, a Chinaman "sees an especial connection between cookery and civilization."[7] For most Chinese but especially for people from south Guangdong, the linking principle was rice.

A resourceful Pearl River deltan preparing a humble, hasty meal in Gold Rush–era California would have started by collecting exactly the necessary amount of fuel and painstakingly rinsing the necessary amount of rice in clean water before putting it on to cook over lively heat. The usual stove was a small brazier fired with wood or charcoal; a bucket would do for those who didn't have a proper Chinese ceramic brazier. Meanwhile, he (at the time, the number of Chinese females in California was infinitesimal) would also prepare at least one other necessity with unbelievable speed. Before foreign observers could grasp what was going on, he would have grabbed a large, outlandishly proportioned blade and almost instantaneously reduced a handful of other preassembled ingredients to various kinds of small chunks, slices, dices, or shreds, each cut to a certain size or thickness depending on its particular cooking properties.

While the cooked rice rested, all the cut-up components would go—in a prescribed order—into hot oil or lard in a pan. This would most likely have been a cast iron wok made in Foshan, where artisans had perfected the casting of remarkably light iron vessels and where many residents of the poorer Guangdong counties seasonally sought factory work.[8] Almost as soon as the last ingredients were added, the result would be ready to dish up with the rice, needing only the last-minute addition of a few flavorings such as soy sauce. Aside from the wok, the only equipment used in the whole stir-frying performance would have been the strange-looking knife, a cutting surface, and a stirring tool, perhaps nothing but a pair of chopsticks.

As any self-respecting person knew, this was a proper meal because it united cooked rice with some other component designed to share its journey from bowl to belly or, in a common phrase, to "make the rice go down" (Cantonese, *hah faan*; Mandarin, *xia fan*). The rice and the auxiliary element went together like dog and tail, with the understanding that the second could never wag the first. A pot of rice shared among eaters qualified as a meal in its own right even if attended by nothing more than a smidgen of stir-fried vegetable. The assumption was carried to America by all Cantonese immigrants and was drummed into their children and grandchildren until it became instinct. Mary Tsui Ping Yee, who grew up during the 1930s and 1940s as the daughter of Guangdong-born laundry owners in the town of Canonsburg, Pennsylvania, recalled that her mother was "disconsolate" when "supplies of rice ran out for several weeks" during World War II: "As she set down platters of potatoes, bread, or noodles, she sighed, '*Moh fan haek* (No rice to eat)'. What she meant was, 'This is really not a meal; without rice, it's only a snack!'"[9]

The improvised meal described above was a classic Cantonese union of *faan* and *sung*, the helper that made it go down. (Northern Chinese cooks observed the same principle, but for them the *fan* or grain-based element had originally been millet, and later wheat-based noodles and breads; they used the broader word "*cai*" for meat or vegetable dishes that appeared at a meal along with *fan*.) The treatment of ingredients for the stir-fried *sung* had an inevitable logic that Western cooks had a hard time grasping. The great principle was to cut things up in such a way, and add them in such an order, that tougher and tenderer foods should *all reach a desired consistency at the same instant* in a feat of lightning-fast choreography. Major vegetables had to be added in proper sequence, in pieces designed for just so many minutes' cooking and no more. Similarly, any meat or poultry in the dish had to hit the hot fat in slices or other narrow shapes ready to cook through in a very few minutes. The usual aromatics—scallions or other alliums and fresh ginger—might be dissected into tiny bits or hairlike threads that would receive less than a minute's exposure to the heat. The speed with which all these things were accomplished was unimaginable by any standard of Western kitchen operations.

Trying to put such food in one's mouth was equally disconcerting to many Gold Rushers, as it had been to most if not all English people and Americans doing business in China. It is hard to convey to twenty-first-century Western eaters how strange their forebears found the sight of food cut up in small bits before cooking, rather than reaching the table as recognizable steaks, chops, roasts, fowls, and familiar vegetables. Even English or American stews usually involved meat cut into chops or fairly hearty slices. Lacking any adequate descriptive terms for typical Chinese dishes, observers clumsily wrote of "fricassees," "ragouts," "curries," or "hashes"—all words meant to suggest nameless smidgens of mystery meats and vegetables in some kind of strong-flavored sauce. (In genteel culinary parlance, "hash" up to this time had been a dish of cooked meats cut into slices and delicately rewarmed in a savory sauce. In California mining circles, the word was starting to mean any last-ditch anthology of leftovers, the better kind usually being yesterday's meat and potatoes hacked up together and fried.[10])

That anybody found southern Cantonese flavors strong will also puzzle many today. Recalling my own first reaction to Chinese food, I surmise that soy sauce and a cluster of other fermented products were the reason. True, many English and American cooks of the era were brewing condiments (vaguely modeled on ideas that Western voyagers had picked up in the Far East) that they called "soy." But these had nothing to do with Chinese sauces fermented with the mold species *Aspergillus oryzae* and *A. soyae*, which partly digest the carbohydrates of soybeans before a secondary fermentation in a strong brine with another set of microorganisms.[11] At the time, Chinese soy sauce was commonly produced in small batches by local makers or even home preservers. Like other brews rooted in peasant economies, it did not get reduced to any sort of commercial standardization until close to the turn of the twentieth century. The fact that four or more generations of middlebrow Caucasian Americans have now grown up taking factory-made Chinese or Japanese soy sauce for granted does not tell us how people who had never tasted soy sauces in Chinese dishes would have reacted to their unfamiliar fermented notes at around 1850.

At that point soy sauces could be strongly individual in character, and knowledgeable Chinese cooks in wealthy urban households or prominent restaurant kitchens probably had at least as much access to a range of different types as their counterparts today. Modern Guangdong cooks often combine several different kinds of soy sauce (lighter or darker; thinner or more viscous; possibly enriched with mushrooms or sweetenings) to finish their cooking sauces, along with various other fermented pastes of beans or wheat. They may also use small amounts of preserved vegetables (of which there is a large and decidedly pungent repertoire well described in Shiu-ying Hu's *Food Plants of China*[12]) or fermented bean curd (which is made in several mild- or vile-smelling versions). They may add some unfermented oyster sauce—more delicate but puzzling to unhabituated Western palates. It is a foregone conclusion that non-Chinese Gold Rushers had never encountered any of these flavorings. Even a few of the possible additions to cooking sauces, together with the suspicious absence of identifiable objects in most dishes, must have dismayed some Californian diners and helped reinforce a far from romantic sense of mystery.

Western accounts of Chinese eating places frequently mention yet one more drawback: a nasty smell that most people attributed to some kind of oil or perhaps lard. Sinophobic observers had a field day with this unpleasantness. Even thoughtful, sympathetic American and English accounts mention an off-putting odor too often for historians to dismiss the whole thing as ignorant Western prejudice. Certainly soy sauce and other fermentations must have made background contributions to a general Chinese restaurant pong. But I see no reason to doubt the noses of commentators who thought some cooking fat was to blame.

Cooke, who greatly admired Chinese cuisine, found the street-food scene decidedly smelly. What he describes are not *faan/sung* or *fan/cai* meals but quick bites served up amid "a frying of fish and flesh and fowl, and a bubbling of oil in many pans," with an accompanying odor that was "decidedly the weak point of Chinese common cookery. Whether that oil be castor oil, as many say . . . or tea oil, or oil expressed from the cotton seed, or which other of the twenty different vegetable oils in use in China, is of little importance. It is so foul and rancid that the stench it produces is intolerable, and the cookshops add most potently to the fearful scents of a Chinese town or village."[13]

I am not sure that this puzzle will ever be satisfactorily solved. We should first realize that mid-nineteenth-century American and European cooks were familiar with only a small number of cooking fats, mostly animal fats such as butter, beef suet, or lard. (The last was equally popular in China.) The idea of using oil as a cooking medium rather than a salad dressing ingredient was far from universal. The only kind fully accepted in salads was the posh and expensive olive oil. The few other available vegetable oils were widely distrusted as cheap olive oil substitutes. Rapeseed oil had a reputation for harshness. Thomas Jefferson had hoped to introduce sesame oil as an alternative to olive oil, but with scant success. Chinese cooks were fond of it in a form pressed from the toasted seeds, which was prized as a flavoring or condiment to be added to dishes at the last minute but became harsh-smelling over high heat.

In fact, by Gold Rush times the Chinese had gone much further than Westerners in exploring cooking oils extracted from other plant seeds. Recently they had started making oil from peanuts, introduced from the New World during the sixteenth or seventeenth century. Other sources that had been used for generations or centuries were "tea seeds" (from some *Camellia* species related to the tea bush), hempseed, the seeds of various plants in the *Brassica* (cabbage) tribe, castor beans, and, to a small extent, soybeans.[14]

But the technology of oil manufacture was still too crude to turn any of these into facsimiles of the clean-cooking, flavorless, deodorized vegetable oils that would later be introduced to modern kitchens through factory-scale chemical solvent extraction and degumming. All would thus have been somewhat muddier and stickier than the products we are used to, and marked by characteristic odors and flavors. Peanut oil would have tasted and smelled of peanuts (as good Chinese brands still do). Soybean oil—which in any case would remain difficult and expensive to extract until much later—would have had an emphatic beaniness. Tea oil was reputedly pleasant. Hempseed oil was cheap but considered smelly; castor oil was even worse. Any bad original aromas would have been intensified in heating and cruelly magnified if the oil were reused ad infinitum without filtering—also a good recipe for rancidity. The same is true of lard, though it probably was used more carefully because it was expensive.

Whatever the reason for reports of malodorous cooking fats, we can take it for granted that Chinese cookery, like any other, was practiced by both good and bad cooks to splendid or awful effect. We can also assume that non-Chinese eaters greeted it with different degrees of tolerance or intolerance, across an enormous communications gap.

Only the most seasoned and unflappable Western China hands could have recognized that they were encountering something far more subtle, complex, wide-ranging, and heterogeneous than French (or any other European) cuisine. Transforming the raw into the cooked was not in itself an intellectual exercise. But an enormous terminology of connoisseurship—as well as real hands-on skills—grew up around it over the course of many centuries. The concepts involved resist English translation even today. For at least a glimpse of some, consult the appendices and glossary of the English writer Fuchsia Dunlop's pioneering 2001 work *Sichuan Cookery*.[15]

At the time of the California Gold Rush, Chinese cooks in the imperial kitchens or the employ of nobles or wealthy merchants received long, diligent, professional training. Their craft was a vast body of lore and skills; connoisseurs reporting on it singled out dozens (at least) of nuances meaningless to Westerners. People might, for instance, praise the texture of properly cooked ingredients in terms indicating very specific, tactile kinds of softness, tenderness, slipperiness, gelatinousness, crispness, flakiness, firmness, suppleness, sponginess, resilience, rubbery crunch, and so forth. There were names for both the five broad flavor categories—sweet, sour, salt, bitter, and *la* (Mandarin) or *laat* (Cantonese), both meaning pungent or hot—and their effects in different combinations.

There was a body of names for the very shapes into which ingredients should be cut in preparation for cooking, or the different motions of the *dou* (cleaver-shaped knife; Mandarin, *dao*) in dealing with them. The everyday cooking methods of stir-frying and steaming might be practiced with particular added refinements like using only light-colored ingredients for a *qing* (clear, lucid, transparent) effect. Literally dozens of other possible methods existed, including many special kinds of frying, stir-frying, pan-searing, braising, poaching, and stewing as well as ways of combining these. Some methods were chiefly left to cookshops. In Guangdong, the most famous instance has long been a specialized form of *siu* or (Mandarin) *shao*—an untranslatable term often mangled in English as "barbecuing." This method, *cha siu* (or *cha shao*), is one of the few procedures involving meats left whole or in sizable pieces and requires a large, vertically oriented roasting oven that allows freer circulation of heat than any Western oven. The food—large slabs of pork or whole chickens and ducks—is painted with honey or another sweet glaze and suspended on hooks over a very hot charcoal fire until it acquires a glossy or crunchy finish. For non-Chinese fans of Chinese food, the example par excellence of oven roasting is Peking duck.

It is instructive to compare late Qing Chinese cuisine with French cuisine of roughly the same era. Each embraced a spectrum of approaches from the most "mandarinized" rarefaction (for a wealthy clientele) to subsistence-level pot-boiling, with a large middle ground of wonderfully skilled, good cooking that managed to be as practical as it was artful. Each was, as the historians Mary Hyman and Philip Hyman have written of French food, a "multifaceted discipline";[16] each was the highly structured, sometimes pretentious product of a civilization given to systematizing and codifying.

But late Qing culinary culture had not only more ancient intellectual roots but a much older restaurant tradition than its late-nineteenth-century French counterpart. Its actual cooking processes were more intricately detailed. It was more weighted with symbology, more bound up with cosmological and medical beliefs. And if anything beyond these factors set apart the Chinese scene from any other, it was people's sheer adaptability and quick-study savoir faire as cooks, with or without formal training.

George Wingrove Cooke's testimony about his Hong Kong cook's prowess in French dishes deserves to be set beside this flat assertion (in 1852) by a cosmopolitan and witty Frenchman from the southwestern department of Tarn-et-Garonne, the Catholic missionary Évariste Régis Huc: "All the inhabitants of the Celestial Empire, without exception, are gifted with a remarkable aptitude for cookery. If you want a cook, it is the easiest thing in the world to supply the want; you have but to take the first Chinese you can catch, and after a few days' practice he will acquit himself of his duties to admiration."[17]

The Welsh Protestant missionary Griffith John recalled Huc's words a quarter of a century later when wondering whether to appoint one of his converts—Liu Kin-Shan, "a sawyer by trade"—to the post of cook for his small congregation in Hankou: "In England, such a metamorphosis would have been dismissed as ridiculous." But Liu happily accepted the post as a means "of promoting the physical and spiritual well-being of his fellow-men. In this capacity he has given us the utmost satisfaction."[18] No talent of the Chinese more amazed foreigners than this sheer *xiang banfa* ability to cope, in kitchens or any other work situation.

Chinese cuisine (unlike French) was never exported to this country in its most mannered refinements or surpassing extravagances. But it certainly began to be exported in very fine versions during the Gold Rush. Disastrous alignments of the political stars would soon throw the Chinese immigrant community into fear and confusion. Otherwise, I believe that late-nineteenth- and early-twentieth-century America beyond California would have become familiar with excellent representations of Chinese food introduced by both trained pros and nimble-witted improvisers.

In fact, under better circumstances Americans might have learned that the area from which most immigrants came before the 1882 Exclusion Act happened to be China's most celebrated hub of the culinary arts. People everywhere in the kingdom loyally praised their own regional foodways but agreed with surprising consistency that Cantonese cuisine was the most delightful of all. A popular proverb gave the formula for the ideal existence as "being born in Suzhou, dressing in Hangzhou, eating in Guangzhou, and dying in Liuzhou"—thereby profiting from the Middle Kingdom's loveliest surroundings, most exquisite silks, finest food, and best coffin wood.

Where Cantonese cuisine was considered to excel was in the art that conceals art: an unforced freshness, harmony, and balance; a respect for natural flavors; a magical ability to deliver any dish to the table with every ingredient gracefully and absolutely *à point*. But at the same time, diners in Guangzhou and the entire province of Guangdong were also known for what northern Chinese considered grotesque appetites. The emperor's subjects in the far south already had a reputation for disloyalty and lawless pursuits. People in Beijing related with horror, and perfect accuracy, that the perfidious Cantonese actually ate rats, cats, monkeys, snakes (including poisonous ones), and a lively assortment of insects. (Dog was too commonly eaten in most of China to arouse the same kind of disgust.) These were not core elements of everyday menus, but the locals were in no way ashamed of them or their part in the scheme of dietary values. The sharp duality in Chinese outsiders' views of Cantonese cookery—the most elegant in all China but at the same time given to nasty practices—is not unlike some former English attitudes toward French food.

Given the monumental barriers to understanding between Eastern and Western culinary cultures, other Gold Rushers could not have grasped that the new arrivals from the Pearl River Delta possessed the most highly regarded cooking tradition in all China. But for a brief interval, at least some of the true Cantonese culinary gifts would be successfully transplanted to San Francisco and other places of Chinese settlement.

"Celestials" on Gold Mountain

COOKS, MERCHANTS, WORKERS, AND ROLE REVERSALS

Modern accounts of the Chinese American food story sometimes portray the first Guangdong-born Gold Rushers as culinary dimwits marooned in California almost without, as one unwittingly sexist description has it, "a woman in the kitchen to show them how things were done."[1] This version of the saga often goes on to explain that the fare served to Americans in Chinese restaurants until the late twentieth century was a clumsy, half-accidental makeshift cobbled together out of substitutes for unavailable Chinese ingredients.[2] Both ideas are long overdue for correction.

In fact, the assumption that only women would have known their way around a Chinese kitchen is an ignorant cultural bias. No immigrants have ever arrived in the United States with better skills and resources for re-creating their own cuisine than the men who set out from the Pearl River Delta for "Gold Mountain" (the American West) in and after 1849. As for the hybridized American-Chinese cuisine that (beginning at the end of the century) would supply images of Chinese food to the nation at large for close to a century, I later show that it was a cleverly judged construct founded on Cantonese experience in cooking to please Westerners—something that people had been doing along the Pearl River

Delta long before a building contractor noticed something shiny in the stream at Sutter's Mill.

Surviving descriptions indicate that the first eateries founded by Chinese immigrants in San Francisco had a high degree of professional polish and sophistication. There is every reason that they should have. In the first place, restaurant food carefully prepared for well-defined clienteles has had a conspicuous role in Chinese civilization for many centuries. This cannot be said of all world cultures. (Until about the last sixty years, Brahmin society in India was hedged about with so many ritual prohibitions as to exclude the idea of food or drink even *touched* by the wrong hands, much less prepared from start to finish by strangers outside the home.) Cookshops, taverns, and restaurants of various kinds had existed in China since at least the tenth or eleventh century AD, perhaps still earlier. They were skillfully tailored to different classes of patrons, from workingmen grabbing a bowl of noodles at a humble street stall to wealthy merchants for whom trained professional cooks could produce something like scaled-down versions of the banquet fare prepared by the staffs of the imperial court kitchens.

The first great Chinese flowering of a diversified consumer culture took place during the Song dynasty. It grew up initially at the northern Song capital of Kaifeng on the Yellow River (AD 960–1126) and then, after Kaifeng's surrender to invaders from Mongolia, at Hangzhou south of the Yangzi (1127–1279). Observers in twelfth-century Kaifeng and thirteenth-century Hangzhou have left elaborate descriptions of the two cities' numberless eating houses and rich culinary life. Many details are corroborated by Marco Polo, who reached Hangzhou several decades after it too had fallen to the Mongols. But none of the Chinese accounts has been translated into any Western language. The snippets from a few that the French scholar Jacques Gernet cites in his study of Hangzhou's golden age afford tantalizing glimpses into a restaurant scene already at a high pitch of development. Huge numbers of flourishing establishments offered both food and wine, sometimes along with sex, to many differentiated clienteles. They were staffed by professional cooks of whom the great majority were men, though some restaurants are known to have had women cooks. All were attuned to their particular segments of a vast and diverse market.[3]

"The people of Hangchow are very difficult to please," commented Wu Zimu in *Meng liang lu* (Dreaming of the city of abundance), describing a class of large restaurants with flower-decked archways and a choice of seating arrangements:

> Hundreds of orders are given on all sides: this person wants something hot, another something cold, a third something tepid, a fourth something chilled: one wants cooked food, another raw, another chooses roast, another grill. The orders, given in a loud voice, are all different, sometimes three different ones at the same table. Having received the orders, the waiter goes to the kitchen and sings out the orders, starting with the first one. The man who replies from the kitchen is called the Head Dishwarmer, or the Table-setter. When the waiter has come to the end of his list, he takes his tray to the stove and then goes off to serve each customer with the dish ordered. He never mixes them up, and if by any unlikely chance he should make a mistake, the proprietor will launch into a volley of oaths addressed to the offending waiter, will straightaway make him stop serving, and may even dismiss him altogether.[4]

Nothing of comparable pizzazz and efficiency would exist in France, or anywhere else in Europe, for another half-millennium. Other contemporary sources mentioned by both Gernet and Michael Freeman (in an essay on Song dynasty food) make clear that terms like "hot," "cold," "roast," or "grill" don't begin to suggest the richness of the cuisine. Hangzhou, in particular, commanded an infinite wealth of fruits and vegetables, fish, shellfish, meats, and game prepared by still more methods than those mentioned in chapter 2. There were numberless dishes based on wheat (noodles, "ravioli," "pies," and various flatbreads or "cakes"); many different strains of rice were prized by knowledgeable cooks and eaters for special qualities.[5] No body of cooks has ever had an audience better qualified to appraise culinary refinements, from short-order noodle-making skills to prowess at elaborate trompe l'oeil fantasies.

Strange though it may sound, the food that would be served six hundred years later at Chinese restaurants in early San Francisco is much more poorly documented than these Song-era achievements. The explanation is simple enough: local Chinese cooks and restaurateurs themselves had no reason to record it. The only people who produced written accounts were American or European customers almost completely unable to decipher what they were eating.

Of course, the people writing about Song dynasty cuisine at its height had been a class of cognoscenti rather than the cooks and restaurateurs who dished up actual meals. Any gastronomic cognoscenti who may have existed in gold-crazed California were supremely unqualified to appraise Chinese cuisine. The parties to East–West restaurant transactions during this era had as much grasp of each other's culinary terminology as deaf people and blind people trying to decipher each other's words for colors and sounds. But as already noted, the Chinese on their part had already acquired some kind of practical insight into Western preferences that made any formal terminology unnecessary.

By the time the first groups of Chinese disembarked amid the jerry-built beginnings of San Francisco, residents of the southeastern provinces already had a cannier *xiang banfa* sense of what it took to organize and outfit expeditions to distant regions than nearly anyone from the eastern United States. Most of the necessary expertise belonged to the *hua shang*, meaning the merchants and variously specialized commercial operators who knew how to make things happen in defiance of inconvenient Qing dynasty imperial policies. Until the Gold Rush, their main overseas theater of action had been what they considered their rightful backyard: the many bailiwicks of the Nanyang, or Southeast Asia.[6] In China proper, merchantry was at least officially regarded as a debased occupation by comparison with three higher-ranked callings: mandarin scholar-bureaucrat, tiller of the soil, and skilled artisan. Shackled by irksome imperial restrictions at home, would-be moneymakers enjoyed comparative freedom in different corners of the Nanyang. Their activities there would have tremendous importance for both China and (later) the Western powers. Food-related activities were especially crucial.

As early as the Song dynasty, southeastern Chinese had become acquainted with a quick-maturing strain of rice native to Champa on the central coast of today's Vietnam. Soon they were planting this double-cropping variety (more notable for yield than quality) on a large enough scale to revolutionize Chinese agriculture.[7] In the nineteenth century, when even Champa rice proved unable to keep up with the needs of a rampantly increasing population, Chinese growers and brokers penetrated the rice business in Burma, Vietnam, and other areas of the Nanyang. Late in the century, as rice milled and polished to perfect whiteness by Western-devised machinery became the worldwide industry standard, Chinese entrepreneurs would manage first to buy and then to copy and manufacture milling equipment successfully enough to monopolize rice processing and exporting in Thailand for several generations. They set up sugar mills in the Philippines. In other parts of the region, Chinese had achieved firm control of local enterprises ranging from trade in dried fish and shellfish, bird's nests, and the creatures known as "sea cucumbers" or "bêche-de-mer" to sugar refining and pepper growing in, respectively, Thailand and Borneo. They dominated many other trades.[8] In fact, the scope of Chinese activities throughout the Nanyang would dwarf any traffic between China and the United States for a long time to come. It would also incidentally fuel regional anti-Chinese resentments that would be fully unleashed after the Vietnam War of the 1960s and 1970s.

Meanwhile, Gold Rush–era sojourners directly benefited from earlier Chinese experiences in the Nanyang. The *hua shang* had long expertise as protean contrivers outfitting parties of Chinese headed for overseas settlements. As the Western colonial powers boldly expanded their Far Eastern sway, the *hua shang* also acquired immense practical knowhow as labor brokers and bosses dispatching *hua gong*, or Chinese manpower, on a large scale to British and European plantations everywhere in the Nanyang. Suitable provisions were automatically factored into the planning and would continue to be so when fortune seekers set out for the fabled riches of America.

But America wasn't the Nanyang. Neither were Australia and Canada, the sites of other gold fields. All three had already managed to sweep sparse populations of aborigines out of the way and define themselves as societies of white English-speaking transplants. In all three, it would be only a few years before government-backed Sinophobia and some of the most blatantly racist initiatives in the history of Western labor movements confronted new arrivals from southern Guangdong.

The Pearl River Delta Chinese in America would also experience unforeseen rearrangements of traditional Confucian social rankings.

Though laboring men were the descendants of the Chinese peasantry, a class regarded as a peculiarly honorable part of the kingdom's Confucian moral foundations, they would find themselves more defenseless than anyone else against future white campaigns to harass and expel the "inferior" race. The merchants and facilitators, who in their homeland were looked down on by the mandarins as mere moneygrubbers, would not only be exempted from American laws meant to exclude unskilled labor but would to some extent stand as protectors of the *hua gong* as well as the lifeline that kept laborers in touch with families back in Toisan and the rest of the southern Guangdong counties. It was also the *hua shang* who, through thick and thin, would maintain the flow of Chinese cooking necessities and other supplies from the motherland to the overseas Chinese community—eventually to Chinatowns in nearly every one of the United States, but initially to San Francisco's "Little China" and the California mining camps. A network of supply lines from Little China into prospecting territory quickly materialized.[9] Wherever Chinese miners arrived, Chinese cooking ingredients like preserved duck and fermented vegetables also arrived at some hole-in-corner shop run by a Chinese—or sometimes by an American. Prentice Mulford, who prospected during the 1850s, related in 1873:

> The Chinese grocery stores are museums to the American. There are strange dried roots, strange dried fish, strange dried land and marine plants, ducks and chickens, split, pressed thin and smoked; dried shellfish; cakes newly made, yellow, glutinous and fatty, stamped with tea-box characters; and great earthen jars filled with rottenness. I speak correctly if perhaps too forcibly, for when those imposing jars are opened to serve a customer with some manner of vegetable cut in long strips, the native-born American finds it expedient to hold his nose. American storekeepers in the mines deal largely in Chinese goods. They know the Mongolian names of the articles inquired for, but of their character, their composition, how they are cooked or how eaten, they can give no information. It is heathenish "truck," by whose sale they make a profit. Only that and nothing more.[10]

The news of strange discoveries at Sutter's Mill began circulating in February of 1848 and had spread as far as the ports of Valparaíso and Honolulu by summer. The story must have reached Hong Kong and the Pearl River Delta before autumn. No detailed records and statistics survive to tell us just when parties of Chinese started embarking from Hong Kong. But it does not appear that they were exclusively filled with treasure-crazed "Argonauts," the popular label for hopeful prospectors. All signs suggest that many, perhaps most, of the first Chinese Forty-Niners were businessmen who arrived with solid plans for profiting from the future needs of a more sizable Chinese laboring contingent and the immediate needs of everybody else.

For instance, the well-known lack of building materials anywhere near the sandy, scrubby environs of San Francisco inspired the Chinese *hua shang* not only to dispatch bricks and marble slabs across the Pacific (both attested in 1849 Hong Kong shipping records) but to design prefabricated wooden houses in either Western or Chinese styles. Entrepreneurs everywhere from New York to England and Europe were sending their own versions of prefabs, but as the French journalist Étienne Derbec reported in 1850, Chinese models, shipped in panels, were "the prettiest, the best made, and the cheapest; it is possible to have one for fifty or sixty dollars."[11] Guangzhou and Hong Kong carpenters were also busy building chairs and other household furniture for Americans. Additionally, the merchants had foreseen a market for such mementos as ivory fans, embroidered silk shawls, tortoiseshell combs, and parasols, to be bought for white Argonauts' sweethearts or families back East.[12] And they had come prepared to set up restaurants.

The swashbuckling *New-York Tribune* correspondent Bayard Taylor, who visited San Francisco several times between August and late December of 1849, noted three Chinese eateries named "Kong-Sung's," "Whang-Tong's," and "Tong-Ling's." They were, he observed, "much frequented by Americans on account of their excellent cookery, and the fact that meals are $1 each, without regard to quantity."[13] As we have seen, the art of pleasing Western palates was at least a century old in the Pearl River Delta and had been further cultivated in Hong Kong. There is nothing surprising about its rapid transfer to Gold Mountain.

November 19 saw an important meeting at a place unmentioned by Taylor, the Canton Restaurant on Jackson Street. As reported in the *Daily Alta California* on December 10, "some three hundred representatives of the Celestial Empire" had gathered to draft a resolution petitioning a popular local figure, Selim E. Woodworth, to act as "arbitrator and adviser" to the Chinese community—"strangers as we are, in a strange land," who might in future "be at a loss as to what course of action might be necessary for us to pursue."[14]

This episode points to the sort of organizational skills that "Celestials" had already honed in Hong Kong and the Pearl River Delta. The attendance on November 19 may have represented more than a third of California's total Chinese population.[15] The resolution, with its excellent English and deft scriptural allusion (Exodus 2:22), sounds like the work of someone already practiced at reading British or Yankee mentalities. Equally apt was the choice of local advocate. Woodworth, a thirtyish ex–New Yorker, had already evinced political and commercial ambitions as well as an interest in real estate. (In a few years he and his brother Frederick would also be major figures in the crime-plagued city's first "Committee of Vigilance," a stopgap substitute for constituted legal authority.) "The China boys," according to the *Alta* article, subsequently presented "an excellent entertainment" in their new protector's honor to an assembly of guests including such public figures as Alcalde (a Spanish title soon to be amended to "Mayor") John W. Geary.

The meeting place also said much about Chinese restaurants and their place in the new city. In fact, a "Canton Restaurant" had opened earlier in 1849, only to be replaced in autumn by the "New Canton Hotel and Restaurant," announced by an advertisement in the October 4 *Weekly Alta California* as "a new and elegant establishment for the accommodation of the public."[16] Since canvas tents and assorted prefabs in a slough of mud represented the apogee of the Bay Area building trade in the first months of 1849, it's a logical guess that the original Canton had been built for the spring–summer season rather than the ages. That its more ambitious replacement was heralded by a well-written paid ad in an English-language newspaper suggests an alert sense of marketing possibilities in the larger San Francisco community. (Already a few people with good English speaking or writing skills must have been acting as interpreters for other Chinese.) And no one could have built and outfitted a restaurant of three-hundred-person capacity amid the jumbled welter of the infant city without serious fiscal and logistical resources.

The great majority of Chinese activities on the Forty-Niner scene went undocumented. This was undoubtedly true of restaurants and other food-related businesses, few of which could have been on the impressive scale of the Canton. The first city directory, published in 1850, lists only one Chinese restaurant: the "Macoa [sic] and Woosung."[17] The proprietor was Norman Asing, whose name also appears in spellings like "Assing" and "As-sing." (Contemporary anglicizations of Chinese names are hopelessly confused and inconsistent.) Asing—who would later inform California's bigoted governor that he was a Christian and a republican—belonged to a very small scattering of Chinese who had reached the United States decades earlier, though it is unclear whether he had remained there continuously or traveled back to the Far East.

Him Mark Lai, the doyen of bilingual Chinese American historical studies, was able to identify Norman Asing as Sang Yuen, a prominent merchant with a finger in many community pies, who would help found one of the early local mutual-aid associations for emigrants from individual Guangdong districts.[18] A colorful personage even by Gold Rush standards, Asing had been born nearly on the doorstep of Macau (then usually spelled "Macao" in English). The "Woosung" half of the restaurant name is harder to understand unless Asing also had some connection with the east coast town known in Mandarin as Wusong, which played a strategic role in establishing the British as a major trading presence in Shanghai. One of the early prospectors, James O'Meara, long afterward recalled Asing as "the recognized chief of the Chinese" in Forty-Niner days, and his establishment as a highly profitable "Chinese cake and confectionery shop on Kearny Street."[19]

O'Meara's description suggests that the San Francisco "Little China," a district then located roughly between Jackson and Sacramento Streets close to Kearny Street, already supported some specialized businesses such as tea houses or Chinese-style pastry shops. Other Argonauts were only dimly able to grasp the distinctions between various kinds of Chinese eating houses. The ones that Westerners wrote about seem to have combined plenty of atmospheric touches (balconies, lacquered screens, ornate lanterns) with food prepared to either Chinese or English-American taste. The latter was no clumsy afterthought. O'Meara found that the language barrier tended to make any correspondence between what you ordered and what you got somewhat unpredictable, but this was not a majority view.[20] In early days, most accounts praised not only the cheapness of the very first Chinese restaurants but the consistent quality and capable service, sometimes aided by a moderate command of English.

For a short time, Chinese commercial hopes flourished peacefully along with other newcomers' ambitions in San Francisco and other nearby towns. The earliest settlers in post-Mexican California tended to find its chaotic assortment of national origins and languages colorful rather than threatening. To whites, the Chinese seemed stranger than anyone else by virtue of their appearance and speech. But they had quickly made themselves useful in a rough-hewn international fellowship of equals.

Certainly their first restaurants filled a need for well-cooked meals served in pleasant surroundings, at modest prices. San Francisco had almost instantly sprouted innumerable saloons and bars renowned for free lunches, over-the-top decor, and legendary virtuosity at compounding cocktails; a smattering of German beer gardens or other ethnic eating places; and several genuine or purported French restaurants on various levels. All strata of greedy or elegant taste were catered to by someone, somewhere. The English gold-seeker J. D. Borthwick, who arrived in 1851, commented with some favor on the classier French and "principal American" restaurants while less enthusiastically noting the many places serving "corn-bread, buckwheat cakes, pickles, grease, molasses, apple-sauce, and pumpkin pie"—to him, American grub at its grubbiest. The sight of "very nasty Chinese eatables," such as dried fish or ducks, at the stores of "long-tailed Celestials" apparently put Borthwick off trying Chinese restaurants.[21] But many English and American Argonauts knew better.

The wherewithal of enjoyable meals was not easy to come by in those first years, but Pearl River Delta natives attacked all problems with resolution and displayed an uncanny knack for addressing their new neighbors' palates. They were not themselves fond of either beef or mutton but had nonetheless already learned how to prepare both for white men's tables in Guangzhou and Hong Kong, where herds of cattle were kept to please Western appetites. They went on exercising these skills in the Golden West.

Before the transfer to American rule, California's chief sources of revenue had been cattle to furnish hides and tallow as well as sheep raised for wool. Though destined to decline quickly, small local sheep and cattle ranches owned by Spanish-speaking Californios were still the major meat producers.[22] The animals' flesh was undoubtedly stringy and tough, but beef or mutton specially fattened for the table was not yet locally available. Pigs and poultry had been in somewhat scarce supply. But they became more numerous after the arrival of the Chinese, who would pay top dollar for good specimens of either.

Records of the earliest California Chinese restaurant offerings have not survived. We should not envision them as handsomely printed bilingual menus with Chinese characters on one side and English-language listings on the other. (Printing even English, much less Chinese, menus cannot have been cheap for several years at least; all but the grandest local eateries must have initially depended on spoken orders or bills of fare scrawled on boards, eventually graduating to handwritten and later to printed menus.) Our only evidence of what was served comes from Forty-Niners' descriptions. Many details in these suggest a conscious appeal to everyday Anglo-American preferences.

Several early visitors to San Francisco remarked approvingly that Chinese restaurants served not only tea but "excellent" coffee, an article certainly not intended for fellow Chinese.[23] Newcomer James Delavan, nervously anticipating ordeal by chopsticks, was relieved to find a meal presented "in true American style, with knives, forks, spoons, and all the other accessories of the table."[24]

William Shaw, arriving from Australia in 1850 and apparently picking up on the good reputation of local Chinese restaurants, mustered the courage to try Chinese-style "curries, hashes, and fricasees, served up in small dishes, and as they were exceedingly palatable, I was not curious enough to enquire as to the ingredients."[25] Given ubiquitous rumors that the authentic Chinese larder was a chamber of horrors heavily dependent on rat, cat, and still more gruesome articles, readers would generally have understood this to mean "Ask no questions and you'll be told no lies."

Most Anglo-American visitors were content to eat food specifically designed for them, in surroundings notably decent and sanitary by early Gold Rush standards. The English-born William Redmond Ryan, venturing into the Canton in 1849, took pains to mention not only the good food and modest prices but how neat and well-ordered it was: "As I had always been given to understand that these people were of dirty habits, I feel it only right to state that I was delighted with the cleanliness of this place, and I am gratified to bear testimony to the injustice of such a sweeping assertion." As an artist newly retired from the prospecting business, Ryan was especially charmed by the manner in which orders were taken: "Every article that was sold, even of the most trifling kind, was set down, in Chinese characters, as it was disposed of; it being the duty of one of the waiters to attend to this department. This he did very cleverly and quickly, having a sheet of paper for the purpose, on which the article and the price were noted down in Chinese characters, by means of a long, thin brush, moistened in a solution of Indian or Chinese ink."[26]

The report of William Kelly, published in 1851, probably represents a fairly common opinion. Having noted the range of international options on display in San Francisco, he announced, "But amidst the host of competitors the Celestials carry off the palm for superior excellence in every particular. They serve everything promptly, cleanly, hot, and well cooked; they give dishes peculiar to each nation, over and above their own peculiar soups, curries, and ragouts, which cannot be even imitated elsewhere; and such is their quickness and civil attention, they anticipate your wants, and secure your patronage."[27]

We can only hazard educated guesses about what dishes were served for the special pleasure of Americans. If the newly arrived Chinese tried to reproduce the respectable English-descended cooking then common at middling American hotels and restaurants throughout the land, they probably offered a soup or two; a few boiled dishes such as fish with anchovy sauce and leg of mutton with caper sauce; assorted steaks, chops, and roast joints; local game in season; potatoes in one or another simple form; and perhaps some of the delicacies like lobster meat (dispatched in "tin canisters" from the East Coast) or "macaroni" (i.e., Italian pasta) that were already invading the very early Gold Rush dining scene as tokens of extravagance to come.

Beyond question, the wants of newly arrived Chinese were met still more capably. Cantonese diners are notoriously demanding culinary critics. It is not simple racism to guess that most of the Pearl River Delta contingent—even common laborers—were both more particular about quality and better able to judge it than the majority of white Argonauts. And unlikely though it may seem, they enjoyed a better supply of cooking necessities and luxuries than counterparts dependent on sea or overland routes from the East Coast. Prentice Mulford's bemused listing (above) only scratches the surface.

Here again, the sojourning *hua shang* had managed to start laying down a transpacific pipeline as soon as they reached the wharf. The first surviving records of shipments from Hong Kong to San Francisco include dozens of imported food items that Chinese cooks and diners simply could not have done without. In *Dreaming of Gold, Dreaming of Home*, a history of the links maintained between sojourners and their birthplaces, Madeline Y. Hsu points out that "Gold Mountain firms," or *jin shan zhuang* (Cantonese, *gum saan jong*) in Hong Kong kept up an endless flow of cooking necessities. Counterparts in San Francisco distributed them to settlements in the interior. Soy sauce (probably several kinds), rice wine and distilled grain liquors, and various preserved vegetables were imported in their own special ceramic jars. Dried meats and poultry cured by traditional salting or smoking methods rapidly became a common sight in San Francisco Chinese shops and even the mining camps. So did different kinds of dried shellfish (shrimp graded by size, oysters, scallops) and fish, dried mushrooms, preserved eggs, bean curd in several forms, cooking oil, and dried noodles.[28] Good rice was a matter of course. Chinese exporters were not above palming off adulterated tea shipments on Westerners, but Chinese-born purchasers demanded the best. Even rare items like shark's fins and bird's nests could be counted on for special banquets. Chinese gardens filled with any of the newcomers' own favorite food plants that could be acclimated to Gold Mountain soon took root on small plots of ground, supplying fresh produce for restaurant kitchens as well as peddlers' routes.

In short, for a couple of years nobody did more than Chinese facilitators, planners, and cooks to start turning San Francisco into a restaurant town, with unerring re-creations of Pearl River Delta cookery for Chinese patrons and adept versions of Western fare for others. The tiny

Celestial community must have looked like a model for establishing a sound business footing in the fledgling port city.

THE CLIMATE ALTERS

With a luckier throw of the dice, early commercial success might have blossomed into lasting American acceptance of the settlers from south Guangdong, in and beyond the Pacific Coast states. In 1850 Étienne Derbec confidently predicted that "San Francisco will one day be a half Chinese city, and it certainly will not lose by it."[29] It is tempting to imagine an alternate universe in which a whole range of Westernized or less Westernized Chinese eating houses matched to different preferences and pocketbooks could have put down American roots and gone on merging into the national culinary landscape. But that possibility was rapidly doomed by the anti-Chinese hysteria of the next several generations.

In a sense, the *hua shang* were victims of their own success as labor brokers and architects of a transplanted "Little China" on foreign soil. The uncanny re-creation of their own culture—culinary and other—on Gold Mountain echoed earlier Chinese achievements in many parts of the Nanyang. But when they next began organizing an efficient high-volume flow of Pearl River Delta *hua gong* to the American labor market, they were inviting a backlash for which no prior overseas adventure had prepared them.

Statistics for the early American West tend to be rough rather than precise guidelines, especially regarding minority groups. But the estimates in Hubert Howe Bancroft's monumental *History of California* (completed in 1890) show clearly enough where things were headed. Bancroft gauged the Chinese population of California as 54 at the start of 1849, about 790 in January 1850, and about 4,025 in January 1851. Everybody would later point to 1852 as the watershed. Bancroft calculated totals of 7,512 in January of that year, 11,787 in May, and 18,040 in August.[30]

In other words, the Chinese population of California had increased more than twenty-two-fold between 1850 and the late summer of 1852. Meanwhile the state's entire population had less than tripled, from about 92,600 in 1850 by U.S. census figures to about 264,000 according to the first California state census in 1852; other estimates suggest that the full tally of Chinese arriving in 1852 was more than 20,000, perhaps as many as 25,000. (Nationally speaking, the increased Chinese presence was a mere drop in the bucket: The total U.S. population was over 23 million in 1850 and would far exceed 31 million in 1860.)[31]

The job of record keeping got progressively more confusing after 1852 because newcomers started fanning out more rapidly from San Francisco into the hinterland, while in any given year a few hundred or thousand Chinese usually left California on the return voyage to Hong Kong. But in any case, 1852 was the year when public figures started discussing restrictions on Chinese immigration to San Francisco.

At the time, we should realize, Americans had no way of grasping the general concept of "race relations." The first Gold Rushers could comfortably regard a smattering of Chinese newcomers as entertaining oddities who made useful or pretty things and set a good table. Chinese arriving by hundreds or thousands every month triggered other responses only too natural in an avowedly white state unused to recognizing other races as entities in their own right.

For all mid-nineteenth-century American citizens except a few do-gooders of a fervent abolitionist persuasion, such as William Lloyd Garrison and the Beecher family, both black and red people could be categorized as primitives if not savages. Some might deserve kindly Christian regard, but all essentially belonged to rude orders of proto-humanity with no advanced achievements of their own worth weighing against the clear superiority of modern (i.e., white) Western civilization. In fact, before the Gold Rush the vast majority of white Americans had never *seen* members of another race claiming independent status.

When only a few Chinese were on the scene, the first Argonauts might welcome them or shrug them off on an individual basis. But viewed in growing numbers that suggested even larger hordes to come, they began to look like some ghastly vision come to life—a new phenomenon incompatible with thoughts of a justly ordered universe. The racist tide that began to sweep California was outwardly focused on competition for work. But the sheer virulence to which it rose suggests a less rational hatred, a violent and instinctive urge to exclude such beings from any notions about mankind being the Saturday afternoon climax to the story of Creation. Worst of all, unlike the enslaved or obliterated black and red appendages to the human race, they had come from a very large, internationally recognized sovereign state that claimed to have a civilization of its own with accomplishments such as a written history and the ability to count. (In fact, the abacus enabled Chinese shopkeepers to outrace American customers at any feat of computation.)

The more south Guangdong Chinese thronged onto the scene, the more repellent and inhuman features their neighbors claimed to see in them. At an average height of no more than five feet, the alien bipeds appeared comically small by contrast with stalwart American manhood, or at least its idealized image. To other Gold Rushers, their shaven foreheads and yard-long queues looked grotesque; their lack or near-lack of beards suggested an unnatural sexlessness. Their color was not light yellow but a darker shade that contemptuous whites sometimes derided as half negroid; their flattened noses and strangely angled facial contours reinforced the comparison. Their speech—the Toisanese dialect, which even other Cantonese found raucous—was more hideous to Western ears than any other foreign language.

The backlash did not erupt all at once. But throughout the 1850s, American mentions of Chinese restaurants and foodways began to acquire a less friendly tone. Gibes about "rat pies" and the like became more frequent. In 1853 the *Alta California*, which had previously written of the Chinese as welcome additions to the local citizenry, began echoing a call for curbs on "the tide of Asiatic immigration" sounded in the previous year by Governor John Bigler. Citing mining-district rumors about Chinese people's appetite for vermin "of the creeping or crawling kind," the newspaper also complained about the clannish distance they maintained from everyday society and darkly mused, "Good cooks, indeed, many of them are, but it is seldom that they can be disciplined to serve the purposes of a family, and their genius consists principally in managing the culinary affairs of one of their own restaurants, where any person in their confidence may be very comfortably served with a dinner on 'conditions unknown to the public.' "[32]

The real objects of this gathering enmity were the *hua gong*, the waves of Chinese laboring men recruited by the brokers. They spread out from San Francisco in several different directions. At first many headed straight up the Sacramento and San Joaquin Rivers for the nearest gold fields. Later they would make their way across the California borders to the Comstock Lode and the mining districts of Oregon, Idaho, and neighboring U.S. territories as well as British Columbia. (A few thousand South Guangdong gold-seekers had come to western Canada after the 1858 Fraser Canyon gold discovery.) But wherever the Chinese went, white miners soon began ganging up against any who made strikes worth seriously investigating. Most often they were reduced to reworking other parties' half-exhausted claims.[33] In a few years nothing was left to be discovered by cheap, simple panning and placer methods; there was little room for either native or foreign-born Argonauts in the new age of industrial-scale hydraulic and quartz mining.

The Chinese moved into more distant mining districts in the territories or sought out other work opportunities here and there. Some frustrated gold-seekers retreated to Sacramento, Marysville, Stockton, and the many new mining hamlets to found small shops, especially laundries and neighborhood groceries. These choices were no accident. From the first, alert Chinese minds had recognized that local hand-laundry service would infallibly trump the alternative of sending shirts by boat to Honolulu or Hong Kong if not simply throwing them away. And as noted earlier, the Hong Kong and San Francisco *hua shang* had foreseen the need to keep Chinese and other provisions moving to their countrymen in the boondocks.

Some came back to San Francisco, where the first Little China had evolved into a recognized "Chinatown" large enough, and Chinese enough, to arouse the dislike of white neighbors. Here small Chinese-owned factories were carving out niches in the garment, shoemaking, cigar-making, and textile trades.[34] These would employ thousands of laborers over several generations, while hundreds more set up as self-employed laundrymen.

Many resourceful Chinese found a role producing food along the coast or in the nearby countryside. Few Californians had yet grasped that the brightest hopes for the Golden State's economy lay in edible harvests rather than gold. The first people who did had the market almost to themselves. Forward-looking white entrepreneurs began growing wheat on a large enough scale to turn California into the nation's largest wheat and flour exporter by about 1855 (actually supplying flour to Hong Kong and China).[35] The Chinese in North America looked to other avenues.

Nobody had previously sized up the remarkable fish and shellfish stocks of the California coastline. Long experienced in fishing coastal waters off southern Guangdong, the Chinese newcomers soon discovered one of the world's richest supplies of abalone, a prized delicacy in China but unappreciated by Westerners. They found vast amounts of shrimp in San Francisco Bay and elsewhere. As the effort expanded, they were able to bring in oysters, squid, and many kinds of finfish from smelts to Petrale sole. Their small fishing hamlets came to dot the California shoreline from San Francisco southward to (and beyond) Monterey. Most of the catch was salted and dried in the sun; white observers curiously noted the racks or frames that the Chinese built for the purpose and the evil smells that wafted from the sites.[36]

As they had done in the Nanyang, Chinese traders in San Francisco promptly began shipping the preserved bounty back to the mother country. This move reinforced a growing criticism that the clannish aliens never allowed their profits to reach any hands but their own. Some, however, started locally peddling fresh fish to a mixed clientele, especially in San Francisco.

The Chinese also famously took the lead in truck gardening. In this enterprise they expanded more broadly into the larger community. People from hardscrabble districts like Toisan were already old hands at coaxing vegetables from poor soil. They prudently laid in seed stocks for growing fresh greens and vegetables. At the time, any fresh produce in San Francisco usually came to market from some of the nearby ranches that had been founded under Spanish and Mexican rule; it might be both scarce and horribly expensive.

Most Chinese produce was initially grown in small plots close to California mining camps and the outskirts of San Francisco. As the Celestials moved out into other Pacific and Rocky Mountain territories from Northern California to British Columbia, their carefully tended gardens became an invariable fingerprint of their presence. We do not have any complete roster of the crops that were first brought from China. Those that were documented by about 1900 included fresh ginger, some common cabbage relatives like bok choy and choy sum, yard-long beans, a few chive-like or leek-like Far Eastern alliums, and various members of the cucurbit (gourd/melon/cucumber/squash) family.[37]

The Chinese also cultivated vegetables familiar to the white Argonauts. Nothing had frustrated survivors of the grueling east–west overland journey more than the absence of fresh vegetables—above all, greens. Where they were available, people fell on them with a ravenous appetite that we can now recognize as the sum of several vitamin deficiencies.

The produce that Chinese truck gardeners carried to the market or peddled on neighborhood routes throughout the Far West was renowned for freshness, size, and beauty. It enjoyed another sort of renown in anti-Chinese propaganda describing the secret of the unwanted aliens' fertilization methods as "ordure" or "foulness." The idea was simplicity itself: human feces and sometimes urine were collected in pits or tubs and left to mature to hideous smelliness, with the possible addition of some small, luckily discovered animal corpse to enhance the already rich nitrogen content. Eventually the mixture was diluted with water and used to fertilize garden crops.[38] The risk of parasitic infections being spread through this practice varied inversely with the length of the ripening period—ideally, several months, though there was no telling how long anybody had bothered to marinate any given batch. Despite the circumstances of their production, Chinese-grown vegetables soon earned a large white as well as Chinese following. In 1879 an Olympia, Washington, newspaper editorialized that though it stood firm against foreigners undercutting the labor market, "until the arrival of Chinese gardeners, all our earliest small fruits and vegetables came by steamer from San Francisco, for which we paid exorbitant prices. Now, through the native tact and indomitable energy of Chinamen, these fruits and vegetables are raised from our own soil and brought to our doors, weeks earlier than ever they were produced by white men."[39]

THE TIPPING POINT

The events that drastically precipitated the swelling Chinese community onto the late nineteenth-century political stage began with the coming of the transcontinental railroad, undertaken as a government-backed wartime gamble in 1862. At the time, the gold fields were still disgorging thousands of disappointed seekers into Pacific Coast labor markets. But

American ex-Argonauts tended to disdain any really punishing manual labor. The effort that launched the Central Pacific Railroad track line eastward from Sacramento to meet the Union Pacific opposite number being built westward from Omaha soon threatened to stall for lack of capable, disciplined work crews. To the disgust of many, the Central Pacific quadrumvirate of Charles Crocker, Leland Stanford, Collis Huntington, and Mark Hopkins eventually found what they were looking for in the Chinese—who had, as Crocker pointed out to the skeptical Central Pacific construction superintendent, after all built the Great Wall of China.[40]

After hiring an experimental crew, the planners became impressed enough to end up with a workforce of about twelve thousand Chinese to three thousand whites. The men were recruited with the aid of the San Francisco *hua shang* and counterparts in Hong Kong, who negotiated the requisite labor contracts and also supplied the crews with their accustomed food and other necessities. Camp cooks sometimes were part of the arrangement.[41] The fact that Chinese laborers would agree to work longer hours at far less pay than their white rivals was an overwhelming advantage from the entrepreneurs' point of view, a dastardly crime in the eyes of the barely fledged American labor movement.

Observers could scarcely believe the endurance, resourcefulness, and Spartan resolve of these outwardly puny hirees, or the manner in which they outperformed brawny U.S.-born laborers as well as immigrants from England or Ireland. Early in 1869, with the terminal point in sight, the Reverend A. W. Loomis reported in the pages of Bret Harte's *Overland Monthly*: "Foremen and officers on the road speak in the highest terms of their Asiatic laborers. They are reported as prompt on the ground, ready to begin work the moment they hear the signal, and laboring steadfastly and honestly on till admonished that the working hours are ended. . . . Overseers declare that they can drill more rock and move more dirt with Chinamen than with an equal number of men who claim this kind of occupation as their specialty."[42]

But for growing numbers of citizens, such reports merely reinforced an image of the Chinese as swarming, malefic little enemies to the honest workingman. The American workers' movement had been tinged with a whites-only rationale even before the Civil War. By now, cheap yellow labor was fast becoming a convenient symbol for capitalist greed.

The Chinamen's legendary capacity for toil would shortly earn them not goodwill but beatings, torchings, and lynchings throughout the Far Western states and territories.

The young journalist and budding political economist Henry George sounded the alarm in a galvanizing, much-discussed letter to the *New-York Tribune* that appeared on May 1, 1869, as "The Chinese on the Pacific Coast" and was rapidly reprinted in other newspapers. "From San Diego to Sitka, and back into Montana, Idaho, Nevada and Arizona, throughout the enormous stretch of country of which San Francisco is the commercial center, they are everywhere to be found," he warned. "Every town and hamlet has its 'Chinatown'—its poorest, meanest and filthiest quarter, and wherever the restless proprietors open a new district, there, singly or in squads, appears the inevitable Chinaman." If not promptly checked, the effect of their perniciously cheap labor would be "to accelerate the prevailing tendency to the concentration of wealth—to make the rich richer and the poor poorer; to make nabobs and princes of our capitalists, and crush our working class into the dust; to substitute (if it goes far enough) a population of serfs and their masters for that population of intelligent freemen who are our glory and our strength; to rear an empire with its glittering orders round the throne, and its prostrate people below, in place of the Republic of Washington and Jefferson."[43]

Ten days later the junction of the railroads at Promontory Point in the Utah was marked by a ceremony devoid of Chinese dignitaries, and the "Asiatic laborers" who had carried out most of the Central Pacific blasting and track-laying were left to trudge back to California on foot. Many went to work on the smaller rail links and spurs that were now being built everywhere in the Far West; some joined the crews being recruited from south Guangdong to build the fearsomely difficult western stretch of the Canadian Pacific Railway (not completed until 1885). Others were drafted for a task less spectacular than laying road beds and tracks over mountains and chasms but equally Herculean: land reclamation in the Sacramento River–San Joaquin River Delta.

For years California investors and engineers had been talking about draining the malarial wetlands that emptied out of the Central Valley and clearing the soil for farms. The system was a tortuous maze of channels threading through great islands of spongy peat accumulated during the annual growth-and-decay cycle of tall, stubborn rushes called tules (pronounced "tooleys"). Over thousands of years, the tules had sunk dense, tough roots and rhizomes into their islanded peat mats on the floor of an ancient inland sea. Some attempts to turn the region into farm soil were under way by the early 1850s. More ambitious projects followed over several decades. The problem was locating men with the sheer persistence and muscle to build levees and conquer the existing marsh growth.

Like the railroad builders, the reclamation engineers and bosses failed to recruit the necessary gangs of workers among white Californians, for any money. They tried hiring Mexicans, "Kanakas" from the Pacific islands, and Native Americans before finding, in the south Guangdong Chinese, the world's only labor force with centuries of prior experience wresting farmland from an equally large, daunting deltaic system. The tules were a new and different challenge, but Pearl River Deltans met it with their accustomed willingness to perform miracles for low pay and stoic persistence in the face of any obstacle.

With mule- or horsepower, they hauled up incalculable numbers of trees and bushes that had taken root on the tule islands. They cut out and dug up peat or underlying clay and carted it by wheelbarrow to build massive levees (sometimes many hundreds of feet long and as high as fifteen feet) around sections of land newly drained by ditches that they had dug. Standing at times up to the waist in water and surrounded by pestilential armies of mosquitoes, they yanked out the stubborn tule rhizome structures. To plow the tough but treacherously spongy sod that remained, they invented "tule shoes," or detachable horseshoes with large protective outer rings, to keep the animals' hooves from sinking into the soft muck.[44]

We will never know how much arable land the Chinese created through these efforts before steam-powered dredges and pumps arrived in the 1880s—if not the "million acres and more" estimated by a witness before a congressional committee in 1876, at the very least several hundred thousand acres.[45] In effect, they had made possible the growth of industrial-scale California agriculture for generations to come. It is true that the great nineteenth-century swamp-draining projects now stand as a very faulty long-term hydrological and environmental bargain. But at the time, they were an achievement on a par with the railroad itself.

No more fertile soil existed anywhere in the United States than on the virgin peatlands of the delta. Many Chinese managed to lease plots in the reclamation areas as well as other districts of California and the territories, probably cultivating the same assortments of vegetables that they had grown near San Francisco. But the entire structure of Far Western agriculture was being swiftly revolutionized as white investors (along with a handful of ambitious and well-heeled Chinese) recognized the potential of certain crops grown on a gigantic scale, especially in the reclaimed Sacramento–San Joaquin Delta. Thanks to the railroad, the prospective market now stretched from the Atlantic to the Pacific coast.

As always, masses of newcomers from the Pearl River Delta were the ideal labor force. But in the next few decades their visibility as tenders and pickers of crops ranging from pears, strawberries, asparagus, and onions to hops, grapes, and olives became an invitation to harassment or murder.[46]

THE AGE OF PERSECUTION

The Chinese presence had not expanded at a fixed rate since the Gold Rush. There had been spurts and slackenings from year to year. The overall number of Chinese arriving in California had probably topped 20,000 in 1852, the first year in which some whites began to sound public alarms. The estimated Chinese population of the United States was close to 35,000 in 1860 and 63,200 in 1870, the year after the completion of the transcontinental railroad. It was in the next decade that the pull of the rapidly expanding Far Western farm labor market (along with factory-labor opportunities) reached the other side of the Pacific. Between 1870 and 1880 America's Chinese-born population grew by almost 42,270, to a total of nearly 105,500.[47] The same years saw a period of prolonged economic depression that fueled widespread anti-immigrant hysteria among voters. The cry for Chinese exclusion was already at fever pitch by 1880.

In the reign of terror that ensued, no form of manual or factory work guaranteed real security to Chinese employees of substantial farming or manufacturing enterprises. Wherever the *hua gong* were concentrated in their own communities or as a labor corps large enough to attract hostile notice, they became magnets for threats that periodically erupted into violence. The most notorious episode, a murder spree by white coal miners at the Wyoming Territory town of Rock Springs in September 1885, left twenty-eight or more Chinese dead and their small settlement in blackened ruins, and provoked a national and international outpouring of outrage. The United States—shown in a magazine cartoon by Thomas Nast as undeserving to call itself "the head of enlightened nations"—was subjected to the diplomatic wrath of China and eventually forced to pay some $150,000 in indemnities.[48] Acts of violence nonetheless continued, with the open or veiled blessing of local and state officials.

In the Far Western states and territories, Democratic and Republican politicians alike swiftly lined up behind the anti-Chinese cause. Somewhat more cautiously, others climbed on the bandwagon in the East, South, and Midwest. Both parties hoped to translate the call for ridding America of the Chinese menace into an electoral advantage in future presidential campaigns. The rhetoric they adopted invoked the specter of "coolieism" as a virulent successor to the institution of black slavery. The general thinking harmonized with Henry George's argument: rather than having embarked for the United States of their own free will as good-faith immigrants, incoming Chinese were the servile and debased pawns of traffickers eager to shunt conscripted hordes of Asian-born "coolies" halfway around the world. Their supposed aim was to undercut the free, honest labor market that Civil War victories should have guaranteed to all Americans, or all white Americans. The self-appointed opponents to an invasion of coolies were not interested in distinguishing between terrified Chinese forcibly shoved aboard "floating coffins" bound for the Peruvian guano mines and self-directed Chinese who had signed voluntary arrangements to pay back creditors for passage to Gold Mountain. Facts and logic did not matter. For proof of coolieism and its effects, the demagogues simply invited their hearers to shudder at the yellow race's increasing visibility in the republic of the Founding Fathers.[49]

California's Chinese population had increased by more than 14,250 in 1876.[50] In that year alarmists had persuaded Congress to send a bicameral delegation to San Francisco for hearings on the Chinese question. In 1877 the young Irish immigrant Denis Kearney, recently chosen to head the California chapter of the new Workingmen's Party, started a series of rabble-rousing appearances throughout the West meant to unmask the yellow man as a tool of bloated capitalism. Two years later the state constitution was amended to include four provisions meant to curb the numbers of undesirable aliens, forbid the employment of Chinese by corporations or any public body, and fiercely "discourage their immigration" as "foreigners ineligible to become citizens of the United States."[51] (The terms of the 1790 federal Naturalization Act, passed by Congress during George Washington's first term, restricted the privilege of naturalization to free whites.)

The decisive legislative blow came in 1882, when Congress bowed to overwhelming pressure by passing the Chinese Exclusion Act, the first federal law ever meant to categorically bar natives of any other nation from furnishing manual labor in this one. Its chief directive, meant to take effect in ninety days, sweepingly prohibited "any Chinese laborer" from coming to the United States for a period of ten years. Among a host of other provisions, the most important sections dealt with certifying the identity of Chinese already legally in the country. When the law was renewed in 1892 as the Geary Act, that matter was simplified by requiring legal Chinese residents to obtain certificates of residence and produce them on demand.[52]

Here it may be useful to point out how massively the rabble-rousing picture of Mongolian hordes overrunning America differed from any ascertainable facts. At no time from 1850 to 1980 did the number of people entering the United States from China during any ten-year period exceed about 123,000, a figure registered during the peak decade of 1871–1880. Between 1910 and 1920 the number was only about 20,000. On the other hand, nearly 437,000 Irish entered this country between 1870 and 1880, and more than 146,000 between 1910 and 1920. For the intervening decades, their numbers ranged from about 146,200 (1911–1920) to about 655,500 (1881–1890). Approximately 3.6 million Italians would arrive between 1870 and 1920, a period that saw the total U.S. population rise from roughly 38.5 million to 106 million.[53] In other words, the mountains that roused Denis Kearney's acolytes to incendiary raids and sporadic lynchings never amounted to anything more than molehills in the pages of the U.S. census.

Almost from the start of the Gold Rush, the Chinese had been the target of legislative bullying by both California and San Francisco (e.g., the state's 1850 Foreign Miners' Tax and a succession of urban quality-of-life ordinances meant to make their existence as difficult as possible).[54] Now they found themselves not just persona non grata to the nation at large but widely assumed to be guilty of illegal entry until proved innocent (sometimes in spite of proof). Equal hostility was flaring in the Canadian provinces of British Columbia and Alberta.

Little help could be expected from China itself. Faced with stringent pressure from colonial powers in need of cheap plantation labor, the Qing emperors had had to formally grant Chinese subjects liberty to emigrate. One resulting agreement, the 1868 Burlingame Treaty, had put China and the United States on reciprocal most-favored-nation footing and established the right of free Chinese immigration to America. It provided for the maintenance of Chinese consulates in American ports, with some assurances for the safety of Chinese nationals traveling and working in the United States.[55] But under pressure from anti-Chinese agitators, Washington had gotten the treaty amended in 1880 to allow for possible suspension of Chinese immigration. And finally, the Exclusion Act and other unilateral anti-Chinese measures had all but abrogated previous diplomatic guarantees of Chinese nationals' protection. Several American citizens who had agreed to serve as consuls did their best to mount legal defenses for persecuted Chinese, but most people had no representation. China's successful protest against the Rock Springs massacre was an isolated (and, considering the brutality of the affair, puny) gesture.

But the law still left one important class untouched: the "merchants," a term that could be stretched to include *hua shang* of many descriptions, from importers, factory owners, and labor brokers to (in some cases) grocers and peddlers. From the start, the *hua shang* had taken some responsibility for the throngs of *hua gong*, whom they had recruited from Toisan and other South Guangdong districts. Surely they exploited Chinese manual labor as a profitable commodity ensuring generous commissions for themselves. But, to an extent, they also protected workers from the fury of the white community. We shall return later to their role in sponsoring mutual-aid societies based on district of origin, the foundation of persistent legal challenges to discriminatory laws.

Others exercised their wits in the time-honored *xiang banfa* tradition and formed other plans during the decades of anti-Chinese violence.

They decided that the best hope of safety paradoxically lay in relative isolation as self-employed persons in some minimal enterprise requiring little capital and no English-language skills. In virtually all cases, this meant laundries—hand laundries, since large-scale, steam-driven equipment for the purpose was still in the course of development. Hand laundering was work so physically punishing as to daunt the majority of recently arrived whites. That was just why Chinese who were willing to spend decades half-crippling their shoulders, backs, and legs in return for a dependable income were able to carve out a living at it. For thousands of them, survival meant spreading out into villages and hamlets far from the main centers of urban strife and quietly establishing a service that white neighbors found it hard to do without.[56] It is true that isolated laundrymen sometimes found themselves more, not less, vulnerable to anti-Chinese wrath. But on occasion white citizens rallied to their defense.

THE LUCK OF CHINESE COOKS

There remained one other fairly secure and often lucrative option for at least some Chinese with the courage to seek employment on an individual basis rather than as factory personnel or members of work gangs: cooking for whites. All the anti-Chinese hysteria of the era between about 1870 and World War I could not shake a widespread conviction among Westerners (and eventually many people in other parts of the country) that nobody made a more gifted and reliable cook than a Chinaman.

This belief had begun with foreigners living and traveling in China and had been emphatically repeated by writers like George Wingrove Cooke and the Abbé Huc. Almost from the start of the Gold Rush, it took hold in the American and Canadian Far West among two classes of white Westerners. The organizers of mess-hall or other communal-dining facilities at mining camps and lumber camps, large ranches and farms, boarding houses, and fish canneries routinely swore by Chinese cooks, as did some hotel owners (for instance, James Beard's mother; see chapter 2). Their reputation was equally high among many middle-class rural or urban families seeking house servants with decent cooking skills.[57]

In photographs of Far Western logging or ranch crews, an aproned Chinese among the ranks of the men he cooked for was a common sight even when anti-Chinese violence was at its height. The reminiscences of miners, loggers, ranch hands, and others connected with the camps where such people lived abound in mentions of Chinese cooks. They commonly dished up the same breakfast, lunch, and supper dishes that any white (or, less commonly, black) American camp cook would have prepared, from coffee and flapjacks to steaks and apple pie. At times they might add inspirations of their own. Richard Steven Street, the distinguished historian of California farm labor, recounts the story of a San Joaquin Valley ranch cook whose superb roast goose dinners had the crew mightily puzzled about the source of the birds until one man surreptitiously tracked the artist (who was carrying a large hollowed pumpkin with eyeholes cut out) to a nearby waterfowl pond and saw him strip naked.[58] What followed precisely matched the technique that the Spanish Dominican friar Domingo Fernandez de Navarrete had observed in China in the mid-seventeenth century:

> The Chineses [*sic*] . . . go into the Water with their Heads thrust into Calabashes, and walk so slowly, that it looks as if nothing moved but the Calabash upon the Water: Being come up in this manner to the Goose or Duck, which they can see through the holes in the Calabash before their Eyes, they lay hold of it by the Feet and pull it under Water, where they wring the Neck, and put it into a Bag they carry for the purpose; once this is full they then go out again as softly as they went in, without disturbing the rest of the birds.[59]

It is true that not all Chinese made equally good camp or other cooks. "Our Chinese cooks imitate the American style with a painful accuracy," Prentice Mulford wryly observed in 1869. In his horrible example, the fictitious "Polyglot House" in the nonexistent "Hangville," an Italian owner had educated a Chinese "clerk *de cuisine*" in his own ghastly notion of American cooking. Knowing that "a certain amount of meat, flour and vegetables were to be daily prepared after the fashion taught him by his employer," the cook accordingly "exposed [food] to heat on the principle that you season your wood, to burn the easier. American humanity to this Celestial was merely a collection of high pressure flesh and blood machines, for whom he prepared fuel."[60]

By the law of averages, at least some Chinese must have cooked some truly awful meals for camp inmates. The real hurdle was the sheer difficulty of Chinese-speakers and English-speakers trying to hammer out a satisfactory understanding of anything as subtle, intricate, and culturally ingrained as cooking, with almost no linguistic common ground. It took not only forbearance but some mental agility on the part of both instructor and instructed to figure out exactly what was being communicated.

Nonetheless, Chinese camp cooks as a class stood in very high regard for generations. Managers often found them both more reliable (i.e., less habitually drunk) and more naturally talented than the common run of white cooks. Most of them began as boys in their mid-teens—even after the Exclusion Act, which adventurous Chinese indomitably worked to circumvent for decades. They might spend thirty-five or forty years at one job unless they chose to move around; their services were much in demand. In fact, they often commanded higher wages than white cooks, a circumstance enraging to many self-anointed patriots.

Denouncing the un-Americanism of keeping filthy yellow men on payrolls, angry partisans of Denis Kearney's mantra "The Chinese must go!" took to burning or looting camps where they were employed. Some employers bowed to pressure by firing the Chinese cook and promising to observe racial purity in future. Some—often backed up by the other camp employees—refused to cooperate. Similarly, whites who hired Chinese to cook or clean in private homes frequently refused to give in to Kearneyite harassment and threats. Homemakers sometimes wrote to newspapers to give their side of the story, which rested less on benevolence than the bruising truth that keeping house for a family was more than one woman could physically manage on her own.[61]

In an age where the closest thing to any labor-saving household appliance was a cast-iron kitchen range, even badly off middle-class families desperately needed at least one servant to share daily duties with the mistress. The only candidates, however, were immigrants. American-born females of all social classes grew from girls into young women who spurned the role of domestic servant. Even daughters of very poor families considered factory work a far prouder option. In the Far West, the available choices for household servants boiled down to two rival groups: Irishwomen or Chinamen. The latter were at a clear advantage.[62]

Irish immigrants had not been seamlessly absorbed into the American landscape. To a great extent, they still retained the reputation of drunken and pig-ignorant refugees from the most benighted corner of the British Isles. Anti-Irish prejudice especially dogged the thousands of young women who arrived in America looking to enter domestic service. The perceived sins of "Biddy" and "Norah" included coarseness, irresponsibility, Catholicism, thickheadedness, and a tendency to bully hapless employers. By contrast, male Chinese house servants were generally agreed to be deft-handed, quiet, respectful, and phenomenally efficient—in short, jewels, once you had managed to make them understand what you wanted through repeated pidgin-English commands. Like their counterparts in camp kitchens, they could usually command very good wages, an understandably sore point with their female rivals. The Chinese particularly shone as cooks, while Irishwomen were repeatedly pilloried as culinary incompetents who could touch no dish without ruining it. Above all, Chinese servants were too clever to put their employers on the spot with self-interested demands.

Frederick Keller's 1882 cartoon "The Servant Question" in the generally anti-Chinese San Francisco magazine *The Wasp* sums up the prevailing wisdom. It depicts a procession of truculent harpies trooping from an employment office into a home kitchen and bombarding the mistress of the house with a "shorter catechism" of queries like "Wud ye mind givin me sisther's pig a run in the gairden of a Sunday afthernoon?" and "Will ye have breakfast ready fer me when I come from confession?" From an upper corner of the picture the smug genie-like image of a Chinaman gazes down on the scene above the caption "NO QUESTIONS ASKED."[63]

Statistics about how many Chinese cooked for white people during the gathering anti-Chinese storm are impossible to reconstruct. This phenomenon, like many others, was more easily documentable in cities than in the countryside, but notable in both. Certainly the numbers of Chinese hired cooks were minuscule compared to the many thousands of manual labors employed by construction projects, farms, and factories. But their presence had real consequences. Cooking for American employers was at least a small bridge between cultures. In camp kitchens, it helped expose Chinese newcomers to a certain cross-section of the U.S. working-class population, on peaceable terms. In private homes, it brought them in close contact with the American domestic scene, including usual kitchen routines and the ways of middle-class families. In both cases, it kept alive an association between Chinese cooks and excellent food that had started to take hold during the Gold Rush before the era of Yellow Peril hysteria.

A crucial effect was that when the reign of fear finally subsided, a diminished North American Chinese community would be uniquely equipped to enter the restaurant business in far corners of the United States and Canada, with whites rather than Chinese as the target clientele. It was a new survival strategy, made possible through the invention of a novel cuisine that would appear exotic and adventurous to non-Chinese, though in fact it was safely wedded to a middlebrow, white American cultural-culinary frame of reference. And more than a generation afterward, it would help create a class of restaurants economically contingent on something that had hitherto been notably scarce among the world of Chinese in the Americas: actual Chinese families.

FOUR

The Road to Chinatown

I have thus far tried to avoid using the term "immigrants" to characterize the Chinese who arrived from the far side of the Pacific seeking gold or other opportunities in nineteenth- or early-twentieth-century America. Certainly they were not immigrants in the same sense as any European group who came from the other side of the Atlantic during the same period. As suggested earlier, the very words "emigrant" and "immigrant" carry baggage incongruous with their early presence in this country.

The crux of the matter is that the Chinese were far less likely than other newcomers to form immigrant *families*. Only after many decades of struggle on this continent did the broad Chinese community in the United States achieve anything roughly comparable to immigrant footing. The delay has to be seen in relation to the absence of families. The cuisine that they brought with them from southern Guangdong and lovingly preserved among themselves would also, after several decades, "immigrate" into mainstream American foodways with a degree of purposeful reinvention unlike other Old World cuisines that arrived as a natural part of family life.

Well into the twentieth century, women were conspicuously scarce among the Chinese on Gold Mountain. The reason lay partly in obstacles erected by this country's immigration authorities—but also in a prominent feature of overseas Cantonese culture: the custom of long-distance marriage. Marriage, Guangdong-style, was just one of several social institutions that eluded Western understanding, and that were used as arguments for excluding the dirty yellow race from American society. Unfortunately, all such efforts had the effect of driving the community further in on itself, ironically perpetuating just those features of overseas Chinese life that hostile American activists most loved to denounce.

BACHELOR SOJOURNERS

Many or most of the people who sailed from Hong Kong to Gold Mountain were indeed married men. But they were set apart from European immigrants not only by race, an apparently idolatrous religion, and a uniquely baffling language but by a set of interlocking values that revolved around the place of their birth. These beliefs had special force for people in southern Guangdong.

In their world view, the meaning of existence could not be divorced from their native soil—that is, the one village of the Pearl River Delta in which they happened to have been born into a particular clan. Men from southern Guangdong villages had long been accustomed to traveling some distance from the ancestral home not in order to *transfer* family loyalties elsewhere but in order to *fulfill* those loyalties. A conscientious son of the region regarded his own village and lineage as the seat of core values and personal identity. No matter where he went, nothing displaced the home village as the center of his internal magnetic field, with a home district (probably one of the Four Counties; see chapter 1) as a slightly larger frame of reference.[1] The pattern held good for a surprisingly long time in America.

Far from the Pearl River Delta, a sojourner would seek out people from his village, who often had the same surname and spoke a dialect scarcely intelligible to other Cantonese. He would belong to a large assortment of organizations binding him to different aspects of the overseas Chinese community. Wives and womenfolk were barely incidental to this career trajectory.

In the mid-nineteenth century, Pearl River Deltans still commonly followed work and kinship practices rooted in older, originally rural ideas of land stewardship. Families with more than one son ordinarily expected the eldest to succeed his father as lawful property holder in the ancestral village. The rest moved away to become apprenticed to trades in other communities, perhaps cities—or, eventually, Chinese outposts in and beyond the Nanyang (Chinese-settled Southeast Asia). They commonly left in their mid-teens at the latest but remained firmly cemented to the village and the family.[2]

Almost never did wives accompany husbands on these sojourns. After a few years getting started in an occupation, a young man would come home for a family-approved marriage, then depart again for his place of work. At intervals he would return home and stay long enough to father a child. His life's goal, aside from sending home enough money to assist his parents and maintain his wife and children, was final repatriation in his birthplace. With luck, this might occur when he was still able to enjoy it. "He died in his home village, where his grave still is honored by his descendants" was a consummation as devoutly to be wished as "And they lived happily ever after." Otherwise, he would try to make advance arrangements to have his bones shipped back for proper burial in the all-important spot. If he had reached great prosperity, his name might be further immortalized as a village benefactor who had funded a new school or public building project.[3]

During the great nineteenth-century exportation of Chinese labor to destinations as far away as North America, many thousands of *hua gong* continued to adopt the transnational-family model. On Gold Mountain, the result was the most unequal male–female ratio among any group of settlers in the Far West. Virtually all other men reaching 1850s San Francisco and the mining camps had led a bachelor existence for the nonce. But for them, reinforcements of women in the next few decades would bring a shift to more conventional domestic arrangements.

The situation was far different for the Chinese. Only a handful defied the barriers (on both sides) to interracial marriages. Like second and third sons paying conjugal visits to the home village from some nearby city, thousands of others tried to make the nearly seven-thousand-mile voyage from San Francisco to Hong Kong at intervals that might be as short as a few years or longer than a decade. Back in the Pearl River Delta for a few months or perhaps longer, they would be welcomed by their extended families and beget more children. Ideally, the offspring would be sons, who eventually would join their fathers on Gold Mountain and continue the pattern.

In Western eyes, the nonrepresentation of decent females went to prove the heathen state of the Chinese community. The Chinese view was of course quite the reverse. Late Qing-era China was a rigorously patrilineal society ruled by neo-Confucian values that made contemporary North America look like a feminist paradise.

Especially in Guangdong, the expected duty of a girl was to live in deferential seclusion (and with bound feet, unless she belonged to the peasantry) under first a father's and then a husband's authority. Even if widowed, she still belonged body and soul to her husband's family. The thought of independent, self-directed lives required a greater mental leap for Chinese than for Western women.[4] Men, on the other hand, were unfazed by the thought of bachelor housekeeping—for instance, the need to do their own cooking, which seldom came naturally to all-male groups of white gold-seekers.

During the first few centuries of Western contact with the Middle Kingdom, women had not figured even slightly in any East–West commercial exchange. Before the opening of Hong Kong, only a handful of English females had gotten anywhere near the Guangzhou foreign "factories" or other Pearl River Delta sites. On the part of the locals, dealings with Western commercial missions—including cooking for them—were carried out by men; almost without exception, women's existence was closeted within their own domestic sphere.

When San Franciscans gazed upon the first gold-seeking Celestials in 1849 and 1850, Bancroft's *History of California* records the balance of Chinese men to women as 787 to 2. The ratio had reached about 19 to 1 in 1900.[5] Part of the reason for the change was that the overseas business factotums—always less strictly bound by Confucian orthodoxy than other members of Chinese society—had gradually begun sending for their wives and daughters. The far more numerous manual workers seldom did so. For traditionalists, uprooting a wife from the village household that she had entered through marriage disturbed the integrity of the family in a way that her husband's absences did not.

Anti-Chinese propagandists feverishly denounced the twin evils of the transpacific marriage system and what went with it, the sardine-like bachelor accommodations that thousands of laborers found in San

Francisco's Chinese quarter and dozens of smaller Chinese communities throughout the Far West.[6] Few images of sober, decent Chinese family life were available to offset the propagandists' picture of bivouacked aliens bypassing any pretense of local domesticity, intent on bleeding the local economy dry before heading back to the home planet. Most of the Chinese-born women who had made the Pacific crossing were prostitutes; American immigration authorities spent much time and money trying to disprove the claims of any who maintained that they were lawful residents' wives or daughters.

The bleak fact was that poverty and prostitution went hand in hand for people from southern Guangdong, hit especially hard by the many natural and man-made disasters that overtook late Qing-era China. For thousands of struggling households, a daughter (sometimes even a wife) might be the closest thing to a liquid asset. In hard times, selling a girl into prostitution was a family fiscal decision not much more drastic than the usual practice of marrying her off for a bride-price, though it brought in less money.[7]

Again, Hong Kong was the major Far Eastern entrepôt for the overseas trade. Entrepreneurs in the colony were linked to supply rings throughout the Pearl River Delta as well as San Francisco traffickers on the other side. White women might reach California ready to keep house for husbands and cook the day's meals; such expectations were not the norm for newly arrived Chinese women.

Elizabeth Sinn's *Pacific Crossing* (a study of several Hong Kong–San Francisco trade networks) shows that fortunate women might be legally sold under various degrees of compulsion either to sex-trade professionals recruiting whores or to households looking for a bondservant-of-all-work (Mandarin, *mei zai*; Cantonese, *mui tsai*). The less lucky were kidnapped outright.[8]

No matter how they got there, sex workers undoubtedly formed a majority of the female Chinese American population in the early years—by the admittedly lurid accounts of American moralists, an overwhelming majority. Reliable statistics are elusive, but in this case the moralists' claims may have made sense. The demagogues who claimed that the male Chinese laborers streaming into the United States were "coolies," or slaves in all but name, did not understand the varied possibilities of credit ticket arrangements. Where women were concerned, the accusation of quasi-slavery had more merit. Undoubtedly, thousands reached San Francisco and the hinterlands as terrified victims with no hope of escape.

But the story is less cut and dried than that. Many of the procurers and brothel owners were themselves women; these were among the few occupations that afforded women an independent niche in either Hong Kong or San Francisco. From analysis of selected California census statistics, the historian Sucheng Chan has also concluded that prostitutes were often able to graduate from brothels to marriage.[9] Many people who later managed to claim citizenship must have been the children of Chinese-born prostitutes or former prostitutes.

In 1875 wrought-up political posturing against supposed hordes of incoming coolies and sex slaves had produced the Page Act, a predecessor to the 1882 Chinese Exclusion Act. It contained a jumble of provisions meant to keep out forcibly recruited labor from "Oriental" countries and prostitutes from anywhere.[10] Immigration authorities pursued the second aim with a zeal that failed to wipe out Chinatown bordellos but did make it almost insurmountably difficult for women to prove that they had not come from China for immoral purposes. The result was to reinforce existing hindrances to the settlement of families in the Chinese American community.

The first passage and repeated renewals of the 1882 Chinese Exclusion Act further distorted the life of all Chinese—male or female—in the United States. (Similar legal hurdles would soon be enacted in Canada.) Everybody was forced to prove that he or she did not belong to the automatically excluded categories of laborer or prostitute, or was not engaged in prohibited trafficking. Even if most Chinese newcomers had wanted to claim immigrant status in the same sense as others, that option was barred still more rigorously than before.

THE DRUG OF CHOICE

The passage of the Exclusion Act was followed by decades of legal battles and extralegal maneuverings in an atmosphere rife with lurid accusations against Chinese sexual and other vices. Some people hinted that Chinese food was tainted with all manner of filth—if not snakes, cats, and vermin, then probably opium masked by heavy seasonings.[11] Opium prepared for smoking was indeed one of the uglier facts of life for Gold Mountain sojourners, and a crucial element in the Hong Kong–San Francisco commercial pipeline. Along with gambling and visits to prostitutes, it offered some solace to workers eking out a weary existence in cramped, squalid quarters. One of its useful effects in lean times was to dull hunger.

The United States would not prohibit the import of opium until 1909. Until then it was expensive because of high production costs and steep import duties, but lawful and resoundingly popular among both rich and poor Chinese. Sensational if undocumented contemporary estimates suggested that between 30 and 50 percent of the California Chinese were opium smokers during the late nineteenth century.

The drug had been the master key with which the British—later abetted by Americans—opened up the immense market of China by both stealth and force, imposing a disastrous balance of trade on what had been a wealthy exporting nation renowned for tea, silks, and porcelain. Western societies knew the raw version of opium, dried lumps of poppy-head sap that might be eaten in that form or consumed as laudanum, an alcoholic tincture. It was the Chinese who had discovered how to boil down the raw latex to a concentrate that could be smoked in pipes. But it was chiefly the British who throughout the nineteenth century dispatched raw opium from colonial India and parts of the Nanyang to processors in the Pearl River Delta and eventually every port in China, with Hong Kong rapidly becoming the hub of the trade.

Almost every vessel reaching San Francisco from Hong Kong between the Gold Rush and the early twentieth century carried eagerly awaited shipments of Indian opium already prepared for smoking. A handful of large Hong Kong firms usually controlled the importing, processing, and exporting. At the San Francisco end, several major importers distributed the drug to retail outlets in the city as well as Chinese settlements throughout the Far West. A few recognized brand names competed for customer loyalty.[12]

Though opium took a higher economic and physical toll on badly paid manual laborers than anyone else, its use extended to all classes. Like alcohol, it could be devoured by addicts in squalid rooms or savored by recreational users in gracious settings enhanced by elegant accessories. Connoisseurs assessed the fine points of any batch as minutely as lovers of single-malt whiskies, while laborers who habitually worked to the point of scarcely bearable physical exhaustion and pain found grateful relief in even third-rate opium. Their inert euphoria was a bizarre and, to many outsiders, scary contrast to the antics of drunks under the influence of the preferred Western intoxicant.

Anti-Chinese alarmists thundered against opium smoking as yet another threat to decent white Americans. Parties of the latter could often be seen voyeuristically snooping around opium dens (either real or stage-managed for the occasion) in San Francisco Chinatown or a younger counterpart taking shape in New York City, usually guided by police officers with a sideline in horror tourism.[13] The agendas might also include exotica like Chinese restaurants—or, more daringly, brothels.

ORGANIZATION MEN

The *hua shang/hua gong* division altered over time, in response to the shifting political and cultural landscapes of both the United States and China; within a few decades of Exclusion, the original Chinese terms become somewhat anachronistic as applied to the American scene. The many-sided wheeler-dealers, more adroit than other Chinese at finding commercial niches fairly secure against Sinophobic threats, came to resemble not nineteenth-century Chinese or Western "merchants" but twentieth-century American businessmen. The larger class of manual laborers bravely sought their own niches, with more varied success. Undoubtedly the luckier importers and entrepreneurs often thrived at their expense, as purveyors of prostitutes and opium as well as many daily necessities including cooking gear and rice. But the two groups managed to make common cause against racist opponents. They were strengthened by an extraordinary Chinese talent for what is now called networking—or in today's China, *guanxi* (Mandarin) or *gwaanhaih* (Cantonese).

Even in China, southern Cantonese had long shown a penchant for forming themselves into groups, a tendency magnified by the hostile, white-dominated environment of Gold Mountain. English speakers were bewildered by the plethora of organizations that everybody seemed to belong to. Most were called *hui* (Mandarin) or *wuih* (Cantonese), an all-purpose label that could refer to any class of assemblies, associations,

meetings, consortiums, leagues, federations, clubs, caucuses, syndicates, or credit unions. Some were based on lineage—traced back with
a mixture of imagination and Confucian piety to primordial ancestors
supposed to have founded the surnames "Wong," "Lee," and so forth—
and village or at least district of origin. Some resembled the benevolent
societies organized by newcomers from particular corners of Europe.[14]

More titillating to Western curiosity were the *san he hui* (Cantonese,
saam hahp wuih) or "triads," secret brotherhoods obscurely descended
from outlaw groups of diehard Ming dynasty loyalists who had roamed
the rebellious southern provinces for generations after the Qing came
to power. An allied term that might be innocuous or sinister was *tong*
(in Cantonese; Mandarin, *tang*), literally meaning "hall" or "pavilion."
Some tongs were aboveboard business organizations; others were gangs
of racketeers claiming the mantle of the triads. The category glimpsed
on business signs as often as "Co." or "Inc." in English was *gong si* (Mandarin) or *gung si* (Cantonese). It denoted various kinds of trading companies, business firms, and commercial enterprises, though it might
confusingly apply to a tong, triad, or *hui*.

Triad activities shaded into legitimate territory in the many "assembly halls" or *huiguan* (in Mandarin; Cantonese, *wuihgun*), a slew of
mutual aid societies based on Guangdong village or district of origin.
From early Gold Rush days, nearly everyone climbing off the boat in San
Francisco was met at the wharf by representatives of his own *huiguan*,
who steered him to temporary lodgings and oversaw his introduction
to white society.

Hostile Americans professed to find criminality everywhere in the
Chinese community. Chinese settlements in the larger American cities
often saw clashes or sustained feuds between tongs or different *huiguan*
that helped spread the notion. But despite internal rivalries, an overall
agreement on the need for communal solidarity against the coming Chinese Exclusion Act led several separate *huiguan* in 1882 to band into an
umbrella group, the San Francisco Chongwah or Zhonghua (Cantonese
or Mandarin, respectively, for "China") Huiguan. It soon became the
nearest thing to governmental authority in the fractious Chinese community. Headed by members of the traditional *hua shang* or merchant
class, it adjudicated internal disputes and presented the public face of
San Francisco Chinatown to mainstream society. Its unofficial English

name was the "Six Companies." (At one time it had comprised six *hui-guan*, though the actual number fluctuated from year to year.) With the passage of the Exclusion Act, the Six Companies prepared to take on a larger protective role under the name of the Chinese Consolidated Benevolent Association (CCBA).

The developing Chinese communities in midwestern and East Coast cities formed their own CCBAs or Six Companies on the San Francisco model for governing internal affairs and dealing with the outside world. At times the CCBAs were pitted against the tongs in the struggle for community authority. Belatedly recognizing some responsibility for the safety of overseas Chinese, the imperial Qing court began dispatching consuls and other official liaisons to keep the various city benevolent associations and Beijing abreast of each other's affairs, including rivalries with the tongs.[15]

THE CCBA AND WONG KIM ARK

The business leaders who controlled the national (though chiefly San Francisco–based) CCBA were the only Gold Mountain Chinese with the money, lawful residency status, command of English, and political or legal connections to wage public campaigns on behalf of themselves and their poorer compatriots, the now-barred manual laborers. The tenth anniversary of the first Exclusion Act found the community threatened with an even harsher renewal. The CCBA mustered all possible influence and legal advice to stop passage of the new bill, and failed. It was voted into law in May 1892 as the Geary Act, which added muscle to the previous exclusion of Chinese workers by requiring any "Chinese person or person of Chinese descent" already in the country to obtain a certificate of legal residence or be deported after a year's hard labor. The certificates, as issued by the Internal Revenue Service, included a mandatory mug shot of the bearer.[16]

The CCBA dug deep into its pockets to challenge the Geary Act on constitutional grounds, only to see it upheld by the Supreme Court in 1893. There remained one other constitutional hope: the case of *United States v. Wong Kim Ark*. Wong, the son of Chinese-born parents and a cook by trade, was able to prove beyond all doubt that he had been born in San Francisco. Again the CCBA footed the legal costs of pursuing successive appeals all the way to the Supreme Court. This time the effort was successful. In 1898 the Court ruled by a vote of 6 to 2 that, by the terms of the Fourteenth Amendment, any child of Chinese (or other) parents born on American soil was a birthright U.S. citizen.[17]

The decision had one nearly immediate and one more slowly realized consequence. Within a few years of *Wong Kim Ark*, the 1906 San Francisco earthquake and fire sent great masses of birth and customs records up in smoke—a dazzling opportunity for people who could get away with it to concoct fictitious explanations of their presence on Gold Mountain. The longer-term effect was unforeseeable but in hindsight inevitable. Once both boys and girls started being able to claim unchallengeable birthright citizenship on the same grounds as any other children of foreign-born parents, the skewed sex ratio very gradually began to even out. It was the first long-delayed step toward the emergence of Chinese Americans as an immigrant community.

The official and unofficial threats facing Chinese-born working-class people were still dreadful. The CCBA and other Chinese American associations continued to mount legal challenges against deportation proceedings; meanwhile, the Chinese also desperately fought back with extralegal scams inspired by *Wong Kim Ark*.

The great decision would have affected only a handful of people in the short run had not Chinese on both sides of the ocean set about constructing fake identities for thousands. For decades they and the immigration authorities pitted their wits against each other. With false papers, many managed to pass themselves off as American-born citizens. Thousands more produced doctored evidence to prove that, as the Chinese-born children of citizens, they were potentially eligible for citizenship, depending on their fathers' history of residence here and abroad; members of this larger group became popularly known as "paper sons."

The authorities fought back in turn by building a detention center on Angel Island in San Francisco Bay. Starting in 1910, new arrivals from China claiming U.S. citizenship were detained at these grim barracks for exhaustive interrogations meant to weed out liars (as all were assumed to be until cleared by lengthy examination).

The immigration officials had amassed a stunning circumstantial knowledge of street layouts, landmarks, and topographical details in every Toisan village. (Toisan, of course, had produced the vast majority of Chinese laborers trying to enter the United States, or re-enter after conjugal visits to the home village.) Every detainee was required to re-call, with clockwork precision, such minutiae as the number of steps on a staircase in a parent's house, the location of the nearest well, and the years in which brothers or cousins had been married. A frequent question concerned an applicant's mother's feet; to tell the interrogator that they were unbound amounted to confessing one's own status as a mere laborer ineligible for entry. All answers were rigorously checked against those provided by witnesses already residing in this country, who were summoned to testify on behalf of the person under interrogation.[18]

Even legitimate applicants might well get some petty detail wrong or fail to give answers 100 percent consistent with a witness's. The system simply asked to be gamed in any way possible. The most obvious was cribbing. Fabricating crib sheets, or "coaching letters," became a thriving business in Hong Kong and the Pearl River Delta. Witnesses and new arrivals devised ways of surreptitiously exchanging information, often through Chinese American Angel Island employees such as cooks. Among the evidence collected by investigators for the Office of the Superintendent of Immigration—and still preserved in the files of successor agencies—were photographs of a banana skin and a peanut shell that had been adroitly converted into receptacles for coaching letters.[19]

But the resources of the superintendent of immigration and various local authorities, mostly along the Pacific Coast, were far beyond those of poor Toisanese laborers seeking to evade the law. Exclusionary measures could not instantly shut out that supposed enemy, the Chinese manual labor supply. They did, however, shrink the flow to a diminishing trickle, while the masterminds of immigration policy suddenly—if briefly—decided that Japanese workers were the answer to Far West labor shortages.

THE "CHINESE MENACE" ARRESTED

The original Chinese Exclusion Act and its progeny came close to the desired effect, though not all at once. The number of incoming Chinese reached a peak in the decade between 1870 and 1880 and began to decline after 1910. Consequently, the steeply rising U.S. Chinese population leveled off and appeared to be reversing course. Fewer people in

Guangdong or any other part of China even hoped to enter this country through any port city (though daring handfuls managed to survive as undocumented aliens after crossing the Canadian or Mexican border).

About 14,800 Chinese arrived in the United States between 1890 and 1900—a sharp drop compared to the figures for the previous two decades (123,000 from 1870 to 1880; 63,000 from 1880 to 1890). The next few decades saw small increases perhaps partly attributable to "paper son" scams that also gave an edge to what might be called "paper merchants"—people able to tailor their applications to the immigration authorities' definitions of merchantry. The total Chinese or Chinese-descended population in the mainland United States had reached a peak of about 118,750 in 1900 after a previous high of roughly 109,800 in 1890. It fell to approximately 94,400 in 1910 and 85,200 in 1920.[20]

As the architects of anti–Yellow Peril acts had hoped, the remaining Chinese in America were progressively forced out of the unskilled labor market after about 1900. Denouncers of the Chinese presence on American shores must have felt that they had won the battle for good in the years immediately after World War I, an era that saw several heated debates over what kind of society the United States wanted to be. Prohibition and women's suffrage were painfully thorny questions requiring constitutional amendments. By contrast, it was no trouble at all for the voting public at large to agree on a newly restrictive approach to immigration from almost anywhere and for Congress to pass the necessary bills.

By this time, national xenophobia had begun to rely less on violence and more on high-minded appeals to science. Beatings, burnings, and lynchings of unpopular newcomers gradually declined in the first decades of the century. Americans of northwestern European and British origin now turned to the flourishing discipline of eugenics to explain why they alone represented the genetic foundation of a new, improved human race recognizable by fair coloring and commanding height. The rest of the world was awash in short, dark-skinned specimens whose physique denoted their mental and moral inferiority. America owed it to herself to keep them out—Italians and other swarthy sons of southern Europe, Polish or Russian Jews, and of course "Asiatics," an elastic category including anybody born east of Suez but especially damning when applied to Chinese, Japanese, Koreans, and people from all of Southeast Asia.

Senator Albert Johnson of Washington State—which had an aggressive anti-Asiatic history—led the charge in 1921. His "emergency" bill to head off foreigners passed without even token opposition. Aided by postwar controversy over national security threats including Russian Bolshevism and genetic degradation, it established immigration quotas for every nation on earth outside the Western Hemisphere.[21] By 1924 Representative David Reed of Pennsylvania had joined the fray. The 1921 act had set annual quotas at 3 percent of the number of persons from any given nation living in the United States in 1910. Horrified at the thought that this arrangement would loose floods of undesirables into East Coast states to overwhelm "the American born" and defeat the aim of "keeping American stock up to the highest standard," Reed teamed up with Johnson to introduce a much more restrictive bill.[22]

This draconian measure, the Johnson-Reed Act or National Origins Act, set national quotas at 2 percent of 1890 U.S. census figures. Entry for Russians and Poles (code language for Eastern European Jews) was almost eliminated. China's quota would have been effectually reduced to something under 2,200 a year if not for a handy rider forbidding persons ineligible for naturalized citizenship (i.e., nonwhites, under the 1790 Naturalization Act) from coming at all.[23] Among a tiny handful of opponents in either house, thirty-eight-year-old freshman Representative Emanuel Celler of Brooklyn resolved to overturn Johnson-Reed if it took the rest of his career. It did.

In the early years of Exclusion, many Chinese-born manual workers throughout the Far West simply gave up and returned to a motherland now undergoing merciless humiliation at the hands of foreign powers— not least, the Japanese. Meiji Japan, inspired by the plundering zeal of Western interests in the Far East, had first managed to wrest Taiwan and a chunk of southern Manchuria from the enfeebled Qing Empire in the First Sino-Japanese War of 1894–1895. Ten years later the Russo-Japanese War of 1904–1905 resulted in Japanese annexation of all Manchuria, the ancestral home of the Qing. Between these two victories, Japan joined the United States and six European nations in an armed expedition that ended the bloody antiforeigner and anti-Christian insurrection known as the Boxer Rebellion by occupying and sacking Beijing itself in the summer of 1900. If anything could have brought more rage and despair to Chinese workers already battling to maintain a precarious existence in the Pacific Coast states, it was that, at least for the time being, state and federal authorities were inviting China's great Far Eastern enemy to become the preferred source of West Coast farm labor in place of the nearly banished Chinese.

CHINESE ON THE MOVE

Almost from the start of the Gold Rush, the Chinese had simultaneously pursued opportunity and avoided racist violence by fanning out into the boondocks. But when "Chinese Must Go" campaigns intensified after the Civil War, they were still mostly concentrated in California. So were the most rabid anti-Chinese demagogues.

With the changing fortunes of mining and then railroads, Chinese laborers first spread into many parts of the Pacific Coast and Rocky Mountain territories, soon to be states or Canadian provinces. California remained the greatest center of settlement. But Oregon, Wyoming, Idaho, and Montana as well as British Columbia and the Canadian Northwest Territories had begun to attract scattered Chinese communities in the 1850s and 1860s, as shown by Henry George's 1869 complaint about a mean and filthy "Chinatown" blighting every Pacific Coast hamlet. Seeking occupations beyond mining or track-laying, the Chinese found nativist ill-will threatening almost any kind of physical work that they put their hand to. Many or most men of the laboring class eventually would face a toss-up of two career options meant to disguise their laborer status: laundries or restaurants. Other hopes were successively closed in their faces.

Along the California coast, the Chinese who had pioneered in exploiting rich local fisheries were soon driven out of the business by whites. Newly arrived Genoese and Sicilian fishermen used threats, intimidation, and a racially weighted licensing system to rid San Francisco Bay of Chinese competition.[24]

Equal hostility greeted Chinese would-be fishermen farther north. They soon fell back on less independent opportunities as factory workers in the salmon canneries that began opening along the Sacramento

River and the major northern Pacific waterways as far as British Columbia and Alaska during the 1870s and 1880s.[25] But their virtuosic skill at cleaning, gutting, and deboning salmon brought them steady employment only until an automated device began doing the job more than ten times faster than any human. Perfected in the first decade of the twentieth century, the new machine was universally known as the "Iron Chink"—i.e., Chinaman. "There is a suggestion of the Inquisition about that name," a Canadian journalist commented in 1909, "but the 'Iron Chink' is an instrument of good, never of evil. It does away with a large number of Chinamen, and therefore is very popular in British Columbia."[26] The device never eliminated all Chinese labor in the canneries but greatly curtailed it and left the remaining workers dependent on extortionate contracts.

South of the border, Oregon soon became the state with the second-largest concentration of Chinese, most of them clustered in Portland. Like compatriots elsewhere in the Far West, they turned to vegetable gardening and peddling as an endeavor calculated to both put familiar foods on their own tables and appeal to a white clientele. In the mid-1870s a colony of Chinese began erecting shanties west of the Tanner Creek Gulch, directly opposite downtown Portland, and laying out garden plots. For several decades the "Chinese Vegetable Garden" neighborhood supplied much of the city's fresh produce before being squeezed out by an athletic club and field.[27]

In mining country a few hundred miles to the east, still more remarkable patches were sculpted from soil that most American farmers never would have bothered with. Examining a stretch of steep terrain along the South Fork of the Salmon River in Idaho in 1982, the archaeologists Jeffrey M. Fee and Mark Arnold came on an area where Chinese settlers had painstakingly dug and smoothed out the precipitous ground, foot by foot, into an uncanny likeness of the terraced fields their ancestors had built in southern Guangdong. It was one of at least five terraced gardens known to have existed in this vicinity—luckily less hostile to Chinese mining claims than many others—during the 1880s and 1890s.[28]

In most of the Far West, savage anti-"Chink" outbreaks impelled thousands to put a wide distance between themselves and Kearneyite lynch mobs. Some followed the mining trail eastward as either miners or founders of small "service" businesses, trekking through Nevada and Wyoming as far as the Black Hills of South Dakota. (Deadwood, South Dakota, had a well-known Chinese community for sixty or seventy years.) Many were recruited for construction projects in different regions of the country. One famous instance brought a contingent of Chinese laborers to Augusta, Georgia, in 1873 to widen and deepen a pre–Civil War canal originally built to accommodate freight traffic along the Savannah River. It does not appear that anyone else paid them further notice once the canal project was finished. But in succeeding years, handfuls of Chinese managed to put down roots in the city. Others ended up in Atlanta.[29]

The idea of importing Chinese labor from the Far West (or possibly China) occurred to many builders of rail connections in the Southwest and South, and at times brought some months or years of reliable employment to scattered groups. For a few decades after the Civil War, plantation owners frustrated by the loss of slave labor in the Mississippi Delta also tried recruiting Chinese to work cotton or sugar fields. The new employees, however, proved surprisingly stubborn about holding white bosses to the terms of contracts as they (the workers) understood them, and ready to walk off the job for perceived affronts. The main legacy of the experiment was a sprinkling of Chinese who stayed on to found neighborhood grocery stores throughout the delta, sometimes intermarrying with local blacks but mostly occupying an uncertain niche in a society that otherwise recognized only two racial categories.[30] Some gravitated to New Orleans, where a well-known Chinese quarter thrived from the 1880s into the 1920s.[31]

Meanwhile, Pacific Coast and Rocky Mountain Chinese (sometimes together with surreptitious border crossers or loophole-exploiting new arrivals from Guangdong) began finding their way from embattled western outposts into most of the East Coast and midwestern states. They came either singly or in tiny increments that eventually coalesced into substantial Chinatowns or tiny Chinese outposts in major or minor cities as well as some large towns.

THE NEW CHINATOWNS

Chinatowns in the Midwest and along the East Coast tended to follow a somewhat predictable pattern. Most of them got off to an inconspicuous start between 1870 and 1875 with the founding of some pioneer business that attracted others at an accelerating pace. At first, outsiders regarded the larger ones in a somewhat sensationalistic light, as potential haunts of opium fiends or addicts of other forbidden pleasures. (The 1909 disappearance of a New York missionary's daughter named Elsie Sigel, whose body eventually turned up in a Chinatown tenement along with bundles of love letters to two Chinese wooers, pumped much tabloid-fueled energy into this line of thought.[32]) But as time went on, American Chinatowns emerged as accepted parts of city landscapes, generally represented by respectable members of some CCBA who worked at discouraging the more lawless tongs and maintaining courteous relations with mainstream municipal authorities.

Manhattan, a somewhat atypical case, had had handfuls of ill-documented Chinese-born sailors, peddlers, and miscellaneous residents floating around the waterfront for a few decades before a distinct Chinese community began to form. New York Chinatown's first chronicler, Louis J. Beck, cited one Wo Kee and his general merchandise store—originally located in a dockside area of today's Two Bridges neighborhood—as the decisive seed. By the early 1870s Wo Kee, also known as Wong Acton, had made a couple of moves that eventually landed him at a strategic spot on Mott Street, still the heart of today's Chinatown.[33]

St. Louis Chinatown had gotten a slightly more organized start a few years earlier, after some 250 former railroad workers arrived from San Francisco in 1869 looking for employment.[34] Philadelphians have usually identified Lee Fong's laundry on the 900 block of Race Street as the original magnet for the city's Chinatown.[35] The Chinese Historical Society of New England points to three laundries operating on Harrison Avenue, Tremont Street, and Shawmut Avenue in 1875 as founding elements of Boston Chinatown.[36] In Chicago it would be the brothers Moy Dong Chow, Moy Dong Hoy, and Moy Dong Kee, energetic scions of a notable Toisan clan, who got the ball rolling after about 1875.[37]

The usual Cantonese name for any Chinatown was *tong yan gai*, meaning "street of Chinese people."[38] The largest new examples belonged to New York and Chicago. Between 1880 and 1930 their official Chinese populations (certainly smaller than the real totals) rose from, respectively, 747 and 172 to 8,414 and 2,757. Such growth occurred at the expense of the San Francisco Chinese community—which shrank from 21,745 to 16,303 during the same period—and other Far Western Chinatowns.[39]

Most Chinatowns were not just residential communities but supply depots and recreational oases for many Chinese living in other neighborhoods or even some distance away from a particular metropolis or town. Any *tong yan gai* had "service" businesses including Chinese barbershops and doctors' shops as well as grocery stores with the crucial ingredients that had been arriving on Gold Mountain from the beginning. Now, however, they might also stock some imported canned products such as bamboo shoots—especially welcome in the scattered small Chinatowns that were less likely than big cousins to have access to the fresh article.[40]

Restaurants fed the community's cultural lifeblood. People obliged to live in non-Chinese neighborhoods (a growing trend for laundrymen) happily traveled to Chinatown at the end of long work weeks, eager to reconnect with their own culture and enjoy a good restaurant dinner.[41] The arrival of modern gas and electric utilities had made it not easier but more difficult for many workers to prepare a proper meal for themselves than it had been in sardine-style Far Western living quarters, where they could usually cook (either indoors or in the street) in woks on small braziers. In eastern and midwestern cities they were likely to find themselves in rented rooms with even less access to cooking facilities— probably at most an American gas or electric hot plate, nearly useless for stir-frying. The major Chinatown restaurants, however, could give all comers a taste of home. They commanded excellent fresh greens and vegetables grown on nearby Chinese farms. For many years they used big wood-fired brick stoves that could accommodate enormous woks for flash-cooking over the roaring heat that everybody from laundryman to chef recognized as the sine qua non of wok flavor.[42] After about 1910 these would be replaced by powerful gas ranges specially built for the Chinese restaurant industry.

THE CHANGING FACE OF CHINESE LABOR AND CHINATOWNS

The shortness of urban memories ensured that within a generation or so any Chinatown would appear to whites as if it had always been there, complete with laundries, restaurants, and various exotica-laden shops. From the Chinese point of view, the many Chinatowns that had spread out across the United States by 1915 or 1920 offered better shelter than the rudimentary Far Western Chinatowns decried by Henry George more than forty years earlier. Of course, the original labor battle was now officially lost. The problem was finding occupations that the immigration authorities would not construe as infringing on the prerogatives of lawful (i.e., white) American manual labor.

In Chinese communities large and small, the initially preferred line of work was laundering, followed by the restaurant trade. At first, both seemed attractive as enterprises that took relatively little capital to start up, didn't involve large payrolls, and could be conducted with almost no English. These same qualities, however, quickly roused the suspicions of immigration officials on the watch for excluded manual laborers. After all, anyone trying to avoid deportation could wash a couple of shirts or boil a pot of noodles and pretend to be a laundry or eatery. Prudent people soon realized that creating business partnerships involving several principals and a payroll of a few employees was the soundest legal strategy. At least on paper, it put them into the lawful-resident class of businessmen. Many followed the natural (for Cantonese) strategy of going into partnership with "cousins"—that is, men with the same surname and presumed kinship ties.

For a few decades, laundries were the default occupation of most Chinese ex-laborers living in the orbit of city Chinatowns. Their great disadvantages were the physically punishing nature of the work itself and the fact that no one could attract white customers without settling as close as possible to white neighborhoods, at a remove from Chinese companionship. In addition, the business itself was rapidly changing. During the late nineteenth and early twentieth centuries, big mechanized facilities powered by steam were taking over much of the business. (In fact, one of these at Belleville in northern New Jersey had been the first industrial employer to recruit Chinese workers in the vicinity of New York.[43])

The Chinese at first attempted to position themselves as specialists in washing and ironing shirts and other articles that had to be finished by hand with delicate attention to detail. But even in the hand-laundry business, Chinese laundrymen in the major cities incurred hostility and accusations of price gouging from white competitors. During this period many began moving from large to smaller cities with less organized labor opposition. Some even founded hand laundries in dozens of little country towns that might not have a single other Chinese resident. After about 1920, however, a new challenge arose in the form of home washing machines.[44]

Luckily, an alternative to laundering was already at hand. Inspired by trends in the great metropolises, Chinese laundry proprietors in small cities and the hinterlands began to shift to the restaurant business.[45] The whole restaurant enterprise was now acquiring a hugely enlarged emphasis on cooking for non-Chinese patrons in settings saturated with quasi-Chinese atmospheric touches. America's Chinatowns had gained a new allure as tourist attractions. Some tinge of the former vice-district sensationalism remained, but it was quickly being replaced by artificial evocations of local color.

San Francisco had shown the way. After the 1906 earthquake the city's seriously dwindling and shabby Chinatown managed to muster enough political clout to avoid forcible relocation to another district and consolidated this victory by rebuilding its shattered remnants in a deliberately chosen Shangri-La architectural style. This act of self-reinvention proved to be a permanent draw for white visitors marveling at gilded pagodas, tiled roofs with turned-up corners, and other "Oriental" motifs.[46] The neighborhood's Chinese restaurants, already clever at invoking a storied Cathay for the benefit of Western diners, fell in with the chinoiserie ploy.

The growing Chinatowns in the East and Midwest soon adopted elements of the same strategy. None did such an extravagant job of pseudo-Sinification as San Francisco, but most put some thought into atmospheric tourist-geared touches—including tourist-geared restaurant food. A heaven-sent gimmick had appeared a decade earlier, just in time to galvanize the white community's attention.

THE NEW FRONTIER OF CHOP SUEY

By historical destiny or luck, an early stage of the Chinese exodus from the Far West to other regions coincided with one of the journalistic feeding frenzies that fueled turn-of-the-century American newspapers. In 1896 the rapidly sinking Qing regime dispatched the august statesman and general Li Hongzhang—or Li Hung Chang in Cantonese transliteration—on a round of state visits to Western powers including the United States. Arriving in New York on August 28 amid swarms of reporters and even film crews, he was feted for the next few weeks in several American cities before departing for the Pacific Coast via Canadian railway—conspicuously bypassing California, in protest against the state's notorious maltreatment of Chinese. During his stay at the Waldorf Hotel in Manhattan, reporters wrote breathless accounts of seeing the hotel kitchen commandeered by a troop of Chinese master cooks preparing dishes to the distinguished visitor's palate. A handful of supposed recipes appeared in New York newspapers, to be picked up by lesser publications elsewhere.[47] At some point attention became fixated on an exotic masterpiece called "chop sui," and from then on various popular accounts seized on the garbled idea that Li, or his cooks, had introduced America to chop suey.

Today food historians know that Li Hung Chang and his cooks did no such thing. But his obsessively scrutinized visit did have the effect of getting all things Chinese in the news. Chop suey, as understood or misunderstood by the American press, was an immediate benefactor. Thanks to the age's mass communications, by 1900 it was all the rage among fashionable diners everywhere—the first "crossover" dish to leapfrog from any foreign cuisine to American tables throughout the land, and one of the most durable in its new incarnation.

The turn-of-the-century era was marked by an insatiable national hunger for novelty and glamour. The founders of major chop suey restaurants during this period astutely read the market and responded with just what was wanted: an atmosphere that breathed opulent exoticism. In major cities where restaurants could be launched by large, well-funded partnerships, the decor might cost a small fortune. Joy Hing Lo's opening in Chicago in the summer of 1908 was heralded by a full-page puff piece in the *Daily Tribune* fulsomely proclaiming that not only would "chefs who understand every detail of food making in China . . . follow the native recipes to the letter" in preparing "dishes such as are served to the mandarins themselves" in the Celestial Empire, but no expense had been spared on the furnishings:

The walls are of Chinese green and Chinese yellow beautifully inter-
mingled and are paneled alternately with richly colored silk heavily
embroidered and mirrors that reflect the light of thousands of incan-
descent lamps concealed beneath softly shaded oriental lamps and
swinging lanterns. At intervals the great room, which occupies an entire floor, is divided by gilded columns serpentined by dragons richly
carved by native workers. Around these columns at comfortable dis-
tances are the richly carved and ornately inlaid teakwood tables, 68
of them in all.[48]

Restaurants like Joy Hing Lo occupied one glittering stratum in major metropolitan Chinatowns or other districts where white patrons expected a lavishly atmospheric dining experience. In the same neighborhoods, the more plebeian establishments popularly called "chop suey
joints" or "noodle parlors" usually made at least token efforts to invoke
the exotic Orient. Depending on location and marketing strategy, restaurants on both levels might be good enough to attract Chinese patrons as well. The outlying cousins of metropolitan Chinese restaurants
also did their best to provide at least a few Oriental touches in the form
of hanging lanterns and silk tassels.

The success of chop suey would usher in the next stage in Chinese
American career opportunities. American-targeted Chinese restaurants
extolling their authentic chop suey proliferated in all regions of the
country between the eve of World War I and the approach of the next
war. They would lastingly stamp particular notions of "Chinese food"
on the non-Chinese community. Their eventual growth to a permanent
feature of small-town as well as metropolitan life was made possible by
a new demographic bend in the road: an unforeseen resurgence of the
Chinese American population.

FROM A FLOATING TO AN ANCHORED
IMMIGRANT COMMUNITY

By a twist of fate that neither the "America for Americans" partisans
nor the Chinese in America could have anticipated, the enactment of
Johnson-Reed in 1924 occurred just as the natural birthrate of the persecuted community was starting to redraw the picture. Coming as it did

sixteen years into Exclusion, the 1898 *Wong Kim Ark* decision about the birthright-citizen status of children born in this country had narrowly preceded a sharp decline in the total Chinese American population. But a couple of decades later, it was about to produce a lasting turnaround.

The total Chinese or Chinese-descended population in the mainland United States had fallen to a fifty-year low of 85,200 in 1920. After that, however, it began a remarkable comeback not predicted by anybody. The main reason was that only now, forty years after the enactment of the Chinese Exclusion Act, had the distorted male–female ratio had a chance to correct itself through births within the community.

With an improved balance of the sexes, second- and even third-generation Chinese Americans could be born in this country, passing on the privileges of citizenship to their children. Between 1920 and 1930, the number of Chinese in the United States rose to about 102,160.[49] The "paper son" dodge may have accounted for a few thousand. But marriage and childbearing were the chief factor.

This reversal marked the first emergence in seventy years of a Chinese American immigrant community comparable to other immigrant communities. Only now did a family physically present in America become the primary social unit for people of Chinese origin. Thousands of second- and third-generation Chinese American children—daughters as well as sons—now attended American public schools. While still very small they started learning English, the unfathomable language that most of their elders could speak only in broken form and couldn't write at all. Many doors remained closed to them as members of a despised minority. That, however, was true of nearly everyone who couldn't boast English or Teutonic origin. Eventually these youngsters would confront questions of self-definition and American versus old-country loyalties in ways somewhat recognizable to other immigrants' children.

Intense anti-Chinese hostility had died down for several reasons. Now that the Chinese had been substantially drummed out of the farm labor market, Japanese laborers were the usual targets of anti-Asiatic campaigns in the Far West. The insane logic by which white Americans had denounced Chinese men as failing to lead decent family lives and meld into the cultural and economic fabric of the United States while simultaneously barring them from becoming naturalized citizens and discouraging their women from joining them, no longer galvanized protestors. A limited amount of melding took place on at least marginally amicable terms.

Households on the male breadwinner / female homemaker model became more of a norm. So did wives and mothers who cooked for husbands and children as they had done in China, though now with much more independent access to the outside world. For the first time on American soil, meals shared by father, mother, and children became as commonplace among Chinese as anyone else. One clear difference was that Chinese men had a hands-on savvy about cooking seldom matched among male members of other immigrant groups. Almost without exception, men, women, and children alike loved talking about what they were eating, armed with loud opinions and a deep understanding of ingredients and techniques.

The growth in the number of families living together in a relatively safe and peaceful North America was probably the most important factor behind the emergence of family-owned chop suey restaurants well outside the orbit of the older big-city Chinese communities between about 1910 and World War II. During the buildup to Exclusion and the first grim years after its passage, many had found refuge through the road to Chinatown. But as the community managed to regroup on a protected immigrant footing, the road *from* Chinatown would prove equally crucial. It was instrumental in securing Chinese food—in strategically altered form—a lasting acceptance among the larger American public.

PART II

FIVE

The Birth of Chinese American Cuisine

When a fad for Chinese food started making headlines among non-Chinese in the late 1890s, aficionados had to seek it out in the nation's Chinatowns, where restaurants run by men supplied other members of the Chinese bachelor society with meals solidly rooted in a certain culinary tradition. Fifty or sixty years later, the geographical and social circumstances under which restaurants usually served Chinese dishes to white or black Americans would be dramatically rearranged. So would the food itself.

Today's tastemakers routinely dismiss chop suey, chow mein, and other bedrock elements of the Chinese American restaurant cooking style formed during the Exclusion era as horrible excuses for real Chinese cooking. I submit that the usual hauteur needs some tempering. We can learn much from this now-derided food in the light of two easily forgotten realities: It was a chunk of true Americana created, at a time of shameful injustice, by American residents either completely or partly denied the privileges of citizenship. And for more than a century it has given great pleasure to millions who did enjoy those privileges. In fact, it is alive in our day, though not among citizens of any "United States of Arugula."

The cookery now scornfully summed up by some in the mere phrase "chop suey" spoke to non-Chinese patrons across racial boundaries. It was the first purposefully synthesized cooking style ever presented to American eaters—a deliberate, audience-targeted construct whose general outlines took shape between the mid-1890s and about 1910. Before that time, Toisanese men on Gold Mountain had cooked their own food to please themselves, observed with different degrees of apprehensive curiosity by many or most white people. Memories of excellent restaurants where Chinese newcomers served American food to white counterparts in Gold Rush San Francisco had disappeared, along with the culinary-cultural exchange that they had represented.

What the missionary Otis Gibson described as the Chinese way of "cutting everything up fine, and mixing different things together" seemed suspicious or silly to some commentators.[1] The historian Hubert Howe Bancroft slightingly described "the Chinaman" as "having to have everything cut and minced, ready for the stomach," thus sparing "teeth and digestive organs the work which may as well be done by chopper and masher."[2] The English writer George Augustus Sala thought that the cuisine reflected the Chinaman's "predominant shortcomings of faintness and feebleness."[3] Sir Edwin Arnold, Sala's boss at the *Daily Telegraph*, announced with a palpable shudder that a San Francisco Chinese food shop might have supplied the witches in *Macbeth* with "all the ingredients of their cauldron, at one marketing."[4]

For other visitors, it was love at first bite. In the mid-1870s Otis Gibson, himself not wholly comfortable with the smell and taste of Chinese food, took several uninitiated easterners to a San Francisco Chinatown establishment, with some trepidation. To his amazement, one instantly converted clerical guest was just getting warmed up "when I thought he must be about filled," while the man's wife was so delighted that she pitched in with fingers instead of chopsticks.[5] By 1888 several hundred white customers were reported to be regularly dining at New York Chinatown restaurants "in orthodox Chinese fashion, with chopsticks."[6]

A larger contingent, most likely recalling popular wisecracks about lizard soup and cat fricassee, wavered between cautious interest and doubt. Chinese restaurateurs not only managed to win over this public but did so during the bleakest, generally family-deprived days of Exclusion. The Chinese on the West Coast had already shown an uncanny ability—previously developed around Guangzhou and Hong Kong—to cook white people's food for white people. When they came eastward to seek a less violent racial and political climate, they arrived in midwestern and eastern cities equipped with much prior insight into the American palate.

The cooking style that they brought to birth over the last years of the nineteenth century and the first decade of the twentieth could never have had the same impact at any previous moment. Chinese food had been inaccessible to diners in most of the country as long as Chinese workers remained concentrated in western states. Besides, earlier food trends had disseminated only slowly beyond any one neighborhood or city. The moment at which Chinatowns began attracting newspaper attention in major cities also saw regional news wire services coalescing into nationwide networks, allowing small-town papers everywhere to pick up news of glamorous metropolitan doings. The economic demographer Susan B. Carter, who has meticulously studied the spread of Chinese American food during the Exclusion era, points out that it benefited from a sort of media revolution.[7] A reporter's account of a Chinese eatery in New York or Chicago might entertain readers in Arkansas, Kentucky, Nebraska, or even New South Wales within days or weeks. During Li Hung Chang's 1896 visit, big-city newspapers stood ready to rush accounts of the event into print while many more counterparts in country districts waited to reproduce their stories. In the next few years, the sensation dubbed "chop suey" emerged as America's first full-blown nationwide culinary craze.

But despite this new fame, almost no concrete knowledge about *how Chinese cooking worked* ever reached magazines and newspapers for lay readers. In hindsight, we can see that important food-related information did circulate. But it was usually limited to specialized publications.

American botanists and horticulturalists knew of food plants being raised by and for Chinese on the East as well as the West Coasts. An 1888 report in *Garden and Forest* mentions that gardeners at Woodhaven and Astoria in today's New York City borough of Queens were growing some twenty kinds of vegetables "for the Mott Street market-places"; the writer had trouble with names, but the list apparently included bitter melon, yard-long beans, water spinach and several other greens, daikon radish, and "parsley of a high flavor" (that is, the green coriander now usually called cilantro).[8]

More systematic surveys in an 1894 New York State Agricultural Experiment Station bulletin and an 1899 USDA Office of Experiment Stations bulletin were usefully buttressed by photographs, botanical names, and—most important of all—printed Chinese characters.[9] These accounts clearly establish that Chinese restaurant and other cooks had access to fresh bok choy and related brassicas, ginger, jicama (a Meso-american native naturalized in the Far East, sometimes still called "chop suey yam" in Hawaii), lotus root, lily bulbs, Chinese sweet potato culti-vars, taro, cassava, bamboo shoots, fresh ginger, and ginkgo nuts. Sev-eral edible aquatic roots were also available. Today the most important are what we call water chestnuts (*Eleocharis dulcis*); at the time, Chinese cooks also used the somewhat similar "arrowhead" (*Sagittaria sagitti-folia*). Both were often called "Chinese potato." A late-summer favorite, sometimes also confusingly known as "water chestnut," was the pleas-antly mealy-textured, much more chestnut-like water caltrop (*Trapa* spp.). At the time, some of these items probably were being imported from China along with litchis, longans, jujubes, and dried day lily buds. Well before 1900, litchis, pineapple, bamboo shoots, and other perish-able produce were also being put up and exported by a nascent canning and preserving industry in southern China and parts of Southeast Asia. They reached Chinese American communities everywhere through the still-important *jin shan zhuang* pipeline.

In Chinatowns large and small, people often sprouted mung beans indoors on trays or large flat dishes. It is unclear whether Chinese in this country were also planting field crops like red beans (*adzuki*) and different varieties of soybeans. But U.S. agronomists were tremendously interested in the last, which had attracted scattered attention as live-stock feed even before the Civil War. The 1899 bulletin not only gave a fairly detailed description of "the method used by the Chinese of San Francisco in the preparation of the bean cheese used by them" but also mentioned soybean milk and bean milk skin, soy sauce ("resembling the Japanese 'shoju'"), and the condiment now often called "bean paste" or "bean sauce" (Cantonese, *tau ban jeong*; Mandarin, *dou ban jiang*).[10]

Unfortunately, this knowledge had no way of reaching ordinary American food writers or home cooks. Neither did any insight into the cooking equipment and methods behind the culinary effects that first captivated some non-Chinese fans. Most of the relevant factors are clearly mentioned in the entry "Chinese Cookery," with information unsystematically plagiarized from several sources, in an 1889 compilation titled *The Steward's Handbook* by the Chicago hotelier Jessup Whitehead. It is doubtful that Whitehead himself or his readers understood any implications of the comments on equipment and preparation:

> The cooking is done on brick furnaces and with hickory wood, and the half globes of iron set into the glazing coals cook the food with a rapidity that would startle an American cuisinier. . . . Raw materials are prepared for almost every possible order, and seldom require more than five minutes in cooking. All bulky foods are served and eaten in pieces not larger than the end of the thumb. . . .
>
> Another aid to quick cooking is high heat. The almond eyed cook uses kiln dried hickory or oak for fuel, and makes so hot a fire that water over it explodes rather than boils, and oil becomes a seething mass of liquid and vapor. . . .
>
> The boiler in which the staff of life in Southern China—rice—is prepared is made of the thinnest cast iron, so thin that a very slight tap is enough to fracture it, heated over an earthenware vessel containing a few pieces of charcoal; and directly the cooking is completed, each piece of charcoal is carefully lifted out, extinguised [*sic*], and put away for future use. An enterprising European firm once thought to supersede the "gimcrack" native pot by a good substantial article of Birmingham make; but the enterprise proved a failure.[11]

The *Steward's Handbook* entry gave no recipes, and these crucial bits of information probably remained unknown to American diners or cookbook authors. For the next fifty-plus years, a large audience continued to talk about, eat, and sometimes try to cook "chop suey" and the ilk with either imaginary ideas or no ideas of what happened in real Chinese kitchens.

Why wasn't the germane culinary knowledge transmitted more accurately? It did not help that the twentieth century produced an inexhaustible American fondness for hodgepodge dishes rooted in bois-terous anarchy, a club into which chop suey was ignorantly welcomed. But a more crucial reason is the same factor that handicapped Chinese newcomers beyond any other immigrant group for more than a century: the unique language impasse.

"CHOW": THE HIDDEN KEY TO CHOP SUEY

I have compared the position of American and Chinese people trying to exchange culinary information to the position of the blind and the deaf trying to "translate" each other's terms for sounds and colors. In effect, there is no counterpart in American attempts to understand any other foreign group's cooking.

The actual wherewithal of Chinese cooking was too alien to West-erners for helpful English-language description. Moreover, the Chinese simply did not have written recipes on the Western model for cooking either restaurant or home dishes, and for the most part still don't.

Culinary treatises of various kinds had been around for many cen-turies, but by no stretch of the imagination can most of them be called cookbooks. They were generally written not by cooks but by patrician dilettanti. Even when they present formulas with elements like approxi-mate amounts of particular ingredients, only in rare cases would such instructions be recognizable to today's Western cooks as "recipes." The most famous exception, the *Suiyuan Shidan* of the middle-Qing-era poet Yuan Mei, does indeed contain many formulas that to this day could be followed with some exactness by a skilled and knowledgeable Chinese cook.[12] But even this celebrated treatise was conceived more as esthetic manifesto than workaday manual. It can be categorically stated that at the end of the nineteenth century neither professionally trained nor self-taught practitioners, neither men nor women, cooked from written—much less printed—directions.

"As there are no cook books in China the apprentice must learn by watching, tasting, and smelling," the American educator Alice Moore wrote from Beijing to a cousin on Long Island in 1923.[13] Reducing a cook's skills to directions for exact degrees of heat, premeasured amounts of painstakingly labeled ingredients, and stop-watch timings would not have made sense to any Chinese. Conversely, trying to reproduce Chinese dishes without such details would not have made sense to any American. If we possessed even one American-published Chinese-language compilation of Chinese recipes from the Exclusion era, many mysteries would become clearer. But as far as I know, no such magical clue exists. The few Chinese characters included in a handful of early English-language books on Chinese food give very scattered gleams of light.

It was all but impossible for both parties to ask questions and receive answers with any rational understanding. No one could have wrestled Chinese cooking processes into the confines of contemporary American recipe formulas. The few people who tried it deserve our sympathy, not ridicule, for undertaking a task that was nearly doomed by the complete absence of any common culinary vocabulary.

"Chop suey" itself is a case in point. Chinese and non-Chinese American cooks and historians have loudly disputed just what the term means. Some oracles claim that it isn't Chinese at all. Others note that the name certainly exists in Chinese as *tsap sui* (Cantonese) or *za sui* (Mandarin), meaning "miscellaneous fragments" or "broken-up odds and ends." A few follow the lead of the admirable culinary essayist and historian John Thorne, who pointed to *Hong Kong Surgeon*, the autobiography of Li Shu-fan, for a firm assertion that chop suey was being served in Toisan restaurants by 1894.[14] But it's hard to find anyone seriously grappling with the real question: Just what did the early Exclusion-era Chinese in America, or the whites who gradually came to frequent their restaurants, understand by the variously romanized "chop soly," "chop sooy," "chop sui," and so forth?

The contemporary accounts point to one simple, mystery-dispelling conclusion: What turn-of-the-twentieth-century non-Chinese American restaurant-goers and cooks first identified as chop suey were *Cantonese stir-fried dishes as a class*. But the English language lacked words to make sense of these dishes. The very idea of stir-frying long remained as opaque to Western minds as the idea of baking a cake would be in a society that had never seen ovens, cake pans, wheat flour, and the rest of the necessary underpinnings.

Scattered pieces of accurate or inaccurate information began floating around in English-language accounts as early as 1884, when the *Brooklyn Daily Eagle* published an article titled "Chinese Cooking" with the mangled byline of "Wing Chinfoo." The author was in fact the witty, pugnacious, prolific, and publicity-minded Chinese-born journalist and lecturer Wong Chin (or "Ching") Foo, already well known as a defender of his native civilization against ignorant American Sinophobia. As a Mandarin-speaker from Shandong province and an American citizen naturalized in 1874, he came to the task with the advantages of non-peasant, non-Toisanese origin and a considerable Western education. Wong's was the first account by any American to depict the Chinese as a race of culinary sophisticates. It also broke new ground in treating Chinese ingredients and dishes from an informed standpoint. He returned to the subject several times, notably in a series of columns ("The Cook in the Orient," 1885) published in a short-lived culinary newsletter titled *The Cook* and an 1888 article about the New York Chinese written for another new magazine, *The Cosmopolitan*. Because the *Eagle* piece was widely reprinted in other newspapers throughout the country, and bits of his other accounts were cribbed by various writers including Jessup Whitehead, Wong's observations reached a considerable audience, though often without credit. Certainly he sowed the seed for real interest in the Chinese as epicures.

"Chop soly is a ragout and may be justly termed the national dish of China," Wong announced in the 1884 article. "Each cook has his own recipe."[15] This certainly is misleading if we take chop soly/suey to be a single standardized dish like sole Marguery, but has enough truth to be a useful point of departure. The real clue is to be found in the 1888 account, where Wong uses the more precise term "chow chop suey."[16]

Of course, in 1884 or 1888 nobody could have found this phrase on a restaurant menu, or grasped its meaning once found, without being able to read the Chinese characters. To any Chinese patron, the significance of the word now usually romanized as "chow," "chau," or "chao" would have been plain. Unfortunately, no English equivalent could have been devised at the time. It means "stir-fry," a concept that would have defied translation. "Chow/chau/chao" may be justly termed the national cooking method of China.

"Chow chop suey" (Cantonese, *chau tsap sui*; Mandarin, *chao za sui*) might conceivably refer to any assemblage of stir-fried ingredients. It cannot ever have had a fixed composition. But quite often the "odds and ends" (*tsap*, *za*) would include cut-up bits of offal (gizzards, kidneys, liver, and/or tripe), something still observable in Chinese-language entries on menus today where the characters for *gai tsap* or *ji za* indicate a dish made mostly of chicken innards.

But the "chop suey" part of the phrase "chow chop suey" happens to be a red herring in the search for any original meaning, because the majority of *chow/chau/chao* dishes don't involve *tsap sui/za sui*. The most common stir-fries combine some chosen meat or seafood with aromatics (especially ginger) and a few such vegetables as bean sprouts, water chestnuts, dried mushrooms (reconstituted), scallions (possibly onions), bamboo shoots, peppers, celery, or snow peas. There are also all-vegetable versions. The simple stir-fry pan sauces usually involve a little soy sauce with or without some broth and rice wine, often lightly bound with a small amount of starch.

It is self-evident that the Cantonese in America cooked such *chow* or *chau* dishes for themselves, and that some of them were indeed composed of *tsap*. We can easily see how curious Americans could have sampled some odds-and-ends version, tried to ask about it across the unbridgeable language barrier, and confusedly latched onto the wrong end of the phrase "chow chop suey." All who now frequent Chinese restaurants run by people with little English know that such misunderstandings are still routine occurrences. Having no standardized printed source to check the last two words against, they then leapt to the conclusion that these—rather than "chow"—applied to a general category of dishes partly resembling the first one they'd tasted. American eaters thus came to believe in the existence of "shrimp chop suey," "vegetable chop suey," "chicken chop suey," and others named for duck, pork, beef, and so forth, while the Chinese characters on restaurant menus continued to proclaim "chow shrimp," "chow vegetables," "chow chicken," and so on.

Not until 1945 would a whimsical Chinese-born, Western-educated linguist come up with the English term "stir-frying" for *chow/chau/chao* cooking. Before then, no American cook could have grasped the requirements for properly cooking dozens of Chinese dishes. The necessary conditions are a short blast of powerful heat from a stove or brazier designed for the purpose, a properly shaped and briefly preheated cooking vessel, carefully judged amounts of fat (usually oil, sometimes lard) as cooking medium, pieces of food cut into precisely right shapes and sizes and added in precisely right order, and lightning-fast stirring and tossing of the ingredients as they hit the hot fat and metal.

That Westerners identified *chow/chau/chao* cooking with chop suey is clear from the introduction of the commercial-scale "chop suey stove," with removable adaptor rings, at about 1913. This early version of today's "chop suey ranges" was specifically developed for Chinese restaurant kitchens by makers of gas-powered restaurant equipment. "This work requires an intense heat for quick and efficient work," a writer for *American Gas Engineering Journal* explained in 1917. "The chop suey is placed in shallow pans, which are placed on the openings with or without one or more of the loose rings or not as required by the size of pan employed."[17] It should be no surprise that the American observer couldn't follow the train of steps by which "the chop suey" gets into and out of the "shallow pan." But he did grasp that intense heat and quick work must be crucial.

THE "INTANGIBLE SOMETHING" OF THE WOK

The first sustained attempt at an English-language Chinese cookbook was a pretty little unpaginated volume titled *Chinese Cookery in the Home Kitchen* (1911) by Jessie Louise Nolton, a writer for the *Chicago Inter-Ocean*. It assures readers that even a skeptical neophyte "falls under the spell" of glamorous, mysterious Chinese cuisine after a few encounters. "He acknowledges that these Chinese dishes possess an intangible something which no other cooking can approach."[18] This quality—which Nolton herself could not have put a name to—was certainly the *wok hei*, or "vital essence of the pan," prized by Cantonese cooks. We can see in hindsight that the basic technique responsible for the "intangible something" was stir-frying in a wok: "The Chinese Chop Sooy kettle is made of steel with a narrow rounded base and a flaring rim, and with small handles riveted on two sides of the rim." An advertisement by a Chicago restaurant supplier, published in 1920 in *The Chinese Students' Monthly*, settles the question beyond doubt. It contains a photograph of a two-handled wok next to the caption "Manufacture of Hand Hammered Chop Suey Pans."[19]

To Nolton and her readers, "chop sooy" comprised the kinds of dishes that got cooked in this vessel. She explained that chop sooy, "in its various forms, is the foundation of three fourths of all the dishes served in the Chinese restaurants." But it would have been vain to tell readers to buy the right "kettle." (Nolton cannot ever have tried cooking in a wok on an American stove. Though confusedly aware that the shape of the pan mattered in some way, she assured readers that they could use an ordinary "porcelain lined or granite kettle."[20]) The blitzkrieg five-minute performance noted in the *Steward's Handbook* entry, made possible by both explosive stove heat and the contours of the pot, was not reproducible in any home kitchen. Through no fault of her own, the "intangible something" of real *chow* cooking was a closed book to Nolton as well as all white or black American diners. Newspaper writers on food regularly complained that when Chinese chefs could be persuaded to part with recipes for admired dishes, they deliberately left out some secret ingredient. The language barrier and gap between types of equipment didn't permit them to perceive what actually *had* been left out.

The concept of *wok hei* (Mandarin, *huo qi*, though people from the Mandarin-speaking north pay less attention to it than Cantonese) has been elucidated in our time by Grace Young's fine books on wok cookery.[21] *Wok hei* is what Cantonese connoisseurs seek above all in a magnificently realized stir-fry. It is kindled when the searing-hot metal of the wok, lightly glossed with oil, makes brief and breathtaking contact with certain carefully prepared ingredients. *Wok hei* is as unmistakable as the sight of a rainbow, and equally fleeting. Other cooking flavors make only crude comparisons. It captures an arrested stage of high-heat cooking at which food is just on the verge of becoming deeply browned or lightly charred but doesn't quite get there. The word that comes closest to evoking the effect is "smoky," but in this case "closest" really isn't very close.

Chow/chau/chao dishes, as cooked in Chinatown restaurants serving a Cantonese-born clientele that knew *wok hei*, were a magnet for the first Americans to "discover" them. We know that Chinatown restaurants for Chinese had been frequented by some white customers before Li Hung Chang's visit and the ensuing chop suey craze. The same issue of the *New York Journal* that described the great man's meals at the Waldorf also reported that as a result of Li Hung Chang fever, "regular patrons of Chinese restaurants have been very much distressed at the influx of greenhorns. One of them went to his favorite place last night for the first time in a week. There was no seat for him."[22]

With chop suey's publicity-fueled leap to national stardom, a small and somewhat clued-in group of non-Chinese habitués was abruptly swamped by a much larger audience of "greenhorns" who had no culinary frame of reference except the mainstream American cooking of the day. They could not have known that knowledgeable Chinese admired Cantonese cuisine for a subtly judged balance of salty, sweet, sour, and bitter flavors, according to the needs of any individual dish. They were ignorant of everything about the chop suey sensation except that it *was* a sensation. The genius of the Chinatown cooks who developed a novel culinary idiom for this audience was to marry the *chow/chau/chao* technique—unintelligible to American cooks—with a neatly judged blend of certain effects that were as American as apple pie and others that registered on the inexperienced American palate as heady, intoxicating departures.

NEW CLIENTELES, NEW STRATAGEMS

No other corps of either natives or immigrants could have managed to turn a wholly foreign cuisine into a kind of edible pidgin English that Americans could feel proud of having mastered. Chinese American restaurant food *felt* more Chinese to its fans than anything that could have been devised by less skilled mind readers. It had its own calculated equilibrium of flavors and textures, just enough unlike anything else in the intended clientele's experience to strike them with delight. Chinatown cooks manning powerful restaurant stoves could carry it off with bravura and even *wok hei* (though the latter sometimes might have been hard to taste through the accents of the new made-up "language"). That it also travestied a cuisine loved and honored by its creators was part of the price that they had to pay for making a living in Exclusion-era America.

Very soon Chinese restaurateurs realized that if chop suey could draw a sizable non-Chinese clientele to Chinatown, a much larger public was waiting for them beyond the ghetto. In 1903 a *New York Times* article headlined "Chop Suey Resorts: Chinese Dish Now Served in Many Parts of the City" reported that "an ambitious young Chinaman" unaccountably nicknamed "Boston" claimed to have led an exodus of restaurateurs several years earlier from Chinatown to the nearby Lower East Side (Third Avenue near Rivington) and thence uptown to Seventh Avenue around 34th Street. Construction for the new Pennsylvania Railroad Station soon wiped out that neighborhood. A Chinese contingent then settled in a few blocks north, in the Longacre district (today's Times Square), while one adventurer presciently invaded Harlem.[23]

An eager trans-Chinatown black clientele was forming as fast as the white counterpart. An officer of the New York Police Department told the *Times* reporter of "chop suey places patronized exclusively by negroes. In fact, they have developed an extreme fondness for chop suey since places were opened up town. Negroes were afraid to go to Chinatown, for some reason or other. But they like the chop suey well enough, possibly because of the large proportion of chicken in it."[24] In 2002 the historian Huping Ling was informed by an elderly Chinese-born St. Louisan who came to the city as a child that during the early 1930s his father had had "a small Chinese restaurant on Jefferson Avenue that catered to the African American community. . . . The restaurant devised a simple menu of fried rice and duck noodles, and the patrons used forks instead of chopsticks. . . . The restaurant also hired African Americans as servers—one of the early instances of racial collaboration and harmony in pre-desegregated America."[25]

With the removal to non-Chinese neighborhoods, there was little reason for the new crop of restaurants to address the palates of knowledgeable Chinese diners. There was even less when Chinese entrepreneurs began adjusting their sights to target a developing urban nightlife in the next few decades of the twentieth century. New York and San Francisco sprouted a range of colorful Prohibition-era establishments modeled on mainstream honky-tonks, cabarets, or (eventually) nightclubs, with dancing and jazz as entertainment and menus founded on many "chop suey" variations. A Philadelphia reporter exploring the New York Chinese restaurant scene in 1924 noted two theater-district establishments "equipped with jazz bands and large dance floors. They are run like any first-class American eatery." The writer astutely noted that "prices are reasonable—in fact, that is the quaint characteristic of all the Chinese restaurants, which extend from the handsome Port Arthur on Mott street downtown to Sun Hung Far's place away up in the Bronx."[26]

This "quaint characteristic" was one of the signal claims that the new Chinese restaurants exerted on mainstream consumer loyalty. The farther they penetrated into non-Chinese neighborhoods, the better positioned they were to compete with the many urban eating places dependent on short-order service and low prices that had sprung up since the early nineteenth century and were still expanding into new forms (for instance, the self-service cafeterias that began appearing at around the turn of the century). Chinese eateries for non-Chinese had at least two advantages over the rest. Even when furnished on the cheap, they offered more atmospheric surroundings than coffee shops, luncheonettes, and the like. Besides, Cantonese-style stir-fried dishes represented one of the few branches of world cookery in which—American clients' culinary barbarism notwithstanding—lightning-fast service was perfectly compatible with elegant and finished culinary execution.

Some non-Chinese did sense that the popular restaurant dishes often drifted away from any Chinese originals. Qualms on this score set in as early as 1902, when many newspapers picked up a piece from the well-known literary magazine *The Forum* lauding the culinary discernment of real Chinese people and firmly stating, "Chop sooy is made to sell to curious white persons who visit Chinatown."[27] But the craze was already too far gone to be deflected.

SOY SAUCE COMES TO TOWN

The infant cuisine cannot have been one rigidly uniform creation. We can assume that it was practiced with some individuality by different cooks and reflected varying compromises with original Cantonese standards. But wherever it appeared, it displayed several prominent features. Among the most instantly recognizable was a greatly expanded use of soy sauce.

This part of the story is surrounded by confused terminology. Not only are there several different Chinese names for soy sauce, but since the early to mid-nineteenth century, American cookbooks had unsystematically used the word "soy" for a kind of homemade catsup. Wong

Chin Foo grappled with the problem in 1885, when he wrote a short squib for *The Cook* about "Kau-Tsi," the commonest type of dumpling in northern China (modern pinyin, *jiaozi*). No American cook could conceivably have untangled the instructions, and it is impossible to tell whether Wong himself had ever tried to make dumplings. But the piece is historically important as apparently having been the first English-language recipe (with two variants) for any Chinese dish:

The most popular dish in Northern China is Kau-Tsi. It is nothing more than a small dumpling, boiled, baked or fried. The dough (of rice flour or wheat flour) should be rolled until it is thin as card-board, and should be then cut out into circles by a small goblet or large muffin-ring. The filling of the dumpling is left to the cook's taste. A number of recipes are given below. An ounce of filling is the proper weight. The dough is brought together around the filling so as to form a ball, a half-moon or a cocked hat. Place the dumplings in boiling water and boil for ten minutes; then throw in the pot two cups of cold water, raise to boiling and boil again for ten minutes; then raise from water and steam for fifteen minutes. They are now ready to be served, or to be baked or fried. Bake in a hot oven for ten minutes, or fry in hot lard three minutes.

FILLINGS FOR KAU-TSI.
I.
One pound of beef, veal, mutton, lamb, chicken, turkey or duck; one-quarter pound of pork; salt and pepper to taste; one tablespoon-ful Indian soy; one-quarter ounce of ginger; seasoning to taste. Cut all up to a pulp together.
II.
Boil asparagus tips, green peas, cauliflower, carrots, two parsnips, until almost done. To one ounce of each of these when put on the dough, add a small piece of chopped-up fresh pork, and seasoning as in above.[28]

Already soy sauce plays a crucial role in the meat filling. Wong undoubtedly meant to avoid confusion with the American condiment by specifying "Indian soy"—i.e., an article imported from the Far East.

As the puzzling novelty became better known, some American cooks and diners acquired a taste for it either because of or in spite of its singular brewed bouquet. A 1915 chop suey recipe in the *Chicago Tribune* laconically says, "If cooked right soy sauce not needed to color, if the flavor is not liked."[29] Some sophisticates recognized it as the nearly identical twin of a Japanese product being imported as "shoyu" or "shoju," a name originally derived from the Chinese *si yau* (Cantonese) or *chi you* (Mandarin). Louis J. Beck's 1898 survey of Manhattan Chinatown gives the name of the "high flavored" condiment as "See Ow" and describes it as "a popular sauce affected by the Chinese . . . made from beans, star aniseeds and spices, and exposed to the sun."[30] English-language food writers tried many romanizations on the order of "syou" or "see yu," and sent reader-users to Chinatown to buy the unpronounceable stuff. The 1915 edition of *The Settlement Cook Book* cluelessly rendered it as "Shoyn."[31] *The Boston Cooking School Cook Book* was still calling it "shoyu" in 1929.[32]

Part of soy sauce's growing appeal was that it provided an appetizing (at least for Americans) brown tint in contexts where Cantonese would have used it very discreetly or not at all—for instance, stir-fried rice, or the pan sauces of many "chop sueys." Discriminating Cantonese cooks disliked a strong brown color in stir-fried rice and many or most other stir-fries. But they were more than happy to revv up this accent for the sake of their new clientele. They often gratified white patrons' avid preference with a heavy all-purpose brown gravy made from soy sauce and another product that may have started out as a by-product of Chinese sugar refining but eventually devolved into a syrupy cousin of English "gravy browning" (i.e., caramelized sugar dissolved in water with a few other seasonings). The Chinese name was "pearl sauce" or "bead sauce" (Cantonese, *jyu yau*; Mandarin, *zhu you*). Unlike soy sauce, it could be used at will without oversalting a dish, though it did add some sweetness. The Chinese brown gravy that became a standard part of many presentations generally contained a little stock, some starch, and a soy sauce–pearl sauce combination.

Jessie Louise Nolton recommended seasoning "chop sooy" with a mixture of two condiments that she called "Chinese seasoning sauce" and "Chinese flavoring sauce." The first ("A rather salty sauce with a sort of meaty flavor," essential "to obtain the peculiar flavor which makes the chief charm of the dish") was certainly soy sauce. The other ("A sauce which is somewhat like molasses in appearance and is used in most of the Chop Sooy dishes") was most likely pearl sauce.[33]

In a few years soy sauce could be bought in Chinatown shops as "chop suey sauce"; the product that an enterprising New York firm trademarked under that name in 1915 probably was soy sauce.[34] Soon American food writers and home cooks were trying to incorporate soy sauce into their own "Chinese" recipes. The prolific authority Ida Bailey Allen's version of chop suey in *Mrs. Allen's Cook Book* (1917) called for half a cup (with additional salt to taste), an amount suggesting very slender acquaintance with the stuff.[35] She was outdone by Buster Keaton, who called chop suey his favorite dish. His wildly baroque rendition, published in a 1929 fundraising cookbook by a Beverly Hills women's club, featured a fanfare of ingredients including raw pork cubes, water chestnuts, bamboo shoots, "Chinese greens," salted almonds, and the meat of a whole roast chicken, and called for "a cup of 'Soy' sauce added to season it and give it the proper dark color."[36] Mrs. Allen, meanwhile, had become a ubiquitously visible flack for Mazola corn oil. A 1927 newspaper advertisement presented her version of "Chop Suey as the Chinese Make It," featuring Mazola along with products from other Allen clients (Kingsford or Argo cornstarch, Blue Label Karo syrup) and calling for Worcestershire sauce to taste. "Soy sauce, can be used instead of the Worcestershire," she noted. "It can be obtained at Chinese restaurants."[37]

Unfortunately, Westerners no more grasped the varied possibilities of soy sauce than sixteenth-century Aztecs could have grasped the scope of European grape wines. Many different versions of soy sauce exist in various parts of China, Japan, Korea, and Southeast Asia. Some are thick, sweetish, and nearly black; others thin and lighter-colored with a clean, salty flavor. All result from a complex double fermentation of soybeans (usually with wheat) over a period of at least several months; especially prized kinds may take two or three years. All contain innumerable subtle flavor nuances contributed by different by-products of fermentation, especially the glutamic acid salts responsible for the meatiness—"umami" in today's parlance—mentioned by Nolton. Cooks often combine several soy sauces in varying proportions. The Cantonese have famously preferred light, delicate kinds for most purposes and disliked what they consider a coarse overuse of soy sauces in some regional cuisines (e.g., Shanghainese).

Such knowledge lay far outside non-Chinese cooks' and diners' reach at the height of the chop suey era. For several decades, the "syou" or "soy" called for in chop suey recipes came from abroad and had to be inquired for in Chinatown. It could be liable to spoilage since at the time it was not routinely pasteurized. By the early 1930s a domestic alternative had appeared. Applying the already well-known manufacturing technique of acid hydrolysis to soybeans by boiling them in the presence of a strong acid, American know-how presented American consumers with a hydrolyzed soy protein solution that could be cheaply manufactured in weeks, colored brown, heavily salted, and sold as soy or shoyu sauce with no legal objection. The A. E. Staley Company of Decatur, Illinois, pioneered in the bulk manufacture of hydrolyzed soy sauce.[38] The new La Choy company, founded in Detroit in 1922 by a Korean immigrant and a native Michigander who had met as university students, soon started buying the product from Staley for retail bottling and distribution under its own label.[39]

Chinese restaurants continued to cook with imported brewed soy sauce, bumping up amounts to suit Western tastes. But meanwhile, other domestic manufacturers followed the lead of Staley and La Choy. Soy sauce was now free to conquer American palates, in caricatured form. The harsh-tasting hydrolyzed product had none of the fragrant, meaty interplay between brininess and mellowness that distinguished properly brewed soy sauces. But it was easy for grocers to stock anywhere in the country, and nearly imperishable.

CULINARY WAYS AND MEANS

Actual eating experiences in the new Chinese American eateries, from small chop suey joint to cabaret, revolved around a repertoire of effects deeply satisfying to non-Chinese patrons. The most instantly recognizable, after big doses of soy sauce, were glossy, viscous sauces bathing most "chop sueys" (i.e., stir-fries); boneless chunks of meat, poultry, or fish fried in batter-coatings; a heavy hand with sugar; and a rich brown color in nearly everything. All these logically paralleled some flourishing trends in mainstream American cuisine already well known to Chinese who worked as cooks in private homes.

Thick roux-based white sauces were a hallmark of the age. Fritters, croquettes, and cutlets dipped in batters or breadings before frying were enjoying great popularity. The uses of sugar were expanding from the dessert and confection repertoire into new territory as a delirious gelatin-salad vogue overtook the nation and old standbys like baked ham or Boston baked beans acquired a prodigious sweetness. Brown sauces were as admired as the white counterparts—and in fact often were roux-based white sauces doctored with a bit of caramelized sugar or a handy newish product called Kitchen Bouquet. The same trick gave a deeper color to many underbrowned braises and pan gravies.

Chinese cooks, of course, didn't use roux to bind sauces. Their equivalent was starch obtained from water chestnuts, tapioca, or wheat flour from which the gluten had been extracted by a kneading process. Once in North America, many cooks switched to the cheap and readily available cornstarch. All starches gave sauces a translucent gloss while thickening them to any desired degree—and non-Chinese patrons preferred them quite thick, often with a brown tint. Batter-dipped fried foods were not a prominent feature of Cantonese cuisine except as imagined by non-Chinese eaters, who especially liked batter-fried boneless nuggets of pork or chicken set off by another newly conspicuous element: sweet-and-sour sauces made up to please the national sweet tooth.

The actual structure of menus also underwent some rearrangement over time, to satisfy American ideas about the meaning of different courses and the order in which they should appear. At first Chinatown restaurants seem to have set out little dishes of fruits, sweet preserves, and salted seeds or nuts as a starting course. The gesture probably echoed the custom of beginning Chinese formal banquets with prescribed arrays of such items. In a decade or two, the practice faded in meals meant for non-Chinese. It became more usual to greet Westerners with soups—traditionally the last course in Chinese meals—or "appetizers," a word that was gradually driving out the more formal older term "hors d'oeuvre."

The concept of soups presented great obstacles to international understanding. Chinese cuisine is rich in soupy dishes, either savory or sweet, that confound all Western notions of soup. The soul of savory kinds was, of course, a basic stock. The best Guangdong restaurant kitchens were as proud of excellent meat or poultry stocks as any French counterpart. They would never be without *seung tong* (Mandarin, *shang tang*), or literally "superior broth," made with great care from chicken or other poultry, fresh and cured pork, and a few seasonings like ginger and scallion. (*Tong* or *tang* usually refers to clear broths or thin, clear soups made with them.)

From a huge spectrum of possibilities, only wonton soup and a starch-thickened version of egg drop soup took up permanent residence on plebeian Chinese American menus in the "soup" pigeonhole. (Bird's nest and shark's fin soups were favorites at higher-end dining spots, probably more esteemed by Americans as exotic luxury items than from any sense of their merits.) But menus of the period testify to quick and lasting enthusiasm for other standard items from the scarcely translatable repertoire of Chinese "soup noodles" (see below).

American Chinese appetizers usually included sweet-and-sour spare-ribs as well as an innovation called "egg rolls," which weren't sweet but were served with a dipping sauce that more than made up for the lack. Called "plum sauce" or later "duck sauce" (from the supposition that it went with roast duck), it was vaguely modeled on *syun mui jeung* (Cantonese) or *suan mei jiang* (Mandarin), a sweet-sour-salty condiment made from *Prunus mume*, a unique Far Eastern relative of plums and apricots. Egg rolls themselves apparently were invented in New York Chinatown during the chop suey era as a heftier stick-to-the-ribs variant of "spring rolls," a delicate, thin-skinned, and shatteringly crisp fried specialty of the Chinese New Year celebration.[40]

The egg roll filling came to be a general medley of bean sprouts, shredded celery and bamboo shoots, and any other desired vegetable along with bits of pork and (often) shrimp. As with some other naturalized citizens of the Chinese American restaurant kitchen, a sturdy crunch was just what non-Chinese restaurant-goers wanted in the thick wrapping.

The chief fixture of the new menus was, of course, "chop suey" as understood by Americans—i.e., some *chow/chau/chao* dish. "Chicken chop suey" was the most prestigious since at the time chicken was an expensive meat that Americans associated with a fine Sunday dinner.

Though Chinese cooks were used to whacking a chicken into small, flavorful bone-in pieces for stir-fries, Americans were unnerved by chunks of poultry on the bone and considered breast meat the most desirable part of the bird. To them "chicken chop suey" made with breast meat was worth paying extra for. The dish might be embellished with either Chinese or ordinary white mushrooms.

Just plain "chop suey" usually indicated a pork version. Two other popular variations were spawned by Americans' love of beef and the cheapness of veal. (At the time, veal usually came from unwanted bull calves that dairy farmers were eager to get rid of.) Duck, squab, turkey, shrimp, and/or lobster chop suey were often available at large restaurants.

Chow mein, as beloved as chop suey, was equally the victim of mistaken identity. "Mein" really meant "wheat noodles" (Cantonese, *min*; Mandarin, *mian*)—fresh, supple, and usually made with egg. "Chow," again, meant "stir-fried." Cantonese cooks were especially renowned for the *wok hei* of their *chau min*.

Noodles were only beginning to become known to most American diners. Wong Chin Foo, in the 1884 *Brooklyn Eagle* piece, could only lamely mention boiled "pieces of dough," "very much like the 'nudeln' of our German cousins."[41] For *chau min*, the Cantonese boiled and drained the noodles before the dish was assembled. Of the usual procedures, the simplest was to stir-fry aromatics and any other desired ingredients, add the cooked noodles, and swiftly toss everything in the surpassingly hot wok, usually together with a little stock and seasonings. Or the noodles might get a separate stir-frying by themselves before being combined with the other elements. The same approaches were used for dried, soaked, and drained rice vermicelli to create Cantonese *chau fun* (Mandarin *chao fen*); sometimes fresh rice noodle sheets cut into ribbons were the star ingredient.

The "chow mein" that captured the American imagination along with chop suey resembled none of these. What Americans rapidly came to expect in "chow mein noodles"—a phrase as illogical as "chowder soup"—was a crisp crunch utterly unlike the delicate suppleness of the original. The likely source of the notion that the noodles had to be crisp was a popular Hong Kong variant of chow mein, *leung min wong* (Cantonese; the Mandarin is *liang mian huang*). The name means "both sides brown" (or "yellow," which is the same word in Chinese). The dish was made by boiling and draining fine, thin egg noodles and pressing them into a pillowy mass like a pancake. This was lifted out into a little hot oil in a wok and cooked on both sides only until it was golden and slightly crisp on the outside, soft on the inside. Any desired stir-fry of meat, poultry, seafood, or vegetables was then poured over the hot drained noodles. Chinese eaters loved the contrast between the fragile brittleness of the outer "crust" and the suave interior of the loosely formed cake.

I believe that "both sides brown" helped start chow mein on the road to—if not ruin—Americanization as a bed of uniformly crunchy noodles topped with some "chop suey" version. Jessie Louise Nolton's "Chow Mein" recipe is a good instance. She had the cook start with handmade noodles, and continued:

Put olive oil in pan having the oil about one inch deep when heated. Spread the noodles over bottom of pan and let fry slowly till a golden color. Then turn over with wide bladed knife or pancake turner and let fry on the other side until done. Perhaps ten minutes will be right, or fifteen. Remove noodles and drain carefully to remove oil. Put on platter and serve with any of the Chop Sooy dishes you prefer. The Chop Sooy must be ready and hot, and the noodles served immediately when done.[42]

The reason for Nolton's use of olive oil is unclear. (She usually recommends peanut oil.) But, tellingly, she had been taught to understand chow mein as deep-fried noodles served with chop suey. Deep-frying (*ja* in Cantonese; *zha* in Mandarin) is a technique unrelated to *chow/chau/chao*. Probably Chinatown restaurateurs had grasped American patrons' preference for complete crispness and neatly obliged.

Chow mein thus came to be judged by a coarse crunch far removed from the lovely, not-quite-crusty finish of ordinary *chau min* or the pleasing textural contrast of "both sides brown" fresh out of the wok. Andrew Coe's lively history *Chop Suey* cites a 1902 salute to chow mein—uttered in the persona of a birdbrained chorus girl—as something like potato chips in vermicelli form.[43]

Later recipes by American authors followed Jessie Louise Nolton's lead in frying the noodles completely crisp before covering them with chop suey. Within a couple of decades La Choy had perfected a shortcut: thick, heavy noodles baked to a cracker-like crunch that survived being topped by a sauce. Sold in a can by itself, the product was proudly labeled "chow mein" despite a total lack of connection with the *chow/chau/chao* stir-frying method. (La Choy also managed to can bean sprouts and ready-to-heat chop suey.)[44]

A pan-fried noodle dish somewhat closer to real *chau min* did find a place on Chinese American menus: lo mein (Cantonese, *lou min*; Mandarin, *luo mian*, from a word meaning "dredge up" or "stir up"). It differed from *chau min* in requiring only a brief tossing of the noodles in the pan with the other ingredients—too brief to produce the ultimate *wok hei*, but flavorful nonetheless.

As mentioned earlier, the new menus also enlarged the role of "sweet-and-sour" meat or seafood dishes—pork, chicken, fish, shrimp. They were not, as some critics now suppose, invented in North America out of whole cloth. It should be noted that both sugarcane raising and sugar refining were longstanding enterprises in Guangdong province, and that pineapple—frequently used in such dishes—was already being canned there after a few centuries as a plantation crop. But Cantonese antecedents of the newly popularized sweet-and-sour dishes had been fewer and more subtle.

For their new American clientele, Chinatown kitchens rang nimble changes on the theme employing several can't-miss elements: boneless, bite-sized chunks of the main ingredient; an eggy batter; enough fat for deep-frying the coated morsels; and a sauce sweet and sour enough to overpower other flavors. Some versions used canned pineapple with its juice; others, a combination of vinegar and sugar. The sauce often had a dash or a hefty slug of red coloring.

Many Americans were already partial to sweet-sour sauces like the English-style mint sauce that James Beard remembered his mother and their Chinese cook Jue Let arguing over as an accompaniment to leg of lamb. Let thought it drowned out the meat's flavor; Elizabeth Beard half-conceded the point but loved it anyhow.[45] Sugar-vinegar combinations were also familiar enough to German and Eastern European Jewish immigrants to have helped encourage an American fondness for Chinese sweet-and-sour dishes. The higher the sugar content, the happier the audience. By 1903 a writer for the *Brooklyn Daily Eagle* was singing the praises of New York Chinatown's "'sweet and pungent chop suey' which strongly resembles Indian chutney."[46] In the same year an article in the *Minneapolis Journal* mentioned pineapple fish with the approving comment, "No one possibly, tasting it, would imagine it contained fish."[47]

Among the most popular menu standbys were fried rice and "egg foo young," both considerably altered from the originals. Fried rice, which in Cantonese kitchens was supposed to have any meats or vegetables added with discretion and to be as white and delicate as plain rice, became a free-for-all of cooked rice and the usual "chop suey" vegetables (bean sprouts, water chestnuts, green pepper, celery) colored a deep brown with soy sauce. In China, *foo yung* (Cantonese) or *fu rong* (Mandarin) was a dish as simple as it was elegant. It is also the name of several flowers, including the beautiful white Chinese hibiscus. (Some especially delicate versions used only egg whites.) It can be made with any sort of seafood, meat, or poultry added in judicious amounts. But the form that conquered American palates was a thick egg-bound patty studded with the standard chop suey-ish elements and napped with the Chinese brown-gravy-of-all-work.

The "soup noodles" mentioned above comprised several dishes that, for Chinese, were nearly synonymous with humble but excellent fast food often peddled by street vendors. The general concept was not entirely new to American cooks. But the nearest parallel—"vermicelli soup" with thin Italian pasta—originally had other associations; American hostesses had considered it a particularly elegant, refined company dish since the eighteenth century.

The very different egg noodles arrived with German as well as Chinese immigrants. But it was the Chinese who brought soup-and-noodle dishes to thousands of middle-class and working-class eaters wherever Chinese restaurants were to be found. The most popular kinds were yat ca mein (which had variant spellings ranging from "yockamin" to "yet gaw mi"), war mein, and wonton soup.

Yat ca mein (Cantonese, *yat goh min*; Mandarin, *yi ge mian*, meaning "single order of noodles") was dished out in one-person servings by putting boiled and drained noodles into a deep bowl with a few seasonings like sesame oil, pouring hot soup stock over them, and adding a substantial garnish, most often half a hard-boiled egg and a few slivers of roast pork or poached chicken. At its best, it was based on very fine stock. War mein (Cantonese, *wor min*; Mandarin, *wo mian*, from a word for "nest") was usually presented in a large tureen-like vessel and featured thick, absorbent noodles with a wider selection of vegetables, also in a good stock.

There is a postscript to the yat ca mein story: For some reason several U.S. and Canadian cities decided, and believe to this day, that the dish was their own birthright possession. Beef versions now compete with pork or chicken. The New Orleans African American community took a transfigured yat ca mein (spaghetti, beef, Cajun seasonings) to its bosom as a hangover remedy under the nickname of "Old Sober." A catsup-laced relative reached African Americans in the Tidewater-Chesapeake regions of Virginia, Maryland, and Delaware as simply "yock" or "yat."[48]

In the northern Chinatowns where non-Chinese first tasted it, yat ca mein gradually faded away except in very old-style Cantonese rice shops. Wonton soup, on the other hand, became better known and loved after the 1920s and probably underwent less distortion in American Chinese restaurants than any other Chinese dish.

With their usual instinct for tailoring performance to alien expectations, Chinese restaurateurs removed such unpopular items as bean curd, whole fish, duck or chicken feet, and most steamed dishes from bills of fare meant for non-Chinese. They created at least a token section of dessert offerings (almond cookies, sliced pineapple, litchis, preserved ginger). Some put white bread and butter on the table, recognizing that a meal without them would be unintelligible to many patrons. A sizable number of restaurants went further, positioning themselves as split-identity eating houses with both Chinese and mainstream American personas that allowed different members of a party to go the chow mein–spareribs–litchi route or stick with veal cutlets, Virginia ham, and chocolate cake. (Ambitious restaurateurs sometimes saw a Chinese eatery as a stepping stone to opening a high-class Western establishment.) Simultaneously, many large American hotels took to offering chop suey as a sign of cosmopolitan awareness. Versions of the dish eventually became standard on luncheonette and diner menus everywhere in North America.

The huge popularity of chop suey and the other standard offerings was bound to spark a demand for printed recipes. The handicaps to arriving at any sort of adequate formulas were so many and so incomprehensible that it is foolish to criticize the results. It would have taken superhuman effort for anyone to have gotten within hailing distance of Chinese American restaurant dishes without speaking and reading Chinese.

Jessie Louise Nolton, the first writer to make a serious effort, clearly had done her best to take on a daunting task. Her title, *Chinese Cookery in the Home Kitchen*, in itself implies a pitch to American aficionados of Chinatown restaurants. The slender volume contained blank lined pages for a cook's notes opposite each recipe—a clear tip-off that people would need to do much of their own road-map construction. The contents show a struggle to fit a certain amount of real teaching into the context of a ladies' "theme"-entertainment cookbook, complete with suggestions for table decorations and recipes for fruit salads.

Nolton makes game stabs at describing necessary ingredients including "Chinese potatoes" (water chestnuts or arrowhead), "sesamum" oil, preserved ginger, dried mushrooms, and bamboo shoots. She cautions that "American imitations" won't work and shows a laudable insistence on details like the proper handling of rice. She goes so far as to give directions for making noodles from scratch and growing one's own bean sprouts. She argues for peanut oil—then rare in American kitchens—as the most suitable cooking fat in most cases. She understands that a "Chinese Chef . . . is apt to leave the vegetables a little under done, according to the taste of the average American palate"; though she allows a little leeway in the matter, she warns that overdone vegetables "would spoil the dish entirely." Surprisingly, she gives (or at least, tries to give) directions for preparing "Chinese Cured Pork," a homemade version of *cha siu/cha shao* that she regards as indispensable in many dishes.[49]

But lacking the kitchen furnishings necessary for the fast and furious stir-frying process (and having no English name for it), Nolton cannot explain how to replicate it. Her timings for most dishes add up to something more than fifteen minutes—unusually fast by contemporary American standards for cooking combinations of meat and vegetables, but disastrously overlong for the right effect. The amount of knowledge that she managed to absorb and convey despite the linguistic and cultural-culinary barriers is remarkable; she must have spent much time trying to ask the right questions of people with whom she shared no common language. We should not be surprised at her lack of specificity about the particular shapes and sizes in which vegetables and meats must be cut. Chinese cooks who had absorbed this knowledge from the cradle never stopped to puzzle over mathematical details. For American cooks who hadn't, spelling out fractions of an inch would have looked like childish busywork without a clear explanation of why such details affected the outcome of "chop suey."

The number of English-language Chinese cookbooks increased only slowly for several decades. Among them, *Chinese-Japanese Cook Book* by the semifictitious team of Sara Bossé and Onoto Watanna (published by Rand McNally in 1914) is a slapdash affair evincing very little understanding of either Eastern or Western cooking principles.[50] On the other hand, *The Chinese Cook Book* by Shiu Wong Chan is noteworthy on several counts. It was issued in 1917 by Frederick A. Stokes Company, a New York firm that already was carving out a small niche in cookbook publishing. It took the important step of printing the titles of all recipes and a sprinkling of other information in Chinese characters, along with romanized spellings and English translations.[51] The actual characters may not have helped American users at the time, but they provide many retrospective clues to real meanings.

If Jessie Louise Nolton's brave try couldn't overcome the barriers of written/spoken Cantonese added to the barriers of the Cantonese kitchen "idiom," the problem here is the reverse. The unknown author (he was certainly a man, given Chinese women's general lack of access to public venues at the time) clearly was at home with crucial Chinese culinary concepts and cooking terms. He provides recipes for a wealth of dishes that Americans would seldom or never have tasted in run-of-the-mill pre–World War I Chinese American restaurants but that, as the book shows, were being made by Chinese cooks for Chinese patrons. Unfortunately, he had next to no frame of reference for translating the crucial information into English. One pictures him and Nolton gazing at each other from opposite sides of a yet-unbreachable linguistic and culinary-cultural chasm, "so near and yet so far" from each other's comprehension.

The Chinese characters and romanizations, though often garbled, allow us to see that Shiu Wong Chan wanted to introduce Western cooks to many underpinnings of the cuisine. Virtually all of his "chop suey" recipes, whether for bean curd, pigeon, or lobster, bear the character *chow/chau/chao*, directly indicating the stir-fry method. He presents "superior broth"—the foundation stock as necessary to Chinese as to French cooking—under the name of "Primary Soup." He tries to explain how to ferment "Chinese sauce" (soy sauce), grind "sesamum-seed" and peanuts to oil, and make "white cheese" (bean curd) or "red cheese" (a fermented version important as a flavoring) as well as several cured meats, including a few variants of "Chinese frankfurters" (the sausages commonly known as *lap cheung* in Cantonese, *la chang* in Mandarin). The aim here is not complete directions but sketches of what goes into the production of some indispensable cooking materials.

The recipes tantalizingly suggest what a splendid range of dishes Chinese cooks could manage to produce in the United States in the depths of the Exclusion era, from chicken baked in salt to the festive New Year's dish called "raw fish" (Cantonese, *yue sang*; Mandarin, *yu sheng*), made with pieces of uncooked fish and finely cut raw vegetables topped with a seasoned dressing.[52] (It is traditional in parts of southern China as well as the Chinese communities of Singapore and Malaysia.) The bilingual list of ingredients and equipment available from Chinatown sources includes pharmaceuticals (astragalus, the *Cordyceps* caterpillar fungus), rice flour, "sorghum wine," "cooking shovel" (wok spatula), and "frying pan" (iron wok).

The knowledge that went into this pioneering book was sadly destined to remain locked up in its pages, through the author's incomprehensible English and inability to fill in procedural details that would have been terra incognita to his audience. In 1917 serious Chinese-language instruction was becoming established at American universities, but it was far removed from the world of mere cooks. Chinese–English dictionaries paid scant attention to any sort of specialized culinary vocabulary, a failing that persists today. Shiu Wong Chan labored mightily to translate the words for what we now call star anise ("octogon spicery"), taro ("gray potatoes,"), eggplant ("Chinese tomato"), silk squash ("star melon"), ginkgo nuts ("white nuts"), fermented yellow bean sauce ("Chinese sauce residue") and much more.[53] But none of the effort would have gone far to help his readers.

CHOPPING SUEY WITH A VENGEANCE

Of course most of the people trying to teach Americans how to cook Chinese dishes were Americans who spoke no Chinese and couldn't tell what they knew from what they didn't know. Through their diligent efforts we can see chop suey developing a sort of multiple personality disorder over the first decades of the twentieth century.

Cut off from any means of understanding the lightning-fast stir-fry method with its unique equipment, highly structured preparations, and ferocious heat, American observers initially described chop suey as a "hash" but usually came to prefer "stew." That word covered just about any moist-cooked savory dish that wasn't officially called a soup. Nearly the only thing most kinds had in common was that they cooked with liquid over moderate or low heat long enough to "stew" everything to tenderness—the exact opposite of what gave any *chow/chau/chao* dish its dashing brio. To most minds, no particular technique distinguished one stew from another, and the order in which ingredients were added usually didn't matter. No one deeply examined the subtleties behind other ethnic borrowings such as chili con carne or Hungarian goulash, which reached middle-class American kitchens at about the same time as chop suey and were also nonchalantly welcomed into the stew club.

The unstructured American approach to chop suey is well illustrated by a lecture-demonstration at an Indianapolis church in 1906. The instructor, a Mrs. Saunders, knowingly warned her audience, "The brown sauce served with chop suey in some Chinese restaurants is sweetened to hide the opium." (Chop suey joints were sometimes rumored to start customers on a slippery slope toward opium dens.) Her lesson in making it "the American way" averted that peril by substituting Kitchen Bouquet. The other ingredients were cut-up chicken breast and pork tenderloin, onions, celery, button mushrooms, ground salted peanuts, and enough water "almost to cover the ingredients"; the meats were briefly cooked in butter before everything else was thrown in together for a final fifteen minutes.[54]

These directions were not entirely unreasonable for cooks who thought stewing was stewing and, unlike Jessie Louise Nolton and her readers, might have had great difficulty in buying peanut oil, "sesamum oil," or "Chinese Seasoning Sauce" from Chinese groceries. A number of early-twentieth-century authorities stuck to a similar approach, certainly the best that could have been managed without insight into the real technique. Many tried to keep cooking times short by American standards—a worthy idea doomed to failure since cooks were unable to meet other necessary conditions like super-fast tossing and stirring of ingredients over prodigious heat in an appropriate cooking pan. And the authorities themselves weren't always happy with the results of brief cooking. "The chop suey that we buy in restaurants is very often not cooked long enough to suit our American taste," a home economics column for the *Cincinnati Enquirer* observed in 1919.[55] The instinctive national distrust of undercooking explains why many recipes started with already cooked chicken or meat.

The more diligent writers tried to insist on cutting up things into small pieces. Some even had an idea of the principle behind Chinese ways of dicing and slicing. The USDA Bureau of Home Economics scriptwriters who prepared a 1931 installment of the well-loved radio show "Housekeeper's Chat," a household-advice program conducted by the fictitious "Aunt Sammy," managed to work a good deal of accurate information into a broadcast titled "A Chinese Dinner."[56] The script began with a brisk attempt to right popular misconceptions, delivered by Aunt Sammy's savvier friend "Claribel." No, Sammy wouldn't be able to duplicate the menu of a real Chinese dinner; no, chop suey wasn't a real Chinese dish; still, "every Chinese cook I've ever known says it is made according to the best principles of Chinese cookery." (This last claim was completely accurate as regarded the best restaurant chop suey. In fact, perfectly respectable stir-fries can be made from Western vegetables such as globe onions, bell peppers, and American celery as long as proper technique is observed.)

Thus instructed, Sammy embarked on directions for chicken chop suey served with fried noodles and Chinese gravy: "As in most Chinese dishes, all the ingredients are cut up or shredded. Not diced or chopped, as we American cooks would do, but cut in short thin strips, and occasionally sliced. Both vegetables and meat are cut the same size and shape."

The cooking time for Sammy's chop suey was less than ten minutes. Aware that most of her radio audience would be unable to buy water chestnuts, she pointed out the charm of their crunchy texture and suggested substituting sliced Jerusalem artichokes, Brazil nuts, or even apples (very briefly cooked). The other vegetables were shredded green pepper, onion, and celery. Though she didn't require mung bean sprouts in the recipe, she described their virtues (such as vitamin content) and told listeners how to sprout the beans at home. Unwittingly proving the inescapable truth that American authorities who worked hard to get some details right could never quite avoid missing the boat on others, she began the chop suey with cooked chicken and provided a recipe for a gravy—"Chinese" by virtue of a starch thickener and a bit of soy sauce—that apparently was to be poured over the food like Thanksgiving dinner gravy.

Aunt Sammy's creators clearly had striven to arrive at, and conscientiously explain, a formula not altogether divorced from reality. But at least half the recipes in newspapers, cookbooks, and other sources came from people to whom chop suey was simply a popular, infinitely adaptable modern mudpie.

As noted before, the dish's rise to stardom coincided with a growing American fondness for free-spirited culinary mishmashes—for instance, gelatin salads used as edible dumping grounds for anything you felt like throwing in. A couple of decades later, casseroles would prove to be a similar vehicle for the irrepressible national omnium-gatherum approach.

We should note that long before Aunt Sammy, "chop suey" had become a stand-in for any hashed melange of ingredients. By 1903 a soda-fountain industry periodical would offer a recipe for something called a "chop suey sundae," consisting of ice cream topped with a syrupy cooked mixture of figs, dates, and chopped walnuts.[57] More colorful drugstore extravaganzas soon followed. In 1913 a New Jersey sweet shop was advertising chop suey candy at 15 cents a pound.[58] A refreshing hot-weather cold platter of any desired raw vegetables chopped fine and served with pot cheese, popular among Eastern European immigrants, acquired the nickname "Farmer's Chop Suey."[59]

Some thinkers turned to the field of sandwiches, another great twentieth-century anything-goes art form. Perhaps inspired by breakthroughs like Reuben sandwiches, baked bean sandwiches, early versions of subs or hoagies, and the comic-strip exploits of Dagwood Bumstead, pre–World War II pioneers along the Rhode Island and southern Massachusetts shoreline came up with sandwiches involving all the chop suey or chow mein that you could pile into a hamburger bun. St. Louis boasted a kindred inspiration known for some reason as the St. Paul sandwich: a foo young–style egg patty between white bread slices, with the spirited addition of mayonnaise and pickles.[60] Ingredients like bacon and cabbage would later invade pan-cooked chop suey, and American dessert-lovers would invent "Chop Suey Cake."

It needs little guessing to understand why any coupling of the notions "chop suey" and "authentic" did not stir American cooks or eaters to painstaking culinary-cultural analysis. One of the first things ordinary cooks dispensed with was procuring Chinese ingredients. Jessie Louise Nolton might have assured her readers that "it is not a difficult matter to make the necessary purchases," but a short newspaper squib published in the same year as her book expressed the contrary feelings of many:

> "I've got a fine errand," said the man with a grouch. "My wife has just bought a new cook book in which she found a recipe for chop suey. It said that bean sprouts, water chestnuts and other horrible ingredients could be bought at any Chinese merchant's, so she decided that she must try to make it, and I am the goat. I have to go down and do the curious tourist act and buy those things. And then I suppose I'll have to eat it! Wonder what they'll put in the cook books next?"[61]

Interpreting the dish as a motley stew let would-be chop suey artists forgo any list of needed articles, with the usual exception of soy sauce after hydrolyzed versions became universal. Canned bean sprouts, water chestnuts, and bamboo shoots might put in an appearance or be ignored in favor of any familiar vegetable from carrots to potatoes. The more recherché sesame oil, ginger, and Chinese mushrooms were generally omitted. Peanut oil still being relatively rare, American cooks saw nothing wrong with substituting butter. Occasionally someone used lard, which really did belong to the Chinese kitchen.

Some people omitted to cut or slice any ingredient into small pieces. Some took to cooking rice or noodles in the dish itself rather than as an accompaniment. Others streamlined the procedure by putting all the ingredients into the pot at once and covering them with water or stock that would later become a thickened sauce. People accustomed to flour-bound sauces often preferred flour to starch. Many used molasses to color the sauce deep brown, and naturally came to think that sweetness was an intrinsic part of the dish. Cooking times frequently stretched out to the edge of doom. Chop suey also acquired the reputation of being easy to cook for a crowd. *The Settlement Cook Book*'s "Chicken Chop Suey for 15 People," first published in 1915, called for braising a pork-veal combination for several hours before adding cooked chicken, cooking another half hour, binding the sauce with a soy-laced roux, and finally adding the supposedly classic combination of celery, bean sprouts, and canned mushrooms and water chestnuts.[62]

Recipe writers quickly began using the name "American chop suey" for versions with novel touches. At first the term embraced anything from a purportedly Chinese chop suey with extra broth to any long-cooked meat stew, with little rhyme or reason.[63] A Minneapolis church fundraising cookbook from 1920 presents an "American Chicken Chop Suey" with chicken and pork fried in butter, Kitchen Bouquet for coloring, and a cup of ground peanuts. It is followed by "American Chop Suey" with veal and pork fried in butter and lard, two tablespoons of flour, and two tablespoons of Brer Rabbit molasses, the whole being cooked for more than two hours; and "Plain Chop Suey" with cooked hamburger, onions, and spaghetti topped with canned tomato soup and baked for half an hour.[64] This last dish, which essentially fitted the voguish new culinary category of a "casserole," was about to swap names with the other versions.

During the early 1930s, variations on the combination of hamburger, pasta (usually elbow macaroni), and something tomato-ey prepared as baked casseroles came to be semiofficially known as American chop suey—except in regions where they were baptized "goulash" or "chili," with just as much logic. "American chop suey" was the invariable name in New England, where the invention acquired a particularly devoted fan club.

By World War II homemade chop suey of the older persuasion had lost its aura of romance and merged into the ranks of formerly latest old faithfuls, Chinese in the sense that Swedish meatballs were

Swedish. A somewhat similar fate had befallen Chinese American restaurants.

A NEW DEMOGRAPHY TAKES HOLD

The previously noted exodus of Chinese restaurants to white (and sometimes black) city districts was not the only form of out-migration from America's Chinatowns in the early twentieth century. Susan B. Carter has studied nationwide county census records to document a prolonged, little-noticed dispersal of Chinese to lesser population centers, often too small to support any kind of Chinese community.[65] As Carter points out, this long-overlooked development accompanied a steep overall decline in the Chinese American population as enforcement of Exclusion took hold. The economic base of the old communities concurrently shrank, while urban planners routinely targeted Chinatowns—seldom able to fight back—for partial or complete demolition to make room for public works projects.

As before, many Chinese were soon in motion, seeking opportunity elsewhere. Thousands spread out to inconspicuous new homes, sometimes in the chief towns of predominantly rural counties, looking to provide necessary services to whites through the self-employment strategies honed a few decades earlier. As they had in cities with big Chinatowns, most initially set up laundries and subsequently shifted to restaurants. As before, men often recruited a few real or "paper" relatives to form small partnerships in either endeavor.

With the gradual population turnaround after about 1920, another sort of restaurant organization slowly emerged as a practical option in both cities and towns. The partial evening-out of the distorted sex ratio and increase in stateside marriages meant that more wives and children could share the work of a restaurant. Family-run Chinese restaurants became more visible, from major Chinatowns to the boondocks. At first, young children as birthright citizens often were the chief legal bulwark lending countenance to one or both parents' continued residence in America; over time, more restaurant owners were themselves American-born and thus safe against deportation.

Whether they were located in urban Chinatowns or country towns, the new family restaurants nearly always demanded the utmost from every member old enough to do simple tasks. Many firsthand recollections of these businesses have been presented by John Jung in a monograph appropriately titled *Sweet and Sour*; the contributors' memories are abundantly corroborated by shorter accounts in some other histories.

The children of Quong Wong, who founded the New Shanghai Café in Lodi, California, in 1926, described a litany of responsibilities to Jung and another interviewer:

> The children usually did all the assorted menial jobs required in a family restaurant like preparing vegetables, filling small soy sauce bottles, salt and pepper shakers, sorting silverware [white patrons rarely used chopsticks in such establishments], making pots of tea, bussing tables, washing dishes, etc. Depending on their age, the children helped in various ways in the kitchen. All kinds of meat and vegetable had to be chopped, cut, diced or sliced for different dishes. Shrimps have to be shelled. Water urns have to be filled for tea. Other chores included sweeping the dining room floor and keeping a supply of change in the cash register.[66]

Annie Leong, one of Huping Ling's St. Louis informants, recalled how her whole family weathered the Depression through constant work in their restaurant, with her father as chef and her mother supervising the dining room and kitchen:

> We worked seven days a week, from eleven o'clock in the morning to mid-night. . . . We [she and her brothers] did everything. We wrapped wontons, took care of the dining room area, and set up restaurant. Then if they needed us, we could cook too. So we did whatever was needed. It was just natural, and we just did it. We were going to school and had to do our homework. After school, we would study, and it would get busy during dinner hours, and we took care of all the customers. In between, we would study a little, and then took care of customers. After the dinner rush was over, about eight o'clock, we could really have more time to study."[67]

Depending on the restaurant in question and the kind of clientele it addressed, such tasks may or may not have prepared children to appreciate the subtleties of Chinese food. The level of execution must have varied widely from one eatery to the next, and young observers quickly realized that culinary values had to be adjusted for white patrons. In an instance of rapid promotion that occurred a few decades later but cannot have been unique, the future food writer Ken Hom began apprenticing in an uncle's split-menu Chicago restaurant at the age of eleven and was very soon set to cooking short orders of "the stereotypical 'Chinese' food" for white customers: "fried rice; sweet-and-sour pork (much more sweet than sour, and artificially crimson red); and the old standby, chow mein."[68] The food cooked at home by his mother, and by the restaurant chefs for Chinese patrons, belonged to another world of knowledge and appreciation. Sweet-and-sour pork must have been far harder to swallow for people operating restaurants in small towns far from any Chinatown. They were obliged both to address only non-Chinese palates and to do so on very disadvantageous terms.

The earliest Chinese restaurants to attract a scattering of white or black patrons in America's Chinatowns did so without seriously compromising the principles of Cantonese cuisine. They left no documentation of how far they altered (or didn't) any particular dish to please non-Chinese palates. We know that the picture rapidly altered in the late 1890s with the purposeful creation of a Chinese American culinary repertoire. But both major restaurants and hole-in-the-wall eateries in Chinatowns could still count on a knowledgeable Cantonese customer base, no matter who else wandered in.

The situation was far different for those who eventually moved to city locations outside of Chinatown, or small-town locations far from cities. For them, the playing field had to accommodate several new factors.

The spread of Chinese American restaurants beyond Chinatown coincided with the arrival of cooking stoves connected to public utilities. Until recently, most restaurant stoves had burned coal, to which some Chinese establishments had switched after previously using hardwood or charcoal for both large fixed stoves and portable braziers. The brazier had been an ideal wok stove for families or other small groups as well as tiny restaurants and itinerant vendors. But the trend now (reinforced by municipal fire codes) was toward gas or electric ranges. For large Chinatown restaurants sufficiently well capitalized to invest in powerful gas-fired "chop suey stoves" with openings to hold giant woks, there were obvious advantages in getting rid of bulky brick ranges that had to be constantly stoked with solid fuel. The saving in labor costs and storage space might well offset the utility bill.

Smaller operations faced a less attractive tradeoff. So did home cooks. Unfortunately, the home-scale gas and electric ranges that were replacing wood- or coal-burning cast-iron stoves were a terrible fit with Chinese cooking requirements. Most restaurant counterparts were little better. They could not securely accommodate a round-bottomed wok or let it sit close enough to the heat to deliver the terrific pulse of energy necessary for stir-frying.

Though gas companies were advancing outward from the biggest metropolitan areas, there were still gaps in rural coverage; meanwhile, electric utilities and electric stoves were gaining fast on gas. A restaurateur planning to relocate to a little burg with no Chinese competition might be well advised to forgo a chop suey stove and make do with a gas or electric American restaurant model—especially if he had decided to aim for broad customer appeal by adopting a split-menu plan mostly geared toward American dishes with a token chop suey section. In that case, it often made more sense to cook everything in flat-bottomed American pots and pans than to struggle with woks for the Chinese dishes.

Setting up restaurants far from any Chinatown might also mean something relatively new to most Chinese in North America: less reliable access to Chinese foods. For a couple of generations, Chinese on Gold Mountain had been well supplied with ingredients—both those that they grew or fished themselves and others that arrived via the efficient overseas Hong Kong–San Francisco pipeline and the stateside *jin shan zhuang* network. White observers had marveled at the Chinese foods they saw being stocked or cooked with far into mining country. Chinese railroad crews had commanded the wherewithal to cook their own meals to their own satisfaction as Union Pacific construction inched eastward across the mountains to Utah.

Later the transplanted communities in large Midwest and East Coast cities included grocers ready to supply both retail customers and restaurants with a wide range of products shipped from California or directly imported to New York and distributed to more distant locations. Rice and good soy sauce could be taken for granted. Preserved vegetables, dried fish and shellfish, necessary herbs and spices, sesame oil, starch noodles, rice flour, and many condiments were able to reach North American outlets with only minor disruptions. Bean curd, fresh wheat noodles, and cured meats were abundantly available from small producers in San Francisco, Chicago, or New York. The specialty produce raised by Chinese truck gardeners in the orbit of many cities found a ready market in all Chinatowns. (It inspired at least one non-Chinese Michigan farmer to devote herself to the same articles and relate her success story to a Vegetable Growers Association of America conference in 1916.[69])

But people starting Chinese American restaurants in rural counties weren't in the same loop. Getting nonperishable supplies could mean periodic stocking-up trips via train, buggy, or (later) car to a nearby Chinatown—which might not be all that nearby, and which didn't necessarily have the range of specialty ingredients available in Chicago or New York. Restaurateurs might be able to order shipments of produce from Chinese truck gardeners. But given the limitations of their customers' palates, it made little sense for only-game-in-town restaurants to purchase rarefied or unusual-tasting ingredients in large amounts. When they had to, they made do with whatever ordinary American produce was available.

Big-city counterparts with multiethnic clienteles had the knowledge and resources to negotiate flexible compromises between their own standards and the varied preferences of ignorant or semiknowledgeable non-Chinese patrons. And unless they were marginal one-man street operations, they could count on powerful stoves imparting real *wok hei* even to somewhat déclassé "chop suey."

Their food cannot have been uniformly good or bad. It's a reasonable guess that in the nation's Chinatowns some restaurant cooks performed up to very high Cantonese standards even when cooking for outsiders, while some made minor adjustments. All had at least some leeway to cook without wholly abandoning their inbred culinary instincts. But elsewhere, cooks had no guarantee of being within a hundred miles of anyone else who had ever tasted proper Cantonese food or could appreciate some degree of polish in hybridized versions. Even if they had access to the right ingredients and kitchen fittings, they might be best off cooking everything in the way they thought most appealing to uncivilized palates.

The most difficult hardship of all for those who dispersed to the hinterlands was that finding a spot with no Chinese competition also meant being isolated from Chinese companionship, except for the rest of the restaurant staff. This might be a sustaining minicommunity of family and friends, or perhaps a grim handful of men working nearly around the clock to produce meals beneath any standard that they could respect.

In some ways, the transpacific exile from China itself had been less of an exile. Most Gold Mountain sojourners had formed established colonies or lived within easy reach of one; they had never lost the society of people who spoke their own language, celebrated their own festivals, and perfectly understood their own kitchen idiom. Setting out to make a living in remote communities by cooking for strangers who had only a heavily doctored image of the unique Cantonese cuisine, and still less idea of the Cantonese language and culture, was perhaps an even more lonely severance from the known and a more courageous voyage into a new unknown.

If there could be any compensation, it was that the places they founded and the Chinese American food they served in Exclusion-era America genuinely delighted other people in sleepy backwaters as well as major cities. News syndicates, movies, and the radio had in some sense brought rural or small-town America in closer touch with big cities and bright lights. But on another level, modern media had pointed up a cultural divide between metropolis and boondocks, sophisticates and hayseeds. The new communications supplied scattered white communities with compelling images of what was happening—also meaning what they were missing—in the great world. In the confines of provincial existence, a Chinese restaurant serving such fabled delicacies as chop suey and foo young could be a passage to global adventure. One taste of a canned litchi could be a glimpse into a magical unknown.

This is to say that though cooking an artificially distorted version of Cantonese food for people unable to grasp the real principles of the cuisine must have been a sort of tragicomic frustration for hundreds or perhaps thousands of Chinese American restaurant workers, it was not meaningless. It laid down a small but durable foundation of something quasi-Chinese in mainstream American society. And across forbidding cultural and racial boundaries, it gave its creators a lasting claim on the gratitude of neighbors.

SIX

Change, Interchange, and the First Successful "Translators"

CHINESE AMERICA AND POST-IMPERIAL CHINA

During and after the final Qing decline on the western side of the Pacific, Chinese restaurants offered an economic lifeline to thousands of people—an aging population of bachelor "sojourners" along with a younger, family-based contingent—on the eastern side. With a growing generation of birthright citizens, the Chinese community gradually began to achieve a less hazardous footing in U.S. society. But the distorted perspective through which other Americans viewed Chinese food has never wholly disappeared. Indeed, the food that restaurateurs successfully invented for white patrons helped perpetuate a sort of culinary astigmatism. From time to time, English-language writers tried to arrive at a better understanding of Chinese culinary principles and practice—unfortunately without tools of communication intelligible to both parties. Little means of real instruction existed until new intellectual movements and political turmoil, apparently unconnected with culinary issues, arose in China itself.

From their vantage points in North American cities and towns, Chinese-born and American-born members of the Chinese community anxiously watched the unhappy last decades of the moribund Qing Empire. A progressive wing in which the diplomat-soldier Li Hung Chang—he of the durable American chop suey legend—played an internationally renowned role for more than thirty years counseled a national "self-strengthening" agenda through selective adoption of Western business methods and technology. Li and his allies sought to modernize China's army and navy, transportation system, and industrial facilities. They induced the young Guangxu Emperor to think seriously of establishing a constitutional monarchy; they planned sweeping reforms to replace the ancient and much-hated examination system for admitting candidates to the top-heavy, outmoded imperial bureaucracy.

Much of the reformers' agenda was stymied by the emperor's aunt, the empress dowager Cixi, a tireless intriguer who managed to send him into detention in an 1898 coup. But one measure that took hold between the early 1860s and the final toppling of the empire in 1911 was educational reform. All knew that it was a necessary prelude to restructuring the bureaucracy.

Government-sponsored schools offering instruction in foreign languages and some elements of Western university curricula (e.g., modern sciences and mathematics) were set up in Beijing and several of the treaty ports. Some counterparts were founded for younger boys—and even girls, since improving the status of women was a major reformist goal. A number of Western-founded private schools addressed the same needs. Thus it happened that a growing class of outward-looking young men and women already existed in the dying empire when American politicians, businessmen, and intellectuals began acquiring an enlarged view of China's place on the geopolitical stage. As a certain amount of educational interchange developed, Chinese-born students and teachers became a more familiar sight on American campuses in the years between the world wars. By 1930 many universities offered not only courses in Chinese history but actual instruction in Mandarin and perhaps one or two other Chinese languages, sometimes under the auspices of an "Asian Institute" or "Department of Oriental Studies." Further interchange came from an unexpected direction.

The anti-Western, antimissionary Boxer Rebellion that broke out in China in 1900 was savagely suppressed by an alliance of many foreign powers and ended in a humiliating treaty requiring the imperial government to pay large sums of money to all the foreign signatories. Several years later, the United States found that it had actually been paid much more than the stipulated indemnity. The administration of President

Theodore Roosevelt was persuaded to dedicate the surplus to a scholarship program for Chinese students at American universities. Between 1909 and 1930, about 1,300 students traveled to the United States through "Boxer Indemnity" scholarships. Many of them would later return to become political figures, scientists, and well-known writers.

Among the first scholarship recipients were a strong-willed young woman who decided to turn hers down and the young man whom she would later marry. Yuenren Chao (Yuen Ren Zhao or Zhao Yuen Ren in pinyin) traveled to the United States in 1910, returning ten years later with a bachelor's degree in mathematics from Cornell, a PhD in philosophy from Harvard, and an insatiable interest in both China's many languages and the strange byways of English. Back in China, fate threw him into the company of the girl who had declined her indemnity scholarship. She was now Dr. Buwei Yang or Yang Buwei, owner of a degree from Tokyo Women's Medical School, champion of birth control, and director of a small gynecological/obstetrical hospital that she and a female colleague had founded in Beijing.[1]

Dr. Yang was a resourceful, self-taught cook who loved rising to the challenge of any meal, simple or elaborate. After her adoptive father's death, she had astonished her family by producing thirty-three all-vegetarian dishes for the prescribed mourning banquet. Like Mr. Chao, she came to have a great disbelief in outmoded Chinese rituals—for instance, weddings. One day in June of 1921 they invited two friends to an informal four-course meal cooked by Dr. Yang and waited until after tea to produce a statement drafted by Mr. Chao, bearing a legal stamp and affirming that they were man and wife. In fact, the only officially binding formality they needed was to have the guests sign the document as witnesses.

By the time of this anticeremony, the Qing Empire had vanished in a series of great convulsions following the deaths of the Guangxu emperor and the empress dowager within a day of each other in 1908. Already, supporters of reform had jockeyed for more than a decade with advocates of revolution. The overseas Chinese, who shared their compatriots' shame and fury at successive military defeats and diplomatic insults such as the United States' harassment of Chinese nationals, included members of both factions.

Many people in American Chinatowns had long supported the best-known champion of revolution, the self-exiled, Guangdong-born Sun Yat-sen (Sun Zhongshan). Sun cultivated liaisons with the secret societies operating out of American cities. He successfully brought some of the fiercer San Francisco tongs into an international nexus of plots for the overthrow of the "foreign" Qing—Manchu usurpers, not true Han Chinese, as Sun never tired of pointing out—and the defeat of the constitutional-monarchy party, the "Emperor Protection Society." Restaurants were sometimes drawn into the fiscal affairs of one or the other faction. The 1906 opening of the huge, ambitious King Joy Lo in Chicago represented $150,000 or more in contributions from many members of a Chinese businessmen's league dedicated to the aims of the Emperor Protection Society and its chief spokesman.[2] The launch of King Joy Lo would become one of many fiscal scandals surrounding the society; it seems doubtful that most of the money ever went further than the pockets of the manager, the flamboyant restaurateur Chin F. Foin.[3] In any case, the reformers' cause gradually staggered into disarray.

The American Chinese community hung on every news dispatch from China, where several disjointed uprisings in October of 1911 at last coalesced into an armed revolt strong enough to topple the Manchu Empire. But joy at the formal proclamation of the Republic of China early in 1912 was short-lived. The revolutionaries were obliged to arrange terms with the army general Yuan Shikai, a powerful long-time ally of the late empress dowager who installed himself in the presidency of the new republic and within a few years was scheming to advance from lifetime president to emperor.

A few months after Yuan's inauguration, Sun Yat-sen and the thwarted revolutionaries formed a parliamentary opposition titled the Nationalist Party or Guomindang, usually abbreviated to GMD (Kuomintang or KMT in the old Wade-Giles romanization system). But Sun was not destined to preside over the enlightened modern republic he had dreamed of. On Yuan's death in 1916, China fell into an epoch of fragmented scrimmages under local warlords or glorified bandits. Many competing voices—some belonging to Boxer Indemnity scholarship students returned from America—introduced the citizenry to anarchism, socialism, and defiant new artistic and cultural movements founded in a rejection of Confucian institutions. The Chinese Communist Party, formed in 1921 with the aid of the young Soviet Union, powerfully spoke to a disaffected generation.

From a precarious southern power base in Sun's native Guangzhou, the GMD gradually managed to build a creditable army under the leadership of the ambitious Jiang Jie-shi or Chiang Kai-shek (a romanized version of the Cantonese pronunciation). Sun died in 1925; by the end of 1927 Chiang's forces had conquered enough of northern China to establish a GMD government with Nanjing as capital. For the next two decades the regime's nemesis would be an alliance forged between the Chinese Communist Party and what remained of the GMD's former left wing after a course of bloody Chiang-ordered purges.

As the post-imperial era unfolded, the American Chinese community vicariously lived through shock after shock. Overseas sojourners had already seen almost a century and a half of mortifying blows to China's pride and self-determination. Their treatment on Gold Mountain had long testified to the Middle Kingdom's inability or unwillingness to protest affronts to its subjects abroad. Thousands of Chinese nationals suffering under Exclusion in San Francisco, Chicago, New York, and lesser cities had dreamed that the end of Qing rule would mean China's emergence on the global stage as an independent modern power among other powers. Rejoicing at (as they thought) newly recovered national honor, they cut off their queues—a symbol of centuries-long Han subjection to alien Manchu decrees—and exchanged Chinese for Western dress. Some came to acknowledge that daughters might deserve a certain autonomy as citizens of twentieth-century societies, an idea vigorously championed by reforming educators in China and strengthened here by passage of the Nineteenth Amendment in 1919. But all who cared about China and Chinese–American relations soon understood that in some ways Chinese-born people in the land of liberty were men and women without a country.

Many in America's Chinatowns, especially members of the more violent tongs, had detested the Manchu rulers and even plotted for their overthrow. Still, a reigning emperor had never quite ceased to be a unifying symbol of national identity. Had the last emperor been replaced by any plausible constitutional head of state, the overseas Chinese might have found an object of honor to rally around. As it was, they saw their homeland crippled by civil war while a ruthlessly expansionist Japan hovered across the East China Sea, preparing to pick off chunks of territory to add to its seizure of Taiwan in 1895. The GMD, in the eyes of opponents, was more interested in trying (vainly) to destroy the Communists than preparing any defense against the Japanese.

Some rearrangement of loyalties was inevitable. Violent anti-Chinese hostility had partly cooled in the United States since the Chinese had been successfully drubbed out of the manual labor market. Newcomers still contrived to enter the country from China by using the "paper son" ruse, sneaking across borders, or claiming exempt status as students, professionals, or businessmen. Meanwhile, the steady increase of the community through the birth of children cemented the parent generation more securely to the adoptive country.

The children themselves regularly acquired a fluency in English that had eluded most of their elders, as well as some grounding in American culture. They might grow up unhappy at being made to attend the special classes that were necessary for many to master standard (Guangzhou) spoken Cantonese or written Chinese. Such was the case with bright little Pardee Lowe, born in San Francisco in 1904. He applied himself to the challenges of a very good public school with a single-mindedness inspired by a first-grade teacher's ringing declaration to a multiethnic class of boys and girls, "And every single one of you can be President of the United States someday!" He was cured of this error at the age of thirteen, when he went knocking at the doors of ten business firms that had advertised summer office-boy positions. After all ten were slammed in his face, he bleakly acceded to his father's alternative program of improving his Chinese.[4]

The truth was that no amount of education—not even a college degree—offered immigrants' children any reliable escape from the employment ghetto of laundries, restaurants, grocery shops, importing firms, and a few other niche occupations regularly filled by Chinese. Their suspension between two national identities was more painful and more difficult than that of other second-generation immigrants. Unlike their elders, these young men and women had never been threatened with deportation or outright statelessness. But they still remained helpless in the face of racial and cultural prejudice. Their birthright citizenship was in fact second-class citizenship.

At the same time, young Chinese Americans often demurred at or flatly rejected their parents' and grandparents' sense of an identity derived from a particular Pearl River Delta village peopled with owners of the same surname. Some classic Cantonese values—for instance, the importance of returning to a family's "own" hamlet in old age so as to be buried there, or the sacred duty of shipping back the bones of clan members who had died abroad—were less deeply ingrained in them than in men and women born in the Three or Four Counties. Many might well have called themselves proud Americans if America had not furnished them with so many reasons to the contrary.

TRANSCULTURAL EXCHANGE AND THE JOHN DAY COMPANY

Thousands of bright, well-educated, young American-born Chinese continued to work in family-owned businesses like laundries, restaurants, and groceries simply for lack of any alternative. But the situation slowly changed for a few others through new developments in higher learning and the general American intellectual climate. The growth of sociology and allied disciplines set professors and students to examining the details of immigrants' lives. As graduate students at major universities (especially the University of Chicago), some second-generation Chinese Americans produced master's or doctoral theses based on field work in their own communities. (Louis H. Chu's study of New York City Chinese restaurants, written as a New York University master's thesis in 1939, is among the best-known.[5]) White colleagues acquired at least marginal respect for the importance of such work.

Whites were a critical part of other shifting equations during the 1920s and 1930s. Among those who began studying Mandarin (less often Cantonese or other Han Chinese languages) in college language departments were young people inspired by either the glory of Chinese civilization or the prospect of business opportunities in the Far East. (*400 Million Customers*, a breezy survey of warlord-era Chinese society's marketing possibilities by the American-born Carl Crow, a veteran advertising executive long resident in Shanghai, was a 1937 best seller in the United States and England.[6]) Others were attracted to Chinese history and archaeology. As specialized instruction in several aspects of Chinese studies expanded, small interracial and interdisciplinary fellowships of scholars grew up on some campuses. In addition, programs formerly affiliated with Christian missions to China were often reinvented in a secular context (e.g., the Yale-China Association, originally founded in 1901 as the Yale Foreign Missionary Society). Harvard and some other universities established partnerships with sister schools in China.

Such changes also hinted at a broadening interest in Asian affairs on the part of a middle-class American public. China filtered into popular awareness through such dubious channels as the Fu Manchu movies and fashions in brocaded silk dressing gowns but also through general-interest magazines and books. A glossy monthly magazine titled *Asia*, catering to a growing vogue for exotic travel, regaled a posh demographic with accounts of treks to beauty spots or remote fastnesses anywhere from Japan to India. From the mid-1920s, most issues bore spectacularly gorgeous art deco covers testifying to an American hunger for sultry, striking images of the mysterious East.

At about the same time, the Harvard-educated writer and editor Richard J. Walsh founded a book publishing house, not at the outset dedicated to any specialized focus. (By coincidence, he had been a classmate of Earl Derr Biggers, creator of the Charlie Chan mysteries.) The New York–based venture, the John Day Company, had trundled along for a few years without any great breakthrough when Walsh accepted the manuscript of a novel in which a young man appalled his family in China by returning from America with a white wife. The author, a missionary's daughter raised in the east coast province of Zhejiang, clearly knew the society of which she wrote. (In fact, she had grown up speaking the local language more readily than English, and always mentally translated her own work from Chinese to English.)

In 1930 the book appeared to favorable reviews and good sales as *East Wind, West Wind*. The next year saw the publication of her still better-received second novel, the story of a Chinese peasant and his slave-wife trying to wrest a living from his ancestral farm. *The Good Earth* made Pearl S. Buck a household name and the most bankable star in John Day's stable of writers.[7]

What mattered most to Buck about the sudden fame of *The Good Earth* (and the Pulitzer Prize that it won in 1932) was having acquired a national bully pulpit for a supremely important purpose. She harbored no deep illusions about her real abilities as a novelist but rightly thought that she was a born educator. Partly in reaction against the missionary agenda that she had at last rejected, she viewed American ideas of Chinese politics and culture as a mass of ignorant misconceptions begging to be corrected.

She and Walsh became lovers a year or two after the triumph of *The Good Earth*. They divorced their respective spouses and married in 1935. By then Buck was determined to help direct John Day's editorial decisions, and had convinced Walsh that between them they could fill an unpardonable gap in transcultural understanding. They were arguably the most prominent married couple in American publishing.

Buck and Walsh first set out to make John Day the foremost U.S. source of books on Asian and especially Chinese affairs. Her contacts with Chinese thinkers here and abroad, and his in the trade publishing world, gave them access to many representatives of contemporary Chinese literature, philosophy, and art; pioneering teachers at American universities; and influential New York critics or reviewers. Buck's reception of the 1938 Nobel Prize in Literature further enlarged their ambitions.

In 1934 Walsh had acquired *Asia* magazine. The two of them transformed it by degrees into a plainer-looking, more serious vehicle for glimpses into Asian politics and society—for instance, reports on the state of China by the well-known traveler and scholar Owen Lattimore, or a serialization of the Indian nationalist leader Jawaharlal Nehru's letters to his teenaged daughter Indira from a British prison in Uttar Pradesh. America's entry into World War II opened still other opportunities.

The bombing of Pearl Harbor immediately brought the United States in on the side of the Nationalist Chinese government. By now the Japanese had managed to seize all of eastern and southeastern China. Chiang Kai-shek, who had retreated to temporary western headquarters in Chongqing, Sichuan Province, was hailed as America's dauntless ally. In a miraculous reversal of earlier doctrine, the immigration authorities and the State Department decided that the Chinese were no longer the Yellow Peril, while the War Department and the Justice Department clapped thousands of first- and second-generation Japanese immigrants into detention camps.

In December of 1943 Congress passed the Magnuson Act, officially repealing at least parts of the various exclusion acts that had been in force since 1882.[8] People born in China were now explicitly allowed to become naturalized citizens, and a legal immigration quota was established—a pitiful 105 Chinese a year but at least a token step away from the prior zero-tolerance policy. Though it was not the end of hardships for Chinese people in America, it decisively abolished the legal basis of much evil.

By now Buck and Walsh had done a great deal to direct China to the awareness of moderately well-read Americans. They brought the philosopher and novelist Lin Yutang to *Asia* magazine and launched his American career in 1935 with the best-selling book *My Country and My People*. For decades Lin would be the most graceful and congenial interpreter of Chinese culture to an American readership. At John Day, Buck and Walsh also commissioned both popular and specialized works ranging from the autobiography of Arnold Genthe (the photographic documenter of San Francisco Chinatown between about 1898 and 1906) to Elizabeth Colman's contemporary photographic survey *Chinatown, U.S.A.*; a volume of modern Chinese short stories edited by Edgar Snow; and Owen Lattimore's scholarly study *The Mongols of Manchuria*, a region now occupied by the Japanese.

The example of John Day may have created a better climate for authors and other publishers to tackle ideas on Chinese and Chinese American subjects. The early 1940s saw two well-received works that shed real insight into the cultural dilemmas of Chinese Americans. Carl Glick, a community-theater director and eclectic freelance writer who had been introduced to New York Chinatown through a job with the Emergency Works Bureau (a short-lived precursor to the New Deal's Works Progress Administration), became fascinated by every facet of the neighborhood's life. In 1941 his *Shake Hands with the Dragon* achieved widespread notice for a somewhat rose-colored but carefully observed and genuinely respectful account of a society that he felt privileged to have forged ties with. (In a chapter saluting Chinese food as "the best in the world," Glick's closest Chinatown friend one day has the bright idea of going uptown to "have dinner in a Chop Suey Palace. I want to see what chow mein tastes like."[9]) The book attracted enough attention to be picked up at once for a *Reader's Digest* condensation.

Two years later, Pardee Lowe's memoir *Father and Glorious Descendant* gave a far more subtle first-person portrayal of the many tensions between Chinese and American identities in one Bay Area Cantonese family—undoubtedly new mental territory for the large audience of non-Chinese readers who made this a 1943 best seller. Together with a later Chinatown foray by Carl Glick (*Three Times I Bow*), it was chosen for publication in the "Armed Services Edition" roster of books printed as small, cheap, easy-to-carry paperbacks by a publishers' consortium for distribution to members of the Armed Forces. White readers' appetite for glimpses of Chinese American life clearly was at an all-time high.

ENTER THE CHAO FAMILY

In the spring of 1944 Lin Yutang and his wife told Buck and Walsh about a work in progress that had come to their notice, a concise Mandarin–English dictionary that might be available for publication by John Day. They also mentioned that the author's wife was at work on a cookbook.[10] Walsh dispatched a letter of inquiry.

The author in question was Yuenren Chao, by now a professor at Harvard's Department of Asian Studies and one of the great linguists of his generation. He replied with a polite note explaining that the dictionary project was already spoken for, but that the cookbook should soon be finished.[11] Walsh agreed to look at the manuscript.

Since her unconventional wedding to Yuenren Chao in 1921, Dr. Buwei Yang had given up her medical practice to be a full-time wife and mother. She was fifty-five at the time John Day expressed interest in her book and had never published anything except a Chinese translation of *What Every Girl Should Know* by Margaret Sanger, one of her early medical heroes. The Chaos had moved several times between China and the United States, and were now living in Cambridge, Massachusetts, with four daughters ranging in age from thirteen to twenty-two.

Born in Nanjing, Buwei Yang Chao was an outspoken, impetuous woman who had been raised in boy's clothing until the age of thirteen, an occasional custom among families with no sons and a surfeit of daughters. She had had the good luck to be encouraged in blunt speech and unorthodox ambitions by her progressive-minded Yang grandfather, a building supervisor and minor diplomat of catholic intellectual interests. At twenty-five she had had taught herself the elements of Chinese cooking to avoid having to eat Japanese food while studying medicine in Tokyo. As Mrs. Yuenren Chao (a title she wore with pride), she had dealt with kitchens in Nanjing; Beijing; Shanghai; Suzhou (Jiangsu Province); Guangzhou; Changsha (Hunan Province); Kunming (Yunnan Province); Honolulu; New Haven, Connecticut; and Washington, DC. She had traveled extensively in England, Germany, France, and Switzerland. But the cuisine she (like Pearl Buck) felt most at home with belonged to the general orbit of the so-called Jiangnan region—that is, central eastern China south (*nan*) of the Yangzi River ("Jiang"), including parts of Jiangsu, Zhejiang, and southeastern Anhui provinces. In the eyes of people raised there, Jiangnan cuisine rivaled that of Guangdong Province for inspired beauty.

Mrs. Chao's manuscript, originally written in Chinese, was a vast departure from previous attempts to teach Chinese cooking to Americans. Only a few major trade publishers had stuck a toe in these difficult waters. As discussed earlier, Shiu Wong Chan's *The Chinese Cook Book*, published by Frederick A. Stokes in 1917, was a laborious effort doomed by lack of the English-language skills or nimble-mindedness needed to explain utterly foreign culinary concepts to the audience. With one obscure exception, no successor appeared from a mainstream American firm until 1938, when Macmillan published *Cook at Home in Chinese* by Henry Low. (The exception was Stokes's 1936 reissue of a curiosity from the Western-language publishing scene in China: *The Chinese Festive Board* by Corrinne [sic] Lamb, written in Beijing and originally published in 1934 by the firm of Henri Vetch.[12] The slim volume is a fascinating document of food in 1930s Beijing, but it contains only a tiny recipe section with fifty formulas too closely based on local ingredients to have been well understood by American cooks.)

Like the unknown Shiu Wong Chan, Henry Low seems to have been Cantonese since the romanizations of words and names are based on Cantonese pronunciation. He was the head chef of the famous Port Arthur restaurant in New York Chinatown, an establishment mentioned in Louis H. Chu's New York University master's thesis as among "the restaurants which cater chiefly to American diners."[13] He also was, or claimed to be, the originator of the Chinese American "egg roll," for which he provides a recipe with wrappers made from a dough that he had "discovered" thirty years earlier by combining wheat flour with water chestnut starch: "Taking an old Chinese dish, which was served with a dough covering, as a basis, the author further concocted a number of ingredients as a mixture to be wrapped in this new dough, which he named 'Tchun Guen,' or 'Egg Roll.'"[14] ("Tchun Guen" actually means "spring roll.") I doubt that Low's "egg roll" skins much resembled the heavy, floury kind now known by that name. But the shredded and chopped ingredients in the filling—including canned bamboo shoots, Chinese roast pork, shrimps, scallions, water chestnuts, and monosodium glutamate—certainly sound like what would become the standard array.

Low's book is far more polished and sophisticated than Chan's ungainly effort; he hints at having had editorial guidance from an American helper, one Grace S. R. Hillyer. Unlike the earlier work, *Cook at Home in Chinese* does not print the names of recipes in Chinese characters. But it has a longer and better-arranged list of the names for special ingredients, with both Chinese characters and Cantonese romanizations. What it doesn't have is a mindset primed to analyze and remedy either language-based or kitchen-based East–West misunderstandings. It was the best thing of its kind to date but didn't bring truly applicable mental resources to a very complex business.

Mrs. Chao's manuscript was quite another animal. For one thing, it was the first work in the field by a home cook who knew what other home cooks were up against. She was neither a restaurateur, journalist, nor test-kitchen flack like those hired to crank out American soy sauce manufacturers' recipe brochures. Hers was also the first work by anyone acquainted with a broad spectrum of Chinese culinary styles beyond Cantonese (though she had lived in Guangzhou and admired the cuisine). But her book also stood apart from all others for two further reasons. One was the unspoken matter of social and educational status. The second, perhaps even more crucial, was the participation of uniquely qualified translators.

No prior Chinese cookbook addressed to Americans had been produced by a woman or man of higher learning, much less a self-assured cosmopolite who could more than hold her own among Harvard faculty wives. Both Mrs. Chao's cooking and her fearless intelligence were known to a considerable circle in Cambridge. She and her husband had many friends in common with Buck and Walsh—notably, Agnes and William Ernest Hocking. They were respectively the head of a highly regarded progressive school and a well-known student of comparative religion who shared Buck's scathing, highly publicized view of the American missionary presence in China. It was Agnes Hocking who had first suggested that Mrs. Chao write a cookbook.[15]

Of course, the Pearl River Delta Cantonese who lived and cooked in America possessed none of the Chaos' advantages. Most were Four Counties peasants or the children of peasants, cooking by example together with the sort of trained instincts that are synonymous with strongly rooted culinary traditions anywhere from Georgia in the United States to Georgia in the Caucasus. The older generation had worked in the shadow of Exclusion until 1943. Those younger Chinese Americans who had won bachelor's or higher degrees were with rare exceptions shut out from further academic or professional careers. In fact, Mrs. Chao was a privileged newcomer with no experience of the hardships faced by the larger Chinese community in America. Her family had never been threatened with deportation; she had never suffered the double burden imposed on women by white prejudice and Cantonese patriarchal attitudes. Her self-confident written voice radiated a sense of being naturally entitled to address cultivated persons. It could not have been mistaken for that of a first- or second-generation Chinese American, male or female.

Beyond these differences, her book was the first English-language Chinese cookbook to benefit from linguistic awareness—indeed, from the united talents of three people able to grasp the problems of "translating" a cuisine across incredible cultural and language gaps.

Mrs. Chao could make herself understood to American friends in animated but erratic, heavily accented spoken English. She could write short messages confidently enough. But she was perfectly aware of never having mastered the intricacies of English grammar. She and her oldest daughter, Rulan, had spent about three years on the manuscript—Buwei writing in Chinese, Rulan producing working translations of material in progress—with frequent pitched battles between two determined personalities.[16] (Rulan, who would go on to have her own long and distinguished professorial career at Harvard, was at the moment a Chinese-language teaching assistant, working with her father on a special course for U.S. Army personnel.) The whole book had also received interested kibitzing from all the family and a thorough going-over by Professor Chao.

It happened that he not only wrote fluent and spirited English but, as his wife and daughters well knew, was possibly the greatest living expert on the problems of communication among speakers of the many northern and southern, eastern and western Han Chinese languages. He also had been a key player in the early-twentieth-century language reform movement dedicated to educating Chinese of all linguistic backgrounds in a standardized form of spoken Mandarin, the precursor to the *putonghua*, or "common speech," eventually adopted by the People's Republic of China in the 1950s.

Language reform was an issue of immense political importance. It was plain to many former Boxer Indemnity scholars and other intellectuals that China was hopelessly handicapped among world powers by vast accretions of crippling cultural baggage, including speaking and writing systems whose difficulties were nearly insuperable for non-Chinese. These advocates were collectively known as the "New Culture" movement, which also promoted writing in the vernacular style—a revolutionary protest against the educational stranglehold of the learned writing style called "Classical Chinese," derived from two-thousand-year-old literary models. New Culture proponents recognized that any nation with dozens of spoken "dialects" (a wholly inadequate word) that in some cases were as distantly related and mutually unintelligible as Swedish and Provençal could hardly hope to function *as* a nation. Yuen-ren Chao had been deputed to study many branches of regional speech and summarize their most crucial features, with a view to an overall educational strategy.

Most of the Chao family's peripatetic travels in and beyond China had reflected stages of Professor Chao's research on the major Han Chinese language families. Others stemmed from his work on comprehensive schemes of simplifying and standardizing meant to bring a unilingual out of a multilingual China and make the language easier for foreigners (as well as Chinese) to read, write, and speak. He was an urbane, dry-witted man with a lively sense of linguistic absurdity—his first published work had been a Chinese translation of *Alice in Wonderland*—shared by his family. To him, the forbidding language barriers between Chinese and English cooking terminology were so many Gordian knots to be cut through by unexpected strokes of invention.

All three participants brought to the project a quality absent from Shiu Wong Chan's or Henry Low's efforts: delight in teaching something supremely difficult to be taught. They had real pedagogical imagination, a wonderful instinct for imparting shape and structure to a great mass of information outside everyday American experience. All three relished the challenge of remolding Chinese concepts into English words. Buwei, though not proficient in English, certainly grasped the problems at hand well enough to wrestle cleverly with solutions. It was her forceful, irreverent personality—as projected by her collaborators—that gave life to the whole.

The Chaos could not have found a better-qualified judge of their work than Pearl Buck, whose knowledge of the subject came from more than thirty years of living and housekeeping in China. She disdained English-language Chinese cookbooks in general, and the company had turned down several in the past. But as Richard Walsh wrote to Mrs. Chao, "As for the recipes, I can do no better than to say that after reading the manuscript for a short time, Mrs. Walsh dashed to the kitchen and made a complete Chinese meal just for herself and me. I think we shall be trying them one by one for the rest of our lives!"[17] To his son Richard Jr. (a John Day editor), he had already expressed the couple's opinion still more forthrightly: "Mrs. Chao's cook book is splendid and we must certainly have it. . . . Pearl says it is the best Chinese cook book that she has seen."[18]

The John Day Company went through the formality of requesting a reader's report before setting up a production schedule. The reader, a Miss Mills, was lukewarm at best. She was irritated by what she saw as odd tics in the English—for instance, the proposed title "How to Cook and Eat in Chinese." She was dubious about the eccentric coinage "stir-frying," no matter how apt a translation it might be. (This durable phrase has the air of a Yuenren Chao caprice.) She disliked the scattering of informal asides and footnotes based on family discussions of food or

Professor Chao's philological afterthoughts. She also predicted difficulties in production, along with expenses that might or might not be justified.[19]

Buck and Walsh would have none of this. They saw how resourcefully the English style and tone dealt with all that ordinarily defied translation in Chinese vernacular writing and Chinese cooking. They loved Professor Chao's off-the-cuff footnotes well enough to think that more might be added for "the masculine perspective."[20] They were not afraid of the special copyediting, proofreading, and cross-referencing demands of a cookbook. What was more, they were willing to spring for the expense of a bilingual table of recipes at the end of the book, with every entry printed in large, clear Chinese characters as well as English translation—a clue to how thoroughly they entered into the thinking behind the Chao family's effort.

At the time Buck and Walsh accepted the manuscript for publication, they were getting ready to launch a new John Day division called Asia Press. In their enthusiasm for *How to Cook and Eat in Chinese*, they chose it as the first title to bear the imprint "An Asia Press Book."[21] They devised an ambitious publicity campaign that included a teaser, a small prepublication booklet of excerpts titled "Food for Philosophy" that was distributed to influential members of the New York (and national) press as a New Year's gift. *Asia* magazine (now officially retitled *Asia and the Americas*) carried an inside back-cover ad justifying the sister press's inaugural publication of a cookbook with the virtuous if vague declaration, "For we are much more interested in human appetites, human aspirations and all human ways than in the niceties of the experts and the crudities of the exploiters."[22]

Buck herself agreed to contribute a preface to the book. The Chaos arranged for a foreword by their friend Hu Shih, one of the two witnesses at their contrarian wedding in 1921. (He and Professor Chao had been fellow Boxer Indemnity scholarship students at Cornell; Hu had later become the best-known public advocate of the New Culture movement's proposed language reforms and had been Chinese ambassador to the United States between 1938 and 1942.) Buck and Walsh set up a dinner at the Lin Yutangs' home for the purpose of introducing Mrs. Chao (who cooked the entire meal) to influential people including Irita Van

Doren, the editor of the *New York Herald Tribune Book Review*.[23] At the women's page of the *New York Times*, the pseudonymous food reporter "Jane Holt" (Jane Nickerson) was told of the book's importance in time to prepare an intelligently balanced review.[24]

In short, John Day made a point of rolling out its first Asia Press title as a cultural event of the first importance. No American publisher had ever done anything of the kind for a cookbook. The publication date—May 10, 1945—had the bad luck to occur less than a month after the death of President Franklin D. Roosevelt, but the book's reception does not seem to have been dampened. *How to Cook and Eat in Chinese* received much favorable press and radio coverage. Sales were good enough to warrant several more printings by the end of the year.

"USE YOUR HEAD"

Pearl Buck's preface suggested nominating the author for a Nobel Peace Prize in recognition of her "contribution to international understanding" and observed, "As a Chinese, she knows exactly what Americans don't know."[25] Seventy years later, one can only admire Mrs. Chao's apt choices about not just what information to focus on but how to put it across to an audience. The first few paragraphs of her "Author's Note" were enough to convey the flavor of a nimble, down-to-earth mind that united vastly experienced judgment with a natural glee at ridiculing authority. She roundly admitted to finding "most conventions of cooking, serving, and eating to be a little silly," and she swept aside lumbering precepts by pointing out that "nothing takes the place of a little thinking. If you cannot get beef, get pork. If you cannot find an egg-beater, use your head"—the *xiang banfa* spirit in plain English (xii).

Apparently Professor Chao had found Rulan's translation too neatly compressed into proper usage and gone through it in a correctness-be-damned spirit, supplying back-formations with a more original take on Chinese nuances. The result was sentences like "Roughly speaking, *ch'ao* [stir-frying] may be defined as a big-fire-shallow-fat-continual-stirring-quick-frying of cut-up material with wet seasoning" (43). Anyone who has ever seen the action in a Chinese kitchen will recognize this as an unerring slap shot.

Since Buck and the John Day team were as new as the Chaos to the cookbook game, the book had the good luck to escape the attentions of professional cookbook editors bent on translating anything original into "recipese." Thus we encounter a dish named "Mushroom Meets Shrimp Cakes" with "meets" rendering "hui," a method by which several separately prepared ingredients enjoy a brief rencontre in the same cooking pan (120); "leaking ladle" instead of "perforated ladle" (140); "Cut into flying-thin slices" instead of "paper-thin slices" (84); and "The most savorous part [of poached duck] is in the bones" (105).

In another departure from predecessors, the book's culinary coverage gave great weight to the homeland of both Chaos: the central east-coast region running from the Lower Yangzi into the Yangzi Delta. From ancient times, many Chinese have thought of the eastern Yangzi reaches as the real core of Middle Kingdom civilization. To the north lies flatter, drier terrain extending toward the Yellow River and Beijing; to the south are the rich, well-watered soils of Jiangnan. The greatest local city is Shanghai. Westerners sometimes write as if "Shanghai cooking traditions" dominate all the region's kitchens. This is a little like assuming that "New York cuisine," with its many vigorous foreign influences, is *the* cuisine of the northeastern United States.

Centuries before assorted Western powers grabbed trade concessions in Shanghai, the Lower Yangzi was prosperous and powerful, dotted with older merchant towns like Yangzhou, Nanjing, Suzhou, and Hangzhou that enjoyed their own lofty culinary reputations. Since for centuries the region was linked with Beijing by the Grand Canal, it managed to unite many culinary blessings of north and south. It produced excellent rice but also imported wheat from northerly breadbasket provinces (and grew a little of its own, north of the river). Local waters supported a wealth of both freshwater and saltwater fish and shellfish.

The Lower Yangzi is known throughout China for the rice wine made in Shaoxing, the wonderful black rice wine vinegar from Chinkiang (officially "Zhenjiang" in pinyin), and the "hairy crabs" or "mitten crabs" that appear in local waters in autumn. It has its own repertory of *dian xin* specialties corresponding to the Cantonese "dim sum," including various steamed or pan-fried wheat-flour rolls raised with yeast, savory dumplings, and filled buns. Like the Cantonese, people from the region are adept at stir-frying and steaming.

But the techniques that Chinese cognoscenti most associate with the Lower Yangzi are long, gentle stewing and braising. Many of the classic local stewed dishes are called "red-cooked" (Mandarin, *hong shao*; Cantonese, *hung siu*) for the red-brown color the sauce acquires from a mixture of soy sauce and rice wine. Large pieces of meat (e.g., pork shoulder) or cuts with much natural cartilage and gelatin (pigs' feet or hocks) are often given this treatment. In all dishes, red-cooked or otherwise, discreetly blended flavors are valued over aggressive accents. Fresh ginger, small amounts of sugar, and rice wine are the most common seasonings, sometimes with the addition of scallion.

How to Cook and Eat in Chinese provided many 1940s American cooks and readers with their first glimpse of the Jiangnan or Lower Yangzi cooking style, and provides a scarcely surpassed glimpse today. It gives more than two dozen recipes for red-cooked dishes of all kinds. Mrs. Chao also offers what appear to be the first English-language recipes for *man-t'ou* or *mantou* (steamed yeast rolls), *pao-tzu* or *baozi* (filled sweet or savory dumplings using the same yeast dough), and scallion pancakes, along with one of the first recipes for fried *jiaozi*, or pork dumplings. (The Chaos dubbed these "wraplings" and called wontons "ramblings," coinages that failed to catch on like "stir-fry.") She essays pork meatballs in the style of the region's famous "Lion's Head." She gives recipes for smoked fish (very briefly hot-smoked over brown sugar), Nanjing "salt-water" duck (fresh-salted, poached, and chilled), and fresh-salted pork cooked until it can be pressed flat, chilled, and sliced like an aspic for serving with Chinkiang vinegar.

Mrs. Chao also presents a good many recipes representing Beijing and the north. These too were a novelty in an American cookbook— "sour-hot soup" in the original Beijing version with peppercorns instead of hot red pepper, "soy jam noodles" (usually called *zha jiang mian* [Mandarin] or *ja jeung min* [Cantonese], and made by tossing wheat noodles with a mixture of minced pork and hoisin sauce), and a sweet-meat of dried peas cooked to a puree with sugar. There are recipes for cold jellied lamb and the equally classic Beijing-style "rinsed lamb," a cousin of the celebrated Mongolian fire pot, along with other fire pots of various origins and occasional borrowings from other regions, such as Sichuan twice-cooked pork.

What Buwei Yang Chao doesn't attempt is as significant as what she does. She never claims to be presenting an encyclopedic, region-by-region picture of Chinese cuisine in all its vastness and complexity. She doesn't guarantee surefire success with every recipe or pretend that every detail is flawlessly "authentic." Her book's authenticity lay (and lies today) first and foremost in evoking the shape and feeling of the major Chinese cooking techniques and putting them to simple use in her recipes. It also depends on much hard work at conveying Chinese attitudes toward food. The first five recipe chapters are all for "Meat," occupying twenty-five pages in all—but as the author has already explained, "when we [Chinese] say meat, we mean pork unless some other kind of meat is specified" (15). Beef, by contrast, gets only one seven-page chapter.

Sometimes Mrs. Chao refuses to use an American ingredient—notably, crabs. In her opinion, "fresh-water crabs are so much better than sea crabs that any crab dish made with sea crabs would be a caricature of the Chinese dish" (124). But most recipes stick to a fairly simple range of ingredients that she knew most American cooks could find without trouble, even in wartime. Scallions, soy sauce, and sherry (in place of Chinese rice wine) are her usual seasonings. Mentions of fresh ginger are usually followed by "(if you can get it)"; she allows that dried whole ginger might just possibly be substituted, but not powdered ginger. (Fresh ginger, grown only for the Chinese market, was unknown to non-Asian cooks almost everywhere on the U.S. mainland, though it was a thriving crop on Hawaii.) Despite the number of dishes that really need sesame oil, she is resigned to using plain salad oil instead. She uses fresh white mushrooms for the unavailable dried Chinese kind. These were just the sort of *xiang banfa* expedients that resourceful Chinese have always adopted when they had to, without falsifying the essential Chineseness of the whole approach. "I have been in some places in the United States where I can buy nothing but cabbages, lard, pork, pepper, and salt and such like things, and have still been able to make Chinese dishes," she assures American readers (15).

Of course, the book was written in the midst of a world conflagration—as evidenced by the poor quality of the very paper on which it was printed; all publishers were getting by with whatever could be spared from government paper rationing. The war had interrupted or shut down commercial shipping around the globe, cutting off food imports from China and Southeast Asia. Even in Boston Chinatown, then among the largest in America, crucial Chinese pantry items might be scarce or unavailable. Mrs. Chao scarcely mentions the war (except to remark that friends in China had passed on such new nicknames as "'Bomb Tokyo' for sizzling rice toast in soup" [46]), but it clearly affected some decisions about coverage.

She also refrains from dictating that people must seek out "authentic" Chinese cooking equipment, simply telling reader-users that they ought to have "pots and pans of various sizes" (30). She does explain that a Chinese "vegetable-cutting knife" is endlessly useful and some sort of steamer arrangement absolutely necessary (30–31). As for measuring tools, "The Chinese cook or housewife never measures space, time, or matter," but she had forced herself to get used to measuring cups and the like "so that I can show you how to do it my way. What my way was I could not tell myself until I measured myself doing it" (32–33).

The only odd-looking omission is any mention of a wok, or Mandarin *huo*—and the oddity vanishes when one recalls that woks were then impossible to use on American family kitchen stoves. Because of the round-bottomed shape, a wok had to fit into an aperture that held it securely over the heat source. It is unclear whether manufacturers of Chinese kitchen equipment in America had yet introduced wok rings to balance the wobbly pans on home gas or electric stoves. The fact that the Guangdong cooks who came to Gold Mountain didn't use quite the same type of wok as the cooks of the Chaos' native region may have complicated the issue. (The Cantonese wok is wider and shallower than Lower Yangzi counterparts and hence requires a slightly different stir-frying motion.) For whatever reason, Mrs. Chao decided not to spend time on descriptions of the basic Chinese cooking vessel or stratagems for adapting it to Western cookstoves. She is content to specify "skillets" for stir-frying. Some Cantonese-born home cooks who considered skillets the least bad choice for stir-frying in American kitchens would have agreed with her.

The book also avoids dishes best left to restaurants. Low's *Cook at Home in Chinese* had a dozen recipes involving shark's fins and many others for exorbitant or demanding presentations like chicken boned and filled with a minced fish and lobster mixture. Mrs. Chao, however, never forgot that she was addressing home cooks. She describes shark's fin and its preparation in much detail but gives only two recipes using it. She also registers a certain coolness about a wonder ingredient that had taken Chinese American restaurants by storm in the 1920s and 1930s: monosodium glutamate, known as *wei jing* (Mandarin) or *mei jing* (Cantonese). Henry Low used it in substantial amounts for nearly everything, under the name of "gourmet powder." Mrs. Chao, who calls it "taste-powder," says that its widespread use "has resulted in a lowering of the standard of right cooking and a leveling of all dishes to one flavor" (28). Only in a few "very plain" (usually meatless) dishes does she allow that a small amount might do something to animate other flavors.

The breakthrough work received prompt and admiring publicity. Jane Nickerson's review (as "Jane Holt"), which appeared in the *Times* on the day of publication, described *How to Cook and Eat in Chinese* as "something distinctly novel in the way of a cook book," though warning would-be buyers, "Well seasoned with humor though it is, the volume is not for the novice" and observing that the work required some concentration on Mrs. Chao's actual words if one wanted to follow "practical and good" recipes like the version of red-cooked fish printed in the review. Nickerson, a scrupulous writer who unlike many colleagues didn't try to pass herself off as an expert on all food traditions, nonetheless sensed that the book presented "an authentic account of the Chinese cooking system."[26]

Ida Bailey Allen, now conducting a nationally broadcast radio cooking show from Chicago, devoted part of a program to praising the book and scored a publicity coup of sorts by persuading the world-famous Pearl Buck to send a telegram to the station to be read on the air, explaining the importance of Mrs. Chao's contribution.[27] Several national women's "service" magazines requested permission to print a selection of her recipes. A year later the eminent food and wine writer Julian Street, who at the moment was (anonymously) conducting a monthly newsletter called "Table Topics" for the Bellows liquor distillery, asked permission to quote at length from Mrs. Chao's "delightful" work as part of a long, detailed essay he was preparing on Chinese food as "the only school of cookery that may properly be compared with the high cuisine of France."[28]

How to Cook and Eat in Chinese sold well enough to go into several more printings before the end of the year and achieved more notice in literary circles than was usual for a mere cookbook. In fact, it was successful enough to set the participants thinking about an encore: a memoir by the woman behind the cookbook. It was to be written in Chinese by Buwei and translated into English by Yuenren. Buck and Walsh seriously hoped for a real blockbuster. This wasn't an unreasonable bet at the time, given the popularity of books recalling early-twentieth-century immigrant lives, such as *Mama's Bank Account* (1943) by Kathryn Forbes, based on the story of a Norwegian family in California; or Pardee Lowe's previously mentioned *Father and Glorious Descendant.* All the participants considered the memoir, published in 1947 as *Autobiography of a Chinese Woman*, a work of real importance. The Chaos and the Walshes alike were disappointed when it failed to strike a chord with book buyers. Nonetheless, it remains a wonderfully original evocation of seismic changes in late-Qing and early-republican Chinese society as well as early-twentieth-century America, commonsensically interwoven with the large and small plot lines of family existence.

POSTSCRIPT TO SUCCESS

The cookbook proved to have a more lasting appeal than the memoir—but "lasting" only by the notoriously ephemeral stands of cookbooks. It would survive long enough to be not only read but published by people with short historical memories, before yielding to new competitors in an unimaginably different age.

To the pleasure of the original participants, sales of their pathbreaking effort held up solidly enough to justify a second edition in 1949. Probably for cost-cutting reasons, John Day decided to produce this update with an absolute minimum of changes in typesetting and pagination. The second edition was essentially the first edition printed on better paper, with about a dozen new recipes worked in on the blank space of existing pages or on a few interpolated pages numbered "34a" and so forth. Mrs. Chao had arrived at a few new perspectives, including a brief recommendation of pressure cookers for some "red-cooked" dishes; Pearl Buck had tried to get them mentioned in 1945, but the stubborn author had not then felt familiar enough with them to consent.[29]

With the family now living in Berkeley, she had also softened her stance against American crabs enough to admit the excellence of the "California" (i.e., Dungeness) variety.[30] (Probably Chesapeake blue crabs had been her introduction to North American species, and for anyone accustomed to big, meaty Chinese river crabs, they must have been a bewildering experience.)

Again the Chaos and the Walshes were gratified by reliable sales. The 1949 edition went through at least eight printings. In fact, *How to Cook and Eat in Chinese* was still a desirable property more than a dozen years later. But at that point the John Day Company was a shadow of its older self. Richard Walsh had been incapacitated by a stroke in 1953; Pearl Buck was no longer as closely involved in shaping the firm's publishing agenda. The Chaos took the book to Random House, which issued a third edition in 1963.

The new editor, Jason Epstein, had read the author's introduction with so little comprehension as to form a muddled idea that Mrs. Chao knew no English and her husband had actually written the text.[31] Apparently Random House wanted to update the work's appeal with the smallest possible departure from the plates of the first (and second) edition. The production team arrived at the less than ideal solution of making space by deleting the Chaos' bilingual table of recipes. (It has to be said that few publishers aside from Buck and Walsh could have understood the use of Chinese characters as anything more than window dressing.) Only the English-language index remained for guidance, minus the original Rosetta Stone. The freed-up space was used to add a couple of new chapters: a small one that discussed soybean-based foods and presented a few interesting recipes, and another on the dietary virtues of Chinese cooking. (The latter undoubtedly was meant to appeal to the body of young countercultural types who rejected traditional American diets along with a long litany of other American values.) Several more recipes had been worked in on extra-numbered pages, notably a version of pan-seared dumplings for which the Chaos had come up with the English name "pot sticker."[32] In one minor victory for linguistic barrier-crossing, a list of fourteen important ingredients with Chinese characters, English translations, and both Mandarin and Cantonese pronunciations had been crammed onto the last page of the chapter "Cooking Materials."

The third edition proved even more durable than its predecessors. It remained in print as a hardback book until 1972, when it was reissued under the Random House Vintage paperback imprint. This, too, enjoyed a long run despite the arrival of numerous competitors, along with new fashions in Chinese cuisine (see chapter 7). It went out of print at some point in the 1980s—but not before publisher and authors had managed to produce one last footnote to the story.

The 1970s offered a favorable climate for guides that promised to clue in consumers to chic new Chinese discoveries far beyond the ken of dull, plodding chop suey fans. The Vintage editors and the Chaos decided that the moment might be right for a tiny companion to the much-loved cookbook. *How to Order and Eat in Chinese*, a skinny little paperback, appeared in 1974. It was another mother-father-daughter collaboration, but this time the main translator of Buwei Yang Chao's Chinese text was her third daughter, Lensey Chao Namioka.

Like its better-known predecessor, this short-lived book has not since been surpassed for bundling much knowledge into terse and witty form. It begins with a good deal of information on Chinese meals and manners followed by four chapters on the major regional styles: "Cantonese Cuisine," "Northern Food," "Szechwan Cooking," and "Southern Dishes"—"Southern" being a tradition-hallowed if geographically ambiguous Chinese epithet for the Lower Yangzi or Jiangnan area. The first three areas each received several pages of general description along with bilingual listings (containing printed Chinese characters) of a few dozen typical dishes from the major menu categories. Mrs. Chao elected not to do the same for her own home region, mostly because "there are few Southern restaurants as such in America."[33] (The situation is much altered today, though most diners are not likely to recognize "Southern" food except under the label "Shanghai.")

Perhaps the most useful sections of this clever miniguide are the bilingual listings of dishes; humble though they look compared to the fare at up-to-the-minute restaurants in the second decade of this century, they would be helpful even today to anyone who wanted to carry along the book to dinner and point to Cantonese "Beef Slices with Greens" or Sichuanese "Ants Up a Tree" (spicy cellophane noodles and minced pork or beef). The same is true of a short final section giving nearly seventy practical culinary (and other) terms in Chinese characters with Cantonese and Mandarin pronunciations.

The importance of the Chaos' work was incalculable. It is true that they lived and thought on a plane far removed from the Cantonese Americans who actually cooked for this nation's white (or black) patrons of Chinese restaurants at the time the cookbook appeared. But they were able to help at least some non-Chinese better understand what went into all good Chinese cooking.

Their efforts arose from new kinds of exchange that started to occur during the early twentieth century between certain privileged people of Chinese and non-Chinese ancestry. Only with the arrival of genuinely bicultural women and men like Pearl Buck and Yuenren Chao did such dialogues become possible for others.

Buwei Yang Chao had the good luck to launch one particular conversation just as American approval of China and the Chinese was at an unprecedented height, and to have America's foremost Chinese cultural ambassador-at-large in her corner. She, her husband, and her daughter had exactly the right qualifications to go at the thing with system and gusto. They proved that a tremendously difficult body of knowledge was not after all impossible to convey to Americans who grasped the *xiang banfa* principle well enough to use their heads. Their great breakthrough was to discover the right language for communicating with non-Chinese cooks—to find sturdy, spirited English words for remote Chinese concepts as well as ingenious verbal bridges to the basically nonverbal business of cooking. Their success would eventually give other authors (and cookbook editors) confidence that the Chinese culinary art could be made as accessible to American cooks as any other cuisine.

SEVEN

White America Rediscovers Chinese Cuisine

THE WAR YEARS

By the time Exclusion was abolished in 1943, China's position on the geopolitical stage had radically altered. So had Western attitudes toward the Guomindang (GMD) or "Nationalist" regime that had replaced the Qing Empire. World War II marked the first moment in history at which the United States voluntarily acknowledged China as a great military and political ally vital to America's own security. On this side of the Pacific Ocean, it also marked the first moment at which a precariously positioned Chinese-born population was outnumbered by younger birthright citizens born to Chinese parents in this country—another sign of the shift to an immigrant community at least partly comparable to European-descended immigrant groups.[1]

Chinese Americans had not waited for the end of Exclusion to throw themselves into the war effort. They had watched with mounting horror as Japan seized Manchuria in 1931 and continued to menace China's eastern provinces. Horror turned to militant rage when Japan launched a full-fledged invasion, with no declaration of war, in the summer and autumn of 1937. By the time of the Pearl Harbor attack, the great eastern cities of Shanghai and Nanjing had been in Japanese hands for more than three years, and bombing raids by Japan's highly advanced air force had penetrated far inland. Young Chinese American men had been quick to volunteer for service in the Chinese air force; in a 1942 magazine article, Rose Hum Lee reported that thirty-three trained pilots from Portland, Oregon, had gone to fight on behalf of China before Pearl Harbor.[2]

With America's entry into the war, Chinese Americans found themselves in the novel role of extravagantly cheered poster children for both Chinese and American patriotism—"Americans first," as some boasted, but for the first time ever, free to express pride in a dual Chinese and American identity. Acceptance by white American society now seemed to be something more than a dream.

Chinese American men of military service age signed up in great numbers for the draft. For the rest of the community, the burgeoning wartime economy created an unprecedented wealth of job opportunities beyond the old racially stamped employment ghettos of laundries and restaurants. According to Rose Hum Lee,

> Throughout the Chinatowns in the United States there is a labor shortage. For the first time since Chinese exclusion began, absorption of the Chinese into American industry has been significant. Whether in New York, Los Angeles, San Francisco, Chicago, or Butte, Mont., the service in Chinese restaurants is slow. Four restaurants in New York's Chinatown have closed their doors in the past few months. The proprietor of Li Po, an up-to-date cocktail-chop suey place located in "Chinatown-on-Broadway" in Los Angeles, said sadly: "I was just ready for another venture. But I can't now. No men to run it."[3]

In New York, she added, students who used to moonlight as waiters "have found employment in industries working on lease-lend material for China."[4]

Women, too, were beneficiaries of the expanded job market. In the Bay Area, a resourceful can-do college graduate and future memoirist named Jade Snow Wong snared a position at a Marin County shipyard, where her younger sister was already employed, and soon graduated from typist-clerk in a War Production Drive office to more important personnel-relations positions.[5] Throughout the country, women eagerly poured into defense-related industries or were inducted into the Women's Army Corps or Army Nurse Corps.

Rose Hum Lee's 1942 article suggested that the community's contributions to the war effort showed the necessity of ending the disgraceful legacy of the Exclusion Act and National Origins Act.[6] Congressional dithering over the question ended in 1943 with repeal of Exclusion through the Magnuson Act. The historic vote for Magnuson probably did not indicate that a new band of principled statesmen had seen the light. A more likely motivation was the Roosevelt administration's argument that to continue barring a great contingent of the yellow race from entry would lend embarrassing ammunition—above and beyond the incarceration of Japanese Americans—to Japanese war propagandists.

After 1945 a flood of returning white servicemen partly reversed the wartime employment gains that had been made by women and members of racial minorities. But for American-born Chinese men, the ghetto wall had been decisively breached—the more so with the slow attrition of the aging Chinese-born population to whom the ghettos had been places of refuge. It is true that restaurants continued to be a major source of work. In both 1940 and 1950, they accounted for 29.8 percent of Chinese American employment nationwide.[7] But racist state and local laws (for instance, against Chinese using municipal swimming pools along with whites or buying homes in white neighborhoods) were beginning to crumble, and Chinese with college or higher degrees stood improved chances of well-paying and satisfying careers, rather than a lifetime as (generally nonunionized) cooks or waiters.

THE TAIWANESE CONNECTION

Meanwhile, the world political chessboard had altered even more profoundly since the Japanese surrender. In a very few years, the Cold War converted popular American idealizations of a heroic, freedom-loving China into fearsome images of a Communist-menace China. The Guomindang government, portrayed by the press for four years as our brave comrade-in-arms, was now a needy and difficult ally-in-exile. The linking figure here was Generalissimo Chiang Kai-shek, military commander in chief and president of the Republic of China in its beleaguered, mercilessly bombed wartime Chongqing headquarters and later on Taiwan (usually called "Formosa" by the American news media).

The Republic of China, of course, was a very different entity from the People's Republic of China, which was proclaimed on the mainland in October 1949, while the Nationalist forces were scrambling to escape to the island of Taiwan about a hundred miles off the coast of Fujian Province.

During the war, Chiang and the GMD had played a major role in the Allied Command's Far Eastern theater strategy. One result of America's continuing alliance with the Republic of China was a stream of Nationalist Chinese diplomats and military attachés arriving (with households) in Washington, DC, almost from the day of Pearl Harbor on into the 1950s and 1960s. After the war, still others came to New York City with the Nationalist mission to the newly founded United Nations. (The UN General Assembly was temporarily housed at the former 1939 World's Fair New York City pavilion in Flushing Meadows, Queens, and the tiny precursor to a future Flushing Chinese community took root before the move to permanent UN headquarters on the East Side of Manhattan in 1951.[8]) Some of the newcomers were officially stationed at the U.S. and UN Chinese embassies. Others had been dispatched from different government or trade organizations. Prominent businessmen and financiers accompanied by families and retinues also appeared in major cities, above all Washington and New York.

World War II and the 1949 GMD exodus to Taiwan already had had a certain culinary-cultural impact on people from many regions of China. Starting with the 1937 Japanese invasion, the temporary capital at Chongqing had received perhaps as many as half a million refugees from the war zones.[9] Until 1945 the mountainous Sichuan city would house relocated businesses, schools, and universities as well as the Nationalist government and the Allied Far Eastern military command.

For the duration, all sorts of regional cooking traditions briefly rubbed elbows in Chongqing. Men and women from Shandong, Fujian, Guangdong, or Shanxi might find themselves eating Sichuanese meals or sharing a dish prepared by fellow refugees from some unfamiliar location. At times during the war a scattering of foreign journalists (including luminaries like Theodore White and Emily Hahn) and many Western military personnel also lived in Chongqing long enough to become acquainted with its cuisine.

The 1949 flight to Taiwan had even stronger effects on gastronomic horizons. In a few months it deposited at least a million mainlanders (by some estimates, as many as 2 million) on an island of some 7 million people.[10] At the time, most Taiwan-born people were of Fujianese, or "Hokkienese," descent. (We may briefly note that their cookery was an offshoot of that practiced across the straits in Fujian Province, with some influence from a large minority of Hakkas who had arrived during the Ming dynastic struggles. But neither Hokkienese nor Hakka cuisine would come to the notice of American diners for many years.) They spoke their own version of the Hokkienese or "Minnan" language, unintelligible to the Mandarin-speaking Nationalist leaders.

Taiwan had been liberated from Japan only in 1945, after a half-century of occupation. The merciless, blood-soaked Nationalist takeover was a fresh hell for the population. But it was also one of the most important events in the modern history of Chinese food. The new occupiers included eminent generals, politicians, and businessmen from every part of China, together with the capable kitchen staffs who cooked for them. In an extraordinary concentration of talent, many highly trained professional representatives of different regional culinary schools were now practicing their craft on one island less than twice the size of New Jersey.

In a very short time, tables in the United States would be direct beneficiaries of all these changes. It was an eye-opening experience for Washingtonians and, later, New Yorkers to see Chinese-born people of wealth and political importance moving in the first social circles and hosting impressive entertainments complete with elegant Chinese food. The entourages that had come with them from Taiwan included cooks—often, sizable staffs of cooks able to mount official dinners and other parties. A number of these men had been trained by the last generation of royal or aristocratic household chefs who had ruled over great kitchens before the end of the Qing Empire. Their cooking often amazed Western guests. It represented many prominent Americans' first exposure to Chinese food unconnected with Chinatown, glitzy uptown Chinese nightclubs, or small-town Chinese restaurants—and often conspicuously distinct from the Cantonese culinary style, until now the default image of "Chinese cuisine."

Eventually some of the people brought to this country by the war or Cold War realized that cooking skills might be a passport to careers in America. Among the most important opportunities were restaurants, cooking schools, and cookbook writing. The new arrivals' advantages over the chop suey generation of Chinese cooks included a break with not only culinary but racial stereotypes.

The Han Chinese themselves universally recognized an unscientific but definite contrast between "southern" and "northern" physical types. The Chinatown Cantonese whom U.S. racists had pilloried as yellow rats belonged to the first group. Most were dark-skinned and very short, with broad faces and flattened noses. The northern newcomers were usually several inches taller and fairly light-skinned, with facial features less strange to Western eyes. Few non-Chinese Americans now remembered the old caricatures of hideous little "Chinks" (though caricatures of hideous little "Japs" had flourished throughout the war). But the Mandarin-speaking newcomers' ventures into culinary careers were not hurt by the fact that they tended to look less like the longtime Chinatown residents whose fathers and grandfathers had been thought synonymous with the Yellow Peril than the strategically made-up white actors who usually played Chinese men and women in the movies.

Many or most of the newcomers who opened their own restaurants—at least at the outset—were master cooks with solid experience in the kitchens of grand personages. As individuals, they were of various regional origins. But as professional cooks, they all knew something about the cooking styles of several regions. A rough analogy might be the training of Auguste Escoffier–era chefs in great international hotels; no matter whether they had been born in Portugal or Prussia, they were expected to master a certain repertoire including some important dishes from far-flung European capitals. Similarly, well-schooled, mainland-born Chinese chefs in the first adoptive Chongqing-Taiwan generation had some acquaintance with the cuisine of the north as the former fare of the Manchu emperors in Beijing; the south (that is, Guangzhou-based) as the most refined of all Chinese cuisines; the east (from Zhejiang, Jiangsu, Nanjing, and environs) as the one-time food of a storied Jiangnan merchant elite; and the west (chiefly Sichuan) as both wartime refuge and a celebrated cradle of fierce, startling culinary effects.

Women, who faced more obstacles in becoming restaurant owners or chefs, initially were drawn to culinary teaching and writing. Both offered much scope to ladies of social poise and resourcefulness. Depending on their family backgrounds, the pioneer figures might not have grown up doing their own cooking. But many had made up for it since—often having had to cook from scratch by the exercise of sheer *xiang banfa* ingenuity during wartime uprootings and relocations, certainly having learned to direct kitchen staffs.

Over time, more varied backgrounds and career paths became the norm. Ambitious younger men managed to found their own places after short apprenticeships at popular restaurants; determined women managed to break into the ranks of restaurant owners.

The immigration situation was fluid enough to aid such ambitions. Though the official Chinese quota was fixed at a meager 105 people a year, new wartime and Cold War geopolitical alignments helped many more to enter the United States on humanitarian or diplomatic grounds or simply through high-placed connections. Many members of Nationalist bigwigs' staffs successfully applied for political asylum. The War Brides Act (1945) and Chinese War Brides Act (1946) allowed about six thousand women to bypass the quota and immigrate as wives of servicemen, further improving the sex ratio and soon producing a small American Chinese baby boom. Other measures authorized permanent visas for professors and students who had been stranded in America by the war and the Communist takeover.

The privileged treatment of people connected with the mainland-via-Taiwan Chinese VIP route was a far cry from the openly racist hatred that Cantonese workers had encountered in America during Exclusion. The fact did not endear the new Mandarin-speakers to the existing Chinese American community. Indeed, the years in which non-Cantonese chefs began invading the world of American culinary fashion were difficult ones for old-school Chinese American restaurants in many ways. The base of cooks who had helped create chop suey–parlor cuisine had grown old or died. Though that vogue's first glamour had long since faded, the dishes it had introduced were still sincerely loved by many non-Chinese fans. But the dwindling number of people who continued to supply their wants knew that few bright young descendants of Guangdong-born sojourners saw much of a future behind a restaurant stove, as opposed to studying art history or penetrating new frontiers of technology.

Meanwhile, the Communist victory on the mainland and the GMD's flight to Taiwan had placed the larger American Chinatowns (especially older Chinese-born residents) in a terrible quandary. When American cold warriors led by Senator Joseph McCarthy began pointing fingers at State Department employees and demanding to know what traitors had "lost" China, the Chinese American community saw its recently acquired halo of patriotism abruptly snatched away. During the war, political disagreements about the rival claims of the GMD and the Communists had been successfully papered over to produce unwavering support of Chiang Kai-shek as political heir of the revered Sun Yat-sen and the Nationalist army as defender of the motherland against Japan. Many Chinese Americans had expected that Chiang would again be a legitimate target for opposition after the Japanese surrender. But now anyone rash enough to criticize him in public was likely to bring McCarthyist suspicion on the whole community.

The national and local Chinese Consolidated Benevolent Associations quickly lined up behind the GMD. But the outbreak of the Korean War in 1950 reinforced right-wing suspicions of all American Chinese as potential spies for the People's Republic. Older people born in China—a group still heavily represented among cooks and restaurant owners—were intimidated by a resumption of State Department investigations into "paper son" immigration fraud. It is not hard to see why hard-bitten Toisanese-speaking Chinatown restaurateurs reacted angrily to the arrival of affluent, sophisticated Mandarin-speaking newcomers whose cooking was now admired by white leaders of culinary fads.

Toisan, the largest single source of nineteenth- and early-twentieth-century Chinese labor, had been hit especially hard by World War II when the Japanese occupied Guangdong Province. Money remittances sent by American to Toisanese relatives—nearly the entire basis of the district's economy—had been cut off. Worse was to come during the Korean War, when the United States declared a trade embargo on China. Communication with families on the mainland was again effectually severed. American Chinatown importers, deprived of specialty ingredients from China during the war, once more faced shortages of necessary foods until new ties were established with manufacturers and exporters in Hong Kong, Taiwan, Singapore, and other parts of Southeast Asia. (In any case, many of the articles they prized were no longer being produced in quantity, or at all, in the People's Republic.)

THE NEW FACE OF CHINESE RESTAURANTS

Among the first of the upscale new stateside restaurateurs was the Chinese-trained C. M. Lo, who came to Washington, DC, in 1941 at the age of twenty-three as butler at the Chinese embassy. By the end of the war he had acquired some familiarity with the capital scene. Deciding to put his culinary expertise and local connections to work, he teamed up with several partners in 1947 to launch the Peking restaurant in the Chevy Chase neighborhood of the district.[11] It was the right moment: A budding postwar generation of American sophisticates close to the seat of power now plumed themselves on acquiring a taste for unusual gastronomic experiences matching Washington's status as—in its own and many others' eyes—the citadel of the free world.

The place's title implicitly linked one world capital with another. The far northwest location—miles from the District of Columbia's recently relocated small Chinatown—anticipated chic future trends. In a strategic break with earlier restaurant demographics, it was set in a residential neighborhood overflowing with wealth and prestige. The immediate clientele were members of a Washington smart set that loved the sense of tableside global adventure. Over a few novel dishes, politically connected diners could fancy themselves veteran China hands. This, too, presaged the future appeal of many other elegant Chinese restaurants.

The Peking soon found its niche. It began with and never wholly abandoned a partly Americanized menu. But Lo, himself Canton-born (though of august credentials unknown to most Cantonese-descended Chinatown chefs), put enough northern specialties on the menu to justify the place's title.

In the late 1940s few American restaurant-goers had ever imagined the great size and diversity of mainland China or grasped that it did not have one homogeneous cuisine based on their favorite chop suey–parlor specialties. Once in a while some large Chinatown establishments had ventured to present a few non-Cantonese dishes, little-known here, that enjoyed a nationwide reputation in China. It was terribly difficult for most restaurant waitstaffs to explain their context to non-Chinese patrons. But by the mid-1950s it was worth the effort to pitch unfamiliar specialties to a new clientele hungry for tokens of sophistication such as mu shu pork and Peking duck, two of the Peking's star dishes.

It is not clear whether mu shu pork (Mandarin, *mu xi rou* or *mu xu rou*, a stir-fried melange of pork, vegetables, and scrambled egg bits served with the small, thin pancakes called *bao bing*) had appeared on earlier restaurant menus in San Francisco or New York Chinatown. Certainly Peking duck already had fans in both places. Henry Low's 1938 cookbook gave a recipe, though with yeast-raised folded "lotus-leaf buns" (Mandarin, *he ye juan*) instead of the bao bing that soon came to be more common.[12] The recipe does not mention the finishing touches of hoisin sauce, slivered cucumbers, and scallion brushes that later would become standard.

In a soon-familiar pattern, Lo's hirees used the Peking as a stepping-stone to new career moves. S. Van Lung, son of a former military governor of Yunnan Province, left in 1955 to found the rival Peking Palace only a few blocks away. His ex-employer was not happy. Early in 1956 the Peking filed suit against the Peking Palace, complaining about an allegedly purloined signature dish as well as the restaurant name. The Peking ultimately prevailed in court, forcing the upstart to remove the offending dish (a pork shred/bean curd soup called "O-O soup") from the menu and stop calling itself the Peking Palace. American newspapers had a fine time with this tempest in a teapot. Van Lung and his partners coolly restyled their restaurant "Yenching Palace"—"Yenching," or in modern pinyin "Yanqing" or "Yenqing," being an archaic name for Beijing itself.[13]

The offshoot soon became more popular than the parent restaurant. For decades it was a major venue for power lunches and celebrity sightings. Reports circulated that it had been the site of secret negotiations between Kremlin and U.S. representatives to resolve the Cuban missile crisis in 1962. In the new age of Chinese restaurants combining claims of authenticity with a well-honed appeal to an affluent white clientele, name-dropping in society columns would become an indispensable weapon.

Another Peking staff member, Shanghai-trained T. T. "Tiger" Wang, had come to Washington in 1956 as a chef for the Nationalist ambassador Hollington K. Tong. He decamped to the Peking in 1957 and to New York about a year later. At that time the Manhattan real estate situation was colored by the above-mentioned Cantonese, and especially Toisanese, resentment of northern interlopers. Finding themselves unwelcome in Chinatown locations, non-Cantonese entrepreneurs looked elsewhere. A stretch of upper Broadway in Morningside Heights now began to acquire a scattering of restaurants known for what was loosely called "Shanghai" food, brought by chefs and owners from various parts of the Jiangnan region.

Wang landed at one of these, Shun Lee, on the corner of Broadway and 91st Street. He had been there several years when in 1964 a young American-educated engineer, Michael Tong, was taken by a relative to sample the Shun Lee fare and came away delighted by memorable Shanghai-style, Beijing-style, and even Sichuan-style dishes. The restaurant moved to large, ambitious quarters in the Gramercy neighborhood (Lexington and 23rd Street) before Wang persuaded Tong to join him in a far more expensive gamble, the Shun Lee Dynasty. It opened late in 1965.[14]

Like the Peking, Wang and Tong's new venture occupied a piece of strategically chosen real estate: Second Avenue at 48th Street, handy to deep-pocketed lunchers and diners at the United Nations and many midtown corporate headquarters. To this advantage it added the "wow" factor of a cutting-edge decor (by the celebrated industrial designer Russel Wright) emulating a new breed of wonderland restaurants with breathtakingly planned interiors and fittings. New York's La Fonda del Sol and Four Seasons were the most iconic of these glamorous destinations. Much of Shun Lee Dynasty's instant (and lasting) éclat lay in having been the first Chinese restaurant in Manhattan to stake out such an image for itself—and one of the first to set its sights on the 1960s expense-account clientele.

The menu was a well-judged mixture of American diners' proven favorites with northern, eastern, and western Chinese selections that were new to almost all non-Chinese patrons. The last—"Szechuan" dishes, in pre-pinyin spelling—were destined to become the greatest sensation by virtue of a startling firepower that was new to people raised on usual American Chinatown food.

The partners' gamble was one of the luckiest in New York restaurant history. Its patrons loved the trappings of wealth and success. Their judgment was rapidly confirmed by Craig Claiborne, the *New York Times* food columnist. Enthralled by the mysteries of Chinese cuisine since his small-town Mississippi childhood, he had made himself familiar with many Manhattan Chinese restaurants, including the two previous Shun Lee incarnations. Starting with a New Year's salute to the charms and wind chimes of this "Oriental bazaar" on January 4, 1966, Claiborne would heap increasing praises on Shun Lee Dynasty.[15]

THE THRESHOLD OF A NEW ERA

It was at this juncture—almost exactly coinciding with the 1965 opening of Shun Lee Dynasty—that President Lyndon Johnson succeeded in pushing through passage of the Hart-Celler Act, which forever ended the special plight of Chinese seeking to immigrate. The new law officially took effect in the summer of 1968, a clamorous and sometimes bloody presidential election season preceding Richard Nixon's defeat of Hubert Humphrey.

The political climate had undergone intense shakeups from the time of the Korean War. A real end to the Cold War was still not foreseeable, but leading minds in Washington increasingly thought that the United States had fairly free rein to pursue military objectives in the Far East or Southeast Asia without bringing about the end of civilization. Unlike Korea, the new battleground of Vietnam did not seem certain to draw China into open acts of belligerence. The Chinese American community was no longer under blanket suspicion by right-wingers, partly because it had seldom strayed from public allegiance to the United States and the Nationalist regime on Taiwan. Few of the old "paper sons" were left now to fear deportation if their true past happened to be uncovered. As for the Chinatown restaurant scene, it seemed to have nearly closed one chapter without being quite ready to open another.

One of Nixon's first acts on taking office was to appoint the well-known foreign policy pundit Henry A. Kissinger as national security advisor, giving him an initial brief of preparing America's exit from the

Vietnam War. By now it was an open secret that the Washington foreign policy establishment was heartily sick of Chiang Kai-shek and ready to abandon previous assertions that the mainland Chinese government and the Soviet Union formed one menacing Communist bloc. The rest of the free world (already a half-obsolete term) had gone along for decades with American refusal to recognize the People's Republic of China but seemed increasingly eager to break with earlier policy. Halfway through Nixon's first term, the two great powers began covertly feeling their way toward diplomatic rapprochement, with Kissinger representing the United States and Premier Zhou Enlai the People's Republic. GMD loyalists on Taiwan and in America's Chinatowns suspected that they were about to be left in the lurch.

Zhou and Kissinger had barely concluded their second meeting when, in October of 1971, the UN General Assembly overwhelmingly voted to expel the Republic of China and seat the People's Republic. By now the U.S. State Department had slightly relaxed restrictions on travel to the mainland. The scent of change was in the air, avidly sniffed by the news media. By informed guesses, official American recognition of the "Red China" once denounced by none other than Richard Nixon as our most pernicious Asian enemy was only a matter of time. Zhou and Kissinger were soon smoothing the way for Nixon to visit Beijing in February of 1972. With this trip, the newly unfolding United States–Soviet détente was enlarged to include the People's Republic.

News reporters followed every stage of the trip with rapturous fascination and a special fondness for images of Nixon and his wife wielding chopsticks at official functions. Frequent updates from Beijing throughout the Nixons' stay prefaced a joint communiqué issued at Shanghai on February 26. The bulk of the document contained several intricate pas de deux in which the two powers first stated their differing official views on the Asian geopolitical scene and the future of Taiwan. But in the shorter final sections, both agreed to work together toward full normalization of relations through improved "contacts and exchanges." These would gradually expand until 1979, when détente was followed by the establishment of full diplomatic relations under President Jimmy Carter and the new Chinese head of state, Deng Xiaoping. (The trade embargo officially ended in 1974, though the range of exportable food items still being produced in the People's Republic was limited.) To many leaders of the Chinese American community. it appeared that they and Nationalist Taiwan had been thrown under the bus. But for much of the news-consuming public, the excitement of watching the very symbol of the mysterious East emerge from the enforced invisibility of almost thirty years trumped other considerations.

CULINARY CHINAMANIA

Popular food history would later conflate many developments into one hazy notion that Nixon's watershed 1972 journey to Beijing launched an American era of unprecedented culinary discovery. As the story goes, it suddenly inspired everybody who was anybody to start scarfing up meals at exciting new Chinese restaurants and buying exciting new Chinese cookbooks. The claim is muddled at best. In fact, the 1972 diplomatic breakthrough didn't start a craze for "discovering" unexplored vistas of Chinese cuisine. It reinforced an exploratory vogue that had been under way for decades. By 1972 restaurants like the Peking and Yenching Palace in Washington or Shun Lee Dynasty in New York were familiar to the urban style-setting classes, and people who read about food in small-town newspapers might well have at least seen the term "Szechuan cuisine."

The Sinophile vanguard was based in New York from the mid-1960s on and included two food writers who between them put the restaurant-reviewing profession on the map. Craig Claiborne at the *New York Times* and Gael Greene at *New York* magazine both had immense power to set trend-conscious New Yorkers (and visitors from elsewhere) worshiping places that had received their accolades, or solemnly discussing rival versions of restaurant dishes that they had made famous. And both were mad for Chinese food—though perhaps not as knowledgeable as their older contemporary James Beard, who had had some real exposure to Cantonese-school cooking while growing up on the West Coast. Writing as if an appreciation of the world's oldest great cuisine were de rigueur for modern sophisticates, they spearheaded a near-manic obsession with the latest action on the China front among a certain white urban clique. In a sense, the new Chinese vogue resembled the chop suey craze transposed into another key. Overt racism no longer figured in the equation, but class snobberies did.

Claiborne and Greene eventually brought a wide spectrum of Chinese restaurants to popular notice. But their highest praise was most often reserved for Shun Lee Dynasty together with Wang and Tong's next venture, Shun Lee Palace, which opened on East 55th Street in 1971. Their coverage generally implied that these establishments had introduced America to a version of Chinese haute cuisine as far removed from lowly Chinatown grub as La Côte Basque from a wiener roast. Visible swank often counted for a lot in their reviews. So did any dramatic departure from the trodden ways of previous Chinese American restaurant menus—for instance, hot chile peppers.

Shun Lee Dynasty's Szechuan dishes had struck Claiborne's attention by the end of 1965. On return visits, he seldom missed a chance to mention them, often complaining about inauthenticity if they weren't fiery enough. Between them, he and the Shun Lee team launched a delirious vogue for Chinese food primed with detonators in dried-chile form. Greene, who started at *New York* in 1968, shared the new passion. Soon many New Yorkers were categorically writing off old-style Cantonese American cuisine as dowdy and insipid, while new eateries labeled "Szechuan" multiplied like dandelions in April.

Some of the new craze was based on simplistic notions. It is not true that hot chile peppers—introduced to China from the New World in the sixteenth century—figure only in the food of Sichuan and nearby provinces. They turn up in other regions, though most rarely among the subtlety-loving Cantonese. The Sichuanese culinary style is not a freakish outlier among China's varied cuisines, nor are hot peppers its only distinguishing feature; knowledgeable Chinese diners might point also to a fondness for particular textures or ways of pickling vegetables. On the other hand, the devastating wallop of hot chile, often combined with the "numbing" effect of the native Sichuan peppercorns, required no brains at all for novice devotees to identify, whether or not they appreciated these elements' interplay with other flavors. Proving one's grasp of Sichuanese authenticity was not exactly a blood sport, but it did often mean outfacing all rival chile-heads in the house until somebody was weeping in pain.

Meanwhile, other entrepreneurs were also redrawing the map of American Chinese restaurant food. In New York the cluster of Shanghai-style restaurants on upper Broadway, led by Shanghai Café at 125th

Street and Great Shanghai at 103rd Street, formed an example mentioned as early as 1959 in Kate Simon's *New York Places and Pleasures.* Among the dishes she singled out at Shanghai Café were "fried dumplings and shrimp balls"; "sweet-and-sour bass cooked in a syrup of Oriental nectars"; "spicy pork in black bean sauce"; "the ugly and delectable Chinese black mushrooms"; "thin, elusive, shiny noodles; the beef in oyster sauce."[16] All were clearly appealing departures from anything that Simon—a fearless cosmopolite—had tasted before at Chinese eateries. Her comment that the cooking on display at the new places was "more subtle and varied . . . than the Cantonese, less burdened with garlic and the green of scallions," testifies less to the real qualities of either cuisine than to uptown restaurateurs' successful campaign to discredit Cantonese food as coarse and outmoded.[17]

A revised perspective on Chinese food arrived in Cambridge, Massachusetts, in 1958 with the founding of the eponymous Joyce Chen Restaurant. Chen, a Beijing native who had left China in her early twenties at the time of the Communist takeover, offered an eclectic selection of dishes from several different regions. No more welcoming community could have been imagined. The restaurant rapidly drew crowds from the Harvard and Massachusetts Institute of Technology campuses and exposed hundreds if not thousands of young people to presumably "authentic" Chinese food. (The cookbook that Chen produced in the wake of the restaurant's success does not inspire confidence in the presumption.) For decades it was a favorite destination for dating couples, celebrators of birthdays or anniversaries, and members of high-powered policy cliques (most famously, Kissinger). The location also proved lucky when WGBH, the Boston television station that had made broadcasting history in 1962 with Julia Child's first *French Chef* appearances, was casting about for another cooking project and invited Chen to star in a weekly program. The result, *Joyce Chen Cooks*, was broadcast on public television stations nationwide in 1967 and enlarged the fan club for Chinese dishes not limited to the old Cantonese mold.[18]

At around this time, Sinophile diners like Kate Simon also started talking about a fashion called "Mandarin." The word has no meaning whatever in reference to Chinese cuisine, but for more than half a century restaurateurs had known that it appealed to American notions of ancient Chinese grandeur. This aura still lingered when a young woman named Cecilia Chiang moved from Japan to San Francisco in 1960. Not long afterward her friends talked her into a rash investment in a restaurant startup. Left holding the bag when the other people pulled out, she soldiered on by herself and fashioned a menu based, like Joyce Chen's, on a cross-section of regional dishes. Within a few years her restaurant, the Mandarin, had managed to rekindle the glamour of that term.[19]

Chiang, born to wealthy parents in Wuxi at the heart of the Jiang-nan culinary region, had been raised for the most part in Beijing. In contrast to owners or cooks at most San Francisco Chinese eateries, her bearing effortlessly conveyed that she was a person of education and position. Everything about the Mandarin was conspicuously up-scale and mandarin-worthy, including the prices. Like pathbreaking counterparts in Washington and New York, it was located outside of the city's Chinatown and pointedly distanced from images of Cantonese American food—which, Chiang let it be known, was utterly déclassé. Chop suey and red hanging lanterns would never darken her door, at either the restaurant's original location on Polk Street in Russian Hill or the grander, elegantly appointed Ghirardelli Square quarters to which it moved in 1968.

After about a year at the Polk Street location, the Mandarin was vis-ited by the popular *San Francisco Chronicle* columnist Herb Caen. The next day the paper carried his paean to a "new discovery," announcing, "Here you will find real Chinese food."[20] Chiang's fortune was launched.

As in New York, the rising tide lifted other boats. In 1969 the carefully researched second edition of Doris Muscatine's *A Cook's Tour of San Francisco* commented on the new cluster of restaurants that "have been introducing Americans to Mandarin, Szechwan, Shanghai, and Mongo-lian specialties."[21] They included the Great Shanghai, the North China Restaurant, and the Manchurian (in Chiang's old Polk Street location). Muscatine's description of the now-celebrated Mandarin mentioned such bold decorative touches as the building's original "brick wall and long wooden rafters" and "the Mongolian open barbecue" with seats around the encircling "birch chopping block counter." She singled out such delicacies as "Mandarin tidbits to order," "the Mongolian chafing pot," "prawns a la Szechwan," "beggar's chicken" baked in clay, "Peking or Mandarin duck," and both "pao tzu" (pinyin, *baozi*; steamed yeast-raised dumplings) and "chao tzu" (jiaozi, not yet universally known as "pot stickers").[22]

The term "Mandarin" had already spread across the land. By 1968 even I (quite in the dark about Chinese food) had uncomprehendingly heard tributes to Mandarin cuisine at a restaurant in Philadelphia's tiny Chinatown. In Chicago, Peter and Betty Lo opened the supposedly "Mandarin-style" Chinese Tea House in 1968, followed by Peter Lo's Mandarin restaurant in 1972.[23] In New York, Sichuan-style restaurants were rapidly replacing Shanghai-style predecessors along a good stretch of upper Broadway, driving some of the former owners and cooks to transplant Shanghai or "Mandarin" establishments to new locations.

Emily Kwoh of New York's first Great Shanghai (Broadway and 103rd Street) started the Mandarin East (at Second Avenue and 57th Street) and Mandarin House (in Greenwich Village on West 13th Street; it did not hurt that Craig Claiborne lived in the same building).[24] The Scottish-Chinese Sheila Chang, who also had been at Great Shanghai, began Shanghai East, a luxurious establishment at Third Avenue and 63rd Street.[25] Meanwhile, the Sichuan invasion arrived in Chinatown, where barriers to non-Cantonese restaurant ownership were disappearing as the older generation retired or died off. Even younger Cantonese restaurateurs might now at least consider updating their image to suit a new crew of chile-happy white patrons.

THE COMPETITION EXPANDS

T. T. Wang and Michael Tong, who had inspired the Sichuan vogue and watched others rush to exploit the name, pulled a winning card out of their sleeve in 1972 with a new restaurant called the Hunam, again within the UN orbit (Second Avenue close to 46th Street). Its opening, less than three months after Nixon's visit to China, was a stroke of genius. For one thing, no non-Chinese except a few World War II veterans had ever heard of Hunan Province. (The standard Mandarin pronunciation is "Hunan," but the final consonant has a slightly different nuance in Xiang, the local language.) For another, the restaurateurs were able to claim with complete accuracy that Hunanese food outgunned Sichuanese in sheer firepower.

Claiborne had left the *Times* in 1971. Raymond Sokolov, also a Sichuan-food enthusiast, succeeded to the post of restaurant reviewer. His first feature article for the *Times* was a scoop on a secret Chinese treasure just outside Princeton, New Jersey: a friendly mom-and-pop filling station-cum-lunchroom at which Alex and Anna Shen would gladly cook up magnificent, phenomenally cheap Chinese dishes like hot bean curd, smoked chicken, "real Peking sweet and sour pork," and eggplant with shrimp and hoisin sauce, for customers in the know.[26] (As the chef- and writer-to-be Barbara Tropp—then a Princeton graduate student—later commented, this unsought publicity "resulted in the nice couple becoming very rich in a second, palatial restaurant that featured miserable, steam-table food."[27])

Sokolov lost no time weighing in on the Hunam. Within three weeks of its opening, he had written a four-star review declaring, "By a wide margin, it is the best Chinese restaurant in the city." Grandly informing neophytes that Hunan—not "Peking or Canton or Szechuan or Shanghai or Fukien"—was the source of China's "most celebrated food," he assured them that the restaurant "justifies all the praise lavished on the cuisine of the region by old China hands."[28] Forty-plus years later he would acknowledge in his autobiography, "I was mostly operating in the dark about Chinese gastronomy."[29] This did not matter to the local non-Chinese Chinese fan club, most of whom were still more in the dark; my husband and I with two friends managed to snare a table on the day the review appeared, and we all perused the menu with a reverence exceeded only by ignorance. Crowds nearly battered down the doors of the Hunam in eagerness to sample "honey ham with lotus nuts" and "Lake Tung Ting shrimp." Wang and Tong did not explain—nor did most of us wonder—what their ocean shrimp dish had to do with the freshwater Lake Dongting, or how serving ham in honey sauce squared with the well-known Hunan dislike of sweetness in anything savory. (The dish is famously associated with Yunnan Province.)

The Hunam rapidly acquired a handful of rivals also claiming to specialize in Hunanese cooking. Soon many restaurants that had boasted of their Sichuanese menus were hastily adding the phrase "Hunan cuisine." In a few years the watchword "Hunan" graced restaurants in most large American cities and some midsized towns.

Less than a year and a half after the Hunam had opened, the vogue was well enough advanced for Gael Greene to do a magazine roundup of restaurants boasting some Hunanese connection. She laid down the law as snootily as Sokolov: "Hunan means little to the scholars of Chinese gastronomy." "Beyond ham and sausage and tung hsien cai"—which she identified as "a rare green vegetable" eaten only in Hunan—"the Hunan kitchen is unsung."[30] Such casually dropped bits of lore were great favorites with restaurant critics eager to put Chinese cuisine on the gastronomic glamour map. (In fact, Hunan is one of China's most renowned rice-growing regions, famous for a range of smoke-cured meats but not preeminently for ham or sausage; the leafy green mallow called *dong xian cai* or *dong han cai*—*Malva verticillata*—is not unique to Hunan or even to Asia.)

Greene, whose literary trademark was a form of voluptuary rejoicing over food she loved, hailed the Hunam as "my favorite Chinese restaurant." She went on to discuss two new competitors named Uncle Tai's Hunan Yuan (i.e., "garden") and Uncle Peng's Hunan Yuan, and noted a number of recent Hunan-style additions to the Shun Lee palace menu.

Uncle Tai's was the brainchild of a prominent Wang and Tong rival David Keh, who had already opened several highly regarded Sichuanese restaurants both in Chinatown and in the old Upper West Side Shanghainese stronghold.[31] He and the Shun Lee team had carried out rival scouting expeditions on Taiwan for chefs who knew Hunanese cuisine. T. T. Wang came back with enough dishes to get the Hunam going; seven or eight months later Keh set up the chef Wen Dah Tai in his eponymous establishment nearby.

In New York, Keh would rule a shifting empire of mostly (not exclusively) Chinese restaurants for many years. At the time he started Uncle Tai's, he had recently met a very young, highly starstruck would-be Claiborne named Ed Schoenfeld. The incurably curious youth's initial acquaintance with Chinese food was no greater than that of many other Jewish New Yorkers who frequented Manhattan or Brooklyn citadels of "shar mein"—the preferred pronunciation of aficionados—and wonton soup. (This is as good a place as any to correct the muddled myth that a special passion for Chinese food is a distinguishing mark of American Jews, a claim with little relevance for anybody except New Yorkers or New York expats.) By his late teens Schoenfeld had developed an excellent nose for the Sichuan-style cooking just starting to appear in a few corners of Manhattan. After briefly studying with the well-known cooking teacher Grace Zia Chu and trying his luck as a freelance arranger of Chinese banquets, he convinced Keh to take him on as an aide during the planning for Uncle Tai's opening at the start of 1973.[32]

Schoenfeld was insatiable in the quest for hands-on cooking knowledge. His banquet-hosting ventures had been an ideal means of scoping out the expanding ranks of mainland-trained Chinese chefs in New York. His association with Keh opened still more doors during the first age of Sichuan-style restaurants. Schoenfeld was on hand to encounter the legendary version of cold noodles in sesame sauce that the Sichuan-born chef "Shorty" Tang (Tang Win Fat) introduced to New York at one or two of David Keh's places at around 1970.[33] He appointed himself an informal apprentice to Lou Hoy Yuen, who had come to the New York Sichuanese restaurant scene by way of Brazil and intermittently worked at several Keh enterprises. In a few years he not only knew his way around home and restaurant woks but understood the business side of fashionable, leading-edge Chinese restaurants at least as well as any Chinese colleague.

By 1980 Schoenfeld would be on his way to becoming a mover and shaker—eventually an innovator—in the Chinese American restaurant world. Such a development would have been inconceivable during the chop suey era or the last years of Exclusion. The appearance of a trained, insightful white insider on the scene (as opposed to the few whites who had earlier managed to acquire some notions of Chinese restaurant mechanics and culinary principles) marked a new stage in the American relationship with Chinese food—in a sense, a new psychological stage. By 1960 or 1970, recently arrived Chinese-born cooks and restaurant impresarios who were American citizens or eligible for citizenship could conduct themselves toward whites with a consciousness of equality (in fact, professional superiority) that would have been impossible when the threat of deportation stamped the consciousness of Chinese-born people from the minute they arrived. On the other side, a brash New Yorker like Schoenfeld could sincerely view the chance to penetrate Chinese restaurant circles as an honor and a privilege. And in purely practical terms, the opportunity could not have occurred previously for an inquisitive white youth to spend months and years watching masters of stir-frying and other techniques until the essential motions and timings were in his blood. His presence at Keh's new Hunan venture heralded the emergence of more people who could communicate across the formidable barriers of spoken and culinary idioms.

Uncle Tai's Hunan Yuan was a lively success. Reviewers were soon showering it with superlatives as ecstatic as those for the Hunam. But Uncle Tai himself was canny enough to see how chancy Manhattan restaurant success could be and made an exit when friction developed between him and Keh. In 1979 he lit out for the territories, or at least Houston, where he triumphantly relaunched Uncle Tai's Hunan Yuan. Eventually he relocated to Boca Raton, Florida, where the restaurant is still thriving.

Uncle Tai was not the only Chinese restaurateur to decide that the time was ripe for bringing "new" regional cuisines to the hinterland. In 1973 Sheila Chang had pulled up stakes on Third Avenue and transplanted Shanghai East to the palatial Galleria Mall in Houston. By 1979 it was covering another base by advertising "The First Authentic Szechuan Cuisine in Houston."[34] The Uncle Tai's menu likewise underwent strategic cross-breeding after some years in Texas and later Florida.

In 1973 the brother of a manager at the Washington, DC, Peking opened the Peking Jr. in San Antonio. A local newspaper reviewer reported that the place specialized in "the dishes of Western China," which "originated in Honan [sic] and Szechuan." The owner, known as Karate Hsu by virtue of a black belt, loftily professed a complete lack of interest in "the cuisine of Foochow or Southern China" (i.e, Guangdong).[35] Soon the *Texas Monthly* restaurant reviewer had visited the Peking Jr. and proclaimed that "at its best, the food . . . is simply unbeatable in Texas." With enough notice, Hsu would prepare any dish to order from the menu of the original Peking; but "even if you walk in unheralded, you can expect to find succulent Chinese dishes you didn't even know existed. Simply set aside the menu and tell Karate you want real Chinese food, not chow mein or egg foo young, then sit back and see what he brings."[36]

The same issue of the magazine offered more cautious encomiums of another San Antonio newcomer, the King Wah, that at the time had few parallels in North America. Its creators, two couples both surnamed Leon, were from the Chinese community of Lima, Peru, a seat of Chinese culinary traditions then completely unfamiliar to U.S. fashionistas. They had assembled a restaurant staff somehow able to make themselves understood to each other and the customers in Spanish, Cantonese, Mandarin, and English. Such linguistic feats would eventually be taken for granted in many Chinese American restaurants but must have looked astonishing to 1970s outsiders.

As the King Wah owners told the magazine reporter, they had originally planned to open a restaurant in New York City but changed their minds on seeing the reality of "that declining megapolis."[37] It would be decades before non-Chinese New Yorkers glimpsed the Chinese-Andean heritage represented by the Leons. For the nonce, writers covering the New York food scene were too caught up in the Mandarin-Sichuan-Hunan vogues to understand much else.

SUGAR SELLS: THE GENERAL TSO'S AND LEMON CHICKEN SUCCESS STORIES

Another rising star arrived in New York for a brief but notable interval. David Keh's and T. T. Wang's scoutings on Taiwan had introduced them to a redoubtable chef actually born and raised in Hunan, Chang-kuei Peng or Peng Chang-kuei. Through no fault of his own, his signal mark on Chinese American cuisine was destined to be a dubious blessing.

Peng, born in 1919, was one of the mainland-born chefs who had received classical training in youth from some of the last surviving Qing-era masters or their apprentices before going on to cook for the highest circles of the Nationalist government in exile on Taiwan. Arriving in New York in 1973, he founded an east midtown spot called Uncle Peng's Hunan Yuan that swiftly folded after drawing unfavorable comparisons with the two reigning favorites, the Hunam and Uncle Tai's. (New Yorkers did not immediately realize that Peng had more genuine Hunanese roots than the competition.) He had better luck with two later ventures, Peng's Yunnan Yuan and the tersely named Peng's. All three offered a dish that Peng had originally invented in Taipei and named for a native son of Hunan, the nineteenth-century general Zuo Zongtang (Tso Tsung-t'ang in the old Wade-Giles transliteration system).[38]

A 1977 guide to New York Chinese restaurants describes the Peng's Yunnan Yuan version of "General Tso's Chicken" as "hot but delectable.

Tender chicken cubes are stir-fried in a spicy sauce containing red chilies and crisp scallions."[39] There is no mention of a sweet, sticky red sauce or a thick, crunchy deep-fried coating. But already these featured prominently in a completely different incarnation of General Tso's chicken introduced by T. T. Wang at Hunam and Shun Lee without Peng's knowledge or consent. It was listed on the Hunam menu in English as "General Ching's Chicken" and in Chinese as "Guo Fan Chicken Chunks" (for General Zeng Guofan, a contemporary of Zuo's).[40] Unlike the slightly tart, vinegar-laced original and a somewhat similar version featured at Uncle Tai's Hunan Yuan, the rival dish cleverly addressed the American passion for syrup on anything from ice cream to breakfast sausages. This crunchy creation, usually set on a bed of broccoli and incorporating ever-increasing amounts of sugar, soon marched forth from New York to conquer the nation under the name "General Tso's chicken"; today millions of Americans would probably call it their favorite Chinese dish. Throughout the land, almost the only Chinese restaurants that don't now serve it are ones catering to fresh-off-the-boat Chinese immigrants.

People who considered themselves leaders of advanced taste soon reacted to the mere name "General Tso's" with all the hauteur formerly reserved for "chop suey." Decades later, the elderly Peng (who returned to Taiwan in 1984) was still bemused at how this American cuckoo's chick could have been passed off as having any Hunanese ancestry. "The dish can't be sweet," he emphatically told the questing *New York Times* reporter Jennifer 8. Lee in 2007. "The taste of Hunan cuisine is not sweet." He took umbrage at the idea of serving the chicken over broccoli, and summed up the entire *momingqimiao* (bafflement) in a few well-chosen words: "Chinese cuisine took on an American influence in order to make a business out of it. . . . If you give them real authentic Chinese cuisine, Americans can't accept it."[41]

What they did accept was the sense of being admitted to an inner sanctum. Even in this age of regional newcomers, a few Cantonese-style restaurants still managed to attract an au courant non-Chinese clientele by cultivating an air of privilege. Probably the best-known on the East Coast was Pearl's, a longtime fixture in west Midtown Manhattan. Pearl's represented a certain successful Chinese restaurant school of the age. To start with, it was the creation of a native New Yorker endowed with sangfroid and perfect chic.[42] The slender, glamorous Pearl Wong and her husband, James, were second-generation immigrants with quick instincts for attracting 1960s and 1970s glitterati. She would respond to well-heeled habitués' plea "Feed us, Pearl!" by ignoring the menu and telling the chef, Yook Lum Lee, to improvise something for the party in question.[43] (It was a sensible and natural strategy in any Chinese restaurant but at Pearl's was chiefly practiced by clubby insiders.)

The Wongs had been running the Canton Village on West 49th Street for some years when the owner sold the business out from under them. It was a severe blow to the largest single contingent of Canton Village patrons, the editorial staffs of *Time* and *Life* magazines at their nearby Sixth Avenue headquarters. Someone in this more or less lily-white club suggested raising enough money to start another restaurant by forming themselves into a corporation at five hundred dollars a share. Appealed to through a grass-roots campaign, Canton Village regulars from the theatrical and publishing worlds loyally chipped in, most at a share apiece. The Wongs and Yook Lum Lee were the largest shareholders.[44]

Pearl's opened in 1967 at a very long, narrow space on West 48th Street that the architectural firm of Gwathmey Siegel had managed to imbue with a wonderful sense of cool spaciousness and sunny radiance through the ingenious use of glass and mirrors. It at once joined the Shun Lee restaurants and Uncle Tai's as a venue for celebrity spotting. No one who wrote about it failed to mention names like Jacqueline Onassis, Mike Nichols, Truman Capote, or Danny Kaye. Sokolov, who considered it his mission to educate *Times* readers about "the exciting, if anarchic, revolution in authentic Chinese cooking now in process in this city," regally wrote off the place as "the perfect Chinese restaurant for people who don't really like Chinese restaurants."[45]

Like the Hunam, Pearl's launched a dish now found on innumerable American Chinese restaurant menus. It was called "Lemon Chicken," and had come into being when Yook Lum Lee finished off a presentation of fried boneless chicken breasts and lightly cooked julienned vegetables by throwing one fluid ounce—two full tablespoons—of bottled lemon extract into a luridly sugared sweet-and-sour sauce. By the time of Sokolov's review, it was considered the star attraction at Pearl's. He was not inclined to approve this concoction. The flavor, he tersely noted, was "certainly unusual," but the crowd-pleasing favorite was "not a native Chinese dish."

This was a backhanded swipe at Claiborne, who had fallen in love with Pearl's lemon chicken the minute he tasted it and given it national celebrity by publishing a recipe (headed "Oriental Tang") in the *Sunday Times Magazine* in 1969.[46] (More subtle versions of lemon chicken with real lemon juice or sliced lemons were known in Guangdong and elsewhere.)

The truth was that Greene, Sokolov, Claiborne, and all other non-Chinese arbiters who tackled the subject of Chinese cuisine in the 1960s and 1970s were overwhelmed by the same obstacles to understanding that had bedeviled earlier would-be explicators. They were pioneers unable to draw on the specialized maps that would be available to everyone several decades later. But the prestige that these sometimes inexpert experts conferred on Sichuan or "Mandarin" restaurants played an important role in the eventual creation of such maps by people who really knew the terrain. Though nothing could make the road to mastery of Chinese cooking smooth and foolproof for hopeful Westerners, a new generation of instructors was inspired to rethink the task. Some of the teaching tools that they were looking for would eventually be developed—with help from innovative publishers and editors—in the United States. Some would arrive by way of Taiwan.

EIGHT

An Advancement of Learning

A SEMINAL ERA

Throughout most of the 1960s, members of the non-Chinese dining public who hoped to understand—and possibly cook at home—marvels tantalizingly glimpsed at some acclaimed dining spot had very few printed sources of guidance. *How to Cook and Eat in Chinese*, the Chao family's pioneering 1945 effort, had done about as much to make the unintelligible intelligible to English speakers as could be accomplished with language alone. But it hadn't magically abolished the chasm between Chinese and Western ways of "seeing," "hearing," and otherwise comprehending either language or food. How to convert Chinese characters into either phonetic spellings or English translations, how to make reader-cooks grasp the logical relationships between different parts of an ingredients list or crucial stages in a sequence of directions, were problems that continued to stymie hardworking minds.

Luckily the postwar and Cold War Chinese restaurant craze happened to overlap with two reinforcing trends: an American cooking-class fad that soon attracted capable Chinese-born instructors, and a fascination on the part of leading cookbook editors with expanding the instructional potential of recipes through inventive use of page design, recipe format, illustrations, and perhaps even photography. Their experiments with what could be called supraverbal innovations would especially affect English-language Chinese cookbooks because so much of the above-mentioned chasm wasn't amenable to purely verbal bridging strategies.

At the same time as these developments, Washington policy wonks were paying intense attention to the one nation that the United States officially recognized as "China": Chiang Kai-shek's Republic of China (ROC), in exile on Taiwan. Of course, the People's Republic of China (PRC) had been almost completely invisible to the so-called free world since 1949. By default, the ROC now represented Chinese life and civilization to many Americans, including food lovers. In fact, Taiwan's role as a fount of culinary knowledge, insight, and inspiration for Americans is complex enough to deserve a book in itself. A great number of the advances in understanding Chinese cuisine that took place during the postwar rise of glamorous big-city dining spots owed something to Taiwanese influence or example—or at a slightly later stage, actual immigration in a form previously unimaginable.

"LITTLE DRAGON"–SUPERPOWER INTERCHANGES

For a heady interval after the PRC–ROC split, Washington poured millions of dollars into the coffers of its tiny Cold War ally. The ROC swiftly achieved independent prosperity under Chiang Kai-shek and, after his death in 1975, his son Chiang Ching-kuo. While the PRC remained largely turned in on itself, the transplanted mainlanders made Taiwan into the biggest and richest among the four "little dragons," or newly industrialized states, surging to the economic forefront of the Far East. (The other three were South Korea, Hong Kong, and Singapore.) This success was partly built on the backs of the Hokkien-speaking ethnic majority who had been just recovering from half a century of Japanese occupation when the Nationalist army swarmed in, bringing with it a state of martial law that would last almost forty years.

Taiwan—at least the Mandarin-speaking elite—soon became a sophisticated, affluent consumer society intent on business growth and technological progress. Restaurants offering fine versions of the major mainland regional cuisines flourished in Taipei and other Taiwanese cities. Modern communications kept abreast (or sometimes ahead) of those in First World nations. The culture evolved into a high-powered mixture of Eastern and Western imperatives, though actual Western cooking would not have a dramatic popular impact until the 1980s.

Among many programs for rapid modernization, education for both sexes was a central priority. The National Taiwan University became one of the greatest institutions of higher learning anywhere in Asia, forging ties with scholarly communities in America. At the same time, what might be called lifestyle education—instruction in hobby-and-leisure activities or the domestic arts—was enjoying as great a spurt of growth on Taiwan as in the United States.

The daughters of affluent, educated families flocked to new classes in accomplishments that they would previously have learned at home. Aggressive modernization was helping to create a generation of young women who often had more in common with American businessmen's daughters and wives than with mainland-reared mothers and grand-mothers. Mother–daughter example was no longer enough to equip girls with up-to-date—meaning increasingly Westernized and some-times Japanized—domestic skills. Imparting these in classrooms be-came a growth industry that naturally produced a demand for printed instruction as well. Before the war, cookbooks resembling any Western model would have been useless articles in any Chinese household. Now, however, Taiwanese women could admire American cookbooks as to-kens of modernity.

Academic studies also fostered international exchange in the boom-ing new Taiwan. Taipei received an influx of American college or gradu-ate students drawn by the National Taiwan University or an expanding crop of language schools. Many young Westerners fell in love with the Chinese food of diverse regions as cooked by and for Chinese on Tai-wan. They recognized at once that this experience had nothing to do with eating in either old-style American Chinatown restaurants or hifa-lutin new "Szechuan" and "Mandarin" places with menus cleverly aimed at stylish Washington or New York consumers. Some devotees returned to U.S. campuses obsessed with trying to find or recreate anything half as good as the fare they had regularly devoured from Taipei street carts, holes in the wall, or famous restaurants. For a time, Princeton's Depart-ment of Far Eastern Studies was a small hotbed of informal Chinese gastronomic activity, a few of whose instigators would later go on to write cookbooks.

Some Americans also became aware that pioneering experiments in televised as well as classroom instruction were taking place on Taiwan. A pretty young woman named Fu Pei Mei or Pei Mei Fu began teaching cooking over Taiwan's first television station in 1962—the year that also saw Julia Child's first *French Chef* appearance, and decades before superior hair, teeth, and charm became standard values on American TV cooking programs.[1]

Meanwhile, the Hotai Chemical Corporation, one branch of a Taiwanese family business empire, morphed into a food manufacturing and distribution concern called the Wei-Chuan Foods Corporation. Wei-Chuan quickly set up a home economics department with a school that offered courses in makeup, flower arranging, sewing, and cooking.[2] At about the same time that Pei Mei Fu's broadcasting career was being launched, the cooking part of the Wei-Chuan agenda was split off into a school of its own under another attractive young instructor, Huang Su-Huei or Su-Huei Huang, the daughter of the Hotai founder.

As the economies of the Far Eastern "little dragons" as well as postwar Japan grew, they became important publishing centers, addressing home-grown audiences while also doing increasing amounts of book printing and photographic reproduction for Western publishers. It was inevitable that how-to books loosely corresponding to American models would find a home on Taiwan. Wei-Chuan was an early leader. The school soon acquired a publishing arm and began issuing books by Ms. Huang while the company weighed the idea of English-language or bilingual editions to appeal to potential buyers on Taiwan and even in America itself.

These developments coincided with the start of stateside French, "Continental," and other cooking schools; an upswing in English-language Chinese cookbooks; and some early transpacific exchanges of media influence. If Taiwan was becoming daily more Americanized, it was also true that American students and others returning from Taiwan might well have seen a cooking program by Fu Pei Mei (a household name to television viewers everywhere on the island) or found out about a Wei-Chuan cooking class while shopping for food. By the same token, Taiwanese students were arriving at American universities in increasing numbers, usually missing the excellent Chinese cooking that they had grown up taking for granted and not finding English-language cookbooks well matched to their innate culinary reflexes.

Increasing interchange also exposed the island's modern-minded consumers and communicators to supposedly mouth-watering, profit-stimulating American magazine and advertising photography depicting roast meats, layer cakes, and so forth. Local talent took a while to catch up with American professional standards, but Taiwanese publishers soon saw that photography might be deployed to sell consumers on the Western-inspired publishing novelty of cookbooks. In today's age of digital cameras and YouTube videos, food mavens may not instantly grasp that because of production costs, photographs—especially in color—were used either very sparingly or not at all in most American cookbooks until the mid-1970s. Taiwan got into the game a little earlier.

The first cookbook spinoff of Fu Pei Mei's television program, *Pei Mei's Chinese Cook Book* [*Pei Mei Shi Pu*], was published in Taipei in 1969.[3] (Two additional volumes would follow in 1974 and 1979.) It contained representative dishes from all parts of mainland China organized by region (east, south, west, north) as well as a chapter on dim sum. The two most conspicuous selling points were a bilingual presentation, with Chinese text and rough, sketchy English translations of all recipes on facing pages, and copious use of color photography. There were five substantial color inserts that included studio shots of every dish. All were crude and unimaginative by American as well as later Taiwanese standards, but they point to the growing wants of a market that was also about to acquire international dimensions.

The Wei-Chuan Corporation, meanwhile, began preparing for overseas expansion spurred by the first hints of new Taiwanese outposts that would soon materialize in the San Gabriel Valley east of Los Angeles. At or slightly before 1970, a small cluster of Chinese homes in the San Gabriel town of Monterey Park set wheels spinning in the head of a Chinese-born newcomer with an instinct for real estate speculation. Word went out to Taiwan, where members of the mainlander elite were starting to fear the consequences to themselves of a possible Washington-Beijing rapprochement. Within a few years Monterey Park and several neighboring San Gabriel towns were attracting a strong influx of educated, ambitious Taiwanese professionals along with scatterings of

Hong Kong émigrés, ethnic Chinese from Southeast Asia, and refugees from the dwindling Los Angeles Chinatown. In the past forty years these communities have come to occupy a twenty-five-mile east–west stretch of sprawling and for the most part wealthy Taiwanese-dominated settlements so unlike the old city ghettos that they have earned a sociological label of their own: "ethnoburbs."[4] Monterey Park, the original nucleus, is now home to one of America's largest cookbook publishers, a branch of the Wei-Chuan empire established when Huang Su-Huei and the corporation set their sights on a potential English-language market.

Part of the story began in 1970, when the Wei-Chuan cooking school in Taipei acquired a determined nineteen-year-old pupil named Nina Simonds, a New Englander who had dropped out of the University of Wisconsin in order to study Chinese cooking as close as possible to actual Chinese soil.[5] She had arrived with a somewhat limited command of Mandarin but was also intensively studying the language between sessions at Wei-Chuan. Soon she was playing a part in Ms. Huang's plans for an English-language or bilingual Chinese cookbook.

The English-language attempt was published in 1972 as *Chinese Cuisine: Wei-Chuan Cooking Book*, with Simonds and other people receiving brief credit for help with translation.[6] In hindsight, it was an astute if linguistically shaky effort by a well-organized team, auguring well for future marketing aims. A larger English edition with drastically rearranged contents followed in 1974.[7] In this version, Nina Simonds—by now proficient in Mandarin—was listed as translator, as also in the first (and still more thoroughly revised and expanded) bilingual edition in 1976.[8]

It is improbable that the small community of Americans then engaged in language or other Chinese studies in Taipei could have formed a dependable clientele for these initially clumsy ventures. Neither *Chinese Cuisine* nor another bilingual production by Ms. Huang, *Chinese Snacks* (also translated by Simonds and published in 1974), was primarily addressed to either stateside American cookbook buyers or temporary Taiwan residents.[9] The longer-term audience was the growing body of Chinese professionals looking to move from Taiwan to the San Gabriel Valley and a few other North American ethnoburbs (especially in the vicinity of Houston and Vancouver), often equipped with educational advantages like some command of English that their Cantonese peasant predecessors on Gold Mountain had not possessed.

The Huang family had taken aim at this market as early as 1972 by founding an American branch of Wei-Chuan Foods in Los Angeles. (Today it is one of the chief domestic manufacturers of frozen dumplings, spring rolls, Chinese-style entrees, and many other products.) In 1978 Huang Su-Huei, now married to an American, came to the region to set up Wei-Chuan Publishing in Alhambra and Monterey Park, the biggest new Taiwanese American settlements. A branch of the cooking school had already opened in Alhambra.[10]

Wei-Chuan Publishing also had offices on Taiwan, where most of the actual book printing was done. The American-produced Wei-Chuan cookbook list has grown to number in the dozens, addressing any subject from decorative garnishes to "international baking delights." Bilingual Chinese–English editions, with more professional expertise pumped into the English translations, were soon joined by Chinese–Spanish editions for the Latino market and even a couple of trilingual Chinese–English–Spanish volumes.

The signal feature of the Wei-Chuan books was and is a format that enables every page to be printed with a glamorous close-up color photograph of a finished dish above the recipe-directions. The design requires the recipes to be presented as compactly as possible in order to fit the restricted space. It has been somewhat refined over the years but still relies on the same basic device. The ingredients are arranged in groups marked off by numbered brackets, with the numbers serving as cues at different stages of the execution. Thus, number [1] might include four or five ingredients that need to be stir-fried in a particular sequence; [2] the elements of a starch-and-water slurry; [3] a few final seasonings. The mixing and cooking directions would then say something like "Add [1] in the order listed," "Add [2] and stir to thicken," and "Sprinkle with [3]."

The reason for the method's popularity with Chinese cooks is that they were already used to mentally grouping ingredients *by structural role*. To recognize how 1, 2, and so forth fitted into the action at just the right moment was no stretch of understanding for them. Westerners on Taiwan or back home were inclined to find the format awkward or distracting but often hoped to learn enough from the recipes to buy the books anyhow. Those who persevered acquired insights into Chinese kitchen thinking that usual American recipe formats could not convey. The Wei-Chuan books, which soon found their way into bookstores and variety stores in big-city Chinatowns, vary greatly in quality but represent a vigorous and too-little-noticed intersection of East–West culinary approaches in this country.

A TEACHABLE MOMENT: CHINESE INSTRUCTORS
FIND AN AMERICAN AUDIENCE

Decades before the San Gabriel Valley phenomenon, mainland-born and Mandarin-speaking representatives of the Chinese upper crust began reaching the United States through Washington's alliance with the ROC—and in some cases thinking of food as a promising career option in postwar America.

Unlike the Cantonese predecessors who had founded chop suey restaurants during the Exclusion era, they were not driven to the choice as a last-ditch defense against deportation. Another difference was that women figured proudly among the newcomers. (Not for nothing had Soong Mei-ling—Madame Chiang Kai-shek—made herself into the extravagantly admired public face of the Nationalist regime in America during World War II.) At the outset, virtually all the people who took advantage of a welcoming climate to start new restaurants were highly trained professional cooks—a category virtually limited to men. But their success encouraged sophisticated Chinese-born diplomats', generals', and businessmen's wives or daughters to consider culinary careers of their own. Some would eventually manage to invade the all-male club of restaurateurs. But the field that first opened up to them was culinary instruction.

Cooking schools dedicated to French or other European cuisines had become wildly popular in many American cities. Like their Taiwanese counterparts, they addressed stylish postwar hobby-cooks. The arriving Mandarin speakers were a natural fit with these aspirants to chic, accomplished kitchen globetrotting. Many of them had learned English either at elite schools in prewar China or through years at American private schools and colleges. (From the turn of the twentieth century, sons and daughters of some wealthy, powerful families had attended exclusive U.S. schools quite independently of the Boxer Indemnity scholarship program described in chapter 6.) They were well equipped to capitalize on the new prestige of non-Cantonese cuisine. Whether or not they had grown up with hands-on mastery of Chinese home cooking, they understood its principles well enough to demonstrate them to others.

These women had the self-confidence to stand in front of nervous neophytes and patiently, gracefully show them how to handle cleaver and wok, making sense out of the previously unfathomable for people who couldn't speak Chinese. Their status as teachers would have been far outside the reach of earlier, humbler immigrants from Toisan. And unlike Ed Schoenfeld, most of their American pupils would never have dared to walk into restaurant kitchens and stick around long enough to detect the method in a clamorous whirl of lightning-fast preparations.

Of course, cooking has always been learned more reliably from repeated firsthand example (mother to daughter, master cook to apprentice) than the written word. The close-up sight of a sharp knife at work or a sauce taking on the right consistency cannot be equaled for bringing the essentials to life. This is especially true of Chinese cuisine. Stir-frying in particular resists being explained on paper to the inexperienced about as stubbornly as downhill skiing. It is still poorly grasped by most American cooks. But long before cooking videos, the first American-based teachers gave rise to a generation of communicators who have made it somewhat better understood.

The seeds of the movement were sown at the New York–based China Institute in America, an educational foundation established in 1926 through the efforts of a binational committee including the Chaos' friend Hu Shih and his old Columbia University professor John Dewey. The organizers had managed to get a part of the Boxer Indemnity scholarship fund allocated to setting up a nonprofit cultural center offering language courses and other activities. Eventually the center attracted the support of Henry Luce, the Shandong-born missionary's son and resolute Nationalist supporter who had founded *Time, Life,* and *Fortune* magazines. It was the Luce Foundation that in 1944 presented the institute with "China House," a four-story townhouse on East 65th Street, to serve as new headquarters.

In 1955 someone at the institute decided that a cooking class at China House might appeal to a spectrum of New Yorkers. After a search for an instructor, the post was offered to Grace Zia Chu.[11] This elegant, virtually bilingual woman, always called "Madame Chu," belonged to the corps of Chinese military and diplomatic wives who had spent the war years in the United States. Originally from Shanghai, she had graduated in 1924 from Wellesley (also the alma mater of her acquaintance Madame Chiang Kai-shek, class of 1917) and married an officer in the Nationalist army who was eventually posted to Washington as a military attaché. The couple had broken up after the war, and Madame Chu had tried her hand at several ventures to support herself and her two sons in America before accepting the China Institute position.

Her classes were an instant success. The restless Ed Schoenfeld attended briefly but soon saw that he would be happier in the rough-and-tumble of real restaurant activity. But eager American hobby-cooks, nearly all women, flocked in droves to Madame Chu's China House sessions. In a few years the institute had to hire a second instructor to cope with the tide of applicants, while Madame Chu also began offering classes at other venues, including her own apartment.

Her new colleague at the institute was Florence Lin, who was—like Buwei Yang Chao and Madame Chu—a native of the Jiangnan region, specifically, Ningbo, an ancient silk-trading city about eighty miles east of Hangzhou. She had come to New York in 1947 with her husband, a stockbroker who happened to be a nephew of the writer Lin Yutang.[12] The couple entertained a lot, having entree to various cultural as well as financial circles.

Florence Lin began teaching at the institute in 1960. For some years the two women shared the job of instructor, until Madame Chu set up on her own as founder and principal teacher of Madame Chu's Chinese Cooking School. Lin succeeded her as head of the institute's cooking program, which grew to include several more instructors under her direction.

Classroom instruction in cooking has its limitations. But information conveyed in the presence of students registers in the memory differently from words on a page—especially English words launched across the incredible distance that separates Western cooks from the sui generis "language" of Chinese cuisine. There is no doubt that the live (if artificial) experience of addressing non-Chinese students in teaching kitchens helped cooking instructors recognize other Americans' greatest failures of understanding and seek ways to overcome them through cookbooks—that is, to communicate nonverbal cues on the page for what is after all an intrinsically nonverbal activity.

Other Chinese-born people and a few American-born Chinese began offering cooking classes during the 1960s. New York was the biggest center of activity, but not the only one. A handful of restaurateurs got in on the act: Joyce Chen began teaching Chinese cooking in Boston; Johnny Kan, in San Francisco. Chinese kitchenware shops started to attract white cooking students. A particular favorite in Manhattan's Chinatown was the Oriental Country Store on Mott Street, owned by an entrepreneur named Mailan Lee who had a handful of business ventures. Her mother, Virginia Lee, had some reputation as an accomplished cook. In 1970 Mailan installed a demonstration kitchen above the shop, where Virginia was just about to launch her own cooking course when Craig Claiborne—having heard of her "virtues and talents"—called from the *New York Times* asking to arrange an interview. The resulting article appeared in early September.[13]

Claiborne was already preparing to leave the *Times*, with an eye to starting a food newsletter in partnership with Pierre Franey. The encounter with Virginia Lee gave him a further idea: to study Chinese cuisine to serious purpose. He had already visited and reported on several of the city's Chinese cooking schools. Now, however, he appointed himself a member of Virginia Lee's first series of classes and attended sessions along with her other students. Manhattan food-writing circles were soon rocked by the news that the two were planning to write a cookbook together.

Claiborne's choice of Virginia Lee for coauthor perhaps owed something to the fact that, unlike Madame Chu or Florence Lin, she was his "discovery" rather than an already illustrious figure. The two reigning instructors enjoyed great name recognition. They commanded a large network of contacts and influences in their own right. Through their most eager students, they helped the teaching of Chinese cooking diffuse outward from a handful of privileged big-city fans into a larger, more democratic American white community.

The process began almost at once. Chu's and Lin's most apt students regularly returned for more courses, often becoming assistants to the instructor before seeking their own venues for teaching Chinese cooking. Margaret Spader, a consumer affairs consultant at the Gas Appliance Manufacturers Association who had studied with both women, soaked up all the instruction she could get and eventually started teaching beginner courses for fun in her apartment one evening a week.[14] She also helped Madame Chu and the China Institute team make further contacts at the gas association, a natural ally in promoting Chinese cooking methods. One of Madame Chu's students, Karen Lee (not Chinese, despite the name), founded a well-respected Chinese cooking school of her own. Others secured cooking-demonstration gigs at department stores. Many taught at adult-education centers or in programs run by educational church programs or university extension services. At least half a dozen of Madame Chu's students were hired to conduct live Chinese cooking demonstrations on board the *Queen Elizabeth 2* in the early 1970s.[15] These examples show how broadly the idea of at least dipping into the easier shallows of Chinese cuisine appealed to American hobby-cooks. Instruction in the subject was, if not a growth industry, at least a box-office draw that in one way or another reached a wide public.

THE UNIQUE CHALLENGES OF "COOKING IN CHINESE"

For some time, developments in English-language Chinese cookbooks lagged behind those in cooking classes. One reason was the sheer awkwardness of representing crucial words and ideas on paper. The Chaos had been given their head by the one American trade publisher able to appreciate their command of language issues. They had brilliantly addressed the intractable problems of "translating" between Chinese and English kitchen mentalities, problems that had no real counterpart in English-language cookbooks on French, Italian, or Scandinavian cooking. They had come up with wonderful coinages like "stir-fry" and "pot-sticker." But they had not permanently abolished the many remaining pitfalls of finding English terms for either the "language" formed by the cuisine itself or any actual Chinese language.

In the first place, written Chinese differs from Japanese, Korean, Hindi, and other major East Asian languages in being essentially impossible to convert to any alphabet-based phonetic system. (Today's official pinyin is only the latest in a series of very imperfect attempts.) Though it does have phonetic elements, these are unintelligible unless one already knows the meaning and pronunciation of the characters in one or another Han language. For this reason, postwar writers on Chinese food could not blithely give English equivalents and phonetic pronunciations of even some fairly simple terms. Of course, prewar writers had faced the same obstacle, but it became more egregious as American authors and editors increasingly realized how inadequate the very words "Chinese language" were to the real situation.

Most people had previously taken "Cantonese" and "Chinese" to be synonymous. The arrival of a prominent Mandarin-speaking contingent revealed the error of this idea. Just as Chinese food was acquiring new prestige among movers and shakers, finding ways to represent what was being talked about with the Roman alphabet as basic tool became more confusing.

At the time, many American publishers had adopted the Wade-Giles system for approximating Mandarin pronunciation, along with a slew of hit-or-miss efforts for Cantonese and any other Han Chinese language. Of course no system came very close to actual Mandarin pronunciation (which in any case was not one uniform system) or could correctly indicate the four "sung" Mandarin tones without some further mark over or after each syllable. (Since tone-indications were a useless refinement for Western readers ignorant of how "sung" pitch might affect meaning, only scholarly publications bothered with them.) Where the original language was Cantonese, with its seven or more "sung" tones and an incredible farrago of local sublanguages and dialects, nobody could agree on how to proceed.

One author might elect to transliterate the name of a popular Cantonese American duck dish as "wo sieu ngaap" while another plumped for "wor shu opp" (the most usual spelling on American restaurant menus). Mandarin speakers, meanwhile, would render it as something like "wo shao ya." The lime-treated eggs sometimes known as "thousand-year" or "hundred-year eggs" might appear in a cookbook as "pay daan," "pei don," or (the Mandarin pronunciation) "pi dan." Simply translating the whole name into English didn't necessarily improve matters. In the case of the duck dish, the last word was the only one with an unmistakable English equivalent—"duck." The first two could be variously rendered as "nestled-roasted," "pressed-braised," or a few other hazy approximations of concepts not easy to smuggle across language boundaries. The literal English translation of "pay daan" and so forth was "skin eggs," which was no help to anybody.

Downplaying phonetic spellings (or dispensing with them) and giving the most informative possible English translations accompanied by names in Chinese characters cleared things up for those who could read the latter. It also offered those who couldn't the option of taking the book on dining or shopping excursions and showing the page to waiters or clerks. But it involved extra production expenses and other complexities—for instance, selecting a Chinese typeface or hiring someone to do calligraphy, deciding between traditional Chinese characters as used in American Chinatowns and the simplified forms now being introduced in the People's Republic, and carefully proofreading Chinese against English names. Few cookbook editors at leading publishing houses cared to adopt this procedure in the years when the Chinese market was starting to warm up.

A whole other set of problems revolved around the terrible fit between American recipe conventions and the Chinese cooking mentality. Writers had to set down incredible amounts of information—second nature to Chinese cooks but like differential calculus to anybody new to the proper literal and figurative kitchen "vocabulary"—without drawing out every recipe to ridiculous length. For their part, the users had to make sense out of the shaping concepts on the page, detail by detail, at every moment of a race to the finish line between hauling out the wok and putting a completed dish on the table.

Lists of ingredients were an awful headache. Chinese people understood the structure of Chinese cooking (as shown by the Wei-Chuan books). They knew that even simple dishes often involved several kinds of pre-preparations that had to be sitting at hand, ready to be incorporated, well before the real assembly of elements began. There might be a mixture of egg white, starch, and a little oil for coating and marinating pieces of meat or poultry; some amount of oil to (briefly) fry the meat; a little more oil for a final stir-frying; another mixture involving liquid and starch to bind the pan sauce; and a handful of other seasonings tossed in at the end. All these elements listed in one unbroken sequence had as much structural coherence as an excerpt from the city telephone book.

Telling cooks what to do with the assembled ingredients also imposed a painful stretch on the familiar recipe framework. It was fatally easy to issue a long string of instructions that amounted to directing hikers past one tree after another, ad infinitum, without helping them to gauge their progress through the forest.

More mental exertions would be necessary on the part of trade cookbook editors and publishers before they could adequately deal with the Chinese puzzle in all its interlocked dimensions. Unfortunately, during the first postwar decades these professionals would have been out of their depth in addressing the puzzle even if they hadn't been loath to risk pushing potential buyers beyond received notions of an average housewife's comfort zone. Pearl Buck and Richard Walsh had had not only the rare understanding to grasp the excellence of the Chaos' pathbreaking effort but the guts to throw the John Day / Asia Press resources behind it. For the time being, their example was lost on other publishers. (In a depressing sign of shrunken horizons, Random House would delete the entire fifteen-page bilingual table of recipes from its 1963 reissue of *How to Cook and Eat in Chinese.*)

AN INSPIRED AMATEUR

Given the circumstances, it is little wonder that only one English-language Chinese cookbook displaying anything like the brains of the Chaos' 1945 breakthrough appeared for more than fifteen years. Nor should it be surprising that the work had been dreamed up and executed a couple of thousand miles from usual American trade book publishing channels. It was published in 1950 under the supposed imprimatur of Greenberg: Publisher, a longtime New York cookbook specialist. Greenberg's role, however, really was only that of distributor.

The Joy of Chinese Cooking had been written, produced, and printed in Mexico City. (The authors of *The Joy of Cooking* were anything but pleased by the title.) Its begetter was Doreen Yen Hung Feng, the twenty-seven-year-old daughter of the Nationalist Chinese ambassador to Mexico. At the time, she was a rich playgirl given to exotic hairstyles and expensive amusements such as amateur bullfighting.[16]

The young woman clearly had plunged into the task with toreador-like bravado. Unlike most of the New York star chefs and teachers, she came from a Cantonese family and placed little emphasis on specialties of other regions. Feng was as interesting company on the page as Bu-wei Yang Chao, though with more of a bent for color and atmosphere than brass tacks. Hers was the first important English-language culinary work to dwell at length on Chinese symbolism, cosmology, and myths. She had created a prettier, more evocative volume than the no-nonsense *How to Cook and Eat in Chinese*, copiously illustrated with her own attractive line drawings and instructional diagrams.

The book was something of a vanity production, and all the better for it. Feng barged ahead on her own inspired amateur agenda, unhampered by sage editorial advice about popular appeal. She gave all recipe titles in English, romanized Cantonese pronunciations, and Chinese characters. She also used Chinese characters to identify important methods and ingredients. (Mexico City had its own small Chinese barrio, with shops stocking crucial imports.) The line drawings of major edible plants, including unfamiliar items like cloud ears or bitter melon, were a handsome shopping aid; a section on the chief annual festivals introduced some ten dishes associated with them.

Feng's Latin American background (she had been born in Peru) can be glimpsed in some of her comments: "Chinese parsley" resembles the "variety called cilantro, found in Mexico"; "a water plant called jicama" can do duty for for water chestnuts or bamboo shoots.[17] Occasionally her command of English betrayed her into writing something like "tissue paper" (instead of waxed paper or kitchen parchment) in the "paper-wrapped chicken" recipe.[18] The amateurish index is woefully unhelpful to English speakers. But the work's charm and insight are unmistakable even today.

Feng was not the first author of an American-published cookbook to mention the cooking vessel that she called a "wock." As far as I know, that honor goes to Katherine Bazore, who described "a shallow round-bottomed frying pan called a wak" in her seminal *Hawaiian and Pacific Foods*, published in 1940 by the New York firm of M. Barrows.[19] But Feng seems to have been the first to present a drawing of it—in fact, two.[20] Unfortunately, she could not suggest how to use it on an American home stove.

After a few years of distribution by Greenberg, Feng arrived at an arrangement with another American publisher, Grosset & Dunlap.[21] The book must have sold very reliably, because the Grosset & Dunlap version remained in print until the late 1970s. *The Joy of Chinese Cooking* was thus many American cooks' first introduction to the subject over a period of more than twenty-five years—and actually enjoyed another lease on life in 1992 when it was reissued by Hippocrene Books.[22] It still stands as one of the most genuinely original explorations of Chinese cuisine in the English language.

The field remained fairly untroubled by original thinking for about another dozen years. One mother–daughter team of authors should be mentioned: Tsuifeng Lin and Hsiangju Lin, the wife and youngest daughter of Lin Yutang. In 1956 Prentice-Hall published their maiden effort, *Cooking with the Chinese Flavor*.[23] Certainly the Lin name promised something fresh and unusual. But sadly, neither this work nor an expanded version published in 1960 as *Secrets of Chinese Cooking* aspired to be much more than an amiable quasi-Chinese hodgepodge mostly featuring dishes (from crab soufflé or beef curry to tea-dyed eggs) based on readily available ingredients; a shorter section of "recipes calling for Chinese ingredients" was a little livelier but equally uninformative about the ideas underlying the cuisine.[24]

THE TRANSITIONAL SIXTIES

An expanded role for Chinese cookbooks was nonetheless starting to take shape. The 1960s, a time of vast political and cultural disruption everywhere in America, also ushered in some serious attempts to awaken the cookbook-buying public to the glory of Chinese cooking. As enrollment in cooking classes swelled along with the excited buzz surrounding new high-end Chinese restaurants, writers, editors, and publishers alike began to make less timid efforts at reading the market.

Three works that appeared in quick succession during the first years of the decade show changing ideas of what the cookbook-buying public might be interested in. All not only mention but picture the two most truly Chinese pieces of cooking equipment: kitchen cleavers (with detailed explanations of how particular ways of slicing and cutting affect final results) and woks (with support rings to adapt them to American gas stoves, though only one of the books seriously argued for cooking with woks). Merely identifying these items as major though partly replaceable cogs in a functioning Chinese kitchen system was in itself a serious advance in culinary "translation."

The first of the new teaching stars to secure a cookbook contract with a major publisher was Grace Zia Chu, whose *The Pleasures of Chinese Cooking* was released by Simon & Schuster in 1962.[25] Her reputation at the China Institute, and later her own school, guaranteed the modest-sized work a warm reception and a long afterlife in paperback reprints.

Either Madame Chu or Simon & Schuster chose to avoid challenging reader-cooks by dwelling on factors that set Chinese kitchen civilization apart from other foreign cuisines. All parties seem to have agreed on planing off difficult conceptual edges, ignoring awkward conundrums like Chinese characters, and converting about one hundred dishes into conventional, highly organized formulas accompanied by serving or preparation tips.

These were undoubtedly helpful choices for a large audience, though the book's ambitions look decidedly fainthearted today. Madame Chu knew how to put nervous non-Chinese beginners at ease. She wrote graceful, enjoyable English. Everything about the effort bespeaks a gentle, well-gauged pitch to just the sort of hobby-cooks who might have showed up for the China Institute's first classes.

Menus for orthodox American-style meals (a starch, a meat dish or two, a vegetable dish or two, a dessert) were the backbone of the book. After a brief guide to ingredients, techniques, and other basics, the recipe section encouragingly began with a chapter on familiar Chinese American restaurant standbys like beef chop suey and egg drop soup. Madame Chu worked hard to provide serviceable versions of some good, simple Chinese dishes (steamed fish, plain rice, stir-fried pork shreds with cellophane noodles) but also heavily emphasized a selection of items that reader-cooks could present as cocktail-party nibbles. In fact, ingredients like hoisin sauce got pressed into service as flavorings for sour cream or cream cheese dips and spreads.

The Pleasures of Chinese Cooking certainly did not represent Madame Chu's own ideas of excellence. The main thing that middle-class white women (less frequently, men) wanted from cooking classes like hers was a collection of conversation-worthy new dishes for entertaining guests, together with advice about menus and stratagems for carrying off a dinner or cocktail party. If her way of providing value for their money involved canned or frozen products such as Scandinavian fish balls and prepackaged biscuit or piecrust doughs, no one was complaining at this stage of the game.

The year 1962 also brought a book as rough-edged and clumsy as *The Pleasures of Chinese Cooking* was smoothly sanded down. *Joyce Chen Cook Book*, meant to exploit the success of Chen's Cambridge restaurant, was an outgrowth of her cooking classes at several Boston-area adult-education centers.[26] Apparently the inexperienced author had approached trade publishers expecting to dictate her own terms about design details, including photographs (then an impractical expense for most cookbooks) and the use of Chinese characters to bolster English recipe titles and names of ingredients. When no one was willing to meet her demands, she produced and published the book herself. Only then did the old Philadelphia-based firm of Lippincott agree to distribute it to bookstores.

Chen's naïve overconfidence undercut her effort in many ways. Unlike Buwei Yang Chao, she had no Harvard lecturers in the family to remedy the obvious deficiencies of her English. Professional editorial guidance and production supervision would have spared the book various printing errors, stylistic infelicities, mysteries like "heavy liquid" or "fine hair of bird," and the all-but-unreadable recipe chart that appeared in lieu of an index.[27]

The recipes cover the usual ground that restaurant-goers of the day expected from places advertised as "Mandarin." Some Cantonese American favorites like egg drop soup, shrimp with lobster sauce, and fu yung shared space with dishes ascribed to Shanghai, Peking, Chungking (Chongqing, the wartime capital in Sichuan), Yangzhou, and Hangzhou. Probably the most attractive selections were several whole fish presentations (red-cooked, steamed, sweet-and-sour) and simple vegetable dishes (choy sum cooked in chicken fat, plain wilted spinach, an appetizer of red-cooked dried shiitake mushrooms). Carefully and perhaps accurately second-guessing her audience's preferences and prejudices, Chen eschewed "messy" things like shrimp cooked and served in the shell. She deferred to medical opinion of the day by rejecting Chinese pork belly dishes as "too fat."[28] But she was no trained market researcher. She seemed unsure whether people would be buying a preplucked chicken or "live killed pullet" for best flavor, but on the other hand expected them to start with frozen birds for Peking duck.[29] Her recipe instructed cooks to rub the duck with a mixture of corn syrup, red food coloring, and "brown gravy syrup" (the "pearl sauce" or "bead molasses" that Cantonese restaurateurs had long used to dye gravies and fried rice to American tastes). She got desperately bogged down in trying to explain a roasting method for the bird involving "the rotisserie on your stove," though most household ranges lacked such a device.[30]

To this day, Peking duck remains a feat very difficult to attempt in American home kitchens, though some writers have since managed to work out semipractical methods. The awkward effort to replicate something essentially unsuited to Joyce Chen fans' resources suggests how tricky it was to supply fashion-conscious cookbook readers with what they thought they wanted. Unfortunately, the ambitious Chen was beyond her depth as manual-writer and recipe-scenarist.

Eight Immortal Flavors: Secrets of Cantonese Cookery by Johnny Kan with Charles L. Leong was certainly the most meaningful contribution of the three books.[31] Published in 1963 by Howell-North Books, a Berkeley-based specialist in California-linked histories, it was the most spirited entry in the field since Doreen Yen Hung Feng's. It was also the first (and remains almost the only) English-language Chinese cookbook tinged with some sense of racial and cultural injustice.

Kan, a veteran San Francisco Chinatown restaurateur, and Leong, a pioneering Bay Area newsman, were both American-born and bilingual from the cradle in Cantonese and English. They and the book's illustrator, Jake Lee, shared a great allegiance to the Cantonese American community—more specifically San Francisco Chinatown, the oldest of America's big-city Chinatowns, and then as now the one most deeply rooted in Gold Mountain history. A few years earlier, Lee had contributed a dozen water-color paintings to the Gum Shan or "Gold Mountain" Room of Kan's Grant Avenue restaurant, chronicling Chinese life on Gold Mountain from climbing off the boat to building railroads, tending Sonoma County vineyards, and preparing whole pigs for roasting in big cylindrical brick ovens in a former Chinatown close to the gold mining town of Nevada City, California.[32] The Gum Shan Room paintings reflected both a deeply Chinese homage to forebears and an American immigrant patriotism that was not only forthright but defiant. The cookbook partook of the same spirit.

To celebrate America's Cantonese-descended culinary traditions certainly was not chic in 1963. By now, white cognoscenti unable to read Chinese or speak any form of it confidently belittled Chinatown restaurant fare as the coarse fodder of people who—unlike themselves—didn't know real Chinese food. The scene appeared bleak in other ways for descendants of Pearl River Delta pioneers. The economic underpinnings of San Francisco Chinatown and counterparts elsewhere were rapidly crumbling. Young American-born Cantonese Californians, though better assured of the benefits of citizenship than "paper son" grandparents and sometimes parents had been in the Exclusion era, found those benefits appallingly curtailed by what amounted to latter-day exclusion under the blind, unacknowledged racism of the larger society.

It was either the best or the worst of times for three Cantonese-speaking sons of San Francisco Chinatown to explore a cuisine that, as James Beard's foreword pointed out, "antedates the French." As a child, Kan had occasionally visited Portland cousins who were playmates of Beard's. The two had remained friends, and Beard regarded Kan's celebrated establishment as "the outstanding Chinese restaurant today."[33]

The authors sailed in ebulliently, assuming some brains and enterprise on the part of users. They disdained the sops to timid palates or supposed nutritional authority offered by other writers addressing non-Chinese home cooks. It is true that Kan's food used many stratagems widely deplored today. Monosodium glutamate was an almost ubiquitous seasoning, and the sweet-and-sour sauces (like those in most Cantonese American restaurants) relied heavily on tomato catsup. Nonetheless, some kind of intellectual curiosity, proud culinary ethos, and social conscience spoke from these pages.

Kan made woks (with support rings) sound like "the most practical cooking utensil ever invented by man," not near kin to flying saucers.[34] He took it for granted that non-Chinese could easily learn to appreciate the unique flavor of, say, thousand-year eggs. He expected people to cook with fermented bean curd, salt fish, shrimp paste, dried scallops or squid, bean milk skin, different kinds of preserved vegetables, and other ingredients that Joyce Chen had hesitated to use and Madame Chu had introduced with some circumspection.

The authors offset their romantic images of Chinese cuisine as the rarefied delight of one-time emperors by noting that in the same imperial China, "a simple yet tasty meal of noodles and greens cooked with a pinch of salt and oil" was the daily fare of "a peasant and his family."[35] They tried to convey how certain basic flavors, of which Kan chose eight, form a structural underpinning of all Chinese dishes. As they explained, this holds true whether the menu is "village style" (i.e., simple and modest), "dinner style," or "banquet style."[36] They were as enlightening as the Chaos on the technique of stir-frying—a term that Kan disdained, persuasively arguing for "toss-cooking" as a more graphic translation that helped you see the wok as "a large, *hot* salad bowl, blending ingredients over intense heat."[37]

The roughly 150 recipes, written in a format adapted from *The Joy of Cooking*, were mostly but not exclusively Cantonese in focus; Kan and Leung pointedly noted that "there is no such thing as 'Mandarin food.'"[38] Their directions weren't always polished or exact by professional food editors' standards, but they conveyed what was important about cooking processes. Realists about what home cooks should or shouldn't attempt, they were content with a rhapsodical description of Peking duck "whereby we hope you will understand our reasons for 'no recipe.'"[39] On the other hand, they didn't hesitate to include scenarios for dishes involving time and dedication rather than far-fetched resources. Among the most appealing were a fire pot meal ("Winter Chafing Dish") and "Yee Sang," the same celebratory raw fish dinner that had received a far less intelligible presentation in 1917 by Shiu Wong Chan (see chapter 5).[40]

Even though the excellent guide to major ingredients contained only meager snippets of bilingual information identifying a few plants or seasonings by line drawings matched to Chinese characters and English names, *Eight Immortal Flavors* was and is one of the most treasurable documents of Chinese American cooking. It went through a dozen printings in as many years, and in fact was posthumously reissued by the Kan estate in 1982.[41] More than fifty years later, no latter-day Kans and Leongs have appeared to follow up their tribute to Cantonese American food, though Eileen Yin-Fei Lo has championed the cooking of Guangdong Province in several valuable books, and Ken Hom has commented on the split-personality cooking of Cantonese American restaurants addressing insider and outsider clienteles in *Easy Family Recipes from a Chinese-American Childhood*.[42]

Popular interest in Chinese cooking continued to grow throughout the 1960s. Informed standards did not always keep pace. In 1966 Atheneum Books—enthusiastically equating size with importance—entered the field with a wildly uneven nine-hundred-page effort by Gloria Bley Miller, priced at a then-formidable $20 and titled *The Thousand Recipe Chinese Cookbook*.[43] Miller, who seems to have known no Chinese, had indiscriminately bundled together staggering amounts of information, misinformation, and recipes. Many of the latter had been picked up—without attribution—from Buwei Yang Chao, Doreen Yen Hung Feng, and other writers. Simply by the law of averages, hopeful cooks could usually find some recipes that they liked and ignore what they didn't. The huge anthology of treasures and junk sold well for years.

An entirely more distinguished contribution—another instance of adventurous thinking taking place at a remove from the American trade publishing mainstream—was *Chinese Gastronomy* (1969) produced and copyrighted by the British-American firm of Thomas M. Nelson.[44] Printed in Great Britain and distributed by Hastings House in the United States, it bespeaks a very large production budget for elegant page design and abundant uncredited artwork (lovely, subtle pen-and-ink drawings as well as color-plate sections with photographs of food-related art objects from museums in London and Taipei). The text was by Hsiangju Lin and Tsuifeng Lin, who had made a complete turnaround from the approach of their earlier books.

The Lins were interested less in leading Westerners through cooking scripts than in making them grasp what was unique about the Chinese culinary esthetic. In thoughtfully meandering essays, they introduced and sought to define much of the crucial terminology, for which they supplied Chinese characters. They were the first English-language authors to linger analytically over older Chinese culinary treatises and muse about important national cooking practices in historical context. Their emphasis on rarefied nuances made most competing works look corn-fed. They could be given to pretentious vocabulary, odd lapses of taste like the use of canned consommé in the extremely delicate

Chinese version of simple poached chicken, and haughty dismissals of what rubbed against their subjective prejudices.[45] (As birthright Fujianese cooks, they announced that Cantonese cooks' "handling of flavour lacked the depth which comes from much thought on gastronomy."[46]) And the publisher had provided almost no navigational aids—not even an index—to their intricately organized text. But among English-language Chinese cookbooks of the twentieth century, *Chinese Gastronomy* still stands out for an unexampled quality of mental stimulation. It was a book to be lived with and thought about, not casually mined for dinner party triumphs.

FROM IDEA TO PAGE: THE COOKBOOK DESIGN REVOLUTION

By now the world of American cookbook publishing was beginning to split into many differentiated market niches while editorial experimenters weighed the entire question of how to convey information most clearly to the people they envisioned as buyers.

At the high end of the spectrum, the 1962 success of Alfred A. Knopf and the editor Judith Jones with *Mastering the Art of French Cooking* by Simone Beck, Louisette Bertholle, and Julia Child had started many other editors examining some of its novel features. What was most revolutionary about the actual, physical book was not the recipes per se but the visual experience of using them. The Knopf production team had turned every aspect of page design, recipe format, and illustrations into elaborately marked coordinates for start-to-finish travel maps of all dishes. Different elements (e.g., lists of ingredients or headings to serve as signposts where a new stage of preparation began) were assigned different typographical cues such as boldface or lightface roman or italic type in various point sizes, within a scheme more complex and detailed than anything yet attempted in a cookbook. This was why the recipe for cassoulet occupied six, and boneless stuffed duck seven, roomy pages with leisurely vistas of white space.

Mastering the Art heralded much general rethinking of recipe format and page design. No branch of cooking stood to benefit more from such efforts than Chinese cuisine. As cannot be stressed too often, something transcending words is called for in conveying its processes to Western understanding.

By the mid-1960s, the big trade cookbook editors and publishers had followed the *Mastering the Art* example far enough to try several departures from older recipe formats. The usual strategies involved the use of double columns (ingredients lined up on one side of a page, procedures forming a running sequence on the other side), with some boldface/lightface, roman/italic cues introduced to help a reader's eye interpret what it was seeing on the page of an English-language French, Moroccan, Mexican, or perhaps international-gourmet cookbook. Another means of bypassing the limits of verbal instruction was just becoming practical for U.S. publishers with the advent of more affordable color photography and photographic reproduction toward the end of the 1960s.

MAKING ESSENTIALS VISIBLE

Strangely enough, the first serious cookbook breakthrough in the visual presentation of Chinese cooking for Americans came from a source now often regarded as the embodiment of slick, soulless mass-market publishing: the Time-Life "Foods of the World" cookbook series launched in 1968. All entries were large-format volumes heavily illustrated with photographs, mostly in color and mostly shot by *Life* magazine staff photojournalists. Small auxiliary spiral-bound recipe booklets contained all the recipes for each book, though a sizable selection also appeared in the larger volumes.

The fact that *The Cooking of China* was chosen as one of the inaugural 1968 offerings in the ambitious series shows the rising repute of Chinese cuisine among mainstream food authorities. (It may also have owed something to Henry Luce's ties with the Nationalist regime on Taiwan as well as his influence in the China Institute at its China House headquarters.) The marketing apparatus of Time-Life (the book division of Time, Inc.) guaranteed it wider nationwide sales than any prior Chinese cookbook. Luckily the result justified this unprecedented exposure.

The twenty-seven-book series was bankrolled by a vast American-as-Velveeta corporate machine. Every volume was to a greater or lesser extent a horse designed by a committee, presenting something like the elaborate intertwining of verbal and visual values in a *Life* magazine photoessay with the further complication of recipes. These elements could compete awkwardly for the title of forequarters, midsection, or hindquarters. But in the best books—like this—they were united with some success.

The principal text had been assigned to Emily Hahn, a clever and seasoned observer who had been one of the most prominent American journalists in China from the turbulent late 1930s through World War II. A team of Time-Life researchers and editors had collected a great range of materials for her to work with and imposed an overall organization. The result was the first English-language attempt to survey Chinese cuisine as a reflection of the larger civilization in the light of history and geography. In a set of provocative, wide-ranging essays, Hahn and the Time-Life apparatchiks steered adroitly from one aspect to another of Chinese food by way of strategic anecdotes. T. T. Wang (of the Shun Lee empire), recalled how as a teenaged apprentice at a Shanghai restaurant he was eventually promoted from no salary to one bag of rice a month.[47] Hahn noted the instant reappearance of *xiang banfa* survival instincts in wartime Hong Kong when the Japanese occupation swept away British ordinances about properly kept streets:

> Then the old regulations were void. Famine threatened, and literally overnight the city was transformed. Every Chinese who could lay claim to a scrap of ground, even if it was no larger than a handkerchief, began to cultivate it. . . . Bankers, lawyers, doctors and art dealers were all in it together. Soon crops were growing on every hand, and chickens roamed the streets.[48]

The basic culinary information came chiefly from Florence Lin; Grace Zia Chu was also a consultant. American signs of the times are evident in the comments on rice cookers (which had taken off in Japan in the late 1950s), several mentions of dim sum with a handsome photograph showing eight varieties, and cautions about going easy on monosodium glutamate.[49]

Like other books in the series, *The Cooking of China* owed much to a large Time-Life test kitchen set up for recipe-developing. This was done under Lin's direction with the aid of Madame Chu and the series's consulting editor, the influential cooking-school teacher and writer Michael

Field. Presumably Lin and Madame Chu had made most of the decisions about what dishes and information to include.

The roughly 110 recipes strike a reasonable balance among selections with proven Western appeal (shrimp toast, sweet-and-sour pork, a somewhat simplified home-oven version of Peking duck) and ones that more adventurous non-Chinese eaters were now enjoying in regional restaurants (five-spice beef, steamed Chinese breads, Sichuan-style steamed and deep-fried duck). Field had done or supervised the actual recipe writing. He was known for obsessively dotting and crossing all possible i's and t's—no small task in a job that presupposed much head-banging among Lin, Madame Chu, and a crew of non-Chinese testers steeped in American culinary assumptions. The amount of numerical detail crammed into the recipes can seem cumbrous but was meant for extra insurance: "Set a 12-inch wok or 8-inch skillet over high heat for 30 seconds. Pour in 1 tablespoon of oil, swirl it about in the pan and heat for another 30 seconds, turning the heat down if the oil begins to smoke. Add the shrimp and stir-fry for 1 minute, or until they are firm and light pink."[50]

Considering how new this terrain was to the Foods of the World editors and testers, the recipes are surprisingly un–watered down de-spite occasional compromises like a liquid smoke marinade for "smoked eggs" instead of real smoking, or Tabasco sauce replacing dried chile peppers in a cold cucumber dish. The information on equipment, ingre-dients, and techniques is as useful as that in the book's 1960s competi-tors, and is strengthened by the inclusion of Chinese characters. Recipe titles are given in Chinese, Wade-Giles romanizations, and English translations.

But the real leap forward was in the deployment of visual informa-tion. Only the Foods of the World publishing and marketing resources, including the parent company's experience with photographic repro-duction, could have gotten large, heavily pictorial books printed on coated stock ready to distribute to mail-order series subscribers (and a few large bookstores) at anything but exorbitant prices. At the time, trade publishers simply could not compete.

Most of the photographs were by Michael Rougier, a *Life* staffer. Since the Chinese mainland was largely off-limits to Westerners, the location shots of dinner gatherings, markets, fishing grounds, food stalls, and so forth that crucially figured in all Foods of the World books had had to be rethought. Perhaps this difficulty had encouraged the book's strong reliance on wonderful historical images from museum collections, showing food-related scenes in woodcuts or silk-screen paintings. (For the same reason, Hahn's descriptions of Chinese culinary culture depended heavily on her prewar and wartime memories of Shanghai and Hong Kong.) The location shooting had almost all been done in Hong Kong and Taiwan; a few pictures taken in the PRC by a Swedish photographer eked out the asymmetrical coverage.

But the images that really pointed the way to the future had been shot in the test kitchen and studios at Foods of the World headquarters. Taking important cues from the work being done at *Gourmet* and some of the women's "service" magazines, the art teams for all volumes focused heavily on studio photographs of finished dishes with suitable props and instructional sequences, sometimes buttressed by diagrams or line drawings. In some books of the series, the food photography was not particularly eye-opening. But because Chinese culinary concepts require so much nonverbal "translating," even today *The Cooking of China* has some concrete advantages as a learning tool over many later English-language competitors.

As is often the case, the studio images of theoretically tempting dishes were the least convincing part of the whole. But the instructional shots (both color and black and white) demonstrated a grasp of both what couldn't be conveyed by words alone and how to bring it to life through step-by-step photographs—for instance, wrapping different kinds of wontons and dumplings, or using a cleaver to cut carrots or beef into particular shapes or to reduce chicken breast to a near-puree. No one had previously used such means to address the terrible problems of communicating Chinese culinary notions and skills to Westerners. Apparently Lin and Madame Chu had managed to give Rougier and the art directors, Field and the other editors, and the American test kitchen cooks enough insight into the fundamentals of cutting, dicing, stir-frying, and the crucial principles of the cuisine to inspire them to particularly apt efforts.

The next headline-making contribution to the field was *The Chinese Cookbook* by Craig Claiborne and Virginia Lee. A sizable collection with about 240 recipes drawn from different facets of Chinese cuisine, it appeared a few months after Nixon's 1972 trip to China had electrified the American public. Since the book had been in the works for a while, this coincidence couldn't have been foreseen. But the timing was providential. No name was more luminously visible to fashion-conscious cooks and diners than that of Claiborne. No Chinese cookbook of the postwar era attracted more eager attention or more widespread praise. Nonetheless, it was not an especially well-executed piece of work.

Considering the formidable dimensions of the subject and the fact that one of the authors knew no Chinese, the work had been banged out in record time. Claiborne was already frequenting many of the newer Manhattan Chinese restaurants and had visited a number of Chinese cooking schools. But by his own account he had never thought of seriously "cooking Chinese" until he met Lee in the fall of 1970 and signed up for her cooking classes, initiating the "two-year involvement with Chinese cooking" that produced the book.[51] The actual time he and Lee spent working on the manuscript was more like a year and a half, during which Claiborne was also fulfilling his usual food columnist's duties at the *New York Times*.

A year and a half is an improbably short time for a novice—even one without another full-time job—to not only master the major concepts of Chinese cooking and acquire real technical proficiency but also collaborate on testing and writing up more than two hundred recipes. *The Chinese Cookbook* certainly was not a resource to go to for a thoughtfully planned education in Chinese culinary whys and wherefores. It conveys the impression not of considered planning but of an attempt to get as many formulas onto the page as quickly as possible. The publisher, Lippincott, doesn't seem to have worried greatly about fact-checking (at one point, hoisin sauce is described as being made from pumpkin).[52]

Claiborne and Lee cooked everything together in the kitchen of his Long Island home, with Claiborne tracking measurements and timings and pounding out recipes on his typewriter. But it is not clear how they arrived at some joint culinary and editorial decisions.

By comparison with the Time-Life effort, the authors gave short shrift to the various Chinese cooking methods. They discussed the crucial hand-cutting techniques only briefly and relied more heavily on blender-pureed mixtures than any predecessor. They gave no reason for choices like using crushed cornflakes as a binder in "Lion's Head" meatballs; they finessed the question of using or forgoing monosodium glutamate (already the subject of much debate) by making it optional in dozens of recipes without bothering to discuss the issue.[53]

Judged simply as a recipe anthology, the book offered some pleasures. Many of Claiborne and Lee's recipes were attractive, straightforward choices like "turnip cake" (a well-known dim sum specialty made from daikon radish), cold spiced eggplant, chicken congee, and Mongolian barbecue. But their sloppiness about basic principles and procedures was amazing. Their recipes routinely called for heating oil in a wok, neglecting to explain the correct procedure of first getting the wok very hot. (The preheated surface keeps food from sticking.) And no well-schooled Chinese cook would have unceremoniously thrown two pounds of sliced meat at once into a home-sized wok as required for one of their Sichuan-style stir-fry beef dishes; that amount of meat will limply stew in its own juice instead of cooking with proper *chao* bravura and intensity.[54]

The Claiborne-Lee *Chinese Cookbook* was neither the best nor the worst in a swiftly burgeoning field. Certainly it was rushed into print with very poor preparation. Its real importance was not its quality but the fact that at the height of his fame, the most prestigious American tastemaker of the time had decided to undertake such a project. Whatever the book's failings, the Claiborne name helped decisively establish Chinese cuisine as part of the ongoing gourmet revolution in the eyes of white American reader-cooks. Coming as it did during the publicity fallout from Nixon's mission to China, the work was luckily positioned to send many non-Chinese cooks to bookstores, Chinatown food shops, and kitchen stoves.

An entirely more enlightening window on Chinese food and civilization appeared a couple of years later: *The Mandarin Way* (1974) by Cecilia Chiang (or, as she proudly styled herself on the title page, Cecilia Sun Yun Chiang) with Allan Carr, the collaborator to whom she had dictated many decades' worth of reminiscences. It was a foretaste of a genre that still didn't exist: the food-centered memoir sprinkled with recipes. Between them, Chiang and Carr had managed to impose a semblance of order on a heterogeneous heap of memories and about sixty recipes. A determined user could have extracted valuable information about food by ransacking different corners of the work, but it really hadn't been designed as a cooking manual. It was a brilliant reconstruction of a small, leisured, privileged cosmos as viewed by the young Sun Yun from her family's palace complex in 1920s and 1930s Beijing. Using the changing phases of the lunar year as framing device, the fiftyish Chiang uncannily evoked the whole tone and texture of a strongly woven, apparently inviolable life made possible by phalanxes of servants—or, as she acknowledged, quasi-slaves.

She recalled family cats and dogs greeting spring sunshine on verandas and courtyard stones; trains of laden camels reaching the city from the Gobi Desert in early mornings; the methodical folding of last season's clothes in preparation for the next season; servants beating trees to bring down the chestnuts for special harvest-moon festival dishes; the restaurant master chef hired to put on an elaborate family banquet at home lugging in cookstoves "like large oil drums, thickly lined with mud, for fear the ones he found on arrival would not produce the heat he needed." Such exquisitely etched detail made it all the clearer that she was chronicling a way of life lost beyond all restoring: "The last ten years have completed its destruction."[55] The freshness and contemplative clarity of this wonderfully told life story form a stark contrast with the undigested prattle that now fills most food memoirs.

In the wake of Virginia Lee's collaboration with Claiborne, cooking-school teachers got a stronger foothold in cookbook publishing. Grace Zia Chu's second work, *Madame Chu's Chinese Cooking School*, appeared in 1975.[56] Like the Lins, she was now ready to tackle the enterprise in a bolder spirit. She called for a more adventurous range of ingredients as being both important and available (e.g., amaranth, dried jellyfish, bitter melon, preserved duck). Chinese characters supplemented English names throughout. The scope of recipes had been greatly enlarged since the first book; in the intervening thirteen years, Madame Chu's students clearly had come to welcome dishes like Wu Sih- (Wuxi-) style spareribs or soup with hog's maw, tree ears, and dried bean curd.[57] A chapter with a dozen recipes developed by students suggested how quickly non-Chinese participants in cooking classes were finding their own wings as teachers and caterers.

The year 1975 also saw the first cookbook by Florence Lin. Now the head instructor at the China Institute, she had been working for some years with the institute's perennial student and well-wisher Margaret Spader on what Claiborne, in a *New York Times* article in 1969, called "a definitive book on Chinese cooking."[58] For unknown reasons, the work never appeared. Instead, Lin on her own began a series of books about specialized aspects of Chinese cuisine, starting with *Florence Lin's Chinese Regional Cookbook.*[59] The title itself points to the power of her name as a fixture in the New York gastronomic pantheon. Hawthorn Books, her publisher at the time, quickly followed up with *Florence Lin's Vegetarian Chinese Cookbook* (1976), *Florence Lin's Chinese One-Dish Meals* (1978), and *Florence Lin's Cooking with Fire Pots* (1979).[60]

All these works were notable pioneers in the field. Lin's was the first Chinese vegetarian cookbook, opportunely addressing a market that had been bolstered by growing numbers of sometime or fully committed vegetarians. *Cooking with Fire Pots* was a clever Chinese-themed addition to the ranks of specialty-appliance manuals. The one-dish meals book was well matched to a certain reaction setting in against extravagant chef-d'oeuvres—whether French, Russian, or Chinese—that might leave a cook contemplating more dirty saucepans than there were windows in the house. But the regional cookbook remains the most important of the four. It was the first English-language work to take on a daunting but long-overdue mapping job.

Since the implementation of the Hart-Celler Act in 1968, mainland-born Chinese nationals arriving in American Chinatowns via Taiwan or Hong Kong had started clustering in communities of fellow provincials, or speakers of particular languages, from various corners of China. Unlike the confident newcomers streaming from Taiwan to destinations like the San Gabriel Valley, they were seldom primed for success in the affluent new ethnoburbs. At least in the short term, they could not hope for lucrative professional positions.

These newcomers represented only a tiny foreshadowing of the deluge to come after the liberalization of Chinese emigration policy in the 1980s. But restaurants owned by and aimed at them multiplied quickly enough to draw notice beyond the Chinese community. Unlike the more upscale "Szechuan" or "Mandarin" establishments frequented by white urban sophisticates in desirable neighborhoods, they were often staffed by brusque waiters who spoke no English, and perhaps neither Cantonese nor Mandarin. English menus, if any, might omit the best dishes. Other Chinese might be strangers to the "new" (or newly arrived) cuisines, though, unlike white patrons, they usually had at least a general idea of their place in the larger Chinese culinary geography.

American restaurant reviewers like Greene and Sokolov were hampered by the lack of any English-language guidance to that overall geography. Within China itself, pundits had never unanimously agreed on one fixed scheme of classification. The task was less like categorizing the regional cuisines of France or Italy than imposing some shape on the food of all Western Europe, both within and across language groupings and national boundaries. Besides, factors like Southeast Asian borrowings and the roles of the Yangzi River and the Grand Canal in linking western and eastern, northern and southern kitchens made classifications especially slippery.

Lin did not try to explore every corner of a very complex map. Like most Chinese writers, she grouped the regional cuisines into the four broad categories of north (Beijing, along with Shandong, Hebei, and Henan Provinces), east (Jiangsu and Zhejiang Provinces, embracing the Jiangnan cities of Shanghai, Suzhou, Yangzhou, Hangzhou, and her native Ningbo as well as the hard-to-pigeonhole Fujian Province), south (Guangdong Province), and west (Sichuan and Hunan Provinces). She followed conventional Chinese gastronomic classifiers in mostly ignoring the far northwestern and northeastern provinces, which until some years later would remain as outlandish to the standard authorities as Britain might have seemed to a second-century Roman epicure. (In any case, very few immigrants from these regions had trickled into the United States by 1975.)

Introductory charts in each recipe chapter indicating the origin of individual dishes allowed users to get at least some idea of regional characteristics. For instance, one could compare Cantonese rice congee with the archaic but still-beloved millet congee of the north (a tradition predating the Chinese adoption of rice). Four different noodle dishes showed off the contrasting styles of Guangdong (roast pork lo mein), Fujian (rice noodles from the city of Amoy [Xiamen], Beijing (*zha jiang mian*, or noodles with fried meat sauce), and either Shanghai or Sichuan (represented by cold noodle salad with either a simple soy-vinegar or a spicy peanut-sesame dressing). Dishes like drunken crab, Yunnan-style steamed chicken, fish maw soup, braised spareribs with black beans, or fried fish fillets wrapped in soybean-milk skin could be seen in regional context.

Since the publication of this work, non-Chinese lovers of Chinese food have gotten more accustomed to weighing the vast influence of regional cultures and geographical factors on the many schools of Chinese cuisine. But in the last forty years only a few cookbooks tracing remote or little-known Chinese culinary byways have opened up any frontiers not touched on in Lin's book; it is still the single best collection of regional dishes.

MORE WAYS TO CONVEY MORE INSIGHTS

By the time of Florence Lin's introductions to Chinese regional and vegetarian cuisine, American cookbooks in general were some years into the exploratory design vogue mentioned earlier, inaugurated by *Mastering the Art of French Cooking.* Recipes in prestigious books were getting longer, fed by a wishful supposition that piling on verbal detail made them more foolproof. Few publishers had failed to conclude that at least some discreet juggling of the formerly standard ingredients list / cooking directions sequence could more clearly focus a user's eye and brain on the dovetailing bits of a logical process.

As yet, images were not a dominant teaching element; where they existed, they were usually line drawings, which still tended to be clearer, more informative, and usually more attractive than photographs. (The latter were also beyond most budgets.) Few editors cared to emulate the exorbitant use of page space in *Mastering the Art*, but almost everybody picked up on some of its innovations in design and recipe format. The Time-Life book designers introduced a fairly compact double-column recipe format for dishes in the photographic volumes, with unobtrusive typographical cues like subheadings in small capitals marking off stages of the process (PREPARE AHEAD; TO COOK).

Chinese recipes, which needed all the help they could get, benefited from selective use of such devices. At Hawthorn, Florence Lin and her editor, Elizabeth Backman, used a few simple and soon-to-be-standard touches like italicized headings to break the work into stages (*Preparation, Cooking the Filling, Wrapping and Filling*) for the regional and vegetarian books. In 1974 the Japanese publisher Kodansha, now making inroads on the mainstream U.S. market, achieved a subtle, graceful double-column and numbered-step recipe presentation with directions separated into "To Prepare" and "To Cook" stages for the first serious English-language exploration of Sichuanese cuisine, *The Good Food of Szechwan* by Robert A. Delfs.[61] This was a slim but far from superficial volume with some intelligent attention to cooking and preparation basics and a pleasant selection of recipes that actually drew on several regional cuisines.

Two years later at Harper & Row, another Sichuanese cookbook overseen by the innovative editor Frances McCullough used a lengthier double-column format in which the right-hand column spelled out the directions at length (also marking them off into "Preparation" and "Cooking" stages) while the list of ingredients inched along in step, a few at a time, in the left-hand column.[62]

Both of the Sichuanese books had arisen from American graduate students' gastronomic adventures on Taiwan. Delfs, who had begun by studying Mandarin at Stanford, had later become fascinated by the many excellent Sichuan restaurants on the island and enrolled in cooking classes at the Wei-Chuan school.[63] The Harper & Row contribution, *Mrs. Chiang's Szechwan Cookbook*, had a more tangled parentage. Ellen Schrecker had written the text with the help of her husband, John. It recorded the actual cooking of the Sichuan-born Chiang Jung-feng, whom the couple had hired as cook-housekeeper in 1969 when John Schrecker's study of Chinese brought them and their two young children to Taiwan.[64] Mrs. Chiang and Ellen Schrecker shared the copyright.

The Schreckers had previously lived and studied on Taiwan long enough to realize just how disappointing the usual run of Chinese American restaurant fare was. During their next stay, Mrs. Chiang's cooking not only revived their memories of Chinese food in its glory but inspired them to suggest that she come with them when John Schrecker returned to study at Princeton. The bunch of Princeton graduate students who swapped Chinese cooking lore and investigated promising restaurants during the 1970s included the Schreckers, Delfs, and a young woman named Barbara Tropp, who shortly followed in their Taiwanese footsteps.

People like Delfs and the Schreckers could never have written cookbooks before the world of Taiwan-style academe had opened up to American scholars. The role of insider-outsider observer—the most invaluable qualification for literally and figuratively translating Chinese cuisine to Westerners—had previously been reserved for Chinese-born culinary interpreters and a few American-born Chinese. The two Sichuanese books pointed to a new state of international exchange in which young Americans could directly immerse themselves in many aspects of Chinese life, including its cuisine, rather than picking up information at a remove through supposed authorities. A one-way street was becoming a two-way street littered with fewer educational roadblocks than in the past.

Mrs. Chiang's Szechwan Cookbook exemplified the new possibilities of exchange. Ellen Schrecker's attempts to learn what Mrs. Chiang could teach her about Chinese cooking seven thousand miles from China had been the seed of the book. Since the two women had no common language, John Schrecker had been (as his wife wrote) "our translator, goad, and guide."[65] At Harper & Row, McCullough had understood the threesome's goal of bringing truly relevant information into focus while communicating the spirit behind the details. As a bicultural collaboration, the book was everything that the Claiborne-Lee *Chinese Cookbook* was not. Chiang Jung-feng did not aspire to sudden glory in New York gastronomic circles. Nor was Ellen Schrecker a culinary superstar seeking to dazzle such circles by a dramatic debut in a new repertoire. The aim of the participants was to *get things right*, not to squeeze every possible recipe between endpapers.

A still richer example of an advancing East–West reciprocity in the culinary teaching-learning process was *The Key to Chinese Cooking* by Irene Kuo, published by Knopf in 1978. To this day it is often considered the best of all English-language Chinese cookbooks.[66] Kuo, a Shanghai-born Barnard College graduate with a fine command of English, owned two successful Manhattan restaurants. Her proposal for a general Chinese cookbook reached the desk of Judith Jones, the era's reigning cookbook editor, at around 1971.

Jones had a history of putting together team efforts demanding the utmost from everybody. She was famed for extremely personal, intuition-driven notions of what constituted promise in a writer or a project, refusal to accept anything that didn't chime with her instincts, and stubborn resolve in achieving the result she wanted, no matter how long it took. As she later wrote, she was struck by Kuo's flair for "explosively vivid language" that conjured up the flashing physical energy of Chinese hands and reflexes at work in the kitchen.[67] But she did not expect instant results. The book that came into being more than six years later depended on many complexly meshing contributions, made to look spontaneous and effortless.

The page design was a triumph of subtlety and apparent simplicity. For the recipe format, the Knopf design team had hit on something akin to the Wei-Chuan books' use of brackets (though more graceful-looking and without the number system) that helped lucidly sort out different structural elements. For the names of dishes printed in Chinese characters next to the English recipe titles, someone had found a Chinese typeface beautifully matching the Palatino face of the text. Jones, who would be known for her loyalty to the art of illustration long into the color photography era, had hired the illustrator Carolyn Moy to create a wealth of pen-and-ink drawings that combined extreme delicacy with the sense of purposeful motion.

The actual contents represented a great investment of time and thought. Jones had foreseen that in this case an adequate insider-outsider perspective would require close, prolonged interchange between Kuo and a sounding board. She had recruited Suzi Arensberg, a former Knopf copy editor who had just set up as a freelancer. Arensberg thoroughly understood the nuts and bolts of clear, effective recipe writing but had no special knowledge of Chinese cooking. Her invaluable contribution was a willingness to enter into Kuo's thinking as much as any non-Chinese cook could while keeping a clear eye fixed on what was or wasn't being convincingly communicated.

The manuscript that emerged from this partnership was anything but a rush job. For three and a half years Kuo and Arensberg met every week to discuss and polish pieces of chapters in progress. When they thought they had finished, Jones went through the manuscript and announced that it didn't have the right organization for guiding American cooks from basic culinary concepts to execution. Kuo and Arensberg had to spend another strenuous year and a half taking apart the book and putting it together again in a more shapely manner.[68] The solidity and integrated quality of the final work justify the years spent on fitting everything into its proper place.

The selection of dishes is large (about three hundred recipes) and intelligently planned to include both the obvious and the recherché, the classic and the playful, as well as a range of specialties from every region of China. Kuo is eager to convey what's needed to physically engage with the ingredients:

> Holding a pair of chopsticks as a whisk or using a wooden spoon, stir the shrimp rapidly in a circular, whipping fashion for 1 minute so that all the shrimp skid, bounce, and turn against the side of the bowl.[69]

> Add the noodles and immediately slide a spatula from the side of the pan beneath the noodles, meat, and vegetables. Scoop them up in the air, shake, and shower them back into the pan; repeat these fast sweeping motions in rapid-fire succession from all directions for 3 minutes, until the noodles are heated through, evenly tinted by the sauce, and well mingled with the meat and vegetables.[70]

She loves bringing out the possibilities of humble ingredients (sweet-and-sour cucumber skins, fried chicken gizzards) and singing the praises of regional specialties such as the spaetzle-like Northern-style "dough knots" made by shaving off with a knife blade bits of a soft "marshmallowish dough" into boiling water.[71] But probably the major triumph of the book is a preliminary section that she and Arensberg quarried out of the main recipe chapters at Judith Jones's behest.

This nearly one-hundred-page section is virtually a mini-cookbook in itself. In four chapters on major techniques, the section outlines the principles of four broad categories. They are cooking in liquid (various forms of poaching, simmering, red-cooking, and "flavor-potting"—this last meaning *lu*, or cooking in a richly aromatic "master sauce"), cooking in oil (i.e., stir-frying, shallow-frying, deep-frying), wet-heat cooking (i.e., steaming), and dry-heat cooking (Chinese methods of roasting, smoking, and "barbecuing"). Each important method is accompanied by painstaking notes on general rules and illustrated by at least one "master recipe" that can serve as a procedural guide for tackling any dish from the remaining more conventionally organized subsequent recipe chapters. The patiently and intricately arranged opening chapters lift the book above any predecessor, and most successors, as a one-volume composite of conceptual immersion-course, practical guide, and plentiful recipe anthology.

THE WOK AS LIFESTYLE STATEMENT

If *The Key to Chinese Cooking* marked Chinese cuisine's now-unquestioned stature among affluent U.S. tastemakers at the close of the non-recognition epoch, equal triumphs were being registered among a very different demography. Just at this time, American students and idealistic counterculturalists were wandering to far corners of the globe either with the aid of backpack and sandals or via the kitchen stove. Many were eager to investigate non-Western or non-Eurocentric cuisines that by their lights embodied age-old wisdom, or at least an antidote to modern American food hucksterism.

Some of these young seekers aimed to cook their way through works like Diana Kennedy's *The Cuisines of Mexico* (1972), Madhur Jaffrey's *An Invitation to Indian Cooking* (1973), and Paula Wolfert's *Couscous and Other Good Food from Morocco* (1973) as devotedly as an earlier class of upscale fashion-followers had cooked their way through *Mastering the Art of French Cooking* or Claiborne's *New York Times Cookbook* in the 1960s. Book publishers now recognized fans of "exotic" third-world cuisines as a promising market segment, picking up on clues like the new success of wok manufacturers.

For the young, adventurous, and unmoneyed, lathe-spun sheet-steel woks exactly like those used in thousands of Chinese American households were an ideal cooking vessel. A wok cost a fraction of what a Julia Child disciple might spend on even one mid-sized enameled cast iron or tinned copper saucepan and was said (by fans) to be the only pan you'd ever need. Even if the truth turned out to be a little less simple, a wok made a fine lifestyle statement.

Non-Chinese cooking experts began praising woks in the late 1960s. The 1975 *Joy of Cooking* edition mentioned them, in a newly added description of stir-frying, as a common addition to the "Christmas wish list" of a typical American housewife.[72] Two San Francisco manufacturers, the Atlas Metal Spinning Company and Taylor & Ng, were the leading U.S. suppliers. By 1980 the *Chicago Tribune* food section could report, in a major feature about the pan's new stardom, that Taylor & Ng had sold more than a million since 1968.[73] Taylor & Ng were especially clever marketers. They distributed woks to department stores and cookware shops throughout the country, often as part of boxed gift sets including support rings and such other accessories as a domed lid, a Chinese wok spatula and ladle, and a wooden rice paddle.

The 1980 *Tribune* lead article noted that flat-bottomed models were available. These represented a reasonable compromise between traditional bowl-shaped woks and the kind of surface that best distributed heat on American stove burners. (As *The Joy of Cooking* noted, Chinese American cooks often preferred Western skillets.) It is not clear who first came up with a successful design. Though Joyce Chen is often credited with having introduced flat-bottomed woks, the shape of the one for which she received a patent in 1971 is conspicuously un-woklike, quite unrelated to the wider, less steeply angled pans that rapidly became the most popular alternative to round-bottomed woks.[74] In the true American spirit, various manufacturers began adding other supposed improvements that did nothing but ruin woks for heavy-duty use. Stainless steel and nonstick woks were successfully palmed off on cooks who knew no better; electric woks with self-regulating—in effect, self-defeating—thermostats racked up impressive sales.

From the start of the 1970s, the free-spirited younger wing of the cooking public happily took to its own ideas of wok cooking, with or without any grounding in Chinese technique. Stir-frying or something that went by that name was a favorite method of post-hippies dedicated to simple one-dish meals, though for them it often was synonymous with throwing a bunch of rice (preferably brown) and vegetables into the wok at one fell swoop and letting nature take its soggy course.

Publishers were already addressing age-of-self-discovery cooks through inexpensive paperbacks in funky-looking formats. Wok cookbooks quickly joined the ranks. In California, Nitty Gritty Productions led off the parade in 1970 with *The Wok* (text by Gary Lee, abundant illustrations by Mike Nelson).[75] Yerba Buena Press followed in 1972 with *Wokcraft* (text by Charles Schafer and Violet Schafer, illustrations by Win Ng, a member of the Taylor & Ng firm).[76] Neither was rigorously designed for careful tutoring in Chinese culinary principles and the *chao* method, though a cook already acquainted with these could have prepared some fine Chinese dishes from either book.

Through manufacturers' aggressive promotion campaigns and the 1970s drift of a few post-hippie cults into respectable fashion, woks acquired some standing as a handy tool in any kitchen. Mainstream cooking authorities began praising their aptness for non-Chinese cooking purposes, and recipe developers took up the cause. The Beard Glaser Wolf (James Beard, Milton Glaser, and Burt Wolf) publishing team responsible for the "Great Cooks' Guide" series of small paperback cookbooks on specialized subjects during the 1970s also addressed woks and other Chinese implements in the Chinese section (overseen by Florence Lin) of their big 1977 compilation *The International Cooks' Catalogue*.[77] Their recasting of the material for the paperback series appeared in the same year under the title *The Great Cooks' Guide to Woks, Steamers & Fire Pots*.[78] It contained an eclectic selection of recipes by two dozen well-known cooking teachers and writers whose ideas ran a gamut from simple stir-fried vegetables to Greek-style *tarama* (carp roe) croquettes or "ribbons of veal with cognac, mushrooms and cream." In 1978 *Sunset* magazine published a wok cookbook embracing such diverse purposes as popcorn, fish and chips, "wilted salads in a wok," camp cookery, and pasta carbonara.[79] But leaving no doubt about their own priorities, the *Sunset* team firmly emphasized the special advantages of the stir-fry method for cooking vegetables to a "tender-crisp" state, whether in the Chinese or Mediterranean spirit.[80]

For a time, woks enjoyed crossover popularity in many up-to-date kitchens. But like many of the age's lifestyle discoveries, they eventually stopped making headlines as the elite and popular vanguards moved on to newer thrills. Indeed, the notice paid to Chinese food by leading tastemakers waned somewhat after the early 1980s. Food writers less often pointed out the unique virtues of Chinese cooking methods and materials. In 1984 Julia Child would authoritatively tell a *New York Times* columnist that the very idea of vegetables being cooked "crisp-tender" was nonsense.[81] No one wrote back to comment that properly stir-fried vegetables proved the exact opposite. A certain phase of relations between Mandarin-speaking Chinese cooks and the white audience that they had successfully addressed was coming to a close.

The First Age of Race-Blind Immigration

THE RESTAURANT EXPERIENCE: UNEQUAL
RACIAL EXCHANGES

In the year that saw such exalted events as Nixon's visit to Beijing, the opening of the Hunam Restaurant, and the appearance of Craig Claiborne and Virginia Lee's cookbook, Pantheon Books published a San Francisco oral history project titled *Longtime Californ': A Documentary Study of an American Chinatown*. This unsparing portrait by the husband and wife team of Victor G. Nee and Brett de Bary Nee contained dozens of interviews with local residents old and young. It examined poverty, violence, and other realities hidden behind the community's atmospheric architectural flourishes and colorful paint jobs. Among the sections devoted to labor issues, one of the most disillusioning was the chapter "Why Chinatown Restaurants Are Cheaper." The unvarnished reason, as told to the Nees, was that the enterprises were staffed by nonunionized workers who had no better choice. Employers could dictate the lowest wages for sixty-four-hour weeks to either greenhorn newcomers from Hong Kong who spoke no English or older Cantonese American housing-project dwellers who had been stuck in dead-end waiters' jobs for decades.[1]

Such conditions were not new in the Chinese American restaurant business and still are far from rare today. Since cash and other transactions in the internal economy of America's Chinatowns often have taken place off the books, exact documentation always has been elusive. But regardless of precise dollar figures, this pioneering investigation left no doubt that badly paid behind-the-scenes labor and restaurant patrons' dinners were two sides of the same coin—something still worth pointing out to any non-Chinese fan of Chinese food in America. Unfortunately, separate frames of reference exist for people who own or work in eating places—whether diners, coffee shops, kosher delis, luncheonettes, or Michelin-three-star sensations—and the clients who frequent them. This is especially true when personnel (from owners to dishwashers) and clientele are of different races. Late in my research on this book, a fellow culinary historian expressed a belief that Chinese food in the United States has been declining since a 1970s high point of accomplishment and variety. The claim prompted me to a realization: There is still a terrible disconnect between restaurants as part of the modern Chinese American community and the same places as viewed by white arbiters.

Certainly the late 1960s and 1970s were the apogee of some important developments in Chinese American food. But arguably one of the most important was the self-consequence with which non-Chinese judges of culinary fashion ruled on upscale Chinese restaurants deftly attuned to their fancy. Nothing was further from their minds than fathoming the great geographical, historical, and cultural breadth and depth of food in the worldwide Chinese experience, or questioning their own role in racial exchanges between Chinese American cooks and white customers.

Those exchanges were the product of particular historical circumstances. I have already pointed out that cooking for non-Chinese was a lifeline for desperate victims of Exclusion-era hostility and a profitable career for later Mandarin speakers brought to the United States by the Washington–Taipei alliance. It does not follow that the heirs of Exclusion or the astute postwar generation of restaurateurs will remain permanently wedded to the business of cooking to please outsiders. In fact, an inexorable shift in the relative population shares of white Americans and people of color—above all, Asian Americans—makes it increasingly likely that in an ever-growing number of Chinese restaurants, the presence or absence of white customers will be a negligible factor.

The demographic upheaval in question was triggered by the passage of the Hart-Celler Act in 1965 and its implementation in 1968. One of the law's early effects was an expansion in the numbers of Chinese Americans able to make a living by cooking for other members of the Chinese immigrant community, or often just the segment of it that shared their own regional ethnicity or language. White gourmets took several decades to notice the gathering trend and even then usually interpreted it in self-referential terms, not as a sign of things to come in an increasingly multiracial America. Now, however, it is impossible for students of food history to ignore the implications of a shifting racial balance that is currently projected to make whites a minority of the total U.S. population by about 2040.[2]

Of course, the demographic fallout of Hart-Celler was not to be foreseen in 1968. Between then and the end of the 1980s, many global and domestic forces reshaped the Chinese American food scene in ways that could not have been fully grasped at the time. They include the Western world's formal recognition of the People's Republic of China (PRC) as the legitimate Chinese nation, bloody ethnic rivalries in Southeast Asia, the depopulation and repopulation of old immigrant enclaves along with the founding of new ones in the United States, and the political protest movements of the 1960s. But for many years the only agency of change visible to most American diners was the fickle course of food fashion as ordained by the usual media oracles.

THE MOVING SPOTLIGHT

In hindsight, the late 1960s and 1970s do indeed look like a golden age of Chinese food in America—that is, from the perspective of critics telling people which new restaurant to go to or editors deciding what to publish. After about 1980, the number of dazzling Chinese dining spots mentioned by leading arbiters and ambitious English-language Chinese cookbooks fell off sharply. Admirable Chinese restaurants did not disappear. Neither did intelligent writing about Chinese food. But the excitement of the former scene has never been recaptured.

What ended the supposed golden age was not any sudden dearth of gifted chefs and writers but an increasingly competitive, buzz-driven climate in which simply serving excellent food didn't necessarily make any place either cool or hot in the eye of the vogue-chasing beholder. The fashion spotlight moved on, as spotlights will in an age of shrinking attention spans.

Needing something new to celebrate, some critical champions of up-scale Chinese food began "discovering" Thai food in print. Members of the Chinese American community and the very tiny Thai counterpart didn't get to announce that one cuisine had been discovered as the lat-est rage or the other de-discovered as old hat. That job was handled by white authorities belonging to neither community—usually well-meaning, liberal-minded people who would have been horrified to hear anybody crudely point out the implication that only the dominant race's rating scale mattered. They had no conscious intent to selectively belittle any one Asian people or cuisine. And it would be unjust to ignore what they did to improve non-Chinese understanding of Chinese food. But their profession came more and more to resemble self-preening, trend-hailing coverage of this or that exclusive couturier's spring or fall lines.

Newer fashions were also draining some of the glamour from "cook-ing Chinese" at home with the aid of woks and cookbooks. In many kitchens, do-it-yourself Chinese cooking acquired or reacquired the reputation of being more trouble than it was worth. Cookbook editors, noting decreased enthusiasm for sustained concentration on the part of reader-cooks, now often backed away from arduous earlier struggles with the challenges of Chinese cooking concepts and techniques. Ad-vertising copy tended to stress such watchwords as "quick," "light," and "easy," all of which are fine descriptions of stir-fry cooking as practiced by the practiced but must have made many frustrated beginners gnash their teeth.

Yet Chinese cuisine in America was not about to dwindle into a tired fad in search of updated sales pitches. Too much had already been achieved by too many capable and dedicated people, both Chinese and non-Chinese. There was no going back to the atmosphere of ignorance in which American "experts" and diners had cheerfully identified a dis-torted version of Cantonese cuisine as the height of authenticity. Some enlarged understanding was here to stay, at least for the class of "serious" cooks and restaurant-goers. Just before other Asian culinary vogues be-gan encroaching on the media attention paid to Chinese food, *Gourmet* magazine treated the subject to a prolonged scrutiny that would last-ingly register with influential readers.

AN ICONIC BASTION CONQUERED

Everyone recognized *Gourmet* as the bastion of a culinary value system rooted in misty WASP-but-Francophile notions of past epicurean glo-ries. Loyal readers did know that such places as India, Japan, and China existed. From time to time an isolated tribute to some Asian tradition might appear. Still, the august magazine had been content with distinctly sporadic coverage of anything that wasn't French, regional American, or perhaps Italian. But 1979—by coincidence, the year in which diplomatic relations were established between the United States and the PRC—marked a watershed in *Gourmet*'s approach to Far Eastern cuisines.

The writer who breached the fortress once and for all was Nina Si-monds. She had spent several years in Taipei working with the Wei-Chuan teaching and publishing arms before returning to the United States with an excellent grounding in Mandarin speech and the es-sentials of Chinese cooking methods. The intrepid young woman next transferred herself to Paris for a year's study as a *stagiaire* (student-trainee) at Anne Willan's new and high-powered French cooking school La Varenne.[3] Still filled with a sense of mission about passing on what she had learned on Taiwan, she asked permission to moonlight on the school premises by demonstrating Chinese cooking principles in the evenings to small classes of students.

Among those who attended these informal sessions was Zanne Zak-roff, then on a year's leave from her duties as *Gourmet*'s executive food editor and head of the test kitchen.[4] To Zakroff, the dimensions of the subject being opened up through Simonds's eager advocacy were a revelation.

Nothing more happened for a couple of years. But in 1978 the two women met over lunch in New York to share Paris reminiscences and talk about food. Their conversation turned to possible article ideas. Simonds suggested that the time might have come to examine Chinese cuisine as one of the world's crowning cultural-gastronomic achievements.

Zakroff's encouragement was decidedly cautious. She had little hope that Jane Montant, the magazine's very proper and Francophile editor-in-chief, would entertain any far-reaching proposal on the subject. But to her amazement, Mrs. Montant (as she was always called) not only welcomed the idea of paying more attention to the food of China but ended up accepting a detailed, impressive proposal from Simonds for a series of monthly columns exploring the subject's major facets. Improbably, a *Gourmet* editor apparently wedded to a nearly forty-year-old credo upholding the eternal value of *la grande cuisine française* recognized that Chinese cuisine had comparable (and older) claims to eternal value.

Gourmet had published long serial explorations of particular cuisines before, but they had never strayed from a Eurocentric focus. The time and space that Mrs. Montant finally agreed to devote to this ambitious endeavor were astonishing. After much consideration and planning, she committed the magazine to publishing a two-year run of text-and-recipes monthly columns by Simonds between January 1979 and December 1980. It was an effort more far-reaching and conscientious than any attention previously paid to Chinese cuisine by the Claiborne-led restaurant reviewers and other journalistic pundits. And being sustained over twenty-four months rather than squeezed into a one-shot culinary paean, it had a long time to sink into the awareness of *Gourmet* subscribers.

Though chiefly organized around individual foodstuffs such as eggs, chicken, fish, pork, and so forth, the Simonds series began in 1979 with a careful two-part introduction to crucial seasonings and flavoring principles. Properly and tellingly, the first ingredient to have a column to itself was rice. Presentations on noodles (in two parts), breads, and dumplings followed. Soybeans and bean curd received separate columns; vegetarian cooking was treated at length. Lamb (unusually at the time, since most Chinese restaurateurs in America still came from areas where it was little eaten) received a whole column. Sweets were given two, though Simonds was careful to explain that they didn't really correspond to any Western concept of desserts.

The attention that *Gourmet* devoted to this unprecedented body of instruction was perhaps the most dramatic announcement of change among august food authorities between the start of the Cold War and the first years of official Chinese-American recognition. The series was also the making of Simonds's career as a recognized authority on Chinese cuisine. And Jane Montant's loosening of the magazine's longtime "gourmet-equals-French" conceptual stranglehold would appear all the more enlightened almost fifteen years later when the ex–*New York Times* restaurant reviewer Bryan Miller covertly tried to have his successor, Ruth Reichl, fired for crimes against the paper's previously exalted standards.[5] Sublimely ignorant of Asian culinary traditions, Miller was apoplectic at the mere idea of Japanese soba noodle restaurants deserving three stars on any *Times*-approved scale of values. The Simonds *Gourmet* series was one of the reasons that by then many people writing about food recognized the absurdity of such attitudes.

RETRENCHMENT ON THE BOOK SCENE

In the cookbook field, searches for newer-than-newest trends dampened many trade publishers' and editors' devotion to Chinese cuisine after the late 1970s. But academic publishers began to scent opportunity. In 1977 Yale University Press issued a collection of eight scholarly essays by different hands examining the course of Chinese food over more than four thousand years: *Food in Chinese Culture*, edited by K. C. Chang.[6] For lay readers in love with Chinese cuisine, this unprecedented source of English-language information by bona fide researchers on diet, crops, and material culture from Neolithic to modern times was like a feast to the starving. James Beard greeted it as "long overdue"; Raymond Sokolov called it "a panorama of all Chinese social history, viewed from the kitchen door."[7] Even today it is an unsurpassed introduction to a host of ethnographic and culinary issues in Chinese food history.

An Eater's Guide to Chinese Characters by James D. McCawley, published by the University of Chicago Press in 1985, was another milestone.[8] A small paperback that could be taken to restaurants in a pocket or purse, it was the first and still almost the only serious attack on the fearful language gap that had always stood between English-speaking patrons and real understanding of what they were eating. McCawley, an eminent linguist, had devised a rough-and-ready version of usual Chinese character-recognition systems, enabling users to look up a root element of a word and find more complex words based on it in a glossary containing about two thousand culinary items. Reissued in 2004, it remains the only attempt to date at a Chinese–English culinary dictionary. The long-unmet need for a compact but detailed history of Chinese food was filled in 1988, when Yale published *The Food of China* by the anthropologist E. N. Anderson, one of the contributors to the earlier compendium.[9] Anderson, a trenchant observer and lucid writer, was equally good at compressing masses of specialized scholarship into shapely form and conveying nuances of gastronomic judgment.

These three books, soon indispensable for hard-core Chinese-food enthusiasts, would also be seminal influences on future scholars and food writers. A work of wider popular impact, *The Book of Tofu* by the soy-food advocates William Shurtleff and Akiko Aoyagi, was first published in 1975 by a small New Age press in Massachusetts and reissued as a mass-market paperback by Ballantine Books in 1979.[10] The timing couldn't have been more ideal. Bean curd was just ceasing to be exclusively associated with Japanese or Chinese cuisine and beginning a rise to mainstream success boosted by a (spurious) reputation as a low-fat diet aid. At the same moment, questions about the wastefulness of land use for raising livestock as opposed to high-protein plant crops were moving closer to the center stage of American political debate. Shurtleff and Aoyagi's ecological arguments and their zeal in devising recipes based on tofu triggered prominent debate and moved some serious vegetarians to investigate the huge repertoire of meatless Chinese dishes.

During this time, the major trade publishers showed only fitful interest in following up the Chinese cookbook standouts of the 1960s and 1970s. Houghton Mifflin, however, managed to secure Nina Simonds's first cookbook, a solid, basic manual titled *Chinese Classic Cuisine*.[11] Published in 1982, it thoughtfully revisited and expanded on much of the best material from the *Gourmet* series, and remains one of the best general cooks' introductions to the Chinese kitchen.

An ambitious work that implicitly placed Chinese and French cuisines on the same exalted plane was *Chinese Technique*, published in 1981 by Simon & Schuster.[12] The authors were Ken Hom and Harvey Steiman, respectively a young Berkeley alumnus (and French-traveled champion of East–West fusion cuisine) who was teaching Chinese cooking in the Bay Area and the food-and-wine editor of the *San Francisco Examiner*. The editor was Ann Bramson, who several years before had smoothed the French-born Jacques Pépin's path to American fame by overseeing a pair of pictorial manuals issued by another publisher, *La Technique* and *La Methode*. Each was based on literally hundreds of photographs of Pépin—or usually his hands—demonstrating French culinary procedures in exhaustive step-by-step detail.

The Hom-Steiman book was in effect a replica of the Pépin volumes dedicated to Chinese food and using Hom's hands, with photographs by Willie Kee. Today the black-and-white reproduction looks dated and fuzzy, but the crucial ideas still emerge with clarity. *Chinese Technique* launched Hom's career by bringing him to the notice of a BBC producer who was planning a new television series and looking for a photogenic English-speaking Chinese cook. The resulting show, *Ken Hom's Chinese Cookery*, had made him a superstar in the United Kingdom by the mid-1980s.

Several important projects came from an energetic editor at William Morrow. Maria Guarnaschelli (who much later would introduce the English writer Fuchsia Dunlop to an American public) supervised the decade's one blockbuster Chinese cookbook, Barbara Tropp's *The Modern Art of Chinese Cooking* (1982).[13] Well-focused and astute enough to serve as a good general introduction, it was nonetheless charged with Tropp's fierce individualism and penchant for arranging East–West culinary marriages. Guarnaschelli followed up this success with *Florence Lin's Complete Book of Chinese Noodles, Dumplings and Breads* (1986), which dealt encyclopedically with a subject particularly appealing to American audiences and may have been the veteran author's best-loved book.[14] She went on to oversee the first really extensive cook's-eye survey of Far Eastern foodstuffs, *Bruce Cost's Asian Ingredients* (1988).[15] Bruce Cost, a San Francisco newspaper columnist and cooking instructor as well as a friend of Alice Waters, had managed to interweave an eclectic collection of recipes with descriptions of a pan-Asian array of ingredients ranging from Vietnamese fresh herbs to Chinese rock sugar. The book would stand for years as the most practical reference aid in the field.

Several attractive books testified to the appeal of dim sum, which wasn't absolutely new but had become a big draw among non-Chinese only after the mid-1970s. Florence Lin had actually treated several aspects of the subject in the noodle-dumpling book. So had the thoughtful cooking teacher Mai Leung in *The Chinese People's Cookbook* (1979), a work about snacks and street foods overseen by Frances McCullough at

Harper & Row (1982) and later reissued as *Dim Sum and Other Chinese Street Foods*.[16] More tightly focused on the Cantonese-style teahouse repertoire was *The Dim Sum Book* by the China Institute instructor Eileen Yin-Fei Lo (Crown, 1982).[17] Despite the lucidity and loving detail of Lo's recipes, it is doubtful that many people were able to cook their way through much of this work or a slighter competitor titled *Classic Deem Sum* (Holt, Rinehart, and Winston, 1985) by Henry Chan (proprietor of the well-known San Francisco dim sum parlor Yank Sing) with Yukiko Haydock and Bob Haydock.[18] The problem was that no Chinese recipes are more excruciatingly labor-intensive than the dim sum dumplings that first brought crowds flocking to dim sum parlors like Yank Sing or Hee Seung Fun in New York Chinatown, or require a more dexterous touch in filling and shaping.

THE CROSSOVER CRAZE

Though Thai and Vietnamese establishments siphoned off some of the erstwhile Chinese restaurant clientele, a few Chinese specialties became permanent favorites in an otherwise fickle, hyperactive national food scene. Dumplings—both the northern Chinese *jiaozi* ("pot stickers" or "boiled dumplings," according to how they were cooked) and the kinds belonging to Cantonese dim sum—were rapidly welcomed, along with the great wealth of Chinese wheat-flour and other noodle dishes. As of 1980 northern-style flatbreads were seldom represented by anything but the so-called scallion pancake, but it was such an immediate hit that many Cantonese restaurants were obliged to add it to their menus along with *jiaozi*. Non-Chinese diners responded to such items not as oddities but as congenial counterparts to adoptive citizens like pizza (scallion pancakes often appeared on menus as "Chinese pizza"), ravioli, and spaghetti.

East–West culinary interchanges—depending on one's perspective, confused jumbles or fruitful unions—were a hallmark of the age. In parts of the Far East, versions of packaged white bread and bottled mayonnaise had come to stay; Americans investigating a new crop of city greengroceries run by Korean immigrants might decide to see how rice vinegar tasted in a salad dressing, or some kind of dried noodles in a pasta dish. Brewed soy sauce from Wisconsin (where the Japanese-founded Kikkoman firm had had a plant since 1972) was giving hydro-lyzed American pseudo–soy sauce a run for its money at supermarkets.

At another level, forward-looking restaurants reaped headlines for bending or obliterating boundaries between national cuisines. Some leading mainstream chefs began raiding Japanese or Chinese cuisine for effects that they usually grafted onto French backgrounds. The ensuing "fusion" razzle-dazzle stole a certain amount of thunder from the food of Mandarinized high-end Chinese restaurants. But it also helped underscore the innate grace of Chinese cuisine.

The chief though not the only laboratory for such experiments was California, headquarters for both old San Francisco Chinatown in the north and swathes of affluent new Taiwanese ethnoburbs in the south. The showiest showplace of the French-Chinese fusion vogue was in Los Angeles: Chinois on Main, founded in 1983 by the Austrian-born, French-trained superstar chef Wolfgang Puck.

At China Moon in San Francisco, Barbara Tropp evolved a bolder, edgier style of hybridization. The Bay Area also nurtured links between leaders of the incipient "California cuisine" and prominent local Chinese restaurateurs, especially Cecilia Chiang, a close friend of Alice Waters and other Chez Panisse stalwarts. Nearly everyone in California food circles assumed that all people with any claim to culinary literacy needed an informed appreciation of Chinese food. That idea was also being mightily fostered to the south by Jonathan Gold, a writer for *Los Angeles Weekly*. Starting in 1986, readers of his column "Counter Intelligence" were regularly treated to reviews of San Gabriel Valley Chinese restaurants based on more determined immersion in the cuisine than any American critic had previously attempted.[19] (I once heard Gold describe going back to eat a specialty new and baffling to him—"stinky tofu"—at a Taiwan-style restaurant more than a dozen times before he felt halfway qualified to write a word about it.)

ACTIVISM AND ACADEMIA

To an articulate and angry segment of the Chinese American community, the time that outsiders spent exclaiming over Chinese restaurants was not a compliment but an affront. The same years that saw the passage of Hart-Celler and the Nixon administration's first overtures to mainland China also bred inner-city riots, political assassinations, student "liberations" of university administrators' offices, and mass demonstrations aimed at ending American imperialism. It would have been impossible for the Black Power movement and other militant social-justice campaigns not to inspire kindred rage in the major Chinese American communities.

In a firestorm of protests and strikes during 1968 and 1969, the California State University system was either persuaded or forced to institute some of the nation's first ethnic studies programs at the University of California–Berkeley and San Francisco State College. The spread of such programs was at first sporadic. But within several decades the only college and university curricula that failed to address the concerns of minority groups were at a handful of very reactionary religiously affiliated schools.

Young graduate students and teachers who had welcomed the first California victories immediately began designing courses to redress the earlier neglect of Chinese American history. Among the first fruits was a now classic scholarly reference tool titled *A History of the Chinese in California: A Syllabus*, edited by Thomas W. Chinn, Him Mark Lai, and Philip P. Choy.[20] It was published in 1969 by the Chinese Historical Society of America, of which Chinn had been principal founder in 1963. The society was soon joined by such other organizations as the Chinese Historical Society of Southern California (1975) and the New York Chinatown History Project (1980), a precursor to what is now the Museum of Chinese in America. Today many states from coast to coast have their own Chinese historical societies, maintaining both paper and online archives.

To young political activists, leaders of older community organizations such as the Chinese Consolidated Benevolent Association looked like Uncle Toms and (as perennial supporters of the Chiang Kai-shek regime on Taiwan) tools of American warmongers. The pseudo-Chinese trappings of San Francisco Chinatown were an insult. So was the popular identification of Chinese Americans with two businesses that in the new activists' minds marked them as ghetto victims: laundries and restaurants.

The activists recognized and despised the racism that had doomed their grandparents to years of disenfranchised Exclusion-era drudgery in chop suey joints and kept their parents chained to the same work in spite of supposedly full citizenship. They saw the occupational hardships imposed on contemporary restaurant workers and detailed in the Nees' *Longtime Californ'*. It is not surprising that when well-meaning white allies gushed about their love of Chinatown restaurants, people trying to establish Chinese American history and sociology as a legitimate field of study often reacted like African Americans hearing praise of the old plantation. Their resentment would not soften for many years.

The activists' belief that anti-Chinese racism still enjoyed free rein in America was horrifically reinforced in 1982, when two Detroit auto workers not only ambushed and beat to death a young Chinese American named Vincent Chin, whom they had scuffled with in a bar, but were acquitted of all charges except manslaughter and set free on three years' probation.[21] (The killers—to whom one Asian looked like another—had thought their victim was Japanese.) One of the two was later found guilty on a federal civil rights violation count, but the verdict was overturned on appeal. The Chin murder led to the founding of a Detroit-area Asian American coalition called American Citizens for Justice, which spearheaded a national campaign to hold perpetrators accountable for anti-Asian crimes. It signaled the growth of an Asian American political solidarity that—in contrast to former Chinese–Japanese rivalries—transcended country-of-origin boundaries.

In their own right and as part of the growing Asian American movement, Chinese Americans continued to press for equal justice and opportunity. (Notwithstanding later myths that lumped together all Chinese as a fortunate, high-achieving "model minority," the poor and badly educated had little access to these blessings.) The first university Asian American studies programs meanwhile grew in breadth and depth throughout the 1970s and 1980s, attracting people of both Asian and non-Asian origin. Among the pioneer contributors were the eminent historians Roger Daniels, Him Mark Lai, and Ronald Takaki. Thanks to them and the influential scholars who came in their wake, both specialists and lay people had increasing access to invaluable histories—for instance, Sucheng Chan's detailed study *This Bittersweet Soil: The Chinese in California Agriculture, 1860–1910* and Shih-shan Henry Tsai's compact summary *The Chinese Experience in America* (both 1986).[22]

At the time of the first Asian American studies programs, the Hart-Celler Act was too new to have affected anyone's thinking about later immigration patterns. Philip Hart, Emanuel Celler, and Lyndon Johnson had not dreamed that the act would wreak any startling changes on the American population. Asian Americans themselves were equally ignorant of the future—the more so as diplomatic recognition of the PRC was a yet-unforeseen event.

The first inkling of Far Eastern consequences came during the fallout of America's ill-fated war with Vietnam, which lurched to an end seven years after the implementation of Hart-Celler in 1968. It was a terrible omen for thousands of ethnic Chinese living in the regions of Southeast Asia that they collectively called the Nanyang.

Virtually all of the Nanyang Chinese had come from the southeast coast of China. Cantonese adventurers had founded some settlements. But the great majority were Fujianese or, in their own pronunciation, Hokkienese. In a few areas the Hakka ethnic minority predominated, in others the "Teochiu" or Chaozhou people from a community clustered around the Guangdong-Fujian border. Wherever they went, they had held firm to their languages and sense of group identity. Their cuisine had never lost its Chinese foundations. Happily adopting local ingredients such as lemongrass, basil, coconuts, fish sauce, fermented shrimp paste, taro, or mangoes, they had nonetheless retained the core Chinese cooking techniques and culinary principles.

In far corners of the Nanyang, from the Philippines to Malaysia, the Han Chinese in their hundreds of settled outposts had earned a reputation as profiteering alien merchants and middlemen preying on the societies that they dealt with. The fierceness with which they were hated can be judged from the title of a 1914 pamphlet by King Rama VI of Thailand denouncing the Chinese: *The Jews of the East*.[23] When the aftermath of the Vietnam War left much of Southeast Asia in disequilibrium if not bloody tatters, a tide of anti-Chinese fury broke loose in many of their adoptive homes.

Violent outbreaks against Chinese were not new in the Nanyang. What was new (in addition to the devastation caused by the American war) was the Hart-Celler Act. Thanks to Hart-Celler, thousands of refugees who at one time would have been automatically excluded were able to seek new lives in the United States on the same footing as people from England, Sweden, Belgium, or anywhere else in the world.

Most of the refugees who began crowding onto any boat that would carry them and fleeing from Vietnam in 1977 and 1978 were ethnic Hokkienese who had lived for generations in the Cholon district of Ho Chi Minh City, the former Saigon. Later waves of "boat people" followed over the next ten or dozen years. Sporadic anti-Chinese riots occurred throughout the late twentieth century in Indonesia, Burma, and Malaysia, among other places.

Some U.S. Chinatowns soon began acquiring a scattering of Vietnamese restaurants whose cooking overlapped only in part with the cuisine of other people in northern or southern Vietnam. A little later these outposts were joined by Malaysian restaurants with the strong imprint of the (mostly Hokkienese) Chinese–Malaysian tradition, as distinguished from native Malay, Hindu Indian–Malaysian, and Muslim Indian–Malaysian cooking or various local culinary hybridizations.

The effect of Hart-Celler on Chinese diasporic communities was not limited to the old Nanyang, though for some time that was the biggest general source of new ethnic Chinese immigrants. Mainlanders who had managed to escape to Hong Kong during or after the Communist takeover soon made their way to American destinations, especially San Francisco Chinatown. Most often poor and disadvantaged by lack of English skills, they were a new factor for unrest in that troubled community.

Taiwan, though it lost the diplomatic-recognition battle in 1979, continued to send waves of prosperous and well-educated newcomers to southern California ethnoburbs and (on a smaller scale) New York City's emerging Flushing Chinatown. It also sent enormous amounts of money for investment plans spearheaded by either Taiwanese or new American citizens. Simultaneously, Hong Kong millionaires looking to take their assets elsewhere before 1997 (when the colony was to be returned to the PRC on the expiration of the 1898 British lease) began a spate of ambitious building and restaurant projects in Manhattan Chinatown and Flushing. The Tawa Supermarket (later renamed 99 Ranch Market) and Hong Kong Supermarket chains, created respectively by Taiwanese and Hong Kong entrepreneurs during the 1980s search for investment opportunities, revolutionized food shopping for many thousands of newcomers.[24] The branch stores are spacious emporiums on the model of large, palatial American supermarkets, carrying a vast array of imported Asian food products together with a wide selection of fresh produce, meats, and fish. Most cater to a Taiwanese or other Chinese clientele, but some serve Vietnamese, Indonesian, and other ex-Nanyang immigrant communities.

During this early tide of Taiwanese and Nanyang immigration, other ethnic Chinese groups started reaching America in lesser numbers. Already a few descendants of the Chinese who had worked nineteenth-century Cuban sugar plantations had started coming to America along with a version of *cocina chinacubana* that acquired a small fan club in New York. So had counterparts who had founded a tribe of restaurants popularly called *chifas* in Peru and Ecuador after the decline of the guano mining that had been their chief employment. Representatives of the Hakka settlement that had become the center of the Calcutta leather-working trade would also establish North American niches. Unlike Southeast Asian newcomers, these immigrants didn't necessarily gravitate to existing American Chinatowns, more often clustering in other ethnic neighborhoods along with members of their own communities.

THE START OF MAINLAND EMIGRATION

It took some fifteen years for the effects of the implemented Hart-Celler Act to reach mainland China, since the Mao regime compared favorably with even the most isolationist imperial dynasties for cutting off emigration. Until Mao's death in 1976, undoctored news of the outside world seldom reached citizens of the PRC. The converse was almost equally true. From 1949 until the late 1970s, the U.S. public received only foggy and scattered descriptions of events behind the Bamboo Curtain. Some accounts of the Great Leap Forward (roughly 1958–1960) reached the West but no estimates of the death toll resulting from this "modernization" program's disastrous effects on agriculture. The Cultural Revolution of the late 1960s produced some press reports of state-backed violence against victims identified as "class enemies," but again, Western observers would not understand the full horror for some time to come.

For decades, most Americans' ideas of the mysterious mainland were still shaped more by party lines than solid information. Those with left-leaning convictions went on defending Red China as a noble experiment. Cold War hard-liners (still bitterly opposed to abandoning Chiang Kai-shek and the Nationalists) went on calling it a threat to the free world.

Many also insisted on viewing food through ideological prisms. In 1961 the veteran Hong Kong–based correspondent Peggy Durdin published an article in the *New York Times Magazine*, "Mao's 'Great Crime' Against Cuisine," excoriating the latest communal-kitchen policy and describing the usual fare as a "dull, tasteless, monotonous" travesty of "the world's best, most richly diversified cuisine."[25] A letter to the editor from an angry PRC sympathizer promptly dismissed her account as the let-'em-eat-cake elitism of a "well-traveled gourmet" blind to the plight of hungry masses.[26]

Nixon's 1972 visit to Beijing did not immediately create a flow of information between the two nations. The Watergate scandal, erupting the year after the signing of the Shanghai communiqué, hobbled his administration's foreign policy agenda. The White House could spare no thought or energy on lining up support for the politically risky step of transferring official U.S. recognition from Chiang Kai-shek's Republic of China to the PRC. For a time, Washington could not open an official embassy in Beijing. But it did establish a kind of shadow embassy known as the U.S. liaison office, headed at one point by future president George H. W. Bush.

During this diplomatic limbo, the declining health of Mao and Zhou Enlai left the PRC's entire future in doubt—though in Mao's last years, expatriates living in the United States were granted a little more leeway to visit families on the mainland. Among the few who obtained travel visas was Cecilia Chiang.

The scene that greeted Chiang in 1975 was horrifying enough to spur her to publish a revised edition of *The Mandarin Way* (1980) detailing her experiences. She found her gentle, learned father dying, "after years of privation," in a squalid Beijing hole with essentially no medical attention. His children, who tried to literally carry him through the streets to a hospital on the terrible last day (there was no ambulance), had to bury him in a wretched miscellany of garments.[27]

This nightmare, Chiang made clear, summed up the irrevocable ruin of Chinese culture as she had known it. Food had been one casualty. "As all the best ingredients are exported to obtain foreign exchange, the basic diet is a main dish of cabbage, eggplant or spinach, and sometimes turnip." Cooks trained in anything but rock-bottom basics had died out; formerly celebrated restaurants served clumsy travesties of the old repertoire. "Everywhere I noticed that the skillful cutting and refinement of classical Chinese cooking had departed." In sum, "China will no doubt suffer for the errors of the Cultural Revolution for many years to come."[28]

Cecilia Chiang's visit occurred just on the cusp of tremendous geopolitical shakeups. Both Mao and Zhou died in 1976, having outlived their old enemy Chiang Kai-shek for less than a year. In 1978 Deng Xiaoping emerged victorious from a brief struggle for power, with aggressive reforms in mind. One was to finish the unfinished business of diplomatic recognition. In January of 1979 he and President Jimmy Carter signed the necessary accords; an exchange of ambassadors soon followed. The Republic of China on Taiwan, now replaced by the PRC as the recognized government of China, was given its own shadow embassy and cautiously worded promises of military support.

It was several more years before Deng went on to liberalize the PRC's restrictive emigration policy in the early 1980s. By then he had begun publicly repudiating certain Maoist "errors," limited freedom of travel was opening up, and American news media were establishing Beijing bureaus. For the first time Western journalists were able to form clear ideas of earlier disasters, including crop failures during the Great Leap Forward and savage punishments visited on (among other "enemies") former restaurant chefs during the Cultural Revolution.

The PRC now received a Hart-Celler immigration quota of twenty thousand a year, equivalent to that for Taiwan. Previously most mainlanders who made it to the United States had been lumped in with the Taiwanese quota or a special Hong Kong quota of five thousand. These numbers, together with other influxes from Southeast Asian nations, meant a steep rise in the numbers of Chinese immigrating to the United States. By 1990 the crowds of mainlanders seeking to enter the country were so great that each year's twenty-thousand quota was filled in the blink of an eye. People who didn't make the authorized cut looked to other means. Fujian province, historically a breeding ground of lawbreakers, became the chief source of illegal immigration from the PRC, with hordes of locals incurring massive debts to "snakeheads," or people-smugglers who would clandestinely transport them to U.S. ports or border crossings.[29]

At the time of the new quota arrangements, the old Cantonese-dominated New York City Chinatown had been steadily declining since World War II. The Hart-Celler Act reversed the ebbing tide as undocumented Fujianese poured into the old hub by many tens of thousands. In a sense, Fujian started to become a new Toisan on a far larger scale, the wellhead of a huge transoceanic human pipeline that the immigration authorities constantly struggled to control.[30] A crucial difference was that, even as illegal aliens, the Fujianese in New York were not automatically singled out by racist immigration laws. Fujianese restaurants boldly took root along East Broadway and Forsyth Street, regularly replacing former Cantonese joints. In an equally significant departure, the regular customers were not whites but other Fujianese living in the neighborhood, legally or illegally. People went to Yeung Sun—owned by a highly popular snakehead—and its counterparts to eat the food they loved and talk their own language. The same could be said of many dozens of restaurants that sprang up in Flushing and half a dozen other New York neighborhoods *not* dependent on illegal immigration, after Hart-Celler had cleared the way to admit Chinese from the Nanyang, the mainland, Taiwan, and elsewhere. The majority of these new arrivals came to New York, which surpassed San Francisco as the largest Chinese American population center during the 1980s.[31]

A CHANGED RESTAURANT LANDSCAPE

The new Chinatown restaurants had nothing to do with either chop suey models or the gilded gathering spots founded by earlier Mandarin speakers. They didn't boast the services of chefs whose virtuosic skills harked back to the late Qing Empire. Western lovers of Chinese food now at least faintly glimpsed the truth of what Cecilia Chiang and a few others had reported about the havoc wreaked on the Chinese culinary legacy by the Cultural Revolution. The break with a system of apprenticeship and training that had long supplied magnificent restaurants and great households with *da shi fu* (Cantonese, *daai si fu*)—culinary "grandmasters"—was real and far-reaching. The legacy survived in some strength in the island enclaves of Hong Kong, Singapore, and Taiwan. It was all but extinct on the mainland, and its influence in America would diminish with the loss of aging pioneer chefs like T. T. Wang and C. M. Lo.

But there were substantial compensations. The grandmasters had never represented more than one facet of the Chinese culinary world. Their disappearance did not doom home cooking skills or ordinary people's appreciation of simple beauty in a meal. Once victims of collectivization, hunger, and political purges were free to cook for their own families and communities, Chinese regional cuisines were also free to resurface.

Their distinctive characters would later be somewhat softened by nationwide interchange. But in the first years of emigration under Deng, geography and climate (not to mention rudimentary communications technology) remained potent factors for culinary conservatism. Many of the nation's provinces and autonomous zones were still isolated from the hubs of political and cultural life. The diverse ecosystems of China's many agricultural zones meant strongly differentiated local cuisines, including some that earlier codifiers had never bothered to name among the regional cuisines of China and that American fans of Cantonese, Sichuanese, Hunanese, or Shanghainese cuisine had never heard of. They now began appearing in strength, especially in Flushing and the other new Chinese enclaves in New York City.

There is no general agreement on how many "Chinatowns" were founded by new immigrants in Brooklyn and Queens, but throughout the 1980s Cantonese speakers from Hong Kong and Guangdong flocked to the Brooklyn neighborhood of Sunset Park. They also converged on nearby Bensonhurst, along with an overflow of Fujianese from Manhattan Chinatown. Flushing, a center of Korean and some Indian as well as Chinese immigration, was bolstered by large infusions of Taiwanese money but also attracted disparate settlers from the Nanyang and many mainland regions. Elmhurst in Queens began developing into a smaller pan-Asian hub embracing diverse Chinese elements.

A messy mosaic of languages and provincial origins would eventually appear in all American Chinatowns, but New York remained the chief beneficiary. The Taiwanese were the best educated and most upwardly mobile, quickly gravitating to skilled professions. Many others, especially in Manhattan Chinatown, were trapped in semi–slum housing and badly paying jobs by lack of English. Some (mostly women) found work in a new generation of Chinatown garment-trade sweatshops. Others (mostly men) made their way to a bumper crop of employment agencies that put people on buses to Chinese restaurants anywhere from Georgia to Arizona, where they had been promised jobs as waiters, dishwashers, cashiers, or perhaps cooks.[32] Lucky handfuls, then gathering numbers, managed to found small businesses for neighborhood clienteles, with Fujianese in the old Chinatown forming an aggressive example. Soon restaurants serving particular ethnic Chinese clienteles flourished in all the new Chinatowns. They were seriously baffling to non-Chinese visitors who had thought they knew something about Chinese food. But they were a magnet to a new class of white (and sometimes black) patrons.

Before 1990 two widely different wings were appearing in the ranks of devoted urban restaurant-goers. One consisted of so-called foodies, a word introduced with mildly satirical intent in the early 1980s by the English-based writers Ann Barr and Paul Levy but soon claimed in all seriousness by a U.S. coterie deaf to such nuances. The other was a resolutely disorganized new sect who scorned foodies and cultivated a snobbery-in-reverse devotion to inconspicuous neighborhood beaneries frequented and staffed by recent immigrants from Eastern Europe, South America, Africa, the Near East, and the Far East. In the cyber age to come, they would play a great role in disseminating knowledge about ethnic cuisines through assorted blogs. But from the first they were joyous explorers of the unmapped immigrant food territories annexed to the American larder, as if by some new Louisiana Purchase, as a result of the Hart-Celler Act.

Recognized dining authorities, and the foodies who followed their pronouncements, had an awful time making sense out of anything they tasted in the new immigrant eateries. Reviewers and tastemakers who had learned the difference between Cantonese and two or three other regional categories usually were out of their depth. Restaurant mavens generally winced at the lack of what they considered decor. Where English translations existed for menu items written in Chinese, they might be unintelligible. Waiters or waitresses seldom spoke enough

English to bridge the gap, and impressing the management with any sense of one's importance was usually a lost cause. Sometimes it was possible to make out clues indicating regional or ethnic origin like "Fujian" (or "Hokkien"), "Teochiu" (or other bewildering romanizations), "Hakka," "Xi'an," "Shandong," "Wenzhou," "Yunnan," or "Dongbei." But English-language sources shedding any light on those names scarcely existed.

The contrarians adored such challenges. Unlike mainstream foodies, they perfectly understood that their presence in a neighborhood Turkish or Uzbek restaurant wasn't particularly interesting to the management or anyone else. Eagerly swapping notes about obscure places where they had eaten unfamiliar dishes, they half-accidentally amassed a seat-of-the-pants acquaintance with a number of non-Western cuisines. With only slight exaggeration, Calvin Trillin once explained to *New Yorker* readers that no member of the crew was "likely to spend his time in the latest chic Manhattan bistro while there are Nigerian yam-porridge outposts in Brooklyn left to explore."[33] After some years of noncommunication between the two parties, the foodies and gourmet pundits began discovering that devotees of "alternative eating" or "ethnic eating" were on to something. Exchanges of information about previously remote cuisines grew less haphazard as immigrant communities, together with unpretentious restaurants or street carts serving their needs, became more strongly rooted in American cities. An enlarged idea of the "new" Chinese cuisines began diffusing beyond recently settled Chinese neighborhoods throughout the 1980s.

More windows of culinary exchange have opened up since then, though always lagging behind the pace of enclave-formation from still other Chinese regions or minority populations. Well before the end of the twentieth century, growing numbers of smart, sophisticated, and often bilingual young Chinese Americans started to become magazine test cooks, recipe developers, and food writers. New bicultural sources of knowledge sprang up, famously including a labor-of-love quarterly newsletter titled *Flavor and Fortune* whose editor, Jacqueline M. Newman, diligently sought to fill in one blank space after another on the culinary-cultural map. A younger generation of restaurant critics—not always white—learned to explore the remarkable gamut of Chinese restaurants with a seriousness and humility that hadn't always distinguished mainstream writing on the subject.

FROM HONEYMOON TO DISILLUSIONMENT

Such developments, however, lay some time ahead as Reagan-era America embarked on a sort of honeymoon with Deng-era China reflected in high-level meetings and popular curiosity. Many U.S. citizens thought that they were now looking at a kinder, gentler PRC. So did many higher-ups. Ronald Reagan himself paid a state visit to Beijing in 1984 to discuss expanded economic cooperation. Reports about the PRC's abandonment of collective farming and a full-tilt race to industrialization filled Western news media. The Deng regime launched tourism initiatives that brought thousands of American citizens on carefully supervised visits to Beijing, Shanghai, and many of the provinces. There were even hints that gastronomic tourism might at some point be on the cards. A handful of American food writers were allowed to eat their way around some once-fabled centers of Chinese cuisine. Most famously, in 1986 the former *New York Times* writer Mimi Sheraton (one of the more clear-eyed restaurant reviewers of the day) was dispatched by *Time* magazine to spend a month dining out in seven Chinese cities.[34]

Academic exchange programs grew rapidly. American students' interest in Mandarin classes was exceeded only by Chinese students' enthusiasm for English classes. Western historians of modern China had unprecedented access to crucial materials. Middle-aged Chinese Americans who had been student protesters during the 1960s now learned that youthful counterparts in the 1980s PRC were organizing their own rapidly swelling protests against restrictions on freedom of speech and the press. The news seemed to augur a powerful freedom-seeking tide with history on its side, like the one simultaneously gathering in the old Soviet bloc countries and the Soviet Union itself.

This illusion was shattered in June of 1989, when on Deng Xiaoping's orders the People's Liberation Army brutally crushed a massive pro-democracy rally in the Tiananmen Square plaza of central Beijing. Western governments registered shocked protests. But they lost little time before returning to the course of pragmatic rapprochement with

Beijing. The collapse of all the major Soviet bloc regimes during 1989 and the precarious balancing act of Communist Party secretary (later president) Mikhail Gorbachev in what remained of the Soviet Union spurred rather than discouraged Washington's interest in a strategic alliance with China, the most dramatically rising new powerhouse in all Eurasia.

But many of the well-meaning American welcomers of Deng's reforms who had expected him to supervise a transition to Western-style democracy were lastingly disabused by the 1989 massacre. Never again would they trustingly assume that the PRC had shed its totalitarian past. Tiananmen Square closed the books on a certain hopeful post-Mao phase of U.S.–PRC interchange. American citizens—Chinese and non-Chinese alike—generally stopped hoping for enlightened democracy-to-democracy interchange and accepted the reality of hard-nosed American–Chinese relationships based on self-interest in an unsettled, unsettling post–Cold War world. One result of the bloody Tiananmen Square debacle, however, was a speeded-up flow of immigrants to America's Chinatowns from the PRC, Taiwan, and other parts of the Far East. After 1990 the representation of regional and ethnic Chinese cuisines on American soil became even more diverse.

WHO COOKS FOR WHOM?

When some naive early expectations of the Deng regime ended, a certain chapter of Chinese American food history was also approaching an end, together with earlier assumptions about who cooked for whom and why. In today's romantic haze of fantasies about the glamour of restaurant cooking, it is easy to forget that people don't necessarily spend a lifetime preparing meals for others in sweltering kitchens because it is their dearest ambition. From the 1890s until about forty years ago, the Chinese restaurant story in America meant very different things to those who enjoyed the meals and those who did the actual work. The 1960s activists who founded the first Asian studies programs did everyone a service by refusing to equate Chinese American identity with laundry or restaurant work benefiting a (mostly) white clientele.

The accomplishments of the people who made the meals had been great. They not only consciously strove to cook for Western taste preferences but almost effortlessly succeeded at the task. In the face of appalling threats and hardships, Pearl River Deltans in turn-of-the-nineteenth-century America summoned up the indomitable *xiang banfa* instinct to concoct a stepchild version of Cantonese cuisine that ever since has pushed all the right buttons for millions of white and black diners. After World War II, newly arrived Mandarin speakers pulled off a partly similar feat under much more favorable circumstances. They managed to open stylish restaurants cleverly tailored to the palates of government policy wonks, businessmen, and food writers. What was more, they got their influential clientele talking (if confusedly) about authenticity and regionality. In both cases, Chinese transplants to this country had used food as a linking interest that helped them take the initiative in a certain asymmetrical colloquy or dialogue with non-Chinese Americans.

In retrospect we can see the chop suey restaurants founded in the Exclusion era as symbols of a will not only to endure but to prevail. Today the thousands that still thrive are as all-American as pizza parlors, which they long predated as a crossover national craze. They represent a permanent enrichment of the American table. The joy with which a huge audience has embraced them for some five generations can't be argued away by anyone impatiently dismissing the food as a distortion of Cantonese cuisine.

The smaller contingent of Mandarin speakers who arrived half a century later enjoyed more freedom to make a start in any potential career. But those who chose restaurants (or sometimes cooking schools) had as apt instincts as their predecessors for delighting non-Chinese eaters with sudden discoveries that for a time seemed inexhaustible. They, too, lastingly enlarged America's culinary horizons.

But cooking to please people who don't understand one's birthright culinary "language" can never justify kitchen drudgery in the same way as cooking to the taste of fellow "speakers." More pragmatically: Chinese American restaurant work has often been inseparable from the semi-thralldom of men like those interviewed in *Longtime Californ'*, caught up in bleak poverty while dreaming of escape to better jobs. The family-run chop suey restaurants that dotted the small-town American landscape were not exploitative to the same degree. But by the late twentieth century the demanding routine to which they held every member was usually justified, in parents' eyes, by future bills for the college education that would free their children to pursue other goals. Nor did the more affluent Mandarin speakers who had attracted movers and shakers to elegant establishments necessarily want to hand them down from generation to generation. Their children already had an easier road to lucrative professions than most Cantonese Americans.

This is to say that by 1990 a sizable proportion of the old Cantonese and the postwar Mandarin-speaking communities had *graduated from restaurants*. The pool of talent for running establishments designed to attract a predominantly white clientele had been changed forever by the simple fact that as time went on, fewer of the Chinese already settled in America needed to do it. For the heirs of the first Cantonese Americans, cooking for non-Chinese had long ceased to be a default defense against the immigration authorities. The initial wave of urbane Mandarin-speaking restaurateurs from the mainland via Taiwan had seen its children become lawyers and scientists.

The Chinese Americans who arrived through the Hart-Celler Act and the softening of PRC emigration restrictions did not view cooking for non-Chinese through the same prisms as their predecessors. It is true that many were (and still are) obliged to take initial jobs at chop suey joints in scattered corners of the nation. But restaurateurs in the substantial new Chinatowns of the 1980s were spared the necessity of, so to speak, cooking down to an ignorant non-Chinese clientele. Thus it happened that the numbers of Chinese speakers who understood particular regional or ethnic cuisines, and the ranks of restaurants attuned to their palates, were rapidly growing at the same time that many owners of restaurants dependent on a non-Chinese clientele were leaving the business. With steadily increasing immigration from Asia, and steadily expanding educational and career equality for the heirs of earlier Chinese immigrants, these trends can only accelerate in future.

It's worth noting that some "edgy" twenty-first-century successors to 1970s experiments in East–West chic may stand to contribute profoundly to coming transethnic culinary-cultural conversations. But the old racial dynamic of Chinese American restaurants is beyond recovery. Its passing is not to be lamented.

Life under the Chinese Exclusion Act is now only a memory—though a very bitter memory—for one contingent of a growing Chinese American community that today is unified by nothing except having originated within certain East Asian geographical coordinates. The most recently arrived often endure work every bit as hard and poorly paid as anything their Cantonese predecessors faced and cram themselves into equally wretched sleeping quarters. But they know that they can work toward a future as citizens of a confusedly evolving multiracial America. And simply by being here, they are opening fellow citizens' eyes to the unimaginable diversity of Chineseness. This is the first moment at which a white minority-to-be has had a chance to glimpse—or taste—the huge dimensions of Chinese identity. More than a half-century into the Hart-Celler Act, Gold Mountain may at last be ready to appreciate what Chinese cooks have given other Americans in the past and will give in future.

Postscript

What Might Have Been

It seems fitting to return to the Toisanese and other Pearl River Delta cooks who crossed the Pacific in 1849, eager to place their remarkable skills at the disposal of fellow Gold Rushers. What might Chinese American food have been like if their first friendly reception had not swiftly turned to the most rabid persecution ever visited on any racial group other than African Americans and Native Americans?

It is foolish to suppose that over time they would not have faced at least as much prejudice and disdain as the Irish or Italians, heightened by not only race but what Christian society considered an idolatrous religion. But some other things are obvious beyond question. Had the Cantonese newcomers had the same legal right as anybody else to enter the country, seek employment, and, if they wished, become American citizens, they would have made still greater contributions to the Gold Mountain table. In the Far West and perhaps elsewhere, simply being able to move around safely would have given Cantonese men even greater advantages in seeking jobs cooking for white people. At the same time, more white children would have had something like James Beard's early exposure to Cantonese cooking through the family cook, Jue Let, as well as Johnny Kan's cousins.

In a less hostile climate, the cultural barriers to bringing wives and daughters from ancestral Pearl River Delta villages might well have been more easily overcome. In that case, home cooking for families would have become a norm at an earlier date, along with a swifter evening-out of the distorted sex ratio. The "paper son" dodge, with constant fear of discovery and deportation, would have been unnecessary; children learning English in school and helping parents to overcome the immense language barrier would have become a factor sooner.

Would "chop suey" cuisine ever have been invented? Perhaps. Flawlessly tailored to the culinary American zeitgeist of circa 1900, it looks now like an idea simply waiting to happen. But the need for inventing it would not have been as pressing because the Chinese American community's reliance on the employment ghettos of laundries and restaurants that existed at the behest of a white clientele would have been less desperate. By the same token, the conditions under which Chinese sometimes cooked their own food for non-Chinese patrons would have been less constrained. Long before the 1943 end of Exclusion, some of the latter had begun scorning chop suey and developing a taste for what they saw on Chinese customers' tables. It isn't a stretch to guess that if Exclusion had never been enacted, the path to understanding would have been less obstacle-ridden.

To wonder what might have been lends all the keener edge to thinking of what was. At a time when millions of Americans and their elected representatives were doing their utmost to deny Chinese people any place in this nation's social and cultural fabric, the despised interlopers managed to make an irresistible claim on a small patch of that fabric. The job of cooking to please outsiders was one of the crucial weapons through which they survived threats and persecutions long enough to gradually relax their grip on the restaurant business, or its grip on them. No longer compelled to serve out long terms doing what they did so wonderfully, they have earned the freedom to form other strands in the larger fabric of American life.

Notes

INTRODUCTION

1. A photograph of the incriminating banana is reproduced in Marie Rose Wong, *Sweet Cakes, Long Journey: The Chinatowns of Portland, Oregon* (Seattle: University of Washington Press, 2004), 111.
2. Ellen D. Wu, "The Best Tofu in the World Comes from . . . Indiana?" in *Chinese American Voices: From the Gold Rush to the Present*, ed. Judy Yung, Gordon H. Chang, and Him Mark Lai (Berkeley: University of California Press, 2006), 372–76.

PROLOGUE: A STROKE OF THE PEN

1. Text of Hart-Celler Act is available from the University of Washington (Bothell) legal research database, U.S. Immigration Legislation Online: http://library.uwb.edu/static/USimmigration/1965_immigration_and_nationality_act.html.
2. Among the few nonwhite participants were at least two distinguished Japanese Americans: Senator Daniel Inouye of Hawaii and the official White House photographer, Yoichi Okamoto.
3. Text of Johnson's October 3, 1965, speech is available at http://www.lbjlib.utexas.edu/Johnson/archives.hom/speeches.hom/651003.asp.
4. Text of the Johnson-Reed Act is available at http://library.uwb.edu/static/USimmigration/1924_immigration_act.html.

5. Text of the Chinese Exclusion Act is available at http://library.uwb.edu/static/USimmigration/1882_chinese_exclusion_act.html.

6. Text of the McCarran-Walter Act is available at http://library.uwb.edu/static/USimmigration/1952_immigration_and_nationality_act.html. Text of the 1790 Naturalization Act is available at http://library.uwb.edu/static/US immigration/1790_naturalization_act.html.

1. ORIGINS: THE TOISAN–CALIFORNIA PIPELINE

1. The Nanjing Treaty signing ceremony was commemorated in a well-known engraving based on a painting by John Platt, a British officer in a Bengal Volunteers regiment posted to service in China during the First Opium War.

2. See John Keay, *China: A History* (New York: Basic Books, 2009), 65–66; and Patricia Buckley Ebrey, *The Cambridge Illustrated History of China* (Cambridge: Cambridge University Press, 1996), 179.

3. Lynn Pan, ed., *The Encyclopedia of the Chinese Overseas* (Cambridge, MA: Harvard University Press, 1998), 98; and Thomas W. Chinn, H. Mark Lai, and Philip P. Choy, eds., *A History of the Chinese in California: A Syllabus* (San Francisco: Chinese Historical Society of America, 1969), 12.

4. Lynn Pan, *Sons of the Yellow Emperor: A History of the Chinese Diaspora* (New York: Kodansha America, 1994), 15.

5. See Sucheng Chan, *This Bittersweet Soil: The Chinese in California Agriculture, 1860–1910* (Berkeley: University of California Press, 1986), 18–19.

6. Pan, *Sons of the Yellow Emperor*, 14–15.

7. See the account in Philip A. Kuhn, *Chinese Among Others: Emigration in Modern Times* (Lanham, MD: Rowman & Littlefield, 2008), 55–104.

8. Pan, *Encyclopedia of the Chinese Overseas*, 54.

9. Victor Purcell, *The Chinese in Southeast Asia*, 2nd ed. (London: Oxford University Press, 1965), 25.

10. My treatment of the Canton system draws substantially on Paul A. Van Dyke, *The Canton Trade: Life and Enterprise on the China Coast, 1700–1845* (Hong Kong: Hong Kong University Press, 2005).

11. Ibid., 21–23.

12. Ibid., 7, 12–13, 51–75.

13. Ibid., 77–81.

14. Ibid., 111–13.

15. John King Fairbank and Merle Goldman, *China: A New History*, 2nd ed. (Cambridge, MA: Belknap Press of Harvard University Press, 2006), 168.

16. Pan, *Encyclopedia of the Chinese Overseas*, 26; Frederic E. Wakeman Jr., *Strangers at the Gate: Social Disorder in South China, 1839–1861* (Berkeley:

University of California Press, 1966), 125–38; and Madeline Y. Hsu, *Dreaming of Gold, Dreaming of Home: Transnationalism and Migration Between the United States and South China, 1882–1943* (Stanford, CA: Stanford University Press, 2000), 27–29.

17. Ebrey, *Cambridge Illustrated History*, 240–43; Fairbank and Goldman, *China*, 206–12; and Keay, *China*, 469–74.

18. Text of the Treaty of Nanjing is available at www.international.ucla.edu/asia/article/18421.

19. The best account of the nineteenth-century Hong Kong–San Francisco traffic is Elizabeth Sinn, *Pacific Crossing: California Gold, Chinese Migration, and the Making of Hong Kong* (Hong Kong: Hong Kong University Press, 2013).

20. For Hong Kong's Chinese and non-Chinese population between 1841 and 1910, see *Historical and Statistical Abstract of the Colony of Hongkong* (Hongkong: Noronha & Co. Government Printers, 1911), 1–7.

21. As Philip A. Kuhn points out, there is no real Chinese equivalent for the concept of "emigrant," though setting up a provisional base of action outside one's home was well understood. Kuhn, *Chinese Among Others*, 4 and 5.

22. Wang Gungwu, *China and the Chinese Overseas* (Singapore: Times Academic Press, 1991), 5.

23. Ibid., 6.

24. Cantonese commercial activities in Hong Kong are well described in Sinn, *Pacific Crossing*, 43–91, 191–218.

25. Chan, *This Bittersweet Soil*, 8, 12.

26. Ibid., 16–18.

27. William Poy Lee, *The Eighth Promise: An American Son's Tribute to His Toisanese Mother* (Emmaus, PA: Rodale Books, 2007), 72–73.

28. Chan, *This Bittersweet Soil*, 17.

29. The repatriation of bones is examined at length in Sinn, *Pacific Crossing*, 265–95. See Hsu, *Dreaming of Gold*, 40–54, for an account of Toisan's economic dependence on remittances from sojourners in the United States.

30. See descriptions of the coolie trade in Kuhn, *Chinese Among Others*, 132–34; Sinn, *Pacific Crossing*, 50; Chinn et al., *History of Chinese in California*, 13–14; and Chan, *This Bittersweet Soil*, 21–26.

31. Kuhn, *Chinese Among Others*, 213; Sinn, *Pacific Crossing*, 51–52; Chinn et al, *History of Chinese in California*, 15; and Mary Roberts Coolidge, *Chinese Immigration* (New York: Henry Holt, 1909; repr., New York: Arno Press, 1969), 43–45 (page references are to the 1969 edition).

32. Kuhn, *Chinese Among Others*, 36–37; and Hsu, *Dreaming of Gold*, 23.

33. Kuhn, *Chinese Among Others*, 203; and Hsu, *Dreaming of Gold*, 31–35. The speed with which the Chinese began founding enterprises such as restaurants in San Francisco bespeaks a remarkable amount of business talent assembled in the half-begun settlement as early as the summer of 1849; see chapter 3.

2. THE CULINARY "LANGUAGE" BARRIER

1. See, for instance, Henry Low, *Cook at Home in Chinese* (New York: Macmillan, 1938); and Buwei Yang Chao, *How to Cook and Eat in Chinese* (New York: John Day, 1945).
2. Lynn Pan, *Sons of the Yellow Emperor: A History of the Chinese Diaspora* (New York: Kodansha America, 1994), 130; and G. William Skinner, *Chinese Society in Thailand: An Analytical Study* (Ithaca, NY: Cornell University Press, 1957), 103–4.
3. Charles Frederick Noble, *A Voyage to the East Indies* (London: 1765), 224, cited in Paul A. Van Dyke, *The Canton Trade: Life and Enterprise on the China Coast, 1700–1845* (Hong Kong: Hong Kong University Press, 2005), 62.
4. George Wingrove Cooke, *China: Being "The Times" Special Correspondence from China in the Years 1857–58* (London: G. Routledge, 1859), 236–37.
5. James Beard, *Delights and Prejudices: A Memoir with Recipes* (New York: Collier Macmillan, 1990), 15, 19, 39–40, 54.
6. William Kitchiner, *The Cook's Oracle and Housekeeper's Manual* (New York: J. & J. Harper, 1830), 66–82. Many early- to mid-nineteenth-century English and American cookbooks either closely or loosely adopt Kitchiner's classification of cooking methods.
7. Cooke, *China*, 235.
8. See Donald B. Wagner's translation of a seventeenth-century Chinese account of iron smelting in Guangdong Province in *Ferrous Metallurgy*, vol. 5, part 11 of *Science and Civilisation in China*, ed. Joseph Needham (Cambridge: Cambridge University Press, 2008), 49–52.
9. Mary Tsui Ping Yee, *Chinese Immigrant Cooking* (Cobb, CA: First Glance Books, 1998), 18.
10. Prentice Mulford, "California Culinary Experiences," *Overland Monthly and Out West Magazine* 2, no. 6 (June 1869): 560. "Hashes" of neatly sliced meats begin to disappear from standard cookbooks after about 1870.
11. See E. N. Anderson Jr. and Marja L. Anderson, "Modern China: South," in *Food in Chinese Culture: Anthropological and Historical Perspectives*, ed. K. C. Chang (New Haven: Yale University Press, 1977), 339.

12. Shiu-ying Hu, *Food Plants of China* (Hong Kong: Chinese University Press, 2005), 27–31. The author presents an overview of other fermented products, 32–41.

13. Cooke, *China*, 238.

14. H. T. Huang gives a description of several edible oils in *Fermentations and Food Science*, volume 6, part 5 of *Science and Civilisation in China*, ed. Joseph Needham (Cambridge: Cambridge University Press, 2000), 436–57.

15. Fuchsia Dunlop, *Sichuan Cookery* (London: Penguin Books, 2001), 240–58, or the American edition published as *Land of Plenty* (New York: Norton, 2003), 240–58.

16. Mary Hyman and Philip Hyman, "France," in *The Oxford Companion to Food*, by Alan Davidson, 2nd ed., ed. Tom Jaine (Oxford: Oxford University Press, 2006), 314.

17. Évariste Régis Huc, *The Chinese Empire: A Sequel to Recollections of a Journey Through Tartary and Thibet by M. Huc, Formerly Missionary Apostolic in China*, new ed. (London: Longman, Brown, Green, Longmans, & Roberts, 1859), 128.

18. Griffith John, "North China—Hiau-Kan." In *The Chronicle of the London Missionary Society, April, 1879*, in *The Evangelical and Missionary Chronicle*, vol. 9, new series (London: Hodder & Stoughton, 1879), 260.

3. "CELESTIALS" ON GOLD MOUNTAIN

1. Leslie Brenner, *American Appetite: The Coming of Age of a Cuisine* (New York: Avon Books, 1999), 95–96.

2. Fred Ferretti, "A Rat in the Kitchen," *New York Times*, op-ed article, February 9, 2008, A15.

3. Jacques Gernet, *Daily Life in China on the Eve of the Mongol Invasion, 1250–1276*, trans. M. M. Wright, 2nd ed. (Stanford, CA: Stanford University Press, 1970), 49–51; and Joanna Waley-Cohen, "The Quest for Balance: Taste and Gastronomy in Imperial China," in *Food: The History of Taste*, ed. Paul Freedman (Berkeley: University of California Press, 2007), 111–12.

4. *Meng liang lu*, as cited in Gernet, *Daily Life*, 50–51.

5. Gernet, *Daily Life*, 133–38; and Michael Freeman, "Sung," in *Food in Chinese Culture: Anthropological and Historical Perspectives*, ed. K. C. Chang (New Haven: Yale University Press, 1977), 146–47, 154–55, 161–62.

6. Wang Gungwu, *China and the Chinese Overseas* (Singapore: Times Academic Press, 1991), 188–95.

7. Freeman, "Sung," 146; and E. N. Anderson, *The Food of China* (New Haven: Yale University Press, 1988), 77.

8. Philip A. Kuhn, *Chinese Among Others: Emigration in Modern Times* (Lanham, MD: Rowman & Littlefield, 2008), 183; Victor Purcell, *The Chinese in Southeast Asia*, 2nd ed. (London: Oxford University Press, 1965), 364, 420; and G. William Skinner, *Chinese Society in Thailand: An Analytical Study* (Ithaca, NY: Cornell University Press, 1957), 112.

9. See the description of the services rendered by the contemporary *jin shan zhuang*, or "Gold Mountain firms," in Madeline Y. Hsu, *Dreaming of Gold, Dreaming of Home: Transnationalism and Migration Between the United States and South China, 1882–1943* (Stanford, CA: Stanford University Press, 2000), 34–40.

10. Prentice Mulford, "Glimpses of John Chinaman," *Lippincott's Magazine of Literature and Science* 11 (February 1873): 219–20.

11. Étienne Derbec, *A French Journalist in the California Gold Rush: The Letters of Etienne Derbec*, ed. A. P. Nasatir (Georgetown, CA: Talisman Press, 1964), 170.

12. Such items seem to have been regularly shipped from Hong Kong. See James Delgado, *Gold Rush Port: The Maritime Archaeology of San Francisco's Waterfront* (Berkeley: University of California Press, 2009), 103 and app. 3, 191–203; and Elizabeth Sinn, *Pacific Crossing: California Gold, Chinese Migration, and the Making of Hong Kong* (Hong Kong: Hong Kong University Press, 2013), app. 1, 309–11.

13. Bayard Taylor, *Eldorado: Or, Adventures in the Path of Empire* (New York: G. P. Putnam, 1861), 117.

14. "Meeting of the Chinese Residents of San Francisco," *Daily Alta California*, December 10, 1849, 1.

15. The historian H. H. Bancroft estimated the number of Chinese in California in January 1850 at 787 men and 2 women. Hubert Howe Bancroft, *History of California*, vol. 7, *1860–1890*, of *The Works of Hubert Howe Bancroft*, 39 vols. (San Francisco: History Company, 1890), 336.

16. *Weekly Alta California*, October 4, 1849, advertisement, 3. I am indebted to Erica J. Peters for bringing this notice to my attention.

17. Charles P. Kimball, *The San Francisco City Directory* (San Francisco: Journal of Commerce Press, September 1, 1850), 8.

18. Him Mark Lai, *Becoming Chinese American: A History of Communities and Institutions* (Walnut Creek, CA: AltaMira Press, 2004), 179–80.

19. James O'Meara, "The Chinese in Early Days," *Overland Monthly and Out West Magazine* 3, no. 5 (May 1884): 478.

20. Ibid., 477–78.

21. J. D. Borthwick, *Three Years in California* (Edinburgh: William Blackwood and Sons, 1867), 74–75.

22. Richard Steven Street, *Beasts of the Field: A Narrative History of California Farmworkers, 1769–1913* (Stanford, CA: Stanford University Press, 2004), 80, 97.

23. Taylor, *Eldorado*, 117.

24. James Delavan, *Notes on California and the Placers: How to Get There and What to Do Afterwards* (New York: H. Long & Brother, 1850), 100.

25. William Shaw, *Golden Dreams and Waking Realities* (London: Smith, Elder, 1851), 42.

26. William Redmond Ryan, *Personal Adventures in Upper and Lower California*, vol. 2 (London: William Shoberl, 1852), 267–68.

27. William Kelly, *An Excursion to California*, vol. 2 (London: Chapman & Hall, 1851), 244.

28. Among various reports of foodstuffs available in the Chinese community, probably the most comprehensive is Robert F. G. Spier, "Food Habits of Nineteenth-Century California Chinese," *California Historical Society Quarterly* 37 (March 1958): 79–84, and (June 1958): 129–36.

29. Derbec, *A French Journalist*, 170.

30. Bancroft, *History of California*, 7:336.

31. Population figures compiled from ibid., 7:698n6; *Historical Statistics of the United States: Colonial Times to 1970* (Washington, DC: U.S. Government Printing Office, 1975), part I, page A1–8, Series A 1-5; and Thomas W. Chinn, H. Mark Lai, and Philip P. Choy, eds., *A History of the Chinese in California: A Syllabus* (San Francisco: Chinese Historical Society of America, 1969), 19, table 2.

32. *Alta California*, June 15, 1853, 2.

33. Mary Roberts Coolidge, *Chinese Immigration* (New York: Henry Holt, 1909; repr. Arno Press, 1969), 255–57; and Sue Fawn Chung, *In Pursuit of Gold: Chinese American Miners and Merchants in the American West* (Champaign: University of Illinois Press, 2011), 12–13, 35–45.

34. For information on some industrial Chinese employment opportunities, see Chinn et al., *A History of the Chinese in California*, 49–55.

35. Sinn, *Pacific Crossing*, 181–85.

36. Jack Chen, *The Chinese of America: From the Beginnings to the Present* (New York: Harper & Row, 1980), 97–103; Chinn et al, *A History of the Chinese in California*, 37–41; Coolidge, *Chinese Immigration*, 72–74; and Sandy Lydon, *Chinese Gold: The Chinese in the Monterey Bay Region* (Capitola, CA: Capitola Book Company, 1985), 29–59.

37. See Walter C. Blasdale, *A Description of Some Chinese Vegetable Food Materials*, U.S. Department of Agriculture Bulletin No. 68 (Washington, DC: Government Printing Office, 1899).

38. Sucheng Chan, *This Bittersweet Soil: The Chinese in California Agriculture, 1860–1910* (Berkeley: University of California Press, 1986), 99–100; and Frederick J. Simoons, *Food in China: A Cultural and Historical Inquiry* (Boca Raton, FL: CRC Press, 1991), 470–71.

39. *Washington Standard*, June 20, 1879, cited on Olympia Historical Society and Bigelow House Museum website, olympiahistory.org/wp/market-gardens/.

40. Edwin L. Sabin, *Building the Pacific Railway* (Philadelphia: Lippincott, 1919), 125.

41. Chinn et al., *A History of the Chinese in California*, 44; and Charles Nordhoff, *California: For Health, Pleasure, and Residence* (New York: Harper & Brothers, 1873), 189–90. Nordhoff points out that the cooks were hired (presumably for special wages) by the contractor; the Chinese agents at the San Francisco end must have been able to tap into a supply of qualified applicants.

42. A. W. Loomis, "How Our Chinamen Are Employed," *Overland Monthly*, vol. 2, no. 3 (March 1868): 232.

43. Henry George, "The Chinese in America: Their Habits, Morals and Prospects—The Extermination of the Exterminator," *Defiance Democrat* (Ohio), June 19, 1869, 1. (Originally published in the *New-York Tribune* on May 1, 1869, as "The Chinese on the Pacific Coast.") I am indebted to Michael T. Intranuovo of the Center of Archival Collections at Bowling Green State University for sending me a PDF of this article.

44. Chan, *This Bittersweet Soil*, 158–89; and Street, *Beasts of the Field*, 259–67.

45. Testimony of Col. F. A. Bee in *Report of the Joint Special Committee to Investigate Chinese Immigration*, 44th Congress (Washington, DC: Government Printing Office, 1877), 40–41.

46. Chan, *This Bittersweet Soil*, 106–57.

47. Chinn et al., *A History of the Chinese in California*, 19, table 2.

48. A statement by survivors of the Rock Springs massacre appears in "Memorial of Chinese Laborers at Rock Springs, Wyoming," in *Chinese American Voices: From the Gold Rush to the Present*, edited by Judy Yung, Gordon H. Cheng, and Him Mark Lai, 48–54 (Berkeley: University of California Press, 2006). See also Shih-shan Henry Tsai, *The Chinese Experience in America* (Bloomington: Indiana University Press, 1986), 67–72. The Nast cartoon appeared in *Harper's Weekly*, September 19, 1885.

49. The anti-coolie arguments are summarized by Coolidge, *Chinese Immigration*, 41–54.

50. Ibid., 498.

51. The highly biased proceedings of the joint congressional delegations are summarized by Coolidge, *Chinese Immigration*, 96–108. For the relevant

portions of the 1879 California state constitution, see William L. Tung, *The Chinese in America, 1820–1973: A Chronology and Fact Book* (Dobbs Ferry, NY: Oceana Publications, 1974), 57.

52. For text of the 1882 Chinese Exclusion Act and the Geary Act, see Tung, *Chinese in America*, 58–61 and 71–73.

53. Roger Daniels, *Coming to America: A History of Immigration and Ethnicity in American Life*, 2nd ed. (New York: Harper Perennial, 1990), 189 (table 7.3) and 129 (table 6.5); and *Historical Statistics of the United States*, page A1–8, series A1–55.

54. Chinn et al., *A History of the Chinese in California*, 24–25.

55. For text of the Burlingame Treaty, see Tung, *Chinese in America*, 87–90.

56. For descriptions of laundry working conditions, see Paul C. P. Siu, *The Chinese Laundryman: A Study of Social Isolation*, ed. John Kuo Wei Tchen (New York: New York University Press, 1987), 69–76; and John Jung, *Chinese Laundries: Tickets to Survival on Gold Mountain* (N.p.: Yin & Yang Press, 2007), 126–46.

57. Chan, *This Bittersweet Soil*, 361–68; and Street, *Beasts of the Field*, 243–47.

58. Street, *Beasts of the Field*, 245–46.

59. J. S. Cummins, ed., *The Travels and Controversies of Friar Domingo Navarrete, 1618–1686*, vol. 2 (Cambridge: Hakluyt Society, 1962), 228.

60. Prentice Mulford, "California Culinary Experiences," *Overland Monthly and Out West Magazine* 2, no. 6 (June 1869): 558.

61. See the account of one farm wife, writing to the *Stockton Independent* in 1876, as cited in Chan, *This Bittersweet Soil*, 365.

62. The competition between female Irish and male Chinese household servants is examined in detail by Andrew Theodore Urban in "An Intimate World: Race, Migration, and Chinese and Irish Domestic Servants in the United States, 1856–1920" (PhD dissertation, University of Minnesota, 2009).

63. Reproduced in ibid., 145.

4. THE ROAD TO CHINATOWN

1. Lynn Pan, ed., *The Encyclopedia of the Chinese Overseas* (Cambridge, MA: Harvard University Press, 1998), 23–24.

2. Ibid., 46–47, 75–77; and Jack M. Potter, "Land and Lineage in Traditional China," in *Family and Kinship in Chinese Society*, ed. Maurice Freedman (Stanford, CA: Stanford University Press, 1970), 121–38.

3. G. William Skinner, "Mobility Strategies in Late Imperial China: A Regional Systems Analysis" in *Regional Analysis*, vol. 1: *Economic Systems*, ed. Carol A. Smith (New York: Academic Press, 1976), 327–64; and Elizabeth Sinn, *Pacific*

Crossing: California Gold, Chinese Migration, and the Making of Hong Kong (Hong Kong: Hong Kong University Press, 2013), 265–83.

4. Sinn, *Pacific Crossing*, 224–25; and Judy Yung, *Unbound Feet: A Social History of Chinese Women in San Francisco* (Berkeley: University of California Press, 1995), 18–19.

5. H. H. Bancroft, *History of California*, vol. 7 of *The Works of Hubert Howe Bancroft*, 39 vols. (San Francisco: History Company, 1890), 336. The 1900 ratio is from U.S. census figures as tabulated in Roger Daniels, *Asian America: Chinese and Japanese in the United States Since 1850* (Seattle: University of Washington Press, 1988), 69.

6. As Mary Roberts Coolidge pointed out in 1909, extreme overcrowding in the unventilated, sub-sub-divided, bunk-lined cubicles that constituted living quarters for most Chinese workingmen in San Francisco was largely due to the greed of white landlords. See her *Chinese Immigration* (New York: Henry Holt, 1909; repr. Arno Press, 1969), 412–15.

7. Sinn, *Pacific Crossing*, 226.

8. Ibid., 226, 228–35; see also Yung, *Unbound Feet*, 27–31, 37–41.

9. Sucheng Chan, "Against All Odds: Chinese Female Migration and Family Formation on American Soil During the Early Twentieth Century," in *Chinese American Transnationalism: The Flow of People, Resources, and Ideas Between China and America During the Exclusion Era*, ed. Sucheng Chan (Philadelphia: Temple University Press, 2006), 56; and Yung, *Unbound Feet*, 33–34.

10. The text of the Page Act can be accessed through the University of Washington (Bothell) legal research database, http://library.uwb.edu/static/USimmigration/1875_page_law.html.

11. "How American Women May Make Chop Suey," *Indianapolis News*, February 16, 1906, 7.

12. Sinn, *Pacific Crossing*, 191–216.

13. Josephine Clifford, "Chinatown," *Potter's American Monthly* 14 (May 1880): 353–64.

14. See the introduction to some organizations in Adam McKeown, *Chinese Migrant Networks and Cultural Change: Peru, Chicago, Hawaii, 1900–1936* (Chicago: University of Chicago Press, 2001), 79–80, 111–18, 181–91.

15. Yong Chen, *Chinese San Francisco, 1850–1943: A Trans-Pacific Community* (Stanford, CA: Stanford University Press, 2000), 110–14.

16. For the text of the Geary Act, see William L. Tung, *The Chinese in America, 1820–1973: A Chronology and Fact Book* (Dobbs Ferry, NY: Oceana Publications, 1974), 71–73.

17. For the text of the majority opinion in *Wong Kim Ark*, see Tung, *Chinese in America*, 104–5.

18. Madeline Y. Hsu, *Dreaming of Gold, Dreaming of Home: Transnationalism and Migration Between the United States and South China, 1882–1943* (Stanford, CA: Stanford University Press, 2000), 68–89; and Helen Hong Wong, "Reminiscences of a Gold Mountain Woman," in *Chinese American Voices: From the Gold Rush to the Present*, ed. Judy Yung, Gordon H. Chang, and Him Mark Lai (Berkeley: University of California Press, 2006), 159–60. Other immigration stations were set up at Oregon and Washington State ports. See Marie Rose Wong, *Sweet Cakes, Long Journey: The Chinatowns of Portland, Oregon* (Seattle: University of Washington Press, 2004), 75–148.

19. See photographs of banana and peanut coaching letters in Wong, *Sweet Cakes*, 110–11.

20. Immigration and census figures as tabulated in Pan, *Encyclopedia of the Chinese Overseas*, 262. The collection of data during this era was at times haphazard, and widely varying estimates appear in different sources.

21. The text of the 1921 Emergency Quota Act can be accessed at the University of Washington (Bothell) legal research database, http://library.uwb.edu/static/USimmigration/1921_emergency_quota_law.html.

22. Quoted in George M. Stephenson, *A History of American Immigration* (Boston: Ginn, 1926), 190.

23. The text of the Johnson-Reed Act can be accessed at the University of Washington (Bothell) legal research database, http://library.uwb.edu/static/USimmigration/1924_immigration_act.html.

24. Coolidge, *Chinese Immigration*, 73–74, describes the Italian takeover of the San Francisco fisheries.

25. Jack Chen, *The Chinese of America* (New York: Harper & Row, 1980), 105–7.

26. Harold Sands, "Subduing the Sockeye," *Canadian Magazine* 33, no. 2 (May 1909): 69.

27. Wong, *Sweet Cakes*, 211–20.

28. Jeffrey M. Fee, "Idaho's Mountain Gardens," in *Hidden Heritage: Historical Archaeology of the Overseas Chinese*, ed. Priscilla Wegars (Amityville, NY: Baywood, 1993), 65–96.

29. The Augusta-Atlanta story is examined in Jianli Zhao, *Strangers in the City: The Atlanta Chinese, Their Community, and Stories of Their Lives* (New York: Routledge, 2000).

30. Lucy M. Cohen, *Chinese in the Post–Civil War South: A People Without a History* (Baton Rouge: Louisiana State University Press, 1984), 82–132.

31. Richard Campanella, *Geographies of New Orleans: Urban Fabric Before the Storm* (Lafayette: Center for Louisiana Studies, 2006), 337–55.

32. The Sigel case has been retold by Mary Ting Yi Lui, *The Chinatown Trunk Mystery: Murder, Miscegenation, and Other Dangerous Encounters in Turn-of-the-Century New York City* (Princeton, NJ: Princeton University Press, 2005).

33. Louis J. Beck, *New York's Chinatown: An Historical Presentation of Its People and Places* (New York: Bohemia Publishing, 1898), 11. See also Arthur Bonner, *Alas! What Brought Thee Hither? The Chinese in New York, 1800–1950* (Teaneck, NJ: Fairleigh Dickinson University Press, 1997), 46–47, 61, 71, 103; and John Kuo Wei Tchen, *New York Before Chinatown: Orientalism and the Shaping of American Culture, 1776–1882* (Baltimore: Johns Hopkins University Press, 1999), 236–37.

34. Huping Ling, *Chinese St. Louis: From Enclave to Cultural Community* (Philadelphia: Temple University Press, 2004), 26–27.

35. Lena Sze, "Opportunity, Conflict, and Community in Transition: Historical and Contemporary Chinese Immigration to Philadelphia," in *Global Philadelphia: Immigrant Communities Old and New*, ed. Ayumi Takenaka and Mary Johnson Osirim (Philadelphia: Temple University Press, 2000), 99.

36. Betty H. Lam, "Earliest Chinese Settlement in Boston Dated 1875," *Chinese Historical Society of New England Newsletter* 4, no. 1 (Summer 1998): 2, accessed at http://chsne.org/newsletters/1998.htm.

37. Huping Ling, *Chinese Chicago: Race, Transnational Migration, and Community Since 1870* (Stanford, CA: Stanford University Press, 2012), 30–31.

38. To this day, southern Chinese cling to the otherwise archaic term "*tong yan*" (Mandarin, *tang ren*) or "people of Tang" (referring to the Tang Dynasty, 618–907) as a badge of identity, while Chinese of other regions prefer "*han ren*" (Han people). I am indebted to E. N. Anderson for pointing out the meaning of the name.

39. Susan B. Carter, "Embracing Isolation: Chinese American Geographic Redistribution during the Exclusion Era, 1882—1943" (unpublished paper, 2013), 44, table 4.

40. Hsu, *Dreaming of Gold*, 35.

41. Paul C. P. Siu, *The Chinese Laundryman: A Study of Social Isolation*, ed. John Kuo Wei Tchen (New York: New York University Press, 1987), 144–48; Peter Kwong and Dusanka Miscevic, *Chinese America: The Untold Story of America's Oldest New Community* (New York: New Press, 2005), 133; and Beck, *New York's Chinatown*, 46–47.

42. Jessup Whitehead, *The Steward's Handbook and Guide to Party Catering* (Chicago: Jessup Whitehead, 1903), 279; and Beck, *New York's Chinatown*, 85–90. Smaller Chinatowns also often relied on market gardeners.

43. Siu, *Chinese Laundryman*, 41; Kwong and Miscevic, *Chinese America*, 132–33, 186–89; and Bonner, *Alas! What Brought Thee Hither?*, 26–32.

44. Kwong and Miscevic, *Chinese America*, 186–87; John Jung, *Chinese Laundries: Tickets to Survival on Gold Mountain* (N.p.: Yin and Yang Press, 2007), 71–74, 84–88; and Ronald Takaki, *Strangers from a Different Shore: A History of Asian Americans*, updated and rev. ed. (Boston: Little, Brown / Back Bay Books, 1998), 244–45.

45. Jung, *Chinese Laundries*, 213.

46. Philip P. Choy, "The Architecture of San Francisco Chinatown," in *Chinese American History and Perspectives, 1990* (Brisbane, CA: Chinese Historical Society of America, 1990), 37–66.

47. "Queer Dishes Served at the Waldorf by Li Hung Chung's Chinese Cook," *New York Journal*, September 6, 1896, 29; and "A Chinese Dinner," *Brooklyn Eagle*, September 22, 1896, 8.

48. "Joy Hing Lo," *Chicago Daily Tribune*, July 31, 1908, 18.

49. Population figures as tabulated in Pan, *Encyclopedia of the Chinese Overseas*, 262.

5. THE BIRTH OF CHINESE AMERICAN CUISINE

1. Otis Gibson, *The Chinese in America* (Cincinnati: Hitchcock & Walker, 1877), 70.

2. Hubert Howe Bancroft, "Mongolianism in America," in *Essays and Miscellany*, vol. 38, 309–418, of *The Works of Hubert Howe Bancroft*, 39 vols. (San Francisco: History Company, 1890), 331.

3. George Augustus Sala, *America Revisited*, 6th ed. (London: Vizelly, 1886), 498.

4. Sir Edwin Arnold, *Seas and Lands* (New York: Longmans, Green, 1891), 134.

5. Gibson, *Chinese in America*, 71–72.

6. Wong Chin Foo, "The Chinese in New York," *Cosmopolitan* 5, no. 4 (June 1888): 305.

7. Susan B. Carter, "How the Penny Press 'Educated Up' the American Palate: From 'Rats and Dogs' to 'Chop Suey Mad,'" paper presented at the Roger Smith Food/Tech Conference, April 5, 2014; and Susan B. Carter, "Celestial Suppers: The Political Economy of America's Chop Suey Craze, 1900–1930" (unpublished manuscript, 2009).

8. E. T. Lander, "Chinese Horticulture in New York," *Garden and Forest: A Journal of Horticulture, Landscape Art and Forestry* 1 (December 5, 1888): 483–84.

9. L. H. Bailey, *Some Recent Chinese Vegetables* (Cornell University Agricultural Experiment Station, Horticultural Division, Bulletin 67; Ithaca, NY:

Cornell University, June 1894), 177–201; and Walter C. Blasdale, *A Description of Some Chinese Vegetables and Food Materials, and Their Nutritive and Economic Value*. U.S. Department of Agriculture Bulletin 68 (Washington, DC: Government Printing Office, 1899).

10. Blasdale, *Description of Some Chinese Vegetables*, 35–36.

11. These last comments appear to come from a British observer in Hong Kong and refer to wok cooking on a pottery brazier, not a fixed range. Jessup Whitehead, *The Steward's Handbook and Guide to Party Catering* (Chicago: Jessup Whitehead, 1903), 279.

12. An online translation of the *Suiyuan Shidan* by S. J. S. Chen has been published in installments at https://wayoftheeating.wordpress.com/. A scholarly translation by Beilei Pu, edited by Eugene N. Anderson, is in preparation; see http://www.krazykioti.com/articles/yuan-mei-and-his-suiyuan-shidian-food-book/.

13. Alice Moore, *Chinese Recipes: Letters from Alice Moore to Ethel Moore Rook* (Garden City, NY: Doubleday, Page, 1923), 1–2.

14. John Thorne with Matt Lewis Thorne, *Mouth Wide Open: A Cook and His Appetite* (New York: North Point Press, 2008), 157n.

15. Wing Chinfoo [Wong Chin Foo], "Chinese Cooking," *Brooklyn Daily Eagle*, July 6, 1884, 4.

16. Wong, "Chinese in New York," 304.

17. *American Gas Engineering Journal* 107, no. 24 (December 15, 1917), 539–40. Chop suey stoves are mentioned as an interesting innovation in *American Gas Light Journal* (June 23, 1913), 407.

18. Jessie Louise Nolton, ed., *Chinese Cookery in the Home Kitchen: Being Recipes for the Preparation of the Most Popular Chinese Dishes at Home* (Detroit: Chino-American Publishing Company, 1911).

19. Advertisement of Wm. F. Traub Range Co. in *Chinese Students' Monthly* 16, no. 1 (November 1920): 105.

20. Nolton, *Chinese Cookery*, n.p.

21. See Grace Young and Alan Richardson, *The Breath of a Wok: Unlocking the Spirit of Chinese Wok Cooking Through Recipes and Lore* (New York: Simon & Schuster, 2004) and Grace Young, *Stir-Frying to the Sky's Edge: The Ultimate Guide to Mastery, with Authentic Recipes and Stories* (New York: Simon & Schuster, 2010).

22. "Got the Chinese Craze?" *New York Journal*, September 6, 1896, 33.

23. "Chop Suey Resorts: Chinese Dish Now Served in Many Parts of the City," *New York Times*, November 15, 1903, 20.

24. Ibid.

25. Huping Ling, *Chinese St. Louis: From Enclave to Cultural Community* (Philadelphia: Temple University Press, 2004), 49.

26. Raymond G. Carroll, "Chinese Laundries Gone; Restaurants Are Many," *Los Angeles Times*, March 27, 1924, 6. (Originally published in *Philadelphia Public Ledger*.)

27. Sunyowe Pang, "The Chinese in America," *Forum* 32, no. 5 (January 1902): 606.

28. Wong Chin Foo, "Chinese Recipes," in *The Cook* 1, no. 5 (April 27, 1885): 7. My thanks to Scott Seligman for sending me clear images of the complete Wong series in *The Cook*.

29. Jane Eddington, "Perennial Chop Suey," *Chicago Tribune*, October 29, 1915, 14.

30. Louis J. Beck, *New York's Chinatown: An Historical Presentation of Its People and Places* (New York: Bohemia Publishing, 1898), 56.

31. Mrs. Simon [Lizzie Black] Kander, *The Settlement Cook Book*, 7th ed. (Milwaukee: Settlement Cook Book Co., 1915), 144.

32. Fannie Merritt Farmer and Cora D. Perkins, *The Boston Cooking-School Cook Book*, rev. ed. (Boston: Little, Brown, 1929), 461.

33. Nolton, *Chinese Cookery*, n.p.

34. The U.S. Patent Office recorded a trademark registration for Chop Suey Sauce by the Chop Suey Sauce Company of New York in 1915.

35. Ida C. Bailey Allen, *Mrs. Allen's Cook Book* (Boston: Small, Maynard, 1917), 383.

36. Beverly Hills Woman's Club, *Fashions in Food in Beverly Hills*, 2nd ed. (Beverly Hills, CA: Beverly Hills Citizen, 1930), 73.

37. Advertisement for Mazola, *The Courier-Express* (Dubois, PA), May 24, 1927, 5.

38. Dan J. Forrestal, *The Kernel and the Bean: The 75-year History of the Staley Company* (New York: Simon & Schuster, 1982), 102, 151.

39. See entry 2848 in William Shurtleff and Akiko Aoyagi, *History of Soy Sauce (160 CE to 2012): Extensively Annotated Bibliography and Sourcebook* (Lafayette, CA: Soyinfo Center, 2012), 849–50.

40. It is not clear how or when egg rolls came to be invented. Chinese cooks from all regions generally disdain them as crude, heavy caricatures of spring rolls. See chapter 6 for one not particularly convincing claim by Henry Low.

41. Wing [Wong], "Chinese Cooking."

42. Nolton, *Chinese Cookery*, n.p.

43. Andrew Coe, *Chop Suey: A Cultural History of Chinese Food in the United States* (New York: Oxford University Press, 2009), 168.

44. La Choy urged buyers to create a one-dish chow mein meal by purchasing canned chow mein noodles along with La Choy canned bean sprouts and bottled "soy" and "brown" sauces, and adding any "favorite meat and domestic vegetables." Advertisement in *Indianapolis News*, January 22, 1929, 27.

45. James Beard, *Delights and Prejudices: A Memoir with Recipes* (New York: Collier Macmillan, 1990), 22–23.

46. "Easter Shopping Done in Chinatown," *Brooklyn Daily Eagle*, April 5, 1903, 15.

47. "Chinese Cooking Is a Fine Art," *Minneapolis Journal*, October 24, 1903, section 2, 3.

48. For a brief introduction to yat ca mein under many improbable spellings, see John T. Edge, "Seventh Ward Ramen," *Lucky Peach*, no. 1 (Summer 2011): 45–47.

49. Nolton, *Chinese Cookery*.

50. Sara Bossé and Onoto Watanna, *Chinese-Japanese Cook Book* (Chicago: Rand McNally, 1914). The pseudonymous Watanna (in fact, the novelist Winnifred Eaton) and her sister, the painter Sara Bossé, were of mixed Chinese and English parentage; it is doubtful that either had firsthand knowledge of Chinese or Japanese cooking.

51. Shiu Wong Chan, *The Chinese Cook Book* (New York: Frederick A. Stokes, 1917).

52. Ibid., 91.

53. Ibid., 199–201.

54. "How American Women May Make Chop Suey," *Indianapolis News*, February 16, 1906, 7.

55. "Chinese Dishes," *Cincinnati Enquirer*, July 31, 1919, 5.

56. The script for "A Chinese Dinner" may be accessed at https://archive.org/details/chinesedinner1931unit.

57. *The Spatula: An Illustrated Magazine for Pharmacists*, August 1903, 686.

58. Advertisement, *Red Bank (N.J.) Register*, October 22, 1913, 1.

59. Though there is a durable legend that Harry Houdini craved farmer's chop suey when he lay dying in 1926, I have not been able to ascertain whether it then existed under that name.

60. For an attempt to chronicle the chow mein sandwich, see Imogene L. Lim, "Chinese Cuisine Meets the American Palate: The Chow Mein Sandwich," in *Chinese Cuisine American Palate: An Anthology*, ed. Jacqueline M. Newman and Roberta Halporn, 130–39 (Brooklyn, NY: Center for Thanatology Research & Education), available at https://wordpress.viu.ca.limi/files/2012/008/ChineseCuisineMeetsTheAmericanPalate_CMS.pdf. I am not aware of any similar history of the St. Paul sandwich.

61. "Live Topics about Town," *New York Sun*, October 2, 1911, 7.

62. Kander, *Settlement Cook Book*, 144.

63. "How to Make Chop Suey," *Chicago Daily Tribune*, February 23, 1913, 44.

64. *Lynnhurst Congregational Church Cook Book of Tested Recipes* (Minneapolis: Lynnhurst Congregational Church, 1920), 43.

65. Susan B. Carter, "Embracing Isolation: Chinese American Geographic Redistribution During the Exclusion Era, 1882–1943" (unpublished manuscript, 2013).

66. John Jung, *Sweet and Sour: Life in Chinese Family Restaurants* (N.p.: Yin & Yang Press, 2010), 169.

67. Ling, *Chinese St. Louis*, 49.

68. Ken Hom, *Easy Family Recipes from a Chinese-American Childhood* (New York: Knopf, 1997), 19.

69. "Advice on Vegetables," *Cincinnati Enquirer*, September 27, 1916, 16.

6. CHANGE, INTERCHANGE, AND THE FIRST SUCCESSFUL "TRANSLATORS"

1. For the major facts of the Chaos' careers, I have relied on Buwei Yang Chao, *Autobiography of a Chinese Woman, Put into English by Her Husband, Yuenren Chao* (New York: John Day, 1947).

2. "King Joy Lo: The Finest Chinese-American Restaurant in the World," *Chicago Daily Tribune*, December 22, 1906, 2.

3. Adam McKeown, *Chinese Migrant Networks and Social Change: Peru, Chicago, Hawaii, 1900–1936* (Chicago: University of Chicago Press, 2001), 206.

4. Pardee Lowe, *Father and Glorious Descendant* (Boston: Little, Brown, 1943), 127–48.

5. Louis H. Chu, "The Chinese Restaurants in New York City," master's thesis, New York University, 1939.

6. Carl Crow, *400 Million Customers: The Experiences—Some Happy, Some Sad, of an American in China, and What They Taught Me* (New York: Harper & Brothers, 1937).

7. The best survey of Pearl Buck's career is Peter Conn, *Pearl S. Buck: A Cultural Biography* (Cambridge: Cambridge University Press, 1996). I have drawn on this account and Buck's own memoir, *My Several Worlds: A Personal Record* (New York: John Day, 1954).

8. The text of the Magnuson Act can be accessed at the University of Washington (Bothell) legal research database, http://library.uwb.edu/static/US immigration/1943_magnuson_act.html.

9. Carl Glick, *Shake Hands with the Dragon* (New York: Whittlesey House / McGraw-Hill, 1941), 162.

10. My account of the *How to Cook and Eat in Chinese* publishing story is based on the relevant papers in the John Day Company Archives at the Firestone Library, Princeton University, cited hereafter as JDCA. Walsh's original letter of inquiry was dated March 13, 1944. (For another interesting perspective on "how to cook and eat in Chinese," see John Eng-Wong, "How to Cook and Eat Chinese," Brown University "Year of China" event, May 10, 2012, https://www.brown.edu/about/administration/international-affairs/year-of-china/how-cook-and-eat-chinese; and YouTube, June 4, 2012, https://www.youtube.com/watch?v=FV-xOmtP5NQ).

11. Yuenren Chao to Richard J. Walsh, March 27, 1944 (JDCA).

12. Lamb, born Corrine Goodknight in Sedalia, Missouri, was an American explorer who made several treks into remote areas of China with her husband, Eugene Lamb.

13. Chu, *Chinese Restaurants in New York City*, 63.

14. Henry Low, *Cook at Home in Chinese* (New York: Macmillan, 1938), 214.

15. Buwei Yang Chao, *How to Cook and Eat in Chinese* (New York: John Day, 1945), xiii.

16. Ibid., xiii–xiv.

17. Richard J. Walsh to Mrs. Yuenren Chao, June 2, 1944 (JDCA).

18. Richard J. Walsh to Richard Walsh Jr., May 30, 1944 (JDCA).

19. Memo headed "HOW TO COOK AND EAT IN CHINESE—Mrs. Chao," May 25, 1944 (JDCA).

20. Richard J. Walsh memo on "promotion points," May 30, 1944 (JDCA).

21. Richard J. Walsh to Buwei Yang Chao, December 27, 1944 (JDCA).

22. *Asia* 45, no. 5 (May 1945).

23. Richard J. Walsh to Irita Van Doren, May 2, 1945 (JDCA).

24. Undated memo, M. McManus to Richard J. Walsh (JDCA).

25. Chao, *How to Cook and Eat*, x. Subsequent text references are to this edition.

26. Jane Holt [Jane Nickerson], "News of Food," *New York Times*, May 10, 1945, 20.

27. Telegram, Pearl S. Buck to Ida Bailey Allen, May 7, 1945 (JDCA).

28. Julian Street to the John Day Company, August 27, 1946 (JDCA).

29. Buwei Yang Chao, *How to Cook and Eat in Chinese*, rev., enlarged ed. (New York: John Day, 1949), 34.

30. Ibid., 124.

31. Jason Epstein, "Chinese Characters," *Sunday Times Magazine*, June 13, 2004, 71–72.

32. Buwei Yang Chao, *How to Cook and Eat in Chinese*, 3rd ed. (New York: Random House, 1963), 214a and 214b.

33. Buwei Yang Chao, *How to Order and Eat in Chinese* (New York: Vintage Books, 1974), 76.

7. WHITE AMERICA REDISCOVERS CHINESE CUISINE

1. In 1940 the Chinese population stood at 40,262 American-born and 37,242 foreign-born residents; see Judy Yung, *Unbound Feet: A Social History of Chinese Women in San Francisco* (Berkeley: University of California Press, 1995), table 8, 303.

2. Rose Hum Lee, "Chinese in the United States Today: The War Has Changed Their Lives," *Survey Graphic* 31, no. 19 (October 1949): 419, 444.

3. Ibid., 419.

4. Ibid., 444.

5. Jade Snow Wong, *Fifth Chinese Daughter*, with a new introduction (Seattle: University of Washington Press, 1989), 188–98.

6. Lee, "Chinese in the United States Today," 444.

7. Susan B. Carter, "Embracing Isolation: Chinese American Geographic Redistribution During the Exclusion Era, 1882–1943" (unpublished manuscript, 2013), 47, table 8.

8. Kenneth J. Guest, "From Mott Street to East Broadway: Fuzhounese Immigrants and the Revitalization of New York's Chinatown," in *Chinatowns Around the World: Gilded Ghetto, Ethnopolis, and Cultural Diaspora*, ed. Bernard R. Wong and Tan Chee-Beng (Leiden: Brill, 2013), 32.

9. Rana Mitter, *Forgotten Ally: China's World War II, 1937–1945* (Boston: Houghton Mifflin Harcourt, 2013), 175.

10. Denny Roy, *Taiwan: A Political History* (Ithaca, NY: Cornell University Press, 2003), 76.

11. John De Ferrari, *Historic Restaurants of Washington, D.C.* (Charleston, SC: History Press / American Palate, 2013), 170; and Frank C. Porter, "Chinese Restaurants Keep Going Despite Low Profits," *Washington Post*, April 27, 1959, 69.

12. Henry Low, *Cook at Home in Chinese* (New York: Macmillan, 1938), 144.

13. De Ferrari, *Historic Restaurants*, 171–72; "Oo Soup Is Exclusive," *Huntingdon* (Pennsylvania) *Daily News*, January 20, 1956, 11 (one of many newspaper squibs); and Phyllis C. Richman, "Washington's Bill of Fare," *Washington Post*, March 4, 1982, E1.

14. Craig Claiborne, "T. T. Wang, Influential Master of Chinese Cuisine, Dies at 55," *New York Times*, February 19, 1983; and Michael Tong and Elaine Louie,

The Shun Lee Cookbook: Recipes from a Chinese Restaurant Dynasty (New York: William Morrow, 2007), viii–x.

15. Craig Claiborne, "Chimes Ring in Feasts at Shun Lee Dynasty," *New York Times*, January 4, 1966, 31.

16. Kate Simon, *New York Places and Pleasures* (New York: Meridian, 1959), 153.

17. Ibid., 149.

18. Barbara Ketcham Wheaton, "Chen, Joyce," in *Notable American Women: A Biographical Dictionary*, ed. Susan Ware, vol. 5 (Cambridge, MA: Belknap Press of Harvard University Press, 2004), 116–17. Dana Polan is preparing a study of Chen's television program.

19. See Cecilia Chiang, as told to Alan Carr, *The Mandarin Way*, rev. ed. (San Francisco: A California Living Book, 1980); and Cecilia Chiang with Lisa Weiss, *The Seventh Daughter: My Culinary Journey from Beijing to San Francisco* (Berkeley: Ten Speed Press, 2007).

20. Chiang with Weiss, *Seventh Daughter*, 15–16.

21. Doris Muscatine, *A Cook's Tour of San Francisco*, rev. ed. (New York: Scribner, 1969), 135.

22. Ibid., 146–51.

23. On April 1 and April 3, 2013, a granddaughter of Peter and Betty Lo, writing under the screen name "mixolydian," posted brief histories of their restaurants, Chinese Teahouse, Peter Lo's, and Panda Panda, on a Chowhound thread; see chowhound.chow.com/topics/112187.

24. Death Notice for Emily Kwoh, *New York Times*, January 20, 1998; see also "Farm for 'Hollow Bamboos,'" in "Overseas Chinese," *Taiwan Info*, June 1, 1963, http://taiwaninfo.nat.gov.tw/ct.asp?xItem=164307&ctNode=124; and New York University oral history project "Voices from the Food Revolution" conducted by Judith Weinraub, transcription of interview with Mimi Sheraton, July 2, 2009, dlib.nyu.edu/beard/interviews/mimi-sheraton -interview-1.

25. Sheila Chang obituary, *Houston Chronicle*, March 7, 2103. Chang was the author of a self-published culinary memoir, *Destiny* (2007).

26. Raymond A. Sokolov, "Drivers Who Stop Only for Gas Don't Know What They're Missing," *New York Times*, May 13, 1971, 54.

27. Barbara Tropp, *The Modern Art of Chinese Cooking* (New York: Morrow, 1982), 198n.

28. Raymond A. Sokolov, "For the City's Best in Chinese Cuisine," *New York Times*, May 26, 1972, 43.

29. Raymond Sokolov, *Steal the Menu: A Memoir of Forty Years in Food* (New York: Knopf, 2013), 90.

30. Gael Greene, "Star Struck at Hunam: A Chinese Roundup," *New York*, October 1, 1973, 85.

31. For more on the history of David Keh and Uncle Tai's, see the January 20, 2010, posting by Ed Schoenfeld on the blog of the English writer Fuchsia Dunlop, "General Tso's Chicken (Again)," *Fuchsia Dunlop* (blog), January 6, 2010, www.fuchsiadunlop.com/general-tsos-chicken-again/.

32. For Schoenfeld's accounts of the 1970s New York Chinese restaurant scene, including his own career, see the January 20, 2010, comments on the Dunlop blog (ibid.); Amanda Kludt, "Ed Schoenfeld on the Golden Age of NY Chinese Food," *Eater NY*, November 4, 2011, http://ny.eater.com/2011/11/4/6640057/ed-schoenfeld-on-the-golden-age-of-ny-chinese-food; and Laura Neilson, "Ed Schoenfeld of RedFarm on Domestic Bliss," *Wall Street Journal*, May 10, 2013, http://www.wsj.com/articles/SB10001424127887323628004578459070142111656.

33. Sam Sifton, "The Way We Eat: New York Noodletown," *Sunday Times Magazine*, April 1, 2007.

34. Sheila Chang obituary, *Houston Chronicle*; and *Texas Monthly* advertisement, June 1979, 65.

35. Kennon Crisp, "Weekender Culinary Explorations," *San Antonio Express and News*, June 9, 1973, 3.

36. Griffin Smith Jr., "Pass the Chop Sticks, Por Favor," *Texas Monthly*, July 1973, www.texasmonthly.com/content/pass-chop-sticks-por-favor.

37. Ibid.

38. Different facets of the General Tso's story have been addressed by Fuchsia Dunlop, *The Revolutionary Chinese Cookbook: Recipes from Hunan Province* (London: Ebury Press, 2006; and New York: Norton, 2007), 117–19; Jennifer 8. Lee, *The Fortune Cookie Chronicles: Adventures in the World of Chinese Food* (New York: Twelve, 2009), 66–83; and Ed Schoenfeld, qtd. in Francis Lam, "The Curious History of General Tso's Chicken," *Salon*, January 5, 2010, www.salon.com/2010/01/05/history_of_general_tsos_chicken/; and Schoenfeld, qtd. in the Dunlop blog thread cited above, n28.

39. Stan Miller, Arline Miller, Rita Rowan, and James Rowan, *New York's Chinese Restaurants* (New York: Atheneum, 1977), 130.

40. See the facsimile of a menu page from the Hunam in Andrew Coe, *Chop Suey: A Cultural History of Chinese Food in the United States* (New York: Oxford University Press, 2009), 242.

41. Lee, *Fortune Cookie Chronicles*, 82–83.

42. Eugenia Sheppard, "The Pearl of Pearl's Restaurant," *Kansas City Star*, May 12, 1969, 70.

43. Gael Greene, "Pearl's: The Scrutable Ouch," *New York*, July 26, 1971.

44. Ralph Graves, "Losing a Pearl: A Midtown Empress Leaves Her Throne," *New York*, February 4, 1985, 34.

45. Raymond A. Sokolov, "Standards at Pearl's Have Slipped a Bit," *New York Times*, September 24, 1971, 46.

46. Craig Claiborne, "Oriental Tang," *Sunday Times Magazine*, September 14, 1969, 92.

8. AN ADVANCEMENT OF LEARNING

1. Profiles of Ms. Fu include Amy Lo's "A Woking Ambassador," *Taiwan Info*, September 1, 1992, http://taiwaninfo.nat.gov.tw/fp.asp?xItem=102025&Ct Node=124; and "Fu Pei Mei," Askmar Publishing (n.d.), http://www.askmar publishing.com/authors/pei_mei.html.

2. See advertisements for the Wei-Chuan School's various offerings on the last page of Su-Huei Huang, *Chinese Cuisine: Wei-Chuan Cooking Book*, English-language ed. (Taipei: School of Home Economics, Wei-Chuan Foods, 1972).

3. Fu Pei Mei, *Pei Mei's Cook Book* [*Pei Mei Shi Pu*] (Taipei: Fu Pei Mei, 1969).

4. See Timothy P. Fong, *The First Suburban Chinatown: The Remaking of Monterey Park, California* (Philadelphia: Temple University Press, 1994); and Li Wei, *Ethnoburb: The New Ethnic Community in Urban America* (Honolulu: University of Hawaii Press, 2009). Li is generally credited with having coined the term "ethnoburb."

5. Laurie Ochoa, "My Name's Nina, What's Good?" *Los Angeles Times*, March 9, 1997; and Dianna Marder, "Cookbook Author Nina Simonds' Taste for Chinese Food Dates Back to Childhood," philly.com, January 19, 2012.

6. Huang, *Chinese Cuisine*.

7. Huang Su-Huei, *Chinese Cuisine: Wei-Chuan Cooking Book*, rev. English-language ed., trans. Nina Simonds (Taipei: Department of Home Economics, Wei-Chuan Foods, 1974).

8. Huang Su-Huei, assisted by Lee Mu-Chu, *Chinese Cuisine: Wei-Chuan Cooking Book*, bilingual Chinese–English ed., trans. Nina Simonds (Taipei: Department of Home Economics, Wei-Chuan Foods, 1976).

9. Huang Su-Huei, assisted by Lee Mu Tsun, *Chinese Snacks: Wei-Chuan's Cook Book*, trans. Nina Simonds (Taipei: Department of Home Economics, Wei-Chuan Foods, 1974).

10. See profile of Huang Su-Huei at Zoominfo, http://www.zoominfo.com/s/#!search/profile/company?companyId=302022775&targetid=profile. The

Alhambra cooking school and several Wei-Chuan American distribution centers are mentioned on the back endpaper of *Chinese Snacks.*

11. For a brief biographical sketch of Grace Zia Chu's career, see Sonia Lee, "Chu, Grace Zia," in *Notable American Women: A Biographical Dictionary,* ed. Susan Ware, vol. 5 (Cambridge, MA: Belknap Press of Harvard University Press, 2004), 120–21.

12. Some circumstances of Florence Lin's career are mentioned in Jenny Hu, "In Conversation: Florence Lin and Cecilia Chiang," *SFGate,* September 17, 2013.

13. Craig Claiborne, "Culinary Revolution Topples Chinese Standby," *New York Times,* September 3, 1970, 28.

14. On Margaret Spader, see Cecily Brownstone, "Chinese Cooking Is Her Hobby," *Lewiston* (Maine) *Evening Journal,* October 28, 1978; for an example of Spader's attempts to disseminate Chinese-based culinary approaches to the American cooking public, see "Serve Meals That Say, 'It's Spring,'" *Amsterdam* (New York) *Evening Recorder,* March 31, 1960, 18.

15. Grace Zia Chu, *Madame Chu's Chinese Cooking School* (New York: Simon & Schuster / Fireside, 1975) contains a section headed "Recipes Contributed by My Students" (253–67), describing the cooking engagements of the students.

16. Doreen Yen Hung Feng, *The Joy of Chinese Cooking* (New York: Greenberg, 1950); and Evan Jones, "A Chinese Way with Duck," *Sports Illustrated,* May 30, 1960.

17. Feng, *Joy of Chinese Cooking,* 24, 31.

18. Ibid., 113.

19. Katherine Bazore, *Hawaiian and Pacific Foods: A Cook Book of Culinary Customs and Recipes Adapted for the American Hostess* (New York: M. Barrows, 1940), 50.

20. Feng, *Joy of Chinese Cooking,* 19, 37.

21. Doreen Yen Hung Feng, *The Joy of Chinese Cooking* (New York: Grosset & Dunlap, 1954).

22. Doreen Yen Hung Feng, *The Joy of Chinese Cooking* (New York: Hippocrene Books, 1992).

23. Tsuifeng Lin and Hsiangju Lin, *Cooking with the Chinese Flavor* (Englewood Cliffs, NJ: Prentice-Hall, 1956).

24. Tsuifeng Lin and Hsiangju Lin, *Secrets of Chinese Cooking* (Englewood Cliffs, NJ: Prentice-Hall, 1960).

25. Grace Zia Chu, *The Pleasures of Chinese Cooking* (New York: Simon & Schuster, 1962).

26. Joyce Chen, *Joyce Chen Cook Book* (Philadelphia: J. B. Lippincott, 1962).

27. Ibid., 31–33.

28. Ibid., 127, 143.

29. Ibid., 106.

30. Ibid., 109–10.

31. Johnny Kan, with Charles L. Leong, *Eight Immortal Flavors* (Berkeley: Howell-North Books, 1963). Kan contributed a valuable narrative of 1930s and 1940s San Francisco Chinatown restaurant life to the oral histories collected in Victor G. Nee and Brett de Bary Nee, *Longtime Californ': A Documentary Study of an American Chinatown* (New York: Random House / Pantheon, 1972), 110–16.

32. Eight of the Jake Lee paintings are now in the collection of the Chinese Historical Society of America in San Francisco.

33. James Beard, foreword to *Eight Immortal Flavors*, by Johnny Kan with Charles L. Leong (Berkeley: Howell-North Books, 1963), 6.

34. Kan and Leong, *Eight Immortal Flavors*, 32.

35. Ibid., 15–16.

36. Ibid., 235–38.

37. Ibid., 40.

38. Ibid., 24.

39. Ibid., 148.

40. Ibid., 212–13, 216–19.

41. Johnny Kan with Charles L. Leong, *Eight Immortal Flavors: Secrets of Cantonese Cookery*, rev. ed. (San Francisco: Johnny Kan, 1982).

42. Eileen Yin-Fei Lo, *Eileen Yin-Fei Lo's New Cantonese Cooking* (New York: Viking, 1988); Eileen Yin-Fei Lo, *My Grandmother's Chinese Kitchen* (New York: HP Books, 2006); and Ken Hom, *Easy Family Recipes from a Chinese-American Childhood: 150 Delicious Chinese Dishes for Today's American Table* (New York: Knopf, 1997).

43. Gloria Bley Miller, *The Thousand Recipe Chinese Cookbook* (New York: Atheneum, 1966).

44. Hsiang Ju Lin and Tsuifeng Lin, *Chinese Gastronomy* (New York: Hastings House, 1969).

45. Ibid., 53.

46. Ibid., 139.

47. Emily Hahn and the Editors of Time-Life Books, *The Cooking of China* (New York: Time-Life Books, 1968), 92.

48. Ibid., 103.

49. Ibid., 120, 147, 77–78.

50. Ibid., 86.

51. Craig Claiborne and Virginia Lee, *The Chinese Cookbook* (Philadelphia: J. B. Lippincott, 1972), xiv–xvi, xxi.

52. Ibid., 431.

53. Ibid., 134.

54. Ibid., 182.

55. Cecilia Sun Yun Chiang, as told to Allan Carr, *The Mandarin Way* (Boston: Little, Brown / Atlantic Monthly Press, 1974), 29, 31, 57, 60, 170.

56. Chu, *Madame Chu's Chinese Cooking School.*

57. Ibid., 92, 144.

58. Craig Claiborne, "Steamed Fish—Chinese Style—Gains Something in Translation," *New York Times*, October 23, 1969.

59. Florence Lin, *Florence Lin's Chinese Regional Cookbook* (New York: Hawthorn Books, 1975).

60. Florence Lin, *Florence Lin's Chinese Vegetarian Cookbook* (New York: Hawthorn Books, 1976); *Florence Lin's Chinese One-Dish Meals: The Fastest Way of Cooking Delicious, Economical, Well-Balanced Meals* (New York: Hawthorn Books, Inc., 1978); and *Florence Lin's Cooking with Fire Pots* (New York: Hawthorn Books, 1979).

61. Robert A. Delfs, *The Good Food of Szechwan: Down-to-Earth Chinese Cooking* (Tokyo: Kodansha International, 1974).

62. Ellen Schrecker with John Schrecker, *Mrs. Chiang's Szechwan Cookbook* (New York: Harper & Row, 1976).

63. Virginia Heffington, "The Year of the Dragon," *Long Beach* (California) *Independent Press-Telegram*, January 28 and 29, 1976, F-1.

64. Schrecker, *Mrs. Chiang's Szechwan Cookbook*, xvii–xviii.

65. Ibid., acknowledgments.

66. Irene Kuo, *The Key to Chinese Cooking* (New York: Knopf, 1977).

67. Judith Jones, *The Tenth Muse: My Life in Food* (New York: Knopf, 2007), 101.

68. Author interview with Suzi Arensberg Diacou, October 24, 2014.

69. Kuo, *Key to Chinese Cooking*, 206.

70. Ibid., 441.

71. Ibid., 466.

72. Irma S. Rombauer and Marion Rombauer Becker, *The Joy of Cooking* (Indianapolis: Bobbs-Merrill, 1975).

73. Joanne Will, "The Pan from the Far East That Won the Hearts of the West," *Chicago Tribune*, September 18, 1980, section 7, 1.

74. See images accompanying record of patent grant by the U.S. Patent Office. Joyce Chen, Cooking Utensil, US Patent, 221,397, filed March 9, 1970, and issued August 10, 1971, https://www.google.com/patents/USD221397?dq=USD221397j.

75. Gary Lee, *The Wok: A Chinese Cookbook* (Concord, CA: Nitty Gritty Productions, 1970).

76. Charles Schafer and Violet Schafer, *Wokcraft: A Stirring Compendium of Chinese Cookery* (San Francisco: Yerba Buena Press, 1972).

77. Random House, *The International Cooks' Catalogue: A Beard Glaser Wolf Book*, intro. by James Beard (New York: Random House, 1977), 12–16.

78. Random House, *The Great Cooks' Guide to Woks, Steamers & Fire Pots* (New York: Random House, 1977), 20, 33.

79. Judith A. Gaulke, ed. *Sunset Wok Cook Book* (Menlo Park, CA: Lane Publishing, 1978), 33, 20.

80. Ibid., 74.

81. Marian Burros, "De Gustibus: Vegetables: There's Crispy, Crunchy and Firm," *New York Times*, April 28, 1984.

9. THE FIRST AGE OF RACE-BLIND IMMIGRATION

1. Victor G. Nee and Brett de Bary Nee, *Longtime Californ': A Documentary Study of an American Chinatown* (New York: Random House / Pantheon, 1972), 278–88.

2. See the Pew Research Center's fifty-year projection of racial redistribution, "Modern Immigration Wave Brings 59 Million to U.S., Driving Population Growth and Change Through 2065: Views of Immigration's Impact on U.S. Society Mixed" (Washington, DC: September, 2015), http://www.pew hispanic.org/files/2015/09/2015-09-28_modern-immigration-wave _REPORT.pdf, 10.

3. Anne Willan with Amy Friedman, *One Soufflé at a Time: A Memoir of Food and France, with Recipes* (New York: St. Martin's Press, 2013), 167.

4. Author interview with Zanne [Zakroff] Stewart, October 31, 2014.

5. Ruth Reichl, *Garlic and Sapphires: The Secret Life of a Critic in Disguise* (New York: Penguin, 2005), 235–44.

6. K. C. Chang, ed., *Food in Chinese Culture: Anthropological and Historical Perspectives* (New Haven: Yale University Press, 1977).

7. See blurbs, back cover of ibid.

8. James D. McCawley, *The Eater's Guide to Chinese Characters* (Chicago: University of Chicago Press, 1984).

9. E. N. Anderson, *The Food of China* (New Haven: Yale University Press, 1988).

10. William Shurtleff and Akiko Aoyagi, *The Book of Tofu* (Brookline, MA: Autumn Press, 1975; repr., New York: Ballantine Books, 1980).

11. Nina Simonds, *Chinese Classic Cuisine* (Boston: Houghton Mifflin, 1982).

12. Ken Hom with Harvey Steiman, *Chinese Technique: An Illustrated Guide to the Fundamental Techniques of Chinese Cooking* (New York: Simon & Schuster, 1981).

13. Barbara Tropp, *The Modern Art of Chinese Cooking* (New York: Morrow, 1982).

14. Florence Lin, *Florence Lin's Complete Book of Chinese Noodles, Dumplings and Breads* (New York: Morrow, 1986).

15. Bruce Cost, *Bruce Cost's Asian Ingredients: Buying and Cooking the Staple Foods of China, Japan and Southeast Asia* (New York: Morrow, 1988).

16. Mai Leung, *The Chinese People's Cookbook* (New York: Harper & Row, 1979). Reissued as Harper Colophon paperback in 1982 under the title *Dim Sum and Other Chinese Street Food*.

17. Eileen Yin-Fei Lo, *The Dim Sum Book: Classic Recipes from the Chinese Teahouse* (New York: Crown, 1982).

18. Henry Chan, Yukiko Haydock, and Bob Haydock, *Classic Deem Sum: Recipes from Yank Sing Restaurant, San Francisco* (New York: Holt, Rinehart & Winston, 1985).

19. Gold's reviews were first published as Jonathan Gold, *Counter Intelligence: Where to Eat in the Real Los Angeles* (New York: St. Martin's Press / LA Weekly Books, 2000).

20. Thomas W. Chinn, H. Mark Lai, and Philip P. Choy, eds., *A History of the Chinese in California: A Syllabus* (San Francisco: Chinese Historical Society of America, 1969).

21. Iris Chang, *The Chinese in America: A Narrative History* (New York: Viking, 2003), 320–21.

22. Sucheng Chan, *This Bittersweet Soil: The Chinese in California Agriculture, 1860–1910* (Berkeley: University of California Press, 1986); and Shih-shan Henry Tsai, *The Chinese Experience in America* (Bloomington: Indiana University Press, 1986).

23. Victor Purcell, *The Chinese in Southeast Asia*, 2nd ed. (London: Oxford University Press, 1965), 120.

24. Wei Li, *Ethnoburb: The New Ethnic Community in Urban America* (Honolulu: University of Hawaii Press, 2009), 106–9; and Timothy P. Fong, *The First Suburban Chinatown: The Remaking of Monterey Park, California* (Philadelphia: Temple University Press, 1994), 62.

25. Peggy Durdin, "Mao's 'Great Crime' Against Cuisine," *Sunday Times Magazine*, March 19, 1961, 62.

26. Eric Northrup, letter to the editor, *Sunday Times Magazine*, April 16, 1961, 14.

27. Cecilia Sun Yun Chiang, as told to Allan Carr, *The Mandarin Way*, rev. ed. (San Francisco: California Living Books, 1980), 268–72.

28. Ibid., 273–75.

29. Kenneth J. Guest, "From Mott Street to East Broadway: Fuzhounese Immigrants and the Revitalization of New York's Chinatown," in *Chinatowns Around the World: Gilded Ghetto, Ethnopolis, and Cultural Diaspora*, ed. Bernard P. Wong and Tan Chee-Beng (Leiden: Brill, 2013), 35–54; and Jennifer 8. Lee, *The Fortune Cookie Chronicles: Adventures in the World of Chinese Food* (New York: Twelve, 2008), 107–38.
30. Jennifer 8. Lee draws a similar analogy between Toisan and Fujian in *The Fortune Cookie Chronicles*, 130–31.
31. Min Zhou, *Chinatown: The Socioeconomic Potential of an Urban Enclave* (Philadelphia: Temple University Press, 1992), 122, 186–87.
32. Lee, *Fortune Cookie Chronicles*, 156–59.
33. Calvin Trillin, "New Grub Streets," *New Yorker*, September 3, 2001, 45.
34. Mimi Sheraton, *Eating My Words: An Appetite for Life* (New York: Morrow, 2004), 181–91.

Glossary of Chinese Terms

Most of the following entries represent Mandarin (M) or Cantonese (C) pronunciation, or both, with Mandarin followed by Cantonese romanizations. See also "A Note on Romanization and Terminology."

BAO BING (M): Thin crepe-like pancakes that diners roll around mu xi pork, slices of Peking duck skin, or other fillings.

BAOZI (M): Also "*pao-tzu*" and other romanizations. Filled yeast-raised buns, usually cooked by steaming.

CAI (M): 1. Green vegetables as a class; 2. Cuisine or cooking in general; 3. Dishes served to accompany rice or another starch at a meal (see *fan* and *sung*). In the first two senses, the Cantonese equivalent is *choy*.

CHA SHAO (M), CHA SIU (C): A special roasting technique for pork (or poultry) hung on prongs or hooks in a vertically oriented oven, often mistranslated as "barbecuing."

CHAO (M), CHAU (C): Stir-frying. The word "chow" in early English-language newspaper accounts may have been confusedly picked up from Cantonese "chau."

CHAO FEN (M), CHAU FUN (C): Stir-fried broad rice noodles.

CHAO MIAN (M), CHAU MIN (C): Stir-fried wheat noodles or "chow mein."

CHAO ZA SUI (M), CHAU TSAP SUI (C): Literally, stir-fried mixed fragments. The early romanization "chow chop suey" was the basis of the garbled English term "chop suey."

CHI YOU (M), SI YAU (C): Soy sauce.

COHONG: From Cantonese *gung hong*, the consortium of Guangzhou merchants that functioned as a cartel controlling the movement of imports and exports under the eighteenth-century "Canton system."

DA SHI FU (M), DAAI SI FU (C): A classically trained "grandmaster" chef.

DAO (M), DOU (C): Knife (specifically, the cleaver-shaped Chinese kitchen knife).

DIAN XIN (M), DIM SUM (C): Cantonese-style dim sum or the Northern Chinese counterpart.

DONG XIAN CAI or DONG HAN CAI (M): A variety of mallow (*Malva verticillata*), once well known as a leafy vegetable.

DOU BAN JIANG (M), TAU BAN JEUNG (C): Fermented bean paste, used as a seasoning. The best-known versions are based on fava beans and chili peppers and come from Sichuan Province.

FAN (M), FAAN (C): Cooked rice or other grain-based food, the defining principle of any proper meal. Non-rice dishes (*cai* or *sung*) that accompany *fan* are understood as ancillary factors.

FU RONG (M), FU YUNG (C): Originally a name for the white hibiscus or lotus flower; a dish of eggs (or sometimes egg whites) stir-fried to a lightly scrambled consistency with small amounts of any desired meat, shellfish, or vegetable. In chop suey–era Cantonese American restaurants it became a heavy, thick omelet studded with a medley of meats and vegetables and served with a brown gravy.

GONG SI (M), GUNG SI (C): Business, company, corporation.

GUANGDONG: Canton Province.

GUANGZHOU: Canton City.

GUANXI (M), GWAANHAIH (C): Network of connections and relationships.

HAKKA: A Han Chinese people widely dispersed throughout China and Southeast Asia.

HAN REN (M): Chinese person or people.

HANJIAN (M): Traitor.

HE YE JUAN (M): Lotus leaf bun; a small yeast bun with two folded lobes for "sandwiching" a filling.

HOKKIEN: Fujian Province, as pronounced in the southern Min or Hokkienese language. Colonies of Hokkienese people became widely dispersed throughout Southeast Asia in early modern times.

HONG SHAO (M), HUNG SIU (C): "Red cooking," a form of braising named for the deep color imparted by soy sauce; it is especially identified with the cuisines of the Lower Yangzi River basin east of Nanjing.

HUA GONG (M): Literally, "Chinese labor," the class of manual workers who left China (chiefly Guangdong) in search of work during the late nineteenth century.

HUA SHANG (M): Literally, "Chinese commerce," the class of merchants, traders, and brokers who generally directed the flow of goods and people leaving China in the late nineteenth century.

HUI (M), WUIH (C): 1. A meeting, association, committee, or other group organized for a common purpose; 2. A cooking technique in which a few complementary ingredients briefly "meet" in a pan.

HUIGUAN (M), WUIHGUN (C): An association of people from the same home village or district.

HUO (M), WOK (C): The basic all-purpose Chinese cooking pan.

HUO QI (M), WOK HEI (C): Literally, the "air" or "life force" of the pan, a complex effect slightly resembling smokiness that results from skillful restaurant stir-frying.

JI ZA (M), GAI TSAP (C): Literally, "chicken miscellany," a stir-fry dish of assorted chicken innards.

JIANGNAN: The general region to the south of the Lower Yangzi, encompassing the important culinary centers of Nanjing, Shanghai, Hangzhou, Wuxi, and Suzhou.

JIAOZI or KAU-TSI (M): Small filled dumplings.

JIN SHAN (M), GUM SAAN (C): "Gold Mountain," the usual Chinese name for California and later the American Pacific Coast regions during (and for a time after) the Gold Rush.

JIN SHAN ZHUANG (M), GUM SAAN JONG (C): Exporting–importing businesses that dispatched Chinese goods (including cooking ingredients and equipment) from Hong Kong to North America from Gold Rush times on.

LA (M): Hot in the sense of pungently spiced.

LA CHANG (M), LAP CHEUNG (C): Small, dry-textured cured pork sausages.

LIANG MIAN HUANG (M), LEUNG MIN WONG (C): "Two Sides Brown" or "Two Sides Yellow," fine, cooked egg noodles pressed into a pillow-like shape and lightly crisped on both sides before being served with a stir-fried topping.

LU (M): Cooking in a "master sauce," or intensely deep-flavored sauce or gravy in which poultry or meat is slowly poached. The cooking liquid is saved for poaching another bird or piece of meat, becoming richer with each use. The technique is sometimes called "flavor-potting."

LUO MIAN (M), LOU MIN (C): Stir-fried noodles very quickly, thoroughly tossed and mixed with other ingredients; usually romanized as "lo mein."

MANTOU (M): Steamed wheat-flour buns or mini loaves.

MEI ZAI (M), MUI TSAI (C): Bondwomen, sold as young girls into domestic service as maids of all work.

MIAN (M), MIN (C): Wheat flour, also wheat-flour noodles.

MOMINGQIMIAO (M): Baffling conundrum or puzzle.

MU XI ROU or MU XU ROU (M): A stir-fried pork dish, one of the earliest Northern Chinese dishes to catch on in the United States.

NAN (M): South, southern.

NANYANG (M): Literally, "Southern Ocean," a collective name for all the regions of Southeast Asia in which Han Chinese from the mainland settled, worked, and traded.

PI DAN (M), PAY DAAN (C): "Thousand-year" or "hundred-year" eggs, preserved by curing for several weeks or months in an alkaline mixture.

PINYIN (M): The official transliteration system for *putonghua*, adopted by the People's Republic of China in the 1950s.

PUTONGHUA (M): Literally, "common speech"; the standard spoken language of the People's Republic, principally based on the speech of Beijing. It is roughly synonymous with the inexact older English term "Mandarin."

QIAO (M), KIUH (C): To sojourn or travel overseas from China; overseas sojourner.

QING (M): Clear or pure; a term used to distinguish cooking methods that result in especially light, transparent effects. It is also the name of the last imperial dynasty to rule China.

SAN HE HUI (M), SAAM HAHP WUIH (C): Triads; secret societies derived from underground leagues seeking the overthrow of the Qing dynasty in nineteenth-century Guangdong.

SAN YI (M), SAM YUP (C): The comparatively wealthy Cantonese "Three Counties" or "Three Districts" of Nanhai, Panyu, and Shunde, lying close to Guangzhou; see Si Yi.

SHANG TANG (M), SEUNG TONG (C): "Superior" or "first-class broth," soup stock prepared with particular care and refinement.

SHAO (M), SIU (C): Cooking technique generally corresponding to braising, though in a few specialized cases it may refer to oven-roasting or other methods.

SI YI (M), SZE YUP (C): The relatively poor rural Cantonese "Four Counties" or "Four Districts" of Xinhui, Enping, Kaiping, and Xinning (this last later renamed Taishan or Toisan), some distance west of Guangzhou on the opposite side of the Pearl River; see San Yi. Bitter Sze Yup–Sam Yup rivalries were a shaping force of the Chinese American community for several generations.

SUAN MEI JIANG (M), SYUN MUI JEUNG (C): A jam-like condiment made from a Far Eastern relative of the apricot, the original of the sweeter and blander "duck sauce" or "plum sauce" that became ubiquitous in many Cantonese American restaurants.

SUNG (C): Vegetable or meat dishes meant to be served at a meal with cooked rice, roughly corresponding to Mandarin *cai*.

TANG (M), TONG (C): Derived from a word for "hall"; originally, any sort of association. In American cities the term came to be applied to secret societies involved in organized crime, overlapping with the activities of the *san he hui* or triads.

TONG YAN (C): Chinese person or people. "Tong" here refers to the Tang dynasty, under which the southern provinces were lastingly absorbed into a unified China. The more usual Mandarin term is "*han ren*."

TONG YAN GAI (C): Literally, "street of Chinese people"; the most common Cantonese name for any overseas Chinatown.

WEI JING (M), MEI JING (C): Monosodium glutamate.

WO MIAN (M), WOR MIN (C): "Nested noodles," a Cantonese soup-noodle dish.

XIA FAN (M), HAH FAAN (C): An expression for the non-*fan* components of a meal that "make the rice go down" more palatably.

XIAN (M), SIN (C): County or administrative district.

XIANG BANFA (M), SEUNG BAHNFAT (C): To improvise a stratagem or come up with a plan of action.

YI GE MIAN (M), YAT GOH MIN (C): "One order of noodles," popularly anglicized as "yat ca mein," "ya gaw mein," or "yaka mein," together with a miscellany of abbreviated local U.S. names such as "yat," "yok," or "yock." A simple Cantonese soup-noodle dish that was adopted by non-Chinese in New Orleans, Baltimore, and several other North American cities as a folk hangover remedy. The classic New Orleans name is "Old Sober."

YU SHENG, YUE SANG (C): An elaborate dish of raw fish tossed with seasonings, often served at Chinese New Year.

ZA SUI (M), TSAP SUI (C): Mixed fragments; see *chao za sui*.

ZHA (M), JA (C): Deep-frying.

ZHA JIANG MIAN (M), JA JEUNG MIN (C): "Fried sauce noodles," originally from Beijing; noodles tossed in a ragu-like meat sauce of chopped pork and bean sauce or hoisin sauce.

ZHENG (M), JING (C): In cooking, the steaming technique.

ZHONGHUA (M), CHONGWAH (C): One of the names for China.

ZHONGHUA HUIGUAN (M), CHONGWAH WUIHGUN (C): The San Francisco–founded organization that mounted the principal legal challenges to racist anti-Chinese laws during the Exclusion era.

ZHU JIANG (M), JYU GONG (C): The Pearl River of southern Guangdong.

ZHU YOU (M), JYU YAU (C): "Pearl sauce," a thick, dark, sweetish sauce much used in making the brown gravies that Americans liked in chop suey–era restaurant cooking.

ZHU ZI JUAN (M): Literally, "pigsties," a common name for the prison barracks in which forcibly impressed Chinese were confined while waiting to be transferred to ships bound for New World guano mines or sugar plantations.

Bibliography

Allen, Ida C. Bailey. *Mrs. Allen's Cook Book.* Boston: Small, Maynard, 1917.

Amsterdam (New York) *Evening Recorder.* "Serve Meals That Say, 'It's Spring.'" March 31, 1960, 18.

Anderson, E. N. *The Food of China.* New Haven, CT: Yale University Press, 1988.

Anderson, E. N., Jr., and Marja L. Anderson. "Modern China: South." In *Food in Chinese Culture: Anthropological and Historical Perspectives,* ed. K. C. Chang, 319–82. New Haven, CT: Yale University Press, 1977.

Arnold, Sir Edwin. *Seas and Lands.* New York: Longmans, Green, 1891.

Bailey, L. H. *Some Recent Chinese Vegetables.* Cornell University Agricultural Experiment Station, Horticultural Division, Bulletin No. 67. Ithaca, NY: Cornell University, June 1894.

Bancroft, Hubert Howe. *History of California,* vol. 7, *1860–1890,* of *The Works of Hubert Howe Bancroft,* 38 vols. San Francisco: History Company, 1890.

——. "Mongolianism in America." In *Essays and Miscellany,* vol. 38, 309–418, of *The Works of Hubert Howe Bancroft,* 38 vols. San Francisco: History Company, 1890.

Barbas, Samantha. "'I'll Take Chop Suey': Restaurants as Agents of Culinary and Cultural Change." *Journal of Popular Culture* 36, no. 4 (2003): 669–86.

Barth, Gunther. *Bitter Strength: A History of the Chinese in the United States, 1850–1870.* Cambridge, MA: Harvard University Press, 1964.

Bazore, Katherine. *Hawaiian and Pacific Foods: A Cook Book of Culinary Customs and Recipes Adapted for the American Hostess.* New York: M. Barrows, 1940.

Beard, James. *Delights and Prejudices: A Memoir with Recipes*. New York: Collier Macmillan, 1990.

——. Foreword to *Eight Immortal Flavors*, by Johnny Kan, with Charles L. Leong. Berkeley: Howell-North Books, 1963.

Beck, Louis J. *New York's Chinatown: An Historical Presentation of Its People and Places*. New York: Bohemia Publishing, 1898.

Beverly Hills Woman's Club. *Fashions in Food in Beverly Hills*. 2nd ed. Beverly Hills, CA: Beverly Hills Citizen, 1930.

Blasdale, Walter C. *A Description of Some Chinese Vegetable Food Materials*. US Department of Agriculture Bulletin No. 68. Washington, DC: Government Printing Office, 1899.

Bonner, Arthur. *Alas, What Brought Thee Hither? The Chinese in New York, 1800–1950*. Teaneck, NJ: Fairleigh Dickinson University Press, 1997.

Borthwick, J. D. *Three Years in California*. Edinburgh: William Blackwood and Sons, 1867.

Bossé, Sara, and Onoto Watanna. *Chinese-Japanese Cook Book*. Chicago: Rand McNally, 1914.

Brenner, Leslie. *American Appetite: The Coming of Age of a Cuisine*. New York: Avon Books, 1999.

Brooklyn Daily Eagle. "Easter Shopping Done in Chinatown." April 5, 1903, 15.

Brooklyn Eagle. "A Chinese Dinner." September 22, 1896, 8.

Brownstone, Cecily. "Chinese Cooking Is Her Hobby." *Lewiston* (Maine) *Evening Journal*, October 28, 1978, 15.

Buck, Pearl S. *My Several Worlds: A Personal Record*. New York: John Day, 1954.

Burros, Marian. "De Gustibus: Vegetables: There's Crispy, Crunchy and Firm." *New York Times*, April 28, 1984.

Campanella, Richard. *Geographies of New Orleans: Urban Fabric Before the Storm*. Lafayette: Center for Louisiana Studies, 2006.

Carroll, Raymond D. "Chinese Laundries Gone; Restaurants Are Many." *Los Angeles Times*, March 27, 1924, 6.

Carter, Susan B. "Celestial Suppers: The Political Economy of America's Chop Suey Craze, 1900–1930." Unpublished manuscript, 2009.

——. "Embracing Isolation: "Chinese American Geographic Redistribution During the Exclusion Era, 1882–1943." Unpublished manuscript, 2013.

——. "How The Penny Press 'Educated Up' the American Palate: From 'Rats and Dogs' to 'Chop Suey Mad.'" Paper presented at the Roger Smith Food/Tech Conference, New York City, April 5, 2014.

Chan, Henry, Yukiko Haydock, and Bob Haydock. *Classic Deem Sum: Recipes from Yank Sing Restaurant, San Francisco*. New York: Holt, Rinehart & Winston, 1985.

Chan, Shiu Wong. *The Chinese Cook Book*. New York: Frederick A. Stokes, 1917.

Chan, Sucheng. "Against All Odds: Chinese Female Migration and Family Formation on American Soil During the Early Twentieth Century." In *Chinese American Transnationalism: The Flow of People, Resources, and Ideas Between China and America During the Exclusion Era*, ed. Sucheng Chan, 34–135. Philadelphia: Temple University Press, 2006.

——. *This Bittersweet Soil: The Chinese in California Agriculture, 1860–1910*. Berkeley: University of California Press, 1986.

Chang, Iris. *The Chinese in America: A Narrative History*. New York: Viking, 2003.

Chang, K. C., ed. *Food in Chinese Culture: Anthropological and Historical Perspectives*. New Haven, CT: Yale University Press, 1977.

Chao, Buwei Yang. *Autobiography of a Chinese Woman, Put into English by Her Husband, Yuenren Chao*. New York: John Day, 1947.

——. *How to Cook and Eat in Chinese*. New York: John Day, 1945.

——. *How to Cook and Eat in Chinese*. Rev. ed. New York: John Day, 1949.

——. *How to Cook and Eat in Chinese*. 3rd ed. New York: Random House, 1963.

——. *How to Order and Eat in Chinese*. New York: Vintage Books, 1974.

Chen, Jack. *The Chinese of America: From the Beginnings to the Present*. San Francisco: Harper & Row, 1980.

Chen, Joyce. *Joyce Chen Cook Book*. Philadelphia: Lippincott, 1962.

Chen, Yong. *Chinese San Francisco, 1850–1943: A Trans-Pacific Community*. Stanford, CA: Stanford University Press, 2000.

——. *Chop Suey, USA: The Story of Chinese Food in America*. New York: Columbia University Press, 2014.

Chiang, Cecilia Sun Yun, as told to Alan Carr. *The Mandarin Way*. Boston: Little, Brown / Atlantic Monthly Press, 1974.

——. *The Mandarin Way*. Rev. ed. San Francisco: California Living Books, 1980.

Chiang, Cecilia, with Lisa Weiss. *The Seventh Daughter: My Culinary Journey from Beijing to San Francisco*. Berkeley: Ten Speed Press, 2007.

Chicago Daily Tribune. "How to Make Chop Suey." February 23, 1913, 44.

——. "Joy Hing Lo." July 31, 1908, 18.

——. "King Joy Lo: The Finest Chinese-American Restaurant in the World." December 22, 1906, 2.

Chinn, Thomas W., H. Mark Lai, and Philip P. Choy, eds. *A History of the Chinese in California: A Syllabus*. San Francisco: Chinese Historical Society of America, 1969.

Choy, Philip P. "The Architecture of San Francisco Chinatown." In *Chinese American History and Perspectives*. Brisbane, CA: Chinese Historical Society of America, 1990, 37–66.

Chu, Grace Zia. *Madame Chu's Chinese Cooking School*. New York: Simon & Schuster / Fireside, 1974.

——. *The Pleasures of Chinese Cooking*. New York: Simon & Schuster, 1962.

Chu, Louis H. "The Chinese Restaurants in New York City." Master's thesis, New York University, 1929.

Chung, Sue Fawn. *In Pursuit of Gold: Chinese American Miners and Merchants in the American West*. Champaign: University of Illinois Press, 2011.

Cincinnati Enquirer. "Advice on Vegetables." September 27, 1916, 16.

——. "Chinese Dishes." July 31, 1919, 5.

Claiborne, Craig. "Chimes Ring in Feasts at Shun Lee Dynasty." *New York Times*, January 4, 1966, 31.

——. "Culinary Revolution Topples Chinese Standby." *New York Times*, September 3, 1970, 28.

——. "Oriental Tang." *Sunday Times Magazine*, September 14, 1969, 92.

——. "Steamed Fish—Chinese Style—Gains Something in Translation." *New York Times*, October 23, 1969.

——. "T. T. Wang, Influential Master of Chinese Cuisine, Dies at 55." *New York Times*, February 19, 1983.

Claiborne, Craig, and Virginia Lee. *The Chinese Cookbook*. Philadelphia: J. B. Lippincott, 1972.

Clifford, Josephine. "Chinatown." *Potter's American Monthly* 14 (May 1880): 353–364.

Coe, Andrew. *Chop Suey: A Cultural History of Chinese Food in the United States*. New York: Oxford University Press, 2009.

Cohen, Lucy M. *Chinese in the Post–Civil War South: A People Without a History*. Baton Rouge: Louisiana State University Press, 1984.

Conlin, Joseph R. *Bacon, Beans, and Galantines: Food and Foodways on the Western Mining Frontier*. Reno: University of Nevada Press, 1986.

Conn, Peter. *Pearl S. Buck: A Cultural Biography*. Cambridge: Cambridge University Press, 1996.

Cooke, George Wingrove. *China: Being "The Times" Special Correspondence from China in the Years 1857–58*. London: G. Routledge, 1859.

Coolidge, Mary Roberts. *Chinese Immigration*. New York: Henry Holt, 1909. Reprint, New York: Arno Press, 1969.

Cost, Bruce. *Bruce Cost's Asian Ingredients: Buying and Cooking the Staple Foods of China, Japan and Southeast Asia*. New York: Morrow, 1988.

Crisp, Kennon. "Weekender Culinary Explorations." *San Antonio Express and News*, June 9 1973, 3.

Crow, Carl. *400 Million Customers: The Experiences—Some Happy, Some Sad, of an American in China, and What They Taught Me*. New York: Harper & Brothers, 1937.

Cummins, J. S., ed. *The Travels and Controversies of Friar Domingo Navarrete, 1618–1686*. Cambridge: Hakluyt Society, 1962.

Daily Alta California. "Meeting of the Chinese Residents of San Francisco." December 10, 1849, 1.

Daniels, Roger. *Asian America: Chinese and Japanese in the United States Since 1850*. Seattle: University of Washington Press, 1988.

——. *Coming to America: A History of Immigration and Ethnicity in American Life*. 2nd ed. New York: Harper Perennial, 2002.

De Ferrari, John. *Capital Eats: Historic Restaurants of Washington, D.C.* Charleston, SC: History Press / American Palate, 2013.

DeFrancis, John. *The Chinese Language: Fact and Fantasy*. Honolulu: University of Hawaii Press, 1984.

Delfs, Robert A. *The Good Food of Szechwan: Down-to-Earth Chinese Cooking*. Tokyo: Kodansha International, 1974.

Delavan, James. *Notes on California and the Placers: How to Get There and What to Do Afterwards*. New York: H. Long & Brother, 1850.

Delgado, James P. *Gold Rush Port: The Maritime Archaeology of San Francisco's Waterfront*. Berkeley: University of California Press, 2009.

Derbec, Étienne. *A French Journalist in the California Gold Rush: The Letters of Etienne Derbec*, ed. A. P. Nasatir. Georgetown, CA: Talisman Press, 1964.

Dunlop, Fuchsia. *Revolutionary Chinese Cookbook: Recipes from Hunan Province*. London: Ebury Press, 2006; New York: Norton, 2007.

——. *Shark's Fin and Sichuan Pepper: A Sweet-Sour Memoir of Eating in China*. New York: Norton, 2008.

——. *Sichuan Cookery*. London: Penguin, 2001. Published in slightly revised form as *Land of Plenty: A Treasury of Authentic Sichuan Cooking*. New York: Norton, 2003.

Durdin, Peggy. "Mao's 'Great Crime' Against Cuisine." *Sunday Times Magazine*, March 19, 1961, 62.

Ebrey, Patricia Buckley. *The Cambridge Illustrated History of China*. Cambridge: Cambridge University Press, 1996.

Eddington, Jane. "Perennial Chop Suey." *Chicago Tribune*, October 29, 1915, 4.

Edge, John T. "Seventh Ward Ramen." *Lucky Peach*, no. 1 (Summer 2011): 45–47.

Eng-Wong, John. "How to Cook and Eat Chinese." Brown University "Year of China" event, May 10, 2012. https://www.brown.edu/about/adminis tration/international-affairs/year-of-china/how-cook-and-eat-chinese. YouTube, June 4, 2012. https://www.youtube.com/watch?v=FV-xOmtP5NQ.

Epstein, Jason. "Chinese Characters." *Sunday Times Magazine*, June 13, 2004, 71–72.

Fairbank, John King, and Merle Goldman. *China: A New History*. 2nd ed. Cambridge, MA: Belknap Press of Harvard University Press, 2006.

Farmer, Fannie Merritt, and Cora D. Perkins. *The Boston Cooking-School Cook Book*. Rev. ed. Boston: Little, Brown, 1929.

Fee, Jeffrey M. "Idaho's Mountain Gardens." In *Hidden Heritage: Historical Archaeology of the Overseas Chinese*, ed. Priscilla Wegars, 65–96. Amityville, NY: Baywood, 1993.

Feng, Doreen Yen Hung. *The Joy of Chinese Cooking*. New York: Greenberg, 1950).

——. *The Joy of Chinese Cooking*. New York: Grosset & Dunlap, 1954.

——. *The Joy of Chinese Cooking*. New York: Hippocrene Books, 1992.

Ferretti, Fred. "A Rat in the Kitchen." *New York Times*, February 9, 2008, A15.

Fessler, Loren W. *Chinese in America: Stereotyped Past, Changing Present*. New York: Vantage Press, 1983.

Fong, Timothy P. *The First Suburban Chinatown: The Remaking of Monterey Park, California*. Philadelphia: Temple University Press, 1994.

Forrestal, Dan J. *The Kernel and the Bean: The 75-year History of the Staley Company*. New York: Simon & Schuster, 1982.

Freeman, Michael. "Sung." In *Food in Chinese Culture: Anthropological and Historical Perspectives*, ed. K. C. Chang, 143–76. New Haven, CT: Yale University Press, 1977.

Fu, Pei Mei. *Pei-Mei's Chinese Cook Book* [*Pei Mei Shi Pu*]. Taipei: Fu Pei-Mei, 1969.

Fuller, Sherri Gebert. *Chinese in Minnesota*. St. Paul: Minnesota Historical Society Press, 2004.

Garrett, Valery M. *Heaven Is High, The Emperor Far Away: Merchants and Mandarins in Old Canton*. New York: Oxford University Press, 2002.

George, Henry. "The Chinese in America: Their Habits, Morals and Prospects—The Extermination of the Exterminator." *Defiance Democrat* (Ohio), June 19, 1869, 1. Originally published in *New-York Tribune* May 1, 1869 as "The Chinese on the Pacific Coast."

Gernet, Jacques. *Daily Life in China on the Eve of the Mongol Invasion: 1250–1276*. 2nd ed., trans. M. M. Wright. Stanford, CA: Stanford University Press, 1970.

——. *A History of Chinese Civilization*, trans. J. R. Foster. Cambridge: Cambridge University Press, 1982.

Gibson, Otis. *The Chinese in America*. Cincinnati: Hitchcock & Walker, 1877.

Glick, Carl. *Shake Hands with the Dragon*. New York: Whittlesey House / McGraw-Hill, 1941.

Gold, Jonathan. *Counter Intelligence: Where to Eat in the Real Los Angeles*. New York: St. Martin's Press / LA Weekly Books, 2000.

Graves, Ralph. "Losing a Pearl: A Midtown Empress Leaves Her Throne." *New York*, February 4, 1985, 34.

Greene, Gael. "Pearl's: The Scrutable Ouch." *New York*, July 26, 1971.

——. "A Scrutable Guide to New York's Chinese Restaurants." *New York*, April 2, 1979, 43–58.

——. "Star Struck at Hunam: A Chinese Roundup." *New York*, October 1, 1973, 85.

Gaulke, Judith A., ed. *Sunset Wok Cook Book*. Menlo Park, CA: Lane Publishing, 1978.

Guest, Kenneth J. "From Mott Street to East Broadway: Fuzhounese Immigrants and the Revitalization of New York's Chinatown." In *Chinatowns Around the World: Gilded Ghetto, Ethnopolis, and Cultural Diaspora*, ed. Bernard R. Wong and Tan Chee-Beng, 35–54. Leiden: Brill, 2013.

Hahn, Emily, and the Editors of Time-Life Books. *The Cooking of China*. New York: Time-Life Books, 1968.

Heffington, Virginia. "The Year of the Dragon." *Long Beach* (California) *Independent Press-Telegram*, January 28 and 29, 1976, F-1.

Historical Statistics of the United States: Colonial Times to 1970. Washington, DC: U.S. Government Printing Office, 1975.

Hom, Ken. *Easy Family Recipes from a Chinese-American Childhood*. New York: Knopf, 1997.

Hom, Ken, with Harvey Steiman. *Chinese Technique: An Illustrated Guide to the Fundamental Techniques of Chinese Cooking*. New York: Simon & Schuster, 1981.

Hsu, Madeline Y. *Dreaming of Gold, Dreaming of Home: Transnationalism and Migration Between the United States and South China, 1882–1943*. Stanford, CA: Stanford University Press, 2000.

——. "From Chop Suey to Mandarin Cuisine: Fine Dining and the Refashioning of Chinese Ethnicity During the Cold War Era." In *Chinese Americans and the Politics of Race and Culture*, ed. Sucheng Chan and Madeline Y. Hsu, 173–93. Philadelphia: Temple University Press, 2008.

Hu, Jenny. "In Conversation: Florence Lin and Cecilia Chiang." *SFGate*, September 17, 2013.

Hu, Shiu-ying. *Food Plants of China*. Hong Kong: Chinese University Press, 2005.

Huang, H. T. *Fermentations and Food Science*, vol. 6, part 5 of *Science and Civilisation in China*, ed. Joseph Needham. Cambridge: Cambridge University Press, 2000.

Huang, Su-Huei. *Chinese Cuisine: Wei-Chuan Cooking Book*. English-language ed. Taipei: School of Home Economics, Wei-Chuan Foods, 1972.

——. *Chinese Cuisine: Wei-Chuan Cooking Book*. Rev. English-language ed., trans. Nina Simonds. Taipei: Department of Home Economics, Wei-Chuan Foods, 1974.

——, assisted by Lee Mu-Chu. *Chinese Cuisine: Wei-Chuan Cooking Book*. Bilingual Chinese–English ed., trans. Nina Simonds. Taipei: Department of Home Economics, Wei-Chuan Foods, 1976.

——, assisted by Lee Mu Tsun. *Chinese Snacks: Wei-Chuan's Cook Book*, trans. Nina Simonds. Taipei: Department of Home Economics, Wei-Chuan Foods, 1974.

Huc, Évariste Régis. *The Chinese Empire: A Sequel to Recollections of a Journey Through Tartary and Thibet by M. Huc, Formerly Missionary Apostolic in China*. New ed. London: Longman, Brown, Green, Longmans, & Roberts, 1859.

Huntingdon (Pennsylvania) *Daily News*. "Oo Soup Is Exclusive." January 20, 1956, 11.

Indianapolis News. "How American Women May Make Chop Suey." February 16, 1906, 7.

John, Griffith, "North China—Hiau-Kan." In *Chronicle of the London Missionary Society*, April 1879, 260–63. *The Evangelical and Missionary Chronicle*, vol. 9, new series. London: Hodder & Stoughton, 1879.

Jones, Evan. "A Chinese Way with Duck." *Sports Illustrated*, May 30, 1960.

Jones, Judith. *The Tenth Muse: My Life in Food*. New York: Knopf, 2007.

Jung, John. *Chinese Laundries: Tickets to Survival on Gold Mountain*. N.p.: Yin & Yang Press, 2007.

——. *Sweet and Sour: Life in Chinese Family Restaurants*. N.p.: Yin and Yang Press, 2010.

Kan, Johnny, with Charles L. Leong. *Eight Immortal Flavors*. Berkeley: Howell-North Books, 1963.

——. *Eight Immortal Flavors: Secrets of Cantonese Cookery*. Rev. ed. San Francisco: Johnny Kan, 1982.

Kander, Mrs. Simon [Lizzie Black]. *The Settlement Cook Book*. 7th ed. Milwaukee: Settlement Cook Book Co., 1915.

Keay, John. *China: A History*. New York: Basic Books, 2009.

Kelly, William. *An Excursion to California*. London: Chapman & Hall, 1851.

Kho, Kian Lam. *Phoenix Claws and Jade Trees: Essential Techniques of Authentic Chinese Cooking*. New York: Clarkson Potter, 2015.

Kimball, Charles P. *The San Francisco City Directory*. San Francisco: Journal of Commerce Press, September 1, 1850.

Kitchiner, William. *The Cook's Oracle and Housekeeper's Manual*. New York: J. & J. Harper, 1830.

Kludt, Amanda. "Ed Schoenfeld on the Golden Age of NY Chinese Food." *Eater NY*, November 4, 2011. http://ny.eater.com/2011/11/4/6640057/ed-schoenfeld-on-the-golden-age-of-ny-chinese-food.

Kuhn, Philip A. *Chinese Among Others: Emigration in Modern Times*. Lanham, MD: Rowman & Littlefield, 2008.

Kuo, Irene. *The Key to Chinese Cooking*. New York: Knopf, 1977.

Kwong, Peter, and Dusanka Miscevic. *Chinese America: The Untold Story of America's Oldest New Community*. New York: New Press, 2005.

Lai, Him Mark. *Becoming Chinese American: A History of Communities and Institutions*. Walnut Creek, CA: AltaMira Press, 2004.

Lam, Betty H. "Earliest Chinese Settlement in Boston Dated 1875." *Chinese Historical Society of New England Newsletter* 4, no. 1 (Summer 1998): 2, accessed at http://chsne.org/newsletters/1998.htm.

Lam, Francis. "The Curious History of General Tso's Chicken." *Salon*, January 5, 2010, http://www.salon.com/2010/01/06/history_of_general_tsos_chicken/.

Lander, E. T. "Chinese Horticulture in New York." *Garden and Forest: A Journal of Horticulture, Landscape Art and Forestry* 1 (December 5, 1888): 483–84.

Laudan, Rachel. *Cuisine and Empire: Cooking in World History*. Berkeley: University of California Press, 2013.

Lee, Gary. *The Wok: A Chinese Cookbook*. Concord, CA: Nitty Gritty Productions, 1970.

Lee, Heather R. "A Life Cooking for Others: The Work and Migration Experiences of a Chinese Restaurant Worker in New York City, 1920–1946." In *Eating Asian America: A Food Studies Reader*, ed. Robert Ji-Song Ku, Martin F. Manalansan IV, and Anita Mannur, 53–77. New York: New York University Press, 2013.

Lee, Jennifer 8. *The Fortune Cookie Chronicles: Adventures in the World of Chinese Food*. New York: Twelve, 2009.

Lee, Rose Hum. *The Chinese of the United States of America*. Hong Kong: Hong Kong University Press, 1960.

Lee, Rose Hum. "Chinese in the United States Today: The War Has Changed Their Lives." *Survey Graphic* 31, no. 19 (October 1942): 419.

Lee, Sonia, "Chu, Grace Zia." In *Notable American Women: A Biographical Dictionary*, ed. Susan Ware, vol. 5, 120–21. Cambridge, MA: Belknap Press of Harvard University Press, 2004.

Lee, William Poy. *The Eighth Promise: An American Son's Tribute to His Toisanese Mother*. Emmaus, PA: Rodale, 2007.

Leung, Mai. *The Chinese People's Cookbook*. New York: Harper & Row, 1979.

——. *Dim Sum and Other Chinese Street Food*. New York: Harper Colophon Books, 1982.

Li, Wei. *Ethnoburb: The New Ethnic Community in Urban America*. Honolulu: University of Hawaii Press, 2009.

Lim, Imogene L. "Chinese Cuisine Meets the American Palate: The Chow Mein Sandwich." In *Chinese Cuisine American Palate: An Anthology*, ed. Jacqueline M. Newman and Roberta Halporn, 130–39. Brooklyn, NY: Center for Thanatology Research & Education. Available at http://wordpress.viu.ca/limi/files/2012/08/ChineseCuisineMeetsTheAmericanPalate_CMS.pdf.

Lin, Florence. *Florence Lin's Chinese One-Dish Meals*. New York: Hawthorn Books, 1978.

——. *Florence Lin's Chinese Regional Cookbook*. New York: Hawthorn Books, 1975.

——. *Florence Lin's Chinese Vegetarian Cookbook*. New York: Hawthorn Books, 1976.

——. *Florence Lin's Complete Book of Chinese Noodles, Dumplings and Breads*. New York: Morrow, 1986.

——. *Florence Lin's Cooking with Fire Pots*. New York: Hawthorn Books, 1979.

Lin, Hsiang Ju, and Tsuifeng Lin. *Chinese Gastronomy*. New York: Hastings House, 1969.

Lin, Tsuifeng, and Hsiangju Lin. *Cooking with the Chinese Flavor*. Englewood Cliffs, NJ: Prentice-Hall, 1956.

——. *Secrets of Chinese Cooking*. Englewood Cliffs, NJ: Prentice-Hall, 1960.

Ling, Huping. *Chinese Chicago: Race, Transnational Migration, and Community Since 1870*. Stanford, CA: Stanford University Press, 2012.

——. *Chinese St. Louis: From Enclave to Cultural Community*. Philadelphia: Temple University Press, 2004.

Liu, Haiming. "Chop Suey as Imagined Authentic Chinese Food: The Culinary Identity of Chinese Restaurants in the United States." *Journal of Transnational American Studies* 1, no. 1 (2009), http://escholarship.org/uc/item/2bc4k55r.

Lo, Eileen Yin-Fei. *The Dim Sum Book: Classic Recipes from the Chinese Teahouse*. New York: Crown, 1982.

——. *Eileen Yin-Fei Lo's New Cantonese Cooking*. New York: Viking, 1988.

——. *My Grandmother's Chinese Kitchen*. New York: HP Books, 2006.

Loomis, A. W. "How Our Chinamen Are Employed." *Overland Monthly* 2, no. 3 (March 1868): 232.

Low, Henry. *Cook at Home in Chinese*. New York: Macmillan, 1938.

Lowe, Pardee. *Father and Glorious Descendant*. Boston: Little, Brown, 1943.

Lui, Mary Ting Yi. *The Chinatown Trunk Mystery: Murder, Miscegenation, and Other Dangerous Encounters in Turn-of-the-Century New York City*. Princeton, NJ: Princeton University Press, 2005.

Lydon, Sandy. *Chinese Gold: The Chinese in the Monterey Bay Region*. Capitola, CA: Capitola Book Co., 1985.

Lynnhurst Congregational Church Cook Book of Tested Recipes. Minneapolis: Lynnhurst Congregational Church, 1920.

Marder, Dianna. "Cookbook Author Nina Simonds' Taste for Chinese Food Dates Back to Childhood." philly.com, January 19, 2012.

Mark, Diane Mei Lin, and Ginger Chih. *A Place Called Chinese America*. Dubuque: Kendall Hunt, 1982.

McCawley, James D. *The Eater's Guide to Chinese Characters*. Chicago: University of Chicago Press, 1984.

McKeown, Adam. *Chinese Migrant Networks and Cultural Change: Peru, Chicago, Hawaii, 1900–1936*. Chicago: University of Chicago Press, 2001.

"Memorial of Chinese Laborers at Rock Springs, Wyoming." In *Chinese American Voices: From the Gold Rush to the Present*, ed. Judy Yung, Gordon H. Cheng, and Him Mark Lai, 48–54. Berkeley: University of California Press, 2006.

Miller, Gloria Bley. *The Thousand Recipe Chinese Cookbook*. New York: Atheneum, 1966.

Miller, Stan, Arline Miller, Rita Rowan, and James Rowan. *New York's Chinese Restaurants*. New York: Atheneum, 1977.

Minneapolis Journal. "Chinese Cooking Is a Fine Art." October 24, 1903, section 2, 3.

Mitter, Rana. *Forgotten Ally: China's World War II, 1937–45*. Boston: Houghton Mifflin Harcourt, 2013.

Moore, Alice. *Chinese Recipes: Letters from Alice Moore to Ethel Moore Rook*. Garden City, NY: Doubleday, Page, 1923.

Mulford, Prentice. "California Culinary Experiences." *Overland Monthly and Out West Magazine* 2, no. 6 (June 1869): 556–62.

——. "Glimpses of John Chinaman." *Lippincott's Magazine of Literature and Science* 11 (February 1873): 219–25.

Muscatine, Doris. *A Cook's Tour of San Francisco*. Rev. ed. New York: Scribner, 1969.

Nee, Victor G. and Brett de Bary. *Longtime Californ': A Documentary Study of an American Chinatown*. New York: Random House / Pantheon, 1972.

Neilson, Laura. "Ed Schoenfeld of RedFarm on Domestic Bliss." *Wall Street Journal*, May 10, 2013. http://www.wsj.com/articles/SB10001424127887323628004578459070142111656.

New York Journal. "Got the Chinese Craze?" September 6, 1896, 33.

New York Times. "Chop Suey Resorts: Chinese Dish Now Served in Many Parts of the City." November 15, 1903, 20.

——. "News of Food." May 10, 1945, 20.

Newman, Jacqueline M. *Chinese Cookbooks: An Annotated English Language Compendium/Bibliography*. New York: Garland, 1987.

Nolton, Jessie Louis. *Chinese Cookery in the Home Kitchen: Being Recipes for the Preparation of the Most Popular Chinese Dishes at Home*. Detroit: Chino-American Publishing, 1911.

Nordhoff, Charles. *California: For Health, Pleasure, and Residence*. New York: Harper & Brothers, 1873.

Ochoa, Laurie. "My Name's Nina, What's Good?" *Los Angeles Times*, March 19, 1997.

O'Meara, James. "The Chinese in Early Days." *Overland Monthly and Out West Magazine* 3, no. 5 (May 1884): 477–81.

Pan, Lynn, ed. *The Encyclopedia of the Chinese Overseas*. Cambridge, MA: Harvard University Press, 1998.

——. *Sons of the Yellow Emperor: A History of the Chinese Diaspora*. New York, Tokyo, London: Kodansha America, 1994.

Pang, Sunyowe. "The Chinese in America." *Forum* 32, no. 5 (January 1902): 598–607.

Peters, Erica J. *San Francisco: A Food Biography*. Lanham, MD: Rowman & Littlefield, 2013.

Potter, Jack M. "Land and Lineage in Traditional China." In *Family and Kinship in Chinese Society*, ed. Maurice Freedman, 121–38. Stanford, CA: Stanford University Press, 1970.

Purcell, Victor. *The Chinese in Southeast Asia*. 2nd ed. London: Oxford University Press, 1965.

Random House. *The Great Cooks' Guide to Woks, Steamers & Fire Pots*. New York: Random House, 1977.

——. *The International Cooks' Catalogue: A Beard Glaser Wolf Book*, intro. by James Beard. New York: Random House, 1977.

Reichl, Ruth. *Garlic and Sapphires: The Secret Life of a Critic in Disguise*. New York: Penguin, 2005.

Reid, Anthony, ed. *Sojourners and Settlers: Histories of Southeast Asia and the Chinese*. Honolulu: University of Hawaii Press, 1996.

Report of the Joint Special Committee to Investigate Chinese Immigration, 44th Congress. Washington, DC: Government Printing Office, 1877.

Richardson, Phyllis C. "Washington's Bill of Fare." *Washington Post*, March 4, 1982, E1.

Roberts, J. A. G. *China to Chinatown: Chinese Food in the West*. London: Reaktion Books, 2002.

——. *A Concise History of China*. Cambridge, MA: Harvard University Press, 1999.

Rombauer, Irma S., and Marion Rombauer Becker. *The Joy of Cooking*. Indianapolis: Bobbs-Merrill, 1975.

Roy, Denny. *Taiwan: A Political History*. Ithaca, NY: Cornell University Press, 2003.

Ryan, William Redmond. *Personal Adventures in Upper and Lower California*. London: William Shoberl, 1852.

Sabin, Edwin L. *Building the Pacific Railway*. Philadelphia: J. B. Lippincott, 1919.

Sala, George Augustus. *America Revisited*. 6th ed. London: Vizelly, 1886.

Sands, Harold. "Subduing the Sockeye." *Canadian Magazine* 33, no. 2 (May 1909): 65–71.

Schafer, Charles, and Violet Schafer. *Wokcraft: A Stirring Compendium of Chinese Cookery*. San Francisco: Yerba Buena Press, 1972.

Schrecker, Ellen, with John Schrecker. *Mrs. Chiang's Szechwan Cookbook*. New York: Harper & Row, 1976.

Seligman, Scott D. *The First Chinese American: The Remarkable Life of Wong Chin Foo*. Hong Kong: Hong Kong University Press, 2013.

——. *Three Tough Chinamen*. Hong Kong: Earnshaw Books, 2012.

Shaw, William. *Golden Dreams and Waking Realities*. London: Smith, Elder, 1851.

Sheppard, Eugenia. "The Pearl of Pearl's Restaurant." *Kansas City Star*, May 12, 1969, 70.

Sheraton, Mimi. *Eating My Words: An Appetite for Life*. New York: Morrow, 2004.

Shurtleff, William, and Akiko Aoyagi, *The Book of Tofu*. Brookline, MA: Autumn Press, 1975. Reprint, New York: Ballantine, 1980.

——. *History of Soy Sauce (160 CE to 2012): Extensively Annotated Bibliography and Sourcebook*. Lafayette, CA: Soyinfo Center, 2012.

Sifton, Sam. "The Way We Eat: New York Noodletown." *Sunday Times Magazine*, April 1, 2007.

Simon, Kate. *New York Places and Pleasures: An Uncommon Guidebook*. New York: Meridian, 1959.

Simonds, Nina. "Bean Curd." *Gourmet*, September 1979, 28.

——. "Beef." *Gourmet*, May 1980, 51.

——. "Breads." *Gourmet*, June 1979, 32.

——. "Chicken." *Gourmet*, November 1979, 54.

——. *Classic Chinese Cuisine*. Boston: Houghton Mifflin, 1982.

——. "Duck and Squab." *Gourmet*, December 1979, 58.

——. "Dumplings." *Gourmet*, July 1979, 48.

——. "Eggs." *Gourmet*, October 1979, 38.

——. "Fish." *Gourmet*, January 1980, 26.

——. "Lamb." *Gourmet*, June 1980, 32.

——. "Noodles I." *Gourmet*, April 1979, 44.

——. "Noodles II." *Gourmet*, May 1979, 24.

——. "Pickles and Salads." *Gourmet*, August 1980, 34.

——. "Pork." *Gourmet*, April 1980, 35.

——. "Rice." *Gourmet*, March 1979, 35.

——. "Seafood I." *Gourmet*, February 1980, 26.

——. "Seafood II." *Gourmet*, March 1980, 30.

——. "Seasonings I." *Gourmet*, January 1979, 36.

——. "Seasonings II." *Gourmet*, February 1979, 36.

——. "Soups." *Gourmet*, October 1980, 51.

——. "Soybeans." *Gourmet*, August 1979, 28.

——. "Sweets I." *Gourmet*, November 1980, 54.

——. "Sweets II." *Gourmet*, December 1980, 48.

——. "Vegetables." *Gourmet*, July 1980, 29.

——. "Vegetarian Cooking." *Gourmet*, September 1980, 30.

Simoons, Frederick J. *Food in China: A Cultural and Historical Inquiry*. Boca Raton, FL: CRC Press, 1991.

Sinn, Elizabeth. *Pacific Crossing: California Gold, Chinese Migration, and the Making of Hong Kong*. Hong Kong: Hong Kong University Press, 2013.

Siu, Paul C. P. *The Chinese Laundryman: A Study of Social Isolation*, ed. John Kuo Wei Tchen. New York: New York University Press, 1987.

Skinner, G. William. *Chinese Society in Thailand: An Analytical History*. Ithaca, NY: Cornell University Press, 1957.

——. "Mobility Strategies in Late Imperial China: A Regional Systems Analysis." In *Regional Analysis*, vol. 1: *Economic Systems*, ed. Carol A. Smith. New York: Academic Press, 1976.

Smith, Griffin, Jr. "Pass the Chop Sticks, Por Favor." *Texas Monthly*, July 1973, www.texasmonthly.com/content/pass-chop-sticks-por-favor.

Sokolov, Raymond A. "Drivers Who Stop Only for Gas Don't Know What They're Missing." *New York Times*, May 13, 1971, 54.

——. "For the City's Best in Chinese Cuisine." *New York Times*, May 26, 1972.

——. "Standards at Pearl's Have Slipped a Bit." *New York Times*, September 24, 1971, 46.

——. *Steal the Menu: A Memoir of Forty Years in Food*. New York: Knopf, 2013.

Spier, Robert F. G. "Food Habits of Nineteenth-Century California Chinese." *California Historical Society Quarterly* 37 (March 1958): 79–84, and (June 1958): 129–36.

Stephenson, George M. *A History of American Immigration*. Boston: Ginn, 1926.

Street, Richard Steven. *Beasts of the Field: A Narrative History of California Farmworkers, 1769–1913*. Stanford, CA: Stanford University Press, 2004.

Swislocki, Mark. *Culinary Nostalgia: Regional Food Culture and the Urban Experience in Shanghai*. Stanford, CA: Stanford, University Press, 2009.

Sze, Lena, "Opportunity, Conflict, and Community in Transition: Historical and Contemporary Chinese Immigration to Philadelphia." In *Global Philadelphia: Immigrant Communities Old and New*, ed. Ayumi Takenaka and Mary Johnson Osirim, 96–120. Philadelphia: Temple University Press, 2000.

Takaki, Ronald. *Strangers from a Different Shore: A History of Asian Americans*. Rev. ed. Boston: Little, Brown / Back Bay, 1998.

Taylor, Bayard. *Eldorado: Or, Adventures in the Path of Empire*. New York: G. P. Putnam's Sons, 1861.

Tchen, John Kuo Wei. *New York Before Chinatown: Orientalism and the Shaping of American Culture, 1776–1882*. Baltimore: Johns Hopkins University Press, 1999.

Thorne, John, with Matt Lewis Thorne. *Mouth Wide Open: A Cook and His Appetite*. New York: North Point Press, 2008.

Tong, Michael, and Elaine Louie. *The Shun Lee Cookbook: Recipes from a Chinese Restaurant Dynasty*. New York: Morrow, 2007.

Trillin, Calvin. "New Grub Streets." *New Yorker*, September 3, 2001, 42–48.

Tropp, Barbara. *The Modern Art of Chinese Cooking*. New York: Morrow, 1982.

Tsai, Shih-shan Henry. *The Chinese Experience in America*. Bloomington: Indiana University Press, 1986.

Tsui, Bonnie. *American Chinatown: A People's History of Five Neighborhoods*. New York: Free Press, 2009.

Tung, William L. *The Chinese in America, 1820–1973: A Chronology and Fact Book*. Dobbs Ferry, NY: Oceana Publications, 1974.

Urban, Andrew Theodore. "An Intimate World: Race, Migration, and Chinese and Irish Domestic Servants in the United States, 1856–1920." PhD dissertation, University of Minnesota, 2009.

Van Dyke, Paul A. *The Canton Trade: Life and Enterprise on the China Coast, 1700–1845*. Hong Kong: Hong Kong University Press, 2005.

Wagner, Donald B. *Ferrous Metallurgy*, vol. 5, part 11 of *Science and Civilisation in China*, ed. Joseph Needham. Cambridge: Cambridge University Press, 2008.

Wakeman, Frederic E., Jr. *Strangers at the Gate: Social Disorder in South China, 1839–1861*. Berkeley: University of California Press, 1966.

Waley-Cohen, Joanna. "The Quest for Balance: Taste and Gastronomy in Imperial China." In *Food: The History of Taste*, ed. Paul Freedman, 98–133. Berkeley: University of California Press, 2007.

——. *The Sextants of Beijing: Global Currents in Chinese History*. New York: Norton, 1999.

Wang Gungwu. *China and the Chinese Overseas*. Singapore: Times Academic Press, 1991.

Wang, Xinyang. *Surviving the City: The Chinese Immigrant Experience in New York City, 1890–1970*. Lanham, MD: Rowman & Littlefield, 2001.

Wheaton, Barbara Ketcham. "Chen, Joyce." In *Notable American Women: A Biographical Dictionary*, ed. Susan Ware, vol. 5, 116–17. Cambridge, MA: Belknap Press of Harvard University Press, 2004.

Whitehead, Jessup. *The Steward's Handbook and Guide to Party Catering*. Chicago: Jessup Whitehead, 1903.

Wilkinson, Endymion. *Chinese History: A Manual*. Rev. ed. Cambridge, MA: Harvard University Asia Center, 2000.

Will, Joanne. "The Pan from the Far East that Won the Hearts of the West." *Chicago Tribune*, September 18, 1980, section 7, 1.

Willan, Anne, with Amy Friedman. *One Soufflé at a Time: A Memoir of Food and France, with Recipes*. New York: St. Martin's Press, 2013.

Wing [*sic*] Chinfoo. "Chinese Cooking." *Brooklyn Daily Eagle*, July 6, 1884, 4.

Wong, Bernard P., and Tan Chee-Beng, eds. *Chinatowns around the World: Gilded Ghetto, Ethnopolis, and Cultural Diaspora*. Leiden: Brill, 2013.

Wong Chin Foo. "The Chinese in New York." *Cosmopolitan* 5, no. 4 (June 1888): 305.

——. "Chinese Recipes." *The Cook* 1, no. 5 (April 27, 1885): 7.

Wong, Helen Hong. "Reminiscences of a Gold Mountain Woman." In *Chinese American Voices: From the Gold Rush to the Present*, ed. Judy Yung, Gordon H. Chang, and Him Mark Lai. Berkeley: University of California Press, 2006.

Wong, Jade Snow. *Fifth Chinese Daughter*, with a new introduction. Seattle: University of Washington Press, 1989.

Wong, Marie Rose. *Sweet Cakes, Long Journey: The Chinatowns of Portland, Oregon*. Seattle: University of Washington Press, 2004.

Wu, Ellen D. "The Best Tofu in the World Comes from . . . Indiana?" In *Chinese American Voices: From the Gold Rush to the Present*, ed. Judy Yung, Gordon H. Chang, and Him Mark Lai, 372–76. Berkeley: University of California Press, 2006.

Yee, Mary Tsui Ping. *Chinese Immigrant Cooking*. Cobb, CA: First Glance Books, 1998.

Young, Grace. *Stir-Frying to the Sky's Edge: The Ultimate Guide to Mastery, with Authentic Recipes and Stories*. New York: Simon & Schuster, 2010.

Young, Grace, and Alan Richardson. *Breath of a Wok: Unlocking the Spirit of Chinese Wok Cooking Through Recipes and Lore.* New York: Simon & Schuster, 2004.

Yung, Judy. *Unbound Feet: A Social History of Chinese Women in San Francisco.* Berkeley: University of California Press, 1995.

Yung, Judy, Gordon H. Chang, and Him Mark Lai, eds. *Chinese American Voices: From the Gold Rush to the Present.* Berkeley: University of California Press, 2006.

Zhao, Jianli. *Strangers in the City: The Atlanta Chinese, Their Community, and Stories of Their Lives.* New York: Routledge, 2000.

Zhou, Min. *Chinatown: The Socioeconomic Potential of an Urban Enclave.* Philadelphia: Temple University Press, 1992.

——. *Contemporary Chinese America: Immigration, Ethnicity, and Community Transformation.* Philadelphia: Temple University Press, 2009.

Index

Beard, Elizabeth (Brennan), 27, 121
Beard, James, 27, 121, 178, 231, 239, 261
Beck, Louis J., 89, 114
Borthwick, J. D., 50
Book of Tofu, The (Shurtleff and Aoyagi), 240
Boston Chinatown, 89, 159
Boxer indemnity scholarships, 139–40, 141–42, 152, 199
Boxer Rebellion, 85–86, 139
Bramson, Ann, 240–41
Brooklyn Daily Eagle, 105–6, 121–22
Bruce Cost's Asian Ingredients (Cost), 241
Buck, Pearl S., 145–46, 147, 161, 162; as advocate for Asian affairs coverage at John Day, 145–46, 147; and *How to Cook and Eat in Chinese*, 153–56, 160, 161, 164, 205
Burlingame Treaty (1868), 66
Bush, Pres. George H. W., 249

California agriculture, role of Chinese in growth of, 61–63
California State University system, 244
Canada, Chinese in, 17, 57, 66, 77, 86–88
Canton. *See* Guangdong Province; Guangzhou
Canton Restaurant (San Francisco), 48–49
Canton Village (restaurant; New York), 189
Cantonese cooks: as cooks and servants in Far West, 67–71; and Irish–Chinese rivalry, 70; in late Qing-era China, 25–27, 38–39; skill at reproducing American dishes, 50–52

Cantonese cuisine: arrival in America, 39; and changing American culinary preferences, 171, 179–80, 181, 199; chop suey cuisine as reinvented version of, xvii, 100, 110–23; reputation of in China, 39–40
Cantonese language and dialects, 9, 11, 20, 24, 56; "sung" tones in, 20, 203
Cantonese-speakers and Mandarin-speakers, rivalries of in postwar U.S., 171, 172, 180
Carr, Allan, 220–21
Carter, Pres. Jimmy, 177, 250
Carter, Susan B., 101, 132
CCBA. *See* Chinese Consolidated Benevolent Association
Celler, Emanuel, 1, 2, 246
cha siu (alt., *cha shao*; cooking technique), 38
Chan, Shiu Wong, 125–27, 149–50, 212
Chan, Sucheng, 77
Chang, Sheila, 182, 186
Chao, Buwei Yang: and American kitchen equipment, 159; attitude toward cookbook conventions, 154; educational background of, 148, 150; elucidation of Chinese culinary context by, 158; and home cook's perspective, 150; knowledge of regional Chinese cuisines, 148; marriage to Yuenren Chao, 140; medical career of, 144, 148; memoir of, 161; upbringing of, 148; written voice of, 151; and *xiang banfa* mentality, 155
Chao, Rulan, 151–52, 164

mistaken omission of word *chow*, 106–7; white cooks' improvisations on, 129–30

"chop suey pan" (wok), 108. *See also* wok(s)

"chop suey stoves," 108

chow (alt., *chau, chao*; cooking technique), 106–10, 118

chow chop suey, original meaning of, vii, xix, 106–7. *See also* chop suey

Choy, Philip P., 244

Chu, Grace Zia: consultant on *The Cooking of China*, 216–18; as cooking teacher, 185, 200, 202; *Madame Chu's Chinese Cooking School*, 221–22; *The Pleasures of Chinese Cooking*, 208–9

Chu, Louis H., 144, 149

Cixi, Empress Dowager, 139, 140

Coe, Andrew, 120

cohong, 13–14

Cold War, 167, 176; and American exposure to non-Cantonese Chinese cuisines, 169, 170, 173; impact of on Cantonese American community, 172, 177, 190; and influx of Chinese elite to Washington and New York, 168, 171; and support of Nationalist regime in Taiwan, 192

Convention of Beijing (1860), 15

Cook, The (newsletter), 106, 113

Cook at Home in Chinese (Low), 149–50, 159–60

Cooke, George Wingrove, 26–27, 32, 38, 67

cooking and eating utensils, American vs. Chinese, 51, 109, 159, 230

cooking fats, 35–36, 108, 113, 120, 124, 127, 130

Cooking of China, The (Hahn/Time-Life), 215–18

cooking stoves: braziers as, 32, 107, 134; gas- or electric-powered, 108, 134–35; master chefs', 221; restaurant versions of, 103, 134–35

cooking times, importance of, 32, 33–34, 103, 108–9, 124, 127, 128, 131

Cook's Oracle, The (Kitchiner), 30

Cook's Tour of San Francisco, A (Muscatine), 181–82

coolies and coolieism, 21–22, 64, 76

Cost, Bruce, 241

"Counter Intelligence" (news column), 243

crabs: Chinese freshwater "hairy or "mitten," 156; as compared with Chesapeake blue crabs, 158; as compared with Dungeness crabs, 162

"credit ticket" passage to United States, 22, 64, 76

Crocker, Charles, 60

cuisines of ethnic Chinese sojourners: in Cuba, East India, and Ecuador, 248; in Peru, 186–87, 248; in Vietnam, 247

culinary concepts and terminology, 31, 37–38, 153, 155–56; as barriers to mutual understanding, 26, 34, 44, 69, 104–5, 106–7, 138, 202–5

cutting and dicing (cooking techniques), 32, 33–34, 37, 108, 119, 218, 220

Daniels, Roger, 245

Daoguang Emperor, 7

Delavan, James, 51

Delfs, Robert A., 225

Deng Xiaoping, 177, 250, 255–56

Joyce Chen Cooks (television show), 180

Joyce Chen Restaurant (Cambridge, MA), 180

Kan, Johnny, 201, 210–13, 261, 286n31
Kearney, Denis, 64–65, 69
Keaton, Buster, 115
Keh, David, 184, 186, 187
Keller, Frederick, 70
Kelly, William, 52
Kennedy, Edward, 1
Kennedy, Pres. John F., 1, 3
Kennedy, Robert, 1
Key to Chinese Cooking, The (Kuo), 226–29
Kikkoman, 242–43
King Joy Lo (restaurant; Chicago), 141
King Wah (restaurant; San Antonio), 186
Kissinger, Henry A., 176–77, 180
knives, Chinese kitchen, 30, 32–33, 37, 159, 208. *See also* Chinese cooking implements and vessels
Kodansha, 225
Kong Sung's (restaurant; San Francisco), 47
Korean War, 172
Kuo, Irene, 226–29
Kwoh, Emily, 182
Kuomintang (KMT). *See* Guomindang

La Choy Company, 116, 121, 278n44
Lai, Him Mark, 49, 244, 245
Lamb, Corrine, 149
language reform: as political priority in post-Qing China, 152; Yuenren Chao as proponent of, 152

laundries: as preferred Chinese occupation, 56, 67, 91–92; shift from to restaurant business, 92
Lee, Gary, 231
Lee, Jake, 210–11, 286n10
Lee, Jennifer 8., 188
Lee, Mailan, 201
Lee, Rose Hum, 166
Lee, Virginia, 201, 219–20
Lee, William Poy, 20
lemon chicken, 189–90
Leong, Annie, 133
Leong, Charles L., 210–13
Let, Jue, 27, 121, 261
Leung, Mai, 241–42
Li Hung Chang (Li Hongzhang), 93, 101, 109–10, 138–39
Li Shu-fan, 105
Lin, Florence: as advisor to *The Cooking of China*, 216–18; as cooking teacher, 200, 201, 202, 222; *Florence Lin's Chinese One-Dish Meals*, 222; *Florence Lin's Chinese Regional Cookbook* and rising awareness of regional cuisines in U.S., 222–23; *Florence Lin's Complete Book of Chinese Noodles, Dumplings and Breads*, 241; *Florence Lin's Cooking with Fire Pots*, 222; *Florence Lin's Vegetarian Chinese Cookbook* as pioneer work on meatless Chinese cooking, 222
Lin, Hsiangju, 207, 213–14
Lin, Tsuifeng, 207, 213–14
Lin Yutang, 147, 154, 200, 207
Ling, Huping, 111, 133
Liu Kin-Shan, 39
Lo, Betty, 182
Lo, C. M., 173, 252
Lo, Eileen Yin-Fei, 212–13, 242

Peter Lo's Mandarin Restaurant (Chicago), 182
Philadelphia Chinatown, 89
pinyin romanization system, 16, 24–25, 203
Pleasures of Chinese Cooking, The (Chu), 208–9
plum sauce. *See* duck sauce
Polo, Marco, 42
Port Arthur (restaurant; New York), 149
Portland, OR, Chinese in, 27, 87, 211
Princeton University, 193
prostitution, role of in Chinese American community, 76–77. *See also* Chinese American families; Guangdong: long-distance marriage customs in
Puck, Wolfgang, 243

Qing dynasty, 7–8, 10, 12, 15–16, 18, 21, 66, 81; collapse of, 138, 140–42

race relations, in the United States: and anti-Chinese violence, 55, 63–64, 87; and barriers to Chinese American employment opportunities, 143, 233–34, 244–45; and Chinese Exclusion Act, 65; and cooking as fallback occupation, 67–71; deterioration of in Far West, 55–56, 60–61, 63–64, 69; and eugenics movement, 84–85; as factor in development of chop suey cuisine, xvi, 99, 100; future of, 234–35, 258–59; and Johnson-Reed Act, 85; and perceived status of Chinese American restaurants, 234–35, 236; and restaurant clientele–staff dynamic, 3, 234, 253; shifts in

during 1920s and 1930s, 144–45; shifts in during 1970s and 1980s, 185; and U.S. labor movement, 60–61, 63–65; and World War II, 166–67
railroads, built by Chinese laborers: Canadian Pacific, 61; Central Pacific, 59–61; subsidiary links, 88
Rama VI, king of Thailand, 246
Random House, 162–63, 205
Reagan, Pres. Ronald, 255
red-cooking (cooking technique): and pressure-cooking, 161; as signature cooking technique of Jiangnan region, 157
Reed, David, 2, 85
regional Chinese cuisines, 170, 175–76, 252; Buwei Yang Chao's representation of, 149, 157; Florence Lin's representation of, 222–24; Taiwan as meeting point for, 169, 192–93
Reichl, Ruth, 239
Republic of China. *See* Taiwan
rice: basic cooking of, 32; as core element of Cantonese meal, 33; double-cropping Champa strain of, 44–45; industrial milling of, 45; stir-fried, 114, 122, 134
Rock Springs massacre (WY), 64
Ryan, William Redmond, 52

Sacramento-San Joaquin Delta, land reclamation by Chinese in, 61–63
Sala, George Augustus, 100
San Francisco: and arrival of Chinese in, 22, 23; and California Gold Rush, 17; and Chinese source of building supplies, 47; dispersal from by Chinese prospectors in

Far West, 56, 57; early anti-racist efforts centered in, 80–81; early Chinese restaurants in, 47–52, 53, 100; economic decline of, 89–90; and flow of imported Chinese foods, 53, 135; Hong Kong trade networks with, 17, 53, 76, 78, 135; initial welcome of Chinese in, 48, 50, 57; "Little China," 54, 57; modern Chinese restaurants in, 181–82, 242–43; 1906 earthquake and destruction of Chinatown, 82; portrayal of Chinatown in *Longtime Californ'*, 233; touristic rebuilding of Chinatown, 92

San Francisco Chongwah Huiguan, 80–81

San Gabriel Valley, CA, 195–97, 243

San Yi (or Sam Yup). *See* Three Counties

Schafer, Charles, 231

Schafer, Violet, 231

Schoenfeld, Ed, 184–86, 199, 200

Schrecker, Ellen, 225–26

Schrecker, John, 225–26

Secrets of Chinese Cooking (Lin and Lin), 207

"The Servant Question" (Keller), 70

Shake Hands with the Dragon (Glick), 147

Shanghai, 16, 165; as culinary center, 156; forcible labor recruitment in, 22; and New York restaurants, 179–80

Shanghai Café (New York), 179

Shanghai East (restaurant; New York, Houston), 182, 186

Shanghainese restaurants, 179–80, 182

Shaw, William, 51

Shen, Alex, 183

Shen, Anna, 183

Sheraton, Mimi, 255

Shun Lee (restaurant; New York), 175

Shun Lee Dynasty (restaurant; New York), 175–76

Shun Lee Palace (restaurant; New York), 179

Shurtleff, William, 240

Si Yi (or Sze Yup). *See* Four Counties

Sichuan cuisine: both Chinese and foreigners exposed to during World War II, 168, 170; and U.S. Sichuanese culinary vogue, 179, 182, 186, 225–26

Sigel, Elsie, 89

Simon, Kate, 180

Simon & Schuster, 208, 240

Simonds, Nina: and *Gourmet* magazine series on Chinese cuisine, 237–39, 240; as translator of early Wei-Chuan cookbooks, 196

Sinn, Elizabeth, 76

Six Companies, 80–81

"snakeheads," 251

sojourners and sojourning (*qiao*), Chinese concept of, 18. *See also* immigration/emigration

Sokolov, Raymond, 183, 189–90, 223, 239

Song dynasty, 42, 44

Soong Mei-ling (Madame Chiang Kai-shek), 199, 200

soybeans, 102, 162, 240

soy sauce, 34–35, 112–16; brewed vs. hydrolyzed, 116, 242–43

Spader, Margaret, 202, 222

spring rolls, 118, 149–50, 277n40

steaming (cooking technique), 31, 159

Steiman, Harvey, 240–42

Arts and Traditions of the Table: Perspectives on Culinary History
Albert Sonnenfeld, Series Editor